The Future of Human Rights

PENNSYLVANIA STUDIES IN HUMAN RIGHTS

Bert B. Lockwood, Jr., Series Editor

A complete list of books in the series is available from the publisher.

The Future of Human Rights

U.S. Policy for a New Era

EDITED BY WILLIAM F. SCHULZ

PENN

University of Pennsylvania Press

Philadelphia

2262964.06

Published by
University of Pennsylvania Press
Philadelphia, Pennsylvania 19104-4112

Printed in the United States of America on acid-free paper
10 9 8 7 6 5 4 3 2 1

A Cataloging-in-Publication record is available for the Library of Congress

ISBN 978-0-8122-4111-2

with special appreciation
for the support
of the
Center for American Progress

Contents

Introduction

WILLIAM F. SCHULZ

The great ballet dancer Vaslav Nijinsky was once asked how he managed to leap so high in the air. "The secret," he said, "is this. Most people, when they leap in the air, come down at once. The secret is to stay in the air a little before you return." U.S. foreign policy, so buoyant at the end of the Cold War, has returned to earth with a thud over the past few years and among its crash victims has been American leadership in the struggle for human rights.

Tome after tome has decried the impact of neoconservatism on America's standing in the world, her capacity to fight terrorism and her reputation for integrity.[1] Far fewer analysts have examined how the neoconservative moment has done damage, perhaps lasting, to human rights themselves, often in the name of their promotion. Fewer still have described how the presuppositions of the human rights enterprise have aided and abetted that fiasco.

This volume of essays is intended to point the way out of the morass, at least as far as U.S. international human rights policy is concerned. It is intended as a blueprint for a new administration and a prescription for how the United States can reclaim the mantle of leadership in combating human rights abuses.

To trace that future path with confidence requires that we first understand how we got to where we find ourselves; what challenges now confront the human rights prospect; and how we will need to reconceptualize traditional approaches to human rights if we are to overcome those challenges.

That human rights are worth the effort may be a proposition that all but the most unreconstructed foreign policy "realists" would grant. Human rights have become what Michael Ignatieff has called "the lingua franca of global moral thought."[2] Few world leaders, including the most repressive, fail to dress their regimes in its raiment. The Chinese government, with its hundreds of political prisoners, tens of thousands of people incarcerated without fair trials, persecution of the Falun Gong religious sect, and exorbitant use of the death penalty, claims that it "highly values the protection and promotion of the political, economic, social and cultural rights of its citizens."[3] The Sudanese government, authors of the catastrophe in Darfur, tried to cast itself on the side of the angels by pronouncing the UN Human Rights Council "the conscience of humanity."[4] And even Al Qaeda, according to Thomas Friedman, resists being labeled "genocide perpetrators" because it "affects their street appeal."[5]

Such widespread endorsement might appear to give human rights the advantage. But paradoxically the absence of a reputable competing vision, of a full-throated defense of benevolent authoritarianism, for example, or an unreconstructed plea for privilege, has left human rights flabby, its meaning open to broad interpretation, a cloak of many colors, the possession of many masters, and hence vulnerable to co-optation. And no one has been more eager to claim its cover the last few years than the government of the United States.

A Perfect Storm

One would think Robert Kaplan would have learned his lesson. When his 1993 book *Balkan Ghosts,* with its fatalistic view of ethnic strife in the former Yugoslavia, was cited as having contributed to President Bill Clinton's initial reticence to intervene in the bloody conflict there, Kaplan was taken aback.[6] "This is only a travel book," he contended, not designed to influence policy.[7]

But in 2002 the *Atlantic Monthly* correspondent was back with another book which, though it may never have been read by the sitting president, captured widespread attention among the reigning foreign policy elite. *Warrior Politics: Why Leadership Demands a Pagan Ethos,* coming quickly upon the heels of *The Coming Anarchy* (2000), which had warned ominously of "the dangers of peace," was a call to arms for American primacy.[8] Citing with approval the historian E. H. Carr's observation that "Historically, every approach in the past to a world society has been the product of the ascendancy of a single Power," Kaplan opined that *"We [the United States] and nobody else will write the terms for international society"* and, just to make sure his readers got the point, put the sentence in italics—a sentence that captured the spirit of the times perfectly.[9]

To be fair, the Bush administration's vision of American preeminence long predated Robert Kaplan. Indeed, Kaplan, a self-described realist, had never been smitten with undertaking wars in defense of human rights or pursuit of democracy. He had even warned in *Warrior Politics,* published a year before the invasion of Iraq, that "a single war with significant loss of American life . . . could ruin the public's appetite for internationalism."[10]

The fact is that the "neoconservative moment" was a perfect storm: the result of a confluence of historic American predilections, an ascendant political philosophy, and a unique historic circumstance, all balanced on the shoulders of an ill-prepared president who saw history in simple terms and the future in millennial ones.[11]

First, the predilections. When John Winthrop sailed off for the New World in March of 1630 with his band of Puritans, he did so well aware of his role as a new Moses leading a New Exodus.[12] What the great historian of Puritanism Perry Miller called an "errand into the wilderness" was not prompted by persecution, however, as had been the case with the Pilgrims ten years earlier. It was instead a proactive attempt to establish "a place of Cohabitation . . . under a due form of Government" based upon biblical polity. Such a "City upon a Hill," to use Winthrop's famous phrase, was to be not only a *City* offering its residents potential escape from corruption if they abided by virtue but, just as important, a City *on a Hill*, that is, a City so placed that it could be seen by others as a model of the New Jerusalem. "The eyes of all people are upon us," Winthrop declared, and, if we succeed, they shall say of later plantations "Lord, make it like that of New England."[13]

The Puritans' mission, therefore, was both particular to themselves but universal as well. Naturally those most close at hand were early recipients of the colonists' ministrations. Several generations later Cotton Mather would conjecture that the Devil had intentionally placed the Indians on a continent uninhabited by Christians so that the Gospel of Jesus Christ could never reach their ears but that the arrival of the Puritans had outfoxed him.[14] It was not the Indians, however, whom these first white settlers hoped most to impress and reform but the continent from which they had arrived. England and the rest of Europe were to be transformed by the new model of righteousness the Puritans embodied.

Fast forward 146 years. The Puritan community has long since been rent into a thousand pieces. No longer are the saints "visible"; no longer does religious passion spill in quite the same volume. John Locke has written his *Two Treatises of Government* and *A Letter Concerning Toleration*. The colonies are ripe for independence and the bonds that hold the community together, the political principles that direct its course, are now derived far less from God than from Nature, *unalienable* rights bestowed by a Creator, to be sure, but grounded now in natural law.

Two things are worth noting, however. First, that the Declaration of Independence was not a mere litany of particular grievances by a particular community against a particular king. It was also a statement of precepts about government and consent and duty applicable to everyone everywhere and issued out of a "decent respect for the opinions" not of Parliament or of the king or of the English populace but of "*mankind.*" And second, that among the first order natural rights was *liberty*—a conviction hearkening back to the Puritans' revolt against the Presbyterial system of the Church of England and predicated upon the Christian doctrine of inherent human freedom, the notion that we may *choose* whether we deal falsely or faithfully with God. Winthrop had made it painfully clear that the success of the City on the Hill depended upon his cohort choosing wisely.

The American experience was from its roots characterized by a religious vision to be propagated far and wide and, as the explicitly sectarian nature of that vision diminished with the growth of pluralism and toleration, it transmogrified into a religiously tinged moral mission: to be a model of liberty, a champion of those who had been supplied by Nature with a yearning to be free but cast by political circumstances into chains.

In his recent book *Dangerous Nation*, the neoconservative historian Robert Kagan argues that "the United States has never been a status quo power; it has always been a revolutionary one, consistently expanding its influence in the world in ever-widening arcs," often by military means.[15] We need not agree with every detail of Kagan's analysis (and certainly not with his reason for writing the book)[16] to find truth in the claim that America has rarely been shy about proclaiming its values and model of government superior to others and offering a hand, if not a heel, to those in need of "guidance." The renowned church historian Martin Marty thinks it a telling convenience that Protestantism began to missionize the world, seeking converts and spreading its notions of civilization in the 1790s and years following, just as the new American nation was organizing *itself* and, in tandem with its most popular faith, spreading *its* reach westward and eventually beyond its continental bounds.[17]

Certainly, once America had rid itself of the stain of slavery and entered the industrial age, it found itself well positioned, both ideologically and practically, to indulge its universalizing impulses and fulfill its moral destiny. What it sought, however, was far less physical transformation than moral, less a territorial empire than righteous territory. The best-selling book of 1885 was Congregational minister Josiah Strong's *Our Country: Its Possible Future and Its Present Crisis*, a plea to impose America's Christian values on the world.[18] "We are the chosen people," Strong averred, picking up an echo from the earliest days of European settlement. God was "not only preparing in our Anglo-Saxon civilization the die with which to stamp the people of the earth but . . . also massing behind that die the mighty power with which to press it."[19]

Two world wars, one fought explicitly to "make the world safe for democracy," would reinforce the mightiness of that power. Each would result as well in international institutions designed to modulate the unshackled reach of any one state. But neither war would sidetrack the United States from its fundamental conviction that a desire for liberty beat naturally in every human breast and that this country was uniquely positioned both to model it ourselves and help procure it for others.

These predilections, then, awaited but leaders disposed to exploit them and circumstances that allowed them. They found the former in aficionados of neoconservatism and the latter in a newly acquired enemy both identifiable and ferocious.

The origins of neoconservatism have been described and debated endlessly. I am less interested here in where they came from than what they mean. But in one respect their roots are important: neoconservatism was born out of what Nietzsche called *ressentiment.*

It is not surprising that the lambs should bear a grudge against the great birds of prey, but that is no reason for blaming the great birds of prey for taking the little lambs. And when the lambs say among themselves, "These birds of prey are evil, and he who least resembles a bird of prey, who is rather its opposite, a lamb,—should he not be good?" then there is nothing to carp with in this ideal's establishment, though the birds of prey may regard it a little mockingly, and maybe say to themselves, "We bear no grudge against them, these good lambs, we even love them: nothing is tastier than a tender lamb."[20]

For Leo Strauss, a refugee from Nazi Germany long considered the intellectual progenitor of neoconservatism, the original birds of prey were obvious. But for Strauss and most especially for his followers the aviary grew larger and larger: political scientists who thought politics was a science; academic administrators who failed to stand up to radicals; "flat-souled" students, to use Allan Bloom's phrase from *The Closing of the American Mind,*[21] whose world was "devoid of ideals"; the perpetrators of mass bourgeois culture; political leaders who failed to provide "moral clarity"; secular liberal elites certainly; internationalists of course; and relativists absolutely. Indeed, a special circle of hell was reserved for relativists (or what Strauss called "nihilists") who believed that nothing could be ultimately and absolutely justified. It was a sorry world we lived in.[22]

But there *was* an antidote: natural right. At the beginning of his classic work, *Natural Right and History,* Strauss threw down the gauntlet: "To reject natural right is tantamount to saying that . . . what is right is determined exclusively by the legislators and the courts of the various countries. . . . [But] if principles are sufficiently justified by the fact that they are accepted by a society, the principles of cannibalism are as defensible and sound as those of civilized life."[23] Let Nature be our guide. And no country was more intimately wedded to Nature as a guide to what is right, to natural "unalienable" rights, than America. America, not old, bloodied Europe, was capable of rescuing the world from the scourge of nihilism. But not just any kind of America: only a strong, proud, muscular America, informed by "moral clarity"—that phrase again—and prepared to seek "national greatness."

And how did a people achieve "greatness"? "Because mankind is intrinsically wicked," Strauss once wrote, "he has to be governed. Such governance can only be established, however, when men are united—and they can only be united against other people."[24] In the face of a culture in decline, only a mortal enemy could unify a nation, call it back to its highest ideals, and invest it with transcendent meaning once again. As Robert Kaplan had put it in his 2000 essay "The Dangers of Peace": "Peace . . . leads to a preoccupation with *presentness;* the loss of the past and a consequent disregard of the future. That is because peace by nature is pleasurable, and pleasure is about momentary satisfaction. . . . [C]onvenience becomes the vital element in society." [25] No wonder neoconservatives, far from celebrating the end of the Cold War, found it so dangerous; no wonder Norman Podhoretz, often considered the father of contemporary neoconservatism, bewailed in the collapse of Communism the loss of a "defining foreign demon" and welcomed both the Persian Gulf and Iraq wars as opportunities for the United States to "remoralize" itself again.[26] Faced with the evaporation of one global threat, they found solace, even promise, in the appearance of another. And be it Saddam or terrorism, the only way to defeat a world-historical menace was through the leveraging of a countervailing force of superior power.

The neoconservatives discovered that countervailing force in a faith and a mission, both of which were congruent with the predilections of the American experience. Their faith was, to use the words of their oral amanuensis, George W. Bush, that "freedom is written in our hearts" and that "moral truth is the same in every culture, in every time and in every place,"[27] the latter a universalism breathtaking in its sweep and surely wrong. And their mission was to take the most precious of those moral truths—the inevitable triumph of liberty—and spread it unsparingly, thereby saving both the world and ourselves from the vicious birds of prey: Terror, Tyranny, and Moral Dissipation as well as, not incidentally, the threat to American national sovereignty posed by a growing sense of global community.

This last was just as dangerous in some ways as the first three. As Liah Greenfeld describes in her comprehensive work *Nationalism: Five Roads to Modernity, ressentiment* almost inevitably leads to a celebration of sovereign power—the triumph of the lambs, pure, righteous, and newly robust—and a suspicion of internationalism, a veil behind which lurk the perfidious birds of prey. For after all, if so many elements of *American society*—the media, secular elites, nihilists—are not to be trusted to see the dangers we confront, what possible reason is there to trust world opinion with our very lives? And so, lacking a tragic sense of history—the recognition that life's limits are real and that, no matter what we do, not everyone will be saved—neoconservatives sought to remake the world in their image. It is a commonplace that the Bush administration had tacked on human rights as a rationale for invading Iraq only after no weapons of mass destructions (WMDs) or terror links were discovered. But it is just as likely that WMDs and terror were the excuses for taking out a regime that offended neoconservative sensibilities and whose forced departure, conveniently accomplished *absent* international endorsement, reinforced the mythical vision of an America singularly disposed and equipped to rid the world of bad guys in the name of democracy and "human rights."

That neoconservatism with its revolutionary impulses has little in common with conservatism in a classic sense, ill disposed as the latter is to the adventurous, is ironic surely. Like liberals, neoconservatives believe that, in the words of Patrick Moynihan, "politics can change a culture and save it from itself" while traditional conservatives believe that "it is culture, not politics, that determines the success of a society"[28] and that hence change is a slow, evolutionary process that only fools would try to impose or rush.

Whatever the truth, the consequences of the neoconservative venture have been disastrous, not least for the cause of human rights. But here is the worrisome part: in his mea culpa for his support of the Iraq War, *America at the Crossroads*, Francis Fukuyama lays out his version of the four bedrock principles of neoconservatism. The first two are "a belief that the internal character of regimes matters and that foreign policy must reflect the deepest values of liberal democratic societies" and "a belief that American power . . . could be used for moral purposes, and that the United States needs to remain engaged in international affairs."[29] No American human rights advocate could have said it better.

Cosmic Convergence?

There are only three possible sources for the justification of human rights: God, natural law, or the opinions of "legislatures and courts." Strauss and the neoconservatives derisively dubbed the latter "positivism" (though it is more neutrally called consensualism) and despised it, as we have seen, because, lacking reference to any immutable standards, it could sanction anything, even cannibalism. The advantage to a natural

law theory of rights, which Strauss and the neoconservatives championed, is not only that it sets rights in Nature's stone but makes it easy to
tell the good guys from the bad.

The problem with natural law theory, however, is that it substitutes
for the opinions of those legislatures and courts, representative as they
presumably are of "the people," the idiosyncratic opinions of one philosopher or, at best, of whatever intellectual elite holds sway at the
moment. Hence, when America was founded on principles influenced
by John Locke, the great champion of natural law, it adopted his perception that Nature restricted rights to the male propertied class. The popular nineteenth-century philosopher Herbert Spencer was notorious for
preaching that natural law dictated a minimalist state and that, therefore, "no government should compel vaccination, require children to
be educated, keep small boys from sweeping chimneys, mandate the
construction of sewers, set standards for telegraph systems, or . . . relieve
poverty."[30] The neoconservatives as well found in natural law exactly
what they were looking for: that human rights were coterminous with
the customary notions of civil and political rights embodied in the American tradition (though never social and economic rights such as the
right to food or housing despite the fact that one would think those
needs at least as "natural" as the right to a multiparty system or to a jury
of one's peers). Not unsurprisingly, neoconservative natural law prescribed capitalism over socialism too.[31]

But neoconservatism has not been alone in its attraction to a natural
law theory of rights. Indeed, the first preambular clause of the Universal
Declaration of Human Rights cites natural law as the justification for the
rights listed in that document: "Whereas recognition of the *inherent* dignity and of the equal and *inalienable* rights of all members of the human
family is the foundation of freedom, justice and peace in the world . . .
[emphasis added]." Wary of relegating human rights to the whim of
"legislators and courts," chastened by the criticism that human rights
are a Western phenomenon not applicable to non-Western cultures, and
eager to proclaim the *universal* nature of the rights they champion,
human rights practitioners, no less than neoconservatives, have been
drawn to natural law, eager to derive the principles they cherish—
"moral truths . . . the same in every culture, in every time and in every
place"—from the apparently unchanging nature of the human beast.
And among those natural principles is that "freedom is written in our
hearts." The first article of the Universal Declaration tells us so: "All
human beings are born free and equal in dignity and rights."

Nor is a predisposition to natural law the only thing prevailing human
rights norms share with neoconservative presuppositions. Following on
that natural law theory of rights, the human rights community has also

tended to see its task in moral terms and the world in Manichean, divided between the children of light who would respect human rights and all the children of darkness who would savage them, be they in Pyongyang, Harare, or, yes, Baghdad. It has not been reticent, despite the scruples of a few human rights organizations, to endorse the notion that under some circumstances force may be used—indeed, must be used—to tame those children of darkness. It has not hesitated to look to the United States for leadership in the larger human rights struggle, crediting Franklin and Eleanor Roosevelt for inaugurating the modern human rights era; applauding the U.S. State Department for its unvarnished human rights reports; and chastising this country when it failed to use its military power in pursuit of moral ends—to stop genocide in Rwanda, for example, or to supply a military intervention in Darfur. It, too—the traditional human rights community—has lacked a tragic sense of history, convinced that if nations conform their practices to human rights norms, the world would see an end to misery.[32] It, too, is perfectionist in its ideology, convinced that the right politics can change culture and that you can indeed "legislate morality." It, too, has come to social and economic rights only at a turtle's pace, far more comfortable with rights widely identified with the American, or at least the Western, political and jurisprudential systems. And it, too, has relished the spread of democracy around the globe even while insisting, rightly, that democracy is not sufficient to guarantee that a regime be human rights pure.

None of this of course is to blame the human rights community for decisions of the Bush administration, both because the former lacked decision-making power and because, as we shall see momentarily, there were, despite the similarities, two profound differences in how neoconservatives and mainstream human rights advocates approach the struggle. But it is to explain part of the reputational damage human rights has sustained the past few years and that that damage is not solely because neoconservatives have misappropriated principles or nomenclature. The journalist David Rieff has been relentless in his contention that the human rights cause has, unwittingly or not, provided rationale and cover for the spread of American hegemony[33] and that suspicion is widely shared not only in the Muslim world but even among traditional allies. As the Nobel Prize-winning Iranian human rights lawyer, Shirin Ebadi, for one, put it, "it is hard not to see the Bush administration's focus on human rights violations in Iran as a cloak for its larger strategic interests."[34]

The tragic result is that the United States has been handicapped in providing crucial human rights leadership even where such leadership is desperately needed. Democracy and human rights activists overseas now spurn U.S. support for fear they will be tainted by association with a larger American agenda.[35] President Bush's appeal in his 2005 State of the Union address for desperately needed reform in Saudi Arabia and Egypt was met with derision even by long-time democracy advocates in those two countries.[36] And American military resources and prowess can ill afford to be put at the disposal of efforts to stop genocide in Darfur, not just because they are so overstretched but because the use of American force against another Muslim regime, even one as discredited as Sudan's, would be widely perceived as counterproductive.

How, then, might the pursuit of human rights by the United States be dissociated from a neoconservative program now largely discredited in the world's eyes? The essays that follow lay out a myriad of specific policy recommendations but two general principles—principles that distinguish a normative approach to human rights from a neoconservative one—need to undergird them all.

The first is that human rights must be understood in *comprehensive* terms, not *selective*. Quite apart from whether social and economic rights need to be incorporated into the U.S. government's understanding of rights, no government that picks and chooses among a set of rights those it is comfortable with and those it is not—"yes" to free elections, "no" to due process for all detainees—can ever possibly be credible. This does not mean that the details of human rights law and practice can never change or that the approach the United States takes to the human rights abuses of different countries needs to be identical. But it does mean that human rights cannot be defined narrowly in terms of one particular aspect of the *American* tradition, as neoconservatives are inclined to do.[37]

The protection of individual liberties or the practice of electoral democracy are precious elements of any respectable human rights agenda but they are not the only ones. To equate human rights as a concept with their evolution in the American experience—and then only with selected aspects of that experience (the right to free speech, for example, but not the right to undiluted habeas corpus)—is to forget that the power of human rights is derived not from their national particularity but from the fact that they are supranational, established by regimens that transcend the bounds of any one nation. Without that, they are good for nothing. Robert Mugabe may claim until he is hoarse from shouting that a president in a stratified developing country like Zimbabwe has the right to throw his politically disruptive opponents in jail on a whim or appropriate businesses without compensation, but until he can get other nations to agree with him, he is merely sputtering in the wind. Like the rules of the World Trade Organization, globally recognized human rights must be respected even if they fly in the face of a particular nation's momentary interests.

Which leads to the second general principle the United States must reaffirm: a commitment to *global cooperation* and *respect for international protocols and institutions,* imperfect as they are. Of Francis Fukuyama's four bedrock characteristics of neoconservatism, it is the final one— "skepticism about the legitimacy and effectiveness of international law and institutions to achieve either security or justice"[38]—that most dramatically divides normative human rights practice from neoconservative.[39]

Sophisticated advocates of human rights are not naïve about the failures of the United Nations, the shortcomings of the UN Human Rights Council, the unproven value of the International Criminal Court, or the weakness of unenforceable international law. But to ignore international regimes, much less undermine them, is to sacrifice the best resource the United States has available for convincing the world that we do not suffer from solipsism, immune to the needs and opinions of others; that our intent is benign; and that the most powerful nation on earth is prepared to use its power fairly and wisely. Mighty as we are, we do not live in a cocoon; we cannot solve our problems by ourselves, be they Iraq or terrorism or global warming.

Respect for human rights and the processes by which they are fashioned is one of the best ways to win global friends and influence the passions of people. And whether we think the source of human rights is God, natural law, or consensualism, an international imprimatur lends legitimacy to our pursuit of them. As a study by the Princeton Project on National Security noted recently, "Liberty under law within nations is inextricably linked with a stable system of liberty under law among them."[40] Surely even Condoleezza Rice who, during the 2000 presidential campaign, wrote that "foreign policy in a Republican administration . . . will proceed from the firm ground of the national interest, not the interests of an *illusory* international community [emphasis added]"[41] has come to rue the day she thought the world community no more than a chimera.

Repairing the Damage

The damaging effect of neoconservative policies on human rights goes well beyond reinforcement of the suspicion that American advocacy of human rights is a mere cover for an imperialist agenda. Those policies have undermined the notion that spreading human rights and democracy around the globe are viable goals of U.S. foreign policy. They have weakened international institutions upon which human rights depend. And they have increased a certain natural reticence on the part of the American people to commit U.S. troops to humanitarian and peacekeeping missions, even when they are justified, as they are, for example, in Darfur. Coupled with America's human rights practices as part of its prosecution of the war on terror—secret incommunicado detentions, denial of habeas corpus, winking acceptance of torture—the nation's ability to hold others to account for their own abuses has been severely weakened.

A new administration will certainly have its hands full repairing this damage.

- *It will need to find a variety of ways to signal renewed U.S. support for the international system.* Ratifying one or more international human rights treaties would help do that. Perhaps the Convention on the Rights of the Child, which all countries except the United States and Somalia have ratified, would be a place to start now that the U.S. Supreme Court has removed one of the major objections to the treaty by declaring the execution of juveniles unconstitutional. Or closing Guantánamo Bay. Or removing the reservations to various human rights treaties that declare them nonenforceable in domestic law. Or standing for election to the UN Human Rights Council, flawed though it is, and using that forum to articulate a renewed commitment to a comprehensive human rights agenda. Or revisiting U.S. concerns about the International Criminal Court with an eye toward eventually ratifying the Rome statutes establishing the court, or at least suspending the penalties we have leveraged against those countries that have refused to immunize Americans from prosecution by the court. If Iraq has taught us anything, it ought to have demonstrated that finding ways to deal with tyrants short of military force is to the advantage of all parties.

- *It will need to adopt a more sophisticated, less ham-handed approach to the promotion of democracy around the globe.* It ought to go without saying that human rights are served by an increase in the number of stable democracies in the world. But the key word is "stable," since we know that newly formed, unstable democratic states lacking robust civil societies and strong democratic institutions are especially prone to be breeding grounds for all sorts of mischief, not least the production of terrorists. The tragedy of the Iraq War will only be compounded if the lesson drawn from it is that, because force-feeding democracy proved so destructive, the only alternative is quiescence. While democracy is no magic bullet, tyranny guarantees bullets aplenty. Not every nation is ready to leap into full-blown democracy on a moment's notice. But if, indeed, as worldwide surveys have found, more than 90 percent of Muslims endorse democracy as the best form of government, what is required of us is neither perfectionism nor passivity.[42] What is required of us is patience.

- *It will need to codify the positive obligations of the United States under the newly minted doctrine of the "responsibility to protect."* Just as the Iraq War ought not sour us on promoting democracy, so we must not allow it to impose an unfitting shyness upon us about using military power for humanitarian ends. In 2005 the UN General Assembly endorsed the worldwide responsibility to protect civilian populations at risk from mass atrocities.[43] That does not imply that the United States will have to be the proverbial "world's policeman," committing its troops willy-nilly to the far corners of the globe. But it does mean that the United States will need to take mass atrocities seriously, adopting an early warning system for populations in danger, shoring up weak and failing states, and providing leadership and support for intervention when necessary, even when it itself stays far away from battle. The American people can distinguish between unwise military posturing and morally justified humanitarian interventions. In January 2007, after more than three years and 3,000 U.S. deaths in Iraq, 63 percent of Americans, quite understandably, said that the world has grown more afraid of U.S. military force and that such fear undermines U.S. security by prompting other nations to seek means to protect themselves.[44] Yet, even so, in a poll taken six months later, a plurality of Americans favored deploying U.S. troops as part of a multinational force in Darfur.[45] If the American people can tell the difference between legitimate and illegitimate use of force, the American government ought to be able to also.

- *It will need to conform U.S. practices to international standards on fundamental human rights issues.* The United States will never reclaim its reputation for human rights leadership as long as its own policies on such issues as due process for prisoners taken into custody in the course of the war on terror remain at such radical odds with international law and practice. There is considerable room for debate as to how cases of terror suspects should be adjudicated, especially when highly classified intelligence is involved—whether, for example, the United States should establish special national security courts or integrate such defendants into the regular criminal justice system[46]—but what is beyond doubt is that the current system in which suspects are cast into legal netherworlds of secret detentions and coercive interrogations cannot continue. And in a broader sense, the United States would do well in the eyes of the world to be less defensive about its own domestic practices that may fall short of international standards. Our credibility in criticizing others waxes and wanes in direct proportion to our willingness to acknowledge our own shortcomings. We should, for example, welcome to this country any UN special rapporteur who seeks an invitation to investigate; we should encourage the solicitor general of the United States to draw upon international law to buttress the government's arguments before the Supreme Court, thereby lending encouragement to those members of the court who are beginning to look to such law to inform their opinions;[47] and we should issue an annual report on U.S. human rights practices to complement the State Department's reports on other countries. After all, since the Chinese publish such a report on us each year, it could not hurt to publish a more accurate version of our own.

The Rest of the Story

Important as it is to signal a new beginning in human rights policy, we ought not make the mistake of seeing the human rights context solely through the lens of the neoconservative moment. Several other major developments in the world bear directly on human rights and warrant a rethinking of traditional approaches to the issue. The first of these is terrorism.

Terrorist crimes must be understood as human rights crimes and treated accordingly. Because the Bush administration's war on terror has constituted such an unprecedented assault upon basic human rights and liberties, much of the human rights conversation of the past six or seven years has, quite appropriately, been focused on protecting hard-won first principles—such as the right not to be tortured, the right to know the reasons for incarceration, to gain access to a lawyer, or to be eligible for habeas corpus—from government attack. But the crimes of terrorists are serious human rights crimes as well, violating at their worst one of the most elementary rights in the Universal Declaration: "Article 3: Everyone has the right to life, liberty and security of person." Human rights organizations may be able to survive with a dearth of reports, resources, or campaigning efforts aimed at terrorist groups and their sympathizers but U.S. human rights policy cannot afford such asymmetry. Terrorist crimes must be regarded not just as threats to security but as assaults on fundamental rights. The destruction of Al Qaeda and its affiliates would be an enormous victory for human rights. As the renowned human rights scholar Samantha Power put it recently, "Just because George W. Bush hyped the threat [of terrorism] does not mean that the threat should be played down." And she went on to urge us both to reassert "the moral difference between the United States and Islamic terrorists" and to develop "a 21st century toolbox to minimize actual terrorist threats."[48] A good place to begin is by U.S. human rights officials, not just those responsible for national security policy, being engaged in drafting and advocating for an international treaty on terrorism that provides a standard definition of the term and outlines state obligations to combat the crime.[49]

Such an approach, far from damaging human rights, provides an opportunity to resolve the long-standing conflict between a criminal justice approach to fighting terrorism and a war approach.[50] As Supreme Court Justice Sandra Day O'Connor wrote in her 2004 opinion in *Hamdi v. Rumsfeld*—in which the majority held that any U.S. citizen designated an "enemy combatant" had to be given a meaningful opportunity to contest the factual basis for that detention before a neutral decision-maker—"If the practical circumstances of a given conflict are entirely unlike those of the conflicts that informed the development of the law of war, [the Supreme Court's] understanding of [long-standing law-of-war principles] may unravel."[51] Better that any changes in those understandings be undertaken at the international level than left to the unilateral interpretations of one nation, one president, or even one Supreme Court.

Terrorism is, however, far from the only threat facing the United States. Nuclear proliferation, counterinsurgency, vast disparities in global wealth, climate change, the worldwide spread of disease—all these and more await the attention of the next administration and all of them have implications for human rights—and vice versa.

The next administration should also adopt an integrative approach to human rights, identifying them with broader global development goals and extending the definition of national security beyond military security alone. If the evolutionary biologist Jared Diamond is to be believed, it is no coincidence that Rwanda recorded the highest population density of any country in Africa at the time of the Rwandan genocide in 1994.[52] Certainly we know that encroaching desertification has played an important role in the conflict between pastoral and nomadic tribes in Darfur.[53] Some experts predict that by 2050, as many as 150 million people could be displaced as a result of global warming, leading, as two Australian scientists warn, to "new migrants [who] . . . impinge on the living space of others [and] widen existing ethnic and religious divides."[54] And, to take one more example, scholars have found that countries with severe AIDS epidemics have correspondingly higher levels of human rights abuse because, among other reasons, they produce higher numbers of AIDS orphans vulnerable to exploitation or radicalization. Moreover, AIDS has decimated some African armies, making them ill-prepared to take on peacekeeping duties in places like Darfur.[55]

Contrariwise, depriving populations of their human rights has led repeatedly to larger public problems. No doubt the most pressing current example is Iraq, in which it has become abundantly evident that successful counterinsurgency war requires gaining the confidence of the Iraqi people. As two distinguished Marine Corps commandants wrote recently,

> Victory . . . comes when the enemy loses legitimacy in the society from which it seeks recruits and thus loses its "recuperative power. . . . [U.S. use of] torture methods . . . have nurtured the recuperative power of the enemy. This war will be won or lost not on the battlefield but in the minds of potential supporters who have not yet thrown in their lot with the enemy. If we forfeit our values by signaling that they are negotiable in situations of grave or imminent danger, we drive those undecideds into the arms of the enemy. This way lies defeat, and we are well down the road to it.[56]

Repression (violations of civil and political rights) and deprivation (violations of social and economic rights) almost inevitably lead at some point or another to resentment, instability, and often explosion, none of which are good for security or markets and all of which make for unreliable partners when it comes, for example, to controlling nuclear proliferation or counteracting climate change.[57]

For decades human rights have been understood in narrow terms, isolated from other public policy arenas and pursued, when they have been pursued at all, as an agenda unto themselves. Such an approach is not only foolish; it is dangerous. A new administration must see human rights in far broader terms, as an integral part of our national security strategy and coextensive with a commitment to global development. This means not only that the United States must become comfortable with including social and economic rights in its human rights agenda.[58] It means that human rights advocates, both inside the government and out, must construe such things as population control and climate change, foreign aid and protection against AIDS, as significant elements of our human rights business. And it means that both the government and its counterparts in the NGO community must think in new ways about human rights. They must reach out to nontraditional partners in the military or in business whose decisions and actions have profound implications for human rights. They must understand such issues as the development of nonlethal force or military rules of engagement to have profound human rights implications.[59] They must eschew old debates such as whether economic development alone is sufficient to guarantee improvements in civil and political rights in favor of more sophisticated analyses of the relation between growth and liberty.

Not only does such an approach bear the promise of reducing human suffering more readily; it also expands the circle of those who can support a comprehensive human rights agenda. It was not a political progressive who argued forcefully at a recent forum at the University of Virginia for a foreign policy that took poverty seriously; it was Francis Fukuyama: "[The United States is] being killed in competition with forces like Chavez, Hezbollah, [the] Muslim Brotherhood, Ahmadinejad, and so forth . . . on the . . . social agenda and basically poverty more broadly." He continued: "What we've been offering these people, democracy and free markets, does not get to that constituency [poor people]."[60]

It is also clear that the pursuit of human rights must be undertaken in a manner that is both contextual and nonideological. If human rights are integrated into broader public policy considerations, they will of course play a more capacious role in decision making but, paradoxically, it will also become apparent that they are not and cannot be the singular polestar of U.S. foreign policy. Sometimes other interests will take precedence. The United States quite rightly did not allow pressure on North Korea regarding its atrocious human rights practices, for example, to trump efforts to control its access to nuclear weaponry. "Nonnegotiable demands" on behalf of human rights are rarely either feasible or productive, as the Bush administration has learned to its sorrow. And sometimes human rights norms are simply not as clear-cut as their staunchest advocates would have us believe. What exactly does constitute "proportional use of force"?

Because violations of human rights are often dramatic and psychologically discomfiting, there is an understandable tendency to want to place their eradication at the top of any policy agenda and to be moralistic about those who fail to do so. When it comes to issues like genocide or torture, such moralism is fully justified. But with respect to other human rights abuses, such an approach may in the long run be self-defeating. The achievement of a human rights utopia is a long way off; its realization, if it ever comes, will be slow and evolutionary. A tragic sense of history teaches that, while we may be able to save many individuals, we will simply not be able to save them all and that the rescue of individuals is often more feasible than the transformation of whole societies. Widespread respect for human rights in a society is dependent upon conditions (for example, literacy; a fundamental sense of personal security) and support structures (an independent judiciary; a functioning civil society) that do not develop overnight. The pressure the European Union is currently exerting upon Turkey to improve its human rights practices, for example, is commendable and has borne positive results but, if Turkey's ongoing human rights failings are used as an excuse to exclude her from membership in the EU, the ultimate consequences for human rights victims may be far more damaging than if it were accepted, blemishes and all.

A new administration would, therefore, do well to make clear from the beginning that

- It will not take a zero-sum approach to human rights but will sometimes settle for the good instead of holding out for the best;
- It will adopt different strategies for different countries, recognizing without apology that the United States has different competing interests in relation to different countries, to say nothing of different degrees and methods of leverage;
- And it will accept the fact that sometimes the best thing the United States can do to advance human rights in a particular situation is to do nothing—at least publicly—either because American involvement will be counterproductive or because the time is not ripe for dramatic gestures.

None of this is to offer an excuse for apathy or indifference. New technologies, new strategic partnerships with business, new uses of laws such as the Alien Torts Claims Act, new networks of international contact at the grassroots—all provide a host of innovative ways to exert pressure on human rights offenders. Satellite photography, for example, has documented the destruction of whole villages in Burma (Myanmar)[61] and uncovered new groundwater resources in Darfur that might contribute to a resolution of the conflict there.[62] And even where few tangible alternatives exist, there is much to be said for symbolism and eloquence. The voice of the U.S. president can still carry great weight when he or she is willing to speak out unequivocally on behalf of human rights victims. Outrage has its place. We have only to imagine how much worse human rights conditions would be in Burma or Russia, Congo or China, than they already are if no one, including the world's most powerful country, monitored or criticized them at all. A contextual approach to human rights will not sanction silence but it will ensure that when we do speak, our voice will be resonant and that when we do act, our actions will be clear.

Framing the Issue

Human rights have rarely, if ever, played a major role in American politics. One of the remarkable features of the 2006 congressional campaigns was how little human rights imbued campaign discourse despite all the attention paid in the months preceding the election to issues like Guantánamo, the Iraqi government's torture of detainees, and Darfur. This dearth is reflective of the human rights movement's failure to build a grassroots constituency for human rights comparable to those amassed by the environmental, women's, or gay and lesbian movements. As a result, politicians fear that they will be labeled "soft on terrorism" at worst, or interested in esoteric issues, at best, if they speak of human rights in a political context.

But concern for human rights can readily transcend political differences if it is presented in the right way. After all, the Human Rights Caucus in the U.S. House of Representatives draws serious bipartisan membership. Whether you believe that the principal dynamic at work in the world today is globalization or a clash of civilizations, it is hard not to respond to a person in pain. A 2008 presidential candidate would do well to take three or four key issues—perhaps negotiating a treaty on terrorism, ending the massacres in Darfur, closing Guantánamo, ratifying the Convention on the Rights of the Child, or "resigning" the treaty creating an International Criminal Court in light of our experience in Iraq—as key elements of a human rights platform.

But regardless of what the specific elements may be, human rights need to be framed in positive ways—even emotional ways—to which the American people can respond and, interestingly enough, given their dramatic subject, there are few issues that lend themselves better to such emotional appeals. How, then, ought those issues to be framed to reach as many people as possible and restore bipartisanship to our human rights efforts?

John Winthrop had great hopes for his New Jerusalem. But he knew that their realization turned on just one thing: that the colony would be not just a model for others, a City upon a Hill, but a model of *decency* and *virtue*. If it failed to be that, if it "shall open the mouths of enemies to speak evil of the ways of God," then prayers shall turn into curses and "we shall surely perish out of the good land whither we pass over this vast sea."[63]

America has always thought itself special; always believed itself worthy of imitation; always flirted with hubris. But there is a difference between being a model and being a crusader and a difference between being a model of virtue and a model of zeal. Yes, the United States has far more than once used its military might to impose an unfortunate will on others.[64] But there is more to the American tradition than that. There is also a tradition of generosity and hospitality; of rescue and liberation; of decency and virtue.

That part of the tradition is manifest in a Roger Williams who thought the early colonists ought to pay the Indians for the land they appropriated and in a Judge Samuel Sewall making public apology for his role in the Salem witchcraft trials. It is manifest in the Bill of Rights. It is manifest in a William Lloyd Garrison and a Lydia Maria Child demanding an end to slavery and in an Elizabeth Cady Stanton expressing outrage when the World Anti-Slavery Society in London denied delegate status to women; in a Sojourner Truth leading slaves to freedom and a Lincoln offering his adversaries "malice toward none and charity for all." It is manifest in a nation opening its arms to immigrants and a president dreaming in 1918 of a worldwide consortium of nations dedicated to the preservation of peace. It is manifest in the defeat of fascism; in Roosevelt's Four Freedoms; in Truman's support for the United Nations; in Eleanor Roosevelt's vision of the Universal Declaration; in Eisenhower's stirring conviction that "the only answer to a regime that wages total cold war is to wage total peace";[65] in the civil rights movement and in the ongoing efforts—even today—to bring to justice those who tried to thwart it.

To attract the widest support, America's commitment to universal human rights should be presented as reflecting, indeed embodying, the *best* of the American tradition.

And it should be presented as vital to America's national interests—because it is. As Paul Collier argues in *The Bottom Billion*, getting development right for the billion of the world's people at the bottom of the economic barrel is not just the moral thing to do. [66] "The twenty-first century world of material comfort, global travel, and economic interdependence will become increasingly vulnerable to these large islands of chaos." The 2007 World Health Organization report warns that infectious diseases are emerging at an "unprecedented rate" and can spread around the world far more rapidly than ever before thanks to increased human mobility.[67] Ensuring that new democracies do not fail; retrieving societies from postconflict implosion; reinforcing transparency in trade and business; empowering women (whose economic status is key to growth); stopping genocide before it spreads—all these are not only nice ideas; they are vital to our country's pragmatic interests. If Goldman Sachs is right and the economies of Brazil, Russia, India, and China will be larger than those of the United States, Japan, the United Kingdom, Germany, France, and Italy by 2050, then we certainly better hope that those countries are well enmeshed by then in a variety of global security networks (legal, diplomatic, financial, even military) that make it in *their* best interests to abide by commonly agreed norms and the rule of (international) law.[68]

Charles Kupchan of Georgetown University has observed that "there is little reason to expect liberal internationalism to become the rallying cry of those jockeying for the White House [in 2008]" and he may be right.[69] But the consequences of having repudiated internationalism in both rhetoric and action, particularly in the arena of human rights, have been so severe—our good name sullied; our capacity to provide leadership dulled; our ability to call other nations to account diminished; what former national security adviser Zbigniew Brzezinski calls "global shared resentments" exacerbated;[70] the lives of our troops put in jeopardy by our trashing of the Geneva Conventions; mixed messages sent to allies and adversaries alike about our commitment to democracy; Al Qaeda handed a ready tool for recruitment; weaker nations forced to consider coercive means to defend themselves against our unbridled power; and a message sent to the American people themselves that fear sanctions indulgence of our basest passions and that the ensemble of rights we have always taught our children was a proud characteristic of this nation is in fact a frail and flimsy thing that can be dismantled in a heartbeat—these consequences may be so severe that they may, paradoxically, reawaken a commitment to global cooperation among the American people. After all, an overwhelming majority of Americans want the United States to continue to exert strong leadership in the world—84 percent in a December 2006 poll—but they want it to be *shared* leadership.[71]

That is because they know not only that our resources are limited but our vision is too. Every nation's vision, like every individual's, is blurred at one time or another by its own limitations, its own short-sightedness and misperception, whether intellectual or moral. The wise government, the wise person, is acutely aware of that. The great theologian Reinhold Niebuhr, a favorite of neoconservatives for his robust advocacy of American power but a vigilant critic of self-deception, put it this way in 1952: the only way to overcome the moral hazards of being the most mighty nation in the world, he said, is to come to terms with "the limits of all human striving, the fragmentariness of all human wisdom, the precariousness of all historic configurations of power, and the mixture of good and evil in all human virtue."[72] At our best, we Americans know that. President Harry S. Truman knew that in 1945 when he wrote, "We all have to recognize—no matter how great our strength—that we must deny ourselves the license to do always as we please."[73] And even George W. Bush seemed to know that: "If we're an arrogant nation, [other countries] will resent us," he said in the second presidential debate in 2000. "If we're a humble nation, but strong, they'll welcome us."[74]

We await now a president prepared to implement George Bush's wisdom.

This volume is designed to advise that new president how to do that. First, two caveats. We are focused here on *international* human rights policy, not domestic, important as it is to understand domestic practices such as police brutality as human rights crimes. And second, we cannot hope in one volume to speak in depth to every human rights problem. We only mention in passing, for example, such issues as trading arms with countries that are responsible for human rights crimes, the impunity that has permitted private military contractors to go unregulated, and the rampant abuses of gay, lesbian, transgendered, and bisexual people (LGBT) around the world. The latter remain largely invisible to government and intergovernmental human rights officials, their rights usually unreferenced in international human rights instruments, despite continuing attacks upon their persons and blatant discrimination.[75] The United States should be far more assertive in raising issues of crimes against LGBT persons in bilateral conversations and at appropriate international fora.[76]

The contributors to this volume are drawn from the worlds of human rights activism and academia, government service and private philanthropy. In these pages they tackle some of the toughest questions facing human rights policymakers. *Rachel Kleinfeld* outlines the circumstances and manner in which the United States ought to intervene militarily to stop crimes that "shock the conscience" of humanity. *John Shattuck* and *Catherine Powell* provide broad context for understanding the ways in which America's reputation has suffered internationally since September 11, 2001, and *Elisa Massimino* proposes concrete steps to mitigate the human rights violations committed by the Bush administration during the "War on Terror." *Jennifer Windsor* describes how to rescue democracy promotion from the debacle of Iraq. *Philip Alston* urges us to broaden our understanding of rights to include social and economic. Several authors address evolving issues in key thematic areas, such as women's rights (*Regan Ralph*), refugee policy (*Bill Frelick*), labor rights (*Carol Pier* and *Elizabeth Drake*) and religious freedom (*Felice Gaer*) and others take on mechanisms by which human rights may be advanced: *Debora Spar* describes ways to engage corporate interests in the struggle to improve human rights; *George Lopez* unscrambles the controversial question of sanctions—when they work and when they don't—and *Eric Schwartz*, drawing upon his experience at the National Security Council, elucidates how and where to locate responsibility for human rights policy in the structure of a new administration. Finally, *Alexandra Arriaga* outlines a human rights legislative agenda for a new Congress and a new administration.

Many of the questions that we take on here have no easy answers. The essays represent the opinions of their authors and not necessarily the organizations with which they are affiliated. Needless to say, many who care deeply about human rights may demur from some or even many of the recommendations we offer. But that it is worth struggling with these issues no one would dispute. That the United States can do better than it has in promoting human rights almost goes without saying. The burden of this volume is to begin to sketch a better way.

Chapter 1
Fighting from Strength
Human Rights and the Challenge of Terrorism

Elisa Massimino

Nearly seven years ago, in the immediate aftermath of the 9/11 attacks, this country was awash in fear and anger.[1] The fledgling Bush administration focused urgently—and rightly—on protecting Americans and preventing further attacks. Al Qaeda had declared war on the United States several times during the 1990s, with attacks against Americans and American interests abroad. Finally, in the face of the deaths of nearly 3,000 innocent American civilians on 9/11, the United States reciprocated, declaring a "global war on terror."

Many of the subsequent steps taken to enhance the government's capacity to detect and deter terrorism were sensible and necessary. Few questioned the need for improved coordination among federal, state, and local agencies and between law enforcement and intelligence officials. Likewise, efforts to protect the nation's critical infrastructure and strengthen the preparedness of frontline forces—police, fire, public health, and emergency medical teams—are vital and ongoing.

Perhaps because the government's failure to anticipate—and prevent—the 9/11 attacks was widely seen as a failure of imagination, the Bush administration encouraged government officials charged with counterterrorism responsibilities to be creative, forward-leaning, and to "think outside the box."[2]

But what was "the box" that was seen to constrain the counterterrorism effort? And now, nearly seven years later, are we better off outside it?

Clearly one box that the administration sought to escape was the criminal justice system and the constitutional protections that system affords to suspects. Prior to 9/11, terrorists—from Timothy McVeigh to the Unabomber to the perpetrators of the first World Trade Center attack—were approached as a law enforcement challenge. But after 9/11 that attitude was openly derided by the administration and its supporters as insufficiently muscular to deal with the magnitude of the terrorist threat and too focused on punishment at the expense of prevention.

One way out of this box was to frame counterterrorism operations as a "global *war* on terror."[3] Under the laws of war, combatants captured during wartime are not entitled to the same panoply of rights as criminal defendants and, importantly, once determined to be combatants, can be held without charge or trial until the end of the war. But the same rules that permit prolonged detention in order to remove warriors from the battlefield also require humane treatment and fair trials—another "box" from which the administration seemed determined to escape.

Despite its rhetoric about "taking the fight to Al Qaeda" by seeking to free U.S. actions from the constraints of law, the administration has chosen to contest our terrorist foes on a battlefield of the enemy's choosing, forfeiting our greatest assets in this asymmetric struggle, namely, our values, our ideas, and our commitment to human rights and the rule of law. But, as the hard lessons of the last six years have demonstrated, the way forward in this long struggle requires that, when we take the fight to Al Qaeda, we go into battle armed with these most precious "blessings of liberty."[4]

In his second inaugural address, President George W. Bush declared that "America's vital interests and our deepest beliefs are now one." Yet so many of the missteps of the years since 9/11 are the result of policies grounded in a belief that our values and interests are in conflict. What would it look like to take the president's declaration seriously? An examination of three highly contentious issues—interrogation, detention, and the trials of suspected terrorists—can help us answer that question.

Torture: Reclaiming Who We Are

Few would dispute that intelligence gathering is a necessary—and perhaps the most important—tool in disrupting terrorist networks. Effective interrogations designed to produce actionable intelligence are a legitimate and important part of this effort. Such interrogations can be conducted in a manner fully consistent with the laws and values of the United States.

But that has not been the approach taken by the current administration. Instead, the administration has sought to redefine the rules governing treatment of prisoners, asserting broad executive power under the authority allegedly granted a wartime commander in chief. This approach is epitomized by the Justice Department's infamous "torture memo," which construes the domestic criminal statute prohibiting torture so narrowly that much of what the United States has condemned as torture when done by other governments would not be prohibited. That same memo, which later was withdrawn as "overly broad" but never repudiated, also sought to reassure interrogators that, even if their conduct constituted torture under the memo's narrow definition, they need not worry about being prosecuted under the statute because the president could authorize violations of the law in his power as commander in chief.[5]

The administration took a similar approach to treaty obligations under human rights and humanitarian law. Administration lawyers argued that the United States was not bound by the Geneva Conventions' prohibitions against torture, cruel treatment, and outrages upon personal dignity because, as unlawful combatants, detainees in U.S. custody were not entitled to those protections. The administration likewise sought to evade U.S. treaty obligations under the Convention Against Torture—which requires states to prevent the use of cruel, inhuman, or degrading treatment—by reinterpreting a reservation to the treaty to mean that the United States was not bound by the prohibition on cruelty when it acted against foreigners abroad. When Congress rejected this untenable position by passing the McCain Amendment[6] and required all U.S. personnel—including the CIA—to refrain from cruel, inhuman, and degrading treatment of prisoners, no matter what their location or legal status, the President's signature on the bill was accompanied by a signing statement which in effect reserved the right to bypass the law when he saw fit.[7] Meanwhile, administration lawyers started arguing that the McCain Amendment did not rule out *all* official cruelty but only that which "shocks the conscience"—a standard Vice President Dick Cheney argued was infinitely flexible and "in the eye of the beholder."[8]

Finally, when the Supreme Court ruled in the *Hamdan v. Rumsfeld* case in 2006 that the humane treatment standards of the Geneva Conventions set out in Common Article 3 were binding on the United States in its treatment of all detainees,"[9] the administration tried to convince Congress to replace that standard with its more flexible "shocks the conscience" interpretation. Congress refused. Though it narrowed the range of conduct that would be considered a war crime under domestic law, Congress rejected the administration's proposal to redefine and narrow Common Article 3 itself. Nonetheless, the president concluded, upon signing the bill into law, that the CIA could continue to use a set of "alternative interrogation techniques" beyond those authorized for use by the military. On July 20, 2007 he formalized that conclusion in Executive Order 13440, which purports to interpret Common Article 3 and authorizes a CIA program of secret detention and interrogation. The legal guidance underpinning that order has not been made public but the order itself fails to take off the table any of the torture techniques—including waterboarding,[10] stress positions, and sleep and sensory deprivation—reported to have been authorized previously for use in the CIA program.

Against this backdrop of repeated efforts to circumvent the rules by depriving the words "torture" and "cruelty" of their meaning, the president's claims that "we don't torture" are understandably met with great skepticism at home and abroad. However much we may wish it were not the case, the truth is that we *have* tortured detainees in our custody. According to the Pentagon's own figures, at least eight detainees were literally tortured to death—beaten, suffocated, frozen, hung.[11] And none of these deaths by torture were perpetrated by the "bad apples" featured in the Abu Ghraib photographs. How do we account for this from a country that led the world in drafting the international convention prohibiting torture?

Torture is particularly seductive during times of fear and insecurity. There persists a common American fantasy that if we are ever faced with a "ticking time bomb," we can save the day and avert disaster if only we are willing to "take off the gloves." That kind of wishful thinking is reflected in, and fueled by, popular culture. According to the Parents Television Council, there has been a dramatic rise in the number of scenes depicting torture on television over the last several years—from 4 in 1999 to 228 in 2003. Moreover, while it used to be that only villains tortured, today heroic American characters routinely employ torture. And it almost always works—on the screen.

But real life is not television. No systematic study has ever shown that inflicting torture or other such cruelty yields reliable information or actionable intelligence. To the contrary, a recent report of the Intelligence Science Board published by the National Defense Intelligence College raises serious questions about the supposed effectiveness of abusive interrogations.[12] And there is a substantial body of opinion among serving senior officers and career interrogators that such techniques are not only illegal but ineffective and undermine our ability to elicit reliable intelligence. For example, in releasing the new U.S. Army field manual on interrogation,[13] Lieutenant General John F. Kimmons, deputy chief of staff for Army intelligence, said that "no good intelligence is going to come from abusive practices. I think history tells us that. I think the empirical evidence of the last five years, hard years, tells us that."[14] Likewise, General David Petraeus, the commander of multinational forces in Iraq, recently wrote in an open letter to U.S. troops serving there: "Some may argue that we would be more effective if we sanctioned torture or other expedient methods to obtain information from the enemy. They would be wrong. Beyond the basic fact that such actions are illegal, history shows that they also are frequently neither useful nor necessary."[15]

Nonetheless, the fantasy—that we can use torture to avert catastrophe without fundamentally changing who we are—persists. Enabling that fantasy is the belief that interrogators can walk right up to the torture "line"—"get chalk on [their] cleats," in the words of CIA director Michael Hayden[16]—and not cross it. But that line, while it may exist in theory, is in practice a myth. As former Navy general counsel Alberto Mora wrote in a memo critical of interrogation policies that permitted the use of cruelty and other inappropriate force short of torture: "Once the initial barrier against the use of improper force had been breached, a phenomenon known as 'force drift' would almost certainly begin to come into play. This term describes the observed tendency among interrogators who rely on force. If some force is good, these people come to believe, then the application of more force must be better."[17] This is the logic of torture: in order for it to accomplish its objective—to break a person's will—it must be used until it becomes unbearable.[18]

Just as the use of force tends to "drift" upward, it likewise migrates between agencies. That is why both the prohibition against torture and other cruelty must apply equally to all U.S. personnel, including the CIA. There should be a single standard of humane treatment to which all U.S. military and civilian personnel adhere. Adhering to a single standard of humane treatment does not mean that all detainees must be treated alike. No one argues that suspected 9/11 mastermind Khalid Sheikh Mohammed must be granted the privileges to which prisoners of war are entitled. But there should be no daylight between the baseline humane treatment standards governing military and CIA interrogations. In wartime those standards are found in Common Article 3 of the Geneva Conventions. Outside of armed conflict, they are found in international human rights and domestic law.

Interrogation policy under the executive order forfeits our greatest assets in the asymmetric battle with Al Qaeda—our values, our ideals, and our commitment to human rights and the rule of law that set us apart from our enemies—for little, if any, gain. It is time for a clean break from this approach. For the safety of U.S. personnel and the integrity of fundamental human rights and humanitarian law standards, the United States must make clear—to the American people and to the rest of the world—what it means when it says it will abide by its obligations under Common Article 3. The most effective way to accomplish this would be to hold all government agencies and U.S.-employed private security contractors to the interrogation rules set out in the Army field manual.

The director of national intelligence, Admiral Mike McConnell, in defending the executive order authorizing the CIA program, implied that the United States *wants* detainees to believe that they will be tortured by their American captors. Yet it wants the rest of the world to believe just the opposite. We cannot have it both ways. Our biggest problem now is not that the enemy knows what to expect from us; it is that the rest of the world, including our allies, does not.

There was a time not that long ago when the president declared that the demands of human dignity were "non-negotiable," when no one in the U.S. government questioned the meaning and scope of the humane treatment provisions of the Geneva Conventions and when the rest of the world viewed with great skepticism claims by U.S.-held prisoners that they had been abused.

Today we are in a very different place. Our stand on human dignity seems to be that it *is* negotiable so long as there's no "permanent damage." Common Article 3's prohibition against torture, cruelty, and degradation, clear to our military for more than half a century, is now considered by the administration to be too vague to enforce. And much of the rest of the world believes—not surprisingly, given the administration's refusal to renounce interrogation techniques our own allies consider unlawful—that the United States routinely tortures prisoners in our custody. Interrogation techniques need not cause permanent damage in order to be unlawful. But they *have* inflicted enormous damage on the honor and reputation of the United States and it will be up to the next president to determine whether that damage is permanent.

Detention Without Trial: Abandoning the Guantánamo Experiment

The decision to hold detainees at the U.S. naval base at Guantánamo Bay was driven at least in part by a desire on the part of the administration to insulate U.S. actions taken there—detention, interrogation, and trials—from judicial scrutiny and even from the realm of law itself. Early on one administration official called Guantánamo "the legal equivalent of outer space." That goal—to create a law-free zone in which certain people are considered outside the law—was illegitimate and unworthy of this nation. Any policy bent on achieving it was bound to fail.

The policy at Guantánamo has been a failure in several important respects. First and most obviously, it has failed as a legal matter. The Supreme Court has rejected the government's detention, interrogation, and trial policies at Guantánamo every time it has examined them. And it likely will do so again.

Military commissions at Guantánamo have also failed to hold terrorists accountable for the most serious crimes. Unless you count the plea of the Australian David Hicks who, after five years in U.S. custody, pled guilty to a crime—material support for terrorism—that did not even exist in the laws of war at the time Hicks allegedly committed it, the system has failed to bring a single terrorist to justice.

In addition, fueled by the assertion that it was a "legal black hole,"[19] Guantánamo became the laboratory for a policy of torture and calculated cruelty that later migrated to Afghanistan and Iraq[20] and was revealed to the world in the photographs from Abu Ghraib.[21] These policies aided jihadist recruitment and did immense damage to the honor and reputation of the United States, undermining its ability to lead and damaging the war effort.

But perhaps most important from a security perspective, the policy at Guantánamo—which treats terrorists as "combatants" in a "war" against the United States but rejects application of the laws of war—has had the doubly pernicious effects of degrading the laws of war while conferring on suspected terrorists the elevated status of combatants.

By taking the strategic metaphor of a "war on terror" literally, the United States government has unwittingly ceded an operational and rhetorical advantage to Al Qaeda, allowing them to project themselves to the world—including to potential recruits and a broader audience in the Middle East—as warriors rather than criminals.

Khalid Sheikh Mohammed reveled in this status at his "combatant status review tribunal" hearing at Guantánamo. After reviewing an itemized list of 31 separate attacks and plots for which he claimed responsibility (including the 9/11 attacks and the murder of *Wall Street Journal* reporter Daniel Pearl), he addressed, as if soldier-to-soldier, the uniformed Navy captain serving as president of the military tribunal. Proudly claiming the mantle of combatant ("For sure, I am American enemies"), he lamented, in effect, that war is hell and in war people get killed: "[T]he language of any war in the world is killing . . . the language of war is victims." He compared himself and Osama bin Laden to George Washington ("we consider we and George Washington doing [the] same thing").[22]

Those on the frontlines of the fight with Al Qaeda understand instinctively what a profound error it was to reinforce Al Qaeda's vision of itself as a revolutionary force in an epic battle with the United States. The Army's new counterinsurgency manual, which incorporates lessons learned in a variety of counterinsurgency operations, including Iraq, and was drafted under the leadership of General Petraeus, stresses repeatedly that defeating nontraditional enemies like Al Qaeda is primarily a political struggle, one that must focus on isolating the enemy and delegitimizing it with its potential supporters rather than elevating it in stature and importance. As the manual states: "It is easier to separate an insurgency from its resources and let it die than to kill every insurgent. . . . Dynamic insurgencies can replace losses quickly. Skillful counterinsurgents must thus cut off the sources of that recuperative power."[23]

But U.S. counterterrorism policy has taken just the opposite approach. Prolonged detention at Guantánamo without access to judicial review, interrogations that violate fundamental human rights norms, and flawed military commissions have nurtured the "recuperative power" of the enemy. It will be up to the next president to force a clean break from this misguided approach and begin to construct a counterterrorism policy that conforms to the logic of counterinsurgency operations, adheres to fundamental human rights standards, and capitalizes on the advantages of our system of laws. Here are five first steps down that road.

- *Close Guantánamo.* The human rights and legal challenges posed by the ongoing detention of prisoners at Guantánamo are serious. Closing the prison raises many complex questions about what to do with prisoners being held there—those the United States believes have committed crimes against it and those being held without charge "until the end of the conflict." In many ways it matters less *where* prisoners are held than that their detention, interrogation, and trial comport with U.S. and international law.

It is, however, beyond serious question, even among many who initially supported the decision to detain prisoners at Guantánamo, that the camp has become an enormous diplomatic liability, impairing the capacity of the United States to lead the world not only in counterterrorism operations but on many other issues of priority on which international cooperation is necessary. As Secretary of Defense Robert Gates has said, "There is no question in my mind that Guantánamo and some of the abuses that have taken place in Iraq have negatively impacted the reputation of the United States."[24] Indeed, Guantánamo has become an icon, in much the same way as the picture of the hooded Iraqi prisoner at Abu Ghraib has become an icon, a symbol of the willingness of this country—in the face of security threats—to set aside its core values and beliefs. Respect for the law and fundamental rights is not the only thing that has disappeared into Guantánamo's "black hole"—so has American credibility.

Of course, while it is important to take into consideration the views of our closest allies, all of whom have called on the United States to close the prison, no one argues that we should change U.S. policy simply because other nations do not like it. The most important questions about the current policy are: Is it smart? Is it working? Does it serve the overall objective? Does it comport with our laws and values? Guantánamo fails all those tests.

Secretary Gates has argued that the continued detention of prisoners at Guantánamo is undermining the war effort and that the prison should be shut down as soon as possible. His views echo the conclusion now reached by a broad spectrum of national security policymakers and members of Congress that, whatever its original utility, Guantánamo has outlived its usefulness. State Department and Pentagon officials quoted in the *New York Times* have said that U.S. policy at Guantánamo is "making it more difficult in some cases to coordinate efforts in counterterrorism, intelligence and law enforcement."[25] Former Secretary of State Colin Powell said at the Aspen Institute in July 2006 that "Guantánamo ought to be closed immediately," arguing that the value of continuing to hold the detainees was questionable while the price of holding the detainees was too high.[26] According to the *Washington Post*, former Attorney General John Ashcroft had argued that Guantánamo's liabilities outweighed its usefulness.[27]

None of this is surprising. As the Army's counterinsurgency manual states: "A Government's respect for preexisting and impersonal legal rules can provide the key to gaining widespread and enduring societal support. . . . Illegitimate actions," such as "unlawful detention, torture, and punishment without trial . . . are self-defeating, even against insurgents who conceal themselves amid non-combatants who flout the law."[28]

Despite the self-defeating nature of the policy and the growing consensus that it should end, the administration has continued to transfer new detainees to the prison camp. The administration asserts that one new transferee, Mohammad Abdul Malik, who reportedly confessed to involvement in the 2002 hotel bombing in Kenya, was sent to Guantánamo because he represents a "significant threat." It is increasingly clear, however, that many detainees were sent to Guantánamo, rather than being indicted and tried in federal court, not because that was the smartest or most strategic option available but because it was the one that relieved the government of the burden of making difficult choices. But if U.S. counterterrorism policy consists simply of detaining or killing everyone who harbors hostility toward the United States, we must face the reality that the 385 men at Guantánamo are a drop in that bucket and that continuing to hold them there without charge or trial in fair proceedings will eventually mean that we will need a much bigger bucket.

Former Defense Secretary Donald Rumsfeld once wondered aloud whether we were creating more terrorists than we were killing. That is precisely the right question to ask in a counterinsurgency campaign. But the answer so far is not encouraging. The next administration must solve this problem and chart a way out of the trap that Guantánamo has become, not only for the detainees who have been held there for so many years but for U.S. counterterrorism policy itself. The first step is to shut it down.[29]

• *Release or Transfer Those Not Charged and Bring the Rest to the United States.* In July 2007, President Bush said "I'd like to close Guantánamo, but I also recognize that we're holding some people there that are darn dangerous and that we better have a plan to deal with them in our courts."[30] State Department lawyers continue to shop the world for countries that will agree to take the Guantánamo detainees off our hands but this attempt to "retail" the Guantánamo problem is inadequate and unsatisfactory as it leaves U.S. policy at the mercy of other governments, many of whom have no interest in helping.

Despite the growing sense even inside the administration that the Guantánamo policy is hurting U.S. interests, paralysis has set in and no one in the administration appears to be prepared to move. Part of the reason for this is that the current system lacks incentives that would force decisions about who to try and who to release. Under current policy detainees at Guantánamo can be held without trial for an indefinite period. If they are tried and convicted in a military commission, they remain in detention; if they are tried and acquitted, they may also remain in detention.

If the detainees were brought to the United States, that incentive structure would change and there would be a new sense of urgency to separate those the United States suspects of having committed crimes against it from those it does not. Detainees not suspected of having committed crimes against the United States should be released to their home countries, if possible, in accordance with U.S. obligations under international human rights and humanitarian laws. Where release to the home country is not possible (for example, because there is a fear that a detainee will be subjected to torture), detainees should be released to a third country in accordance with U.S. obligations under international human rights and humanitarian laws.

U.S. allies, particularly the Europeans who have called most loudly for the prison to be closed, should do much more to help on this score. The United States climbed into this box alone but its allies have a shared responsibility to help it get out if they are going to establish a sustainable cooperative framework for fighting terrorism, something both the United States and its allies in this struggle sorely need; this is more than just a U.S. problem now. Manfred Nowak, the Austrian UN special rapporteur on torture, has urged that European governments assume greater responsibility for helping with third country resettlement of these people. "Europe should help empty it," Nowak has said. "No country is eager to accept people who are accused of having Al Qaeda links. But there should be burden-sharing." He's right about that and the sooner the United States moves to regularize its own treatment of detainees, the more likely it is that our European allies will step up to help.

• *Restore Habeas Corpus.* To the extent that there has been a debate about whether detainees at Guantánamo are or should be entitled to raise habeas claims, it has to a large extent been a dialogue of the deaf. On one side is the argument that granting habeas rights to Guantánamo detainees would be unprecedented; prisoners of war have never been entitled to access to the courts to challenge their detention. On the other is the assertion that anyone in U.S. custody is entitled under the Constitution to habeas corpus, a vital mechanism to check the excesses of executive power against the individual, which can only be suspended "when in Cases of Rebellion or Invasion the public Safety may require it,"[31] something Congress has authorized only four times in the nation's history: during the Civil War; in the immediate aftermath of the Civil War to quell rebellions in South Carolina; in the Philippines during a rebellion; and temporarily in Hawaii immediately after the attack on Pearl Harbor.

Both sides are right to a degree. But the argument against habeas assumes its premise: that the detainees at Guantánamo are all properly considered wartime prisoners whose detention is regulated by the laws of war. The past six years have clearly shown that some of the detainees have been wrongly held. Habeas corpus is the safety net designed to ensure that a person deprived of liberty is lawfully detained. Unfortunately, the debate over habeas has been contentious in large part because of the misguided insistence on shoehorning all of these detainees into a combatant framework. Once you step outside of that framework, it is clear that habeas is required. Unless detainees are properly considered to be combatants under the laws of war, courts must be permitted independently to judge the legality of any deprivation of their liberty by the state.

• *Amend the Definition of Enemy Combatant.* Even if the Guantánamo detainees regain the right to habeas, the critical issue of what constitutes an "enemy combatant" remains. The Military Commissions Act (MCA) defines a combatant not only as one who takes part in hostilities but includes people who "purposefully and materially" support hostilities against the United States, including those arrested far from the battlefield. This definition converts people who would never be considered combatants under the laws of war—such as a doctor who operates on a wounded rebel or a permanent resident of the United States who commits a criminal act completely unrelated to armed conflict—into "combatants" who can be placed in military custody and tried by a military commission. Even more troubling, the MCA deems anyone, regardless of whether they fit the above definition, who has been determined to be an "unlawful enemy combatant" based on a determination of a combatant status review tribunal (or "another competent tribunal" established by the president or the secretary of defense) to be an enemy combatant. This "you're a combatant if we say you are" approach not only flies in the face of established humanitarian law, but has ramifications that go far beyond the status of detainees at Guantánamo.

Under the laws of war, combatants may in most situations be lawfully attacked and killed; civilians (unless they take part in hostilities) cannot. The MCA definition blurs that vital distinction with potentially dangerous consequences. For example, is it in the interest of the United States to endorse a definition of enemy combatant that would allow Russian President Vladimir Putin to pick up anyone he deems to have provided "material support" for terrorism (as many human rights NGOs in Russia are accused by the Putin government of having done, simply by virtue of documenting Russian abuses in Chechnya) and treat them as if they were combatants? Would we be comfortable with the Chinese government using this definition to label peaceful Urghurs as enemy combatants or President Álvaro Uribe in Colombia, who once described some members of the political opposition as "terrorists in business suits," adopting its standards to combat his adversaries? What about Amir Mohamed Meshal, the American citizen detained in Kenya, cleared by the FBI of terrorist connections, but deemed by the Kenyan government to have "engaged in guerrilla war against the democratically elected government" of Somalia and rendered by the Kenyans to Ethiopia?[32] If adopted by other governments, the expansive definition of enemy combatant pushed by the Bush administration will strengthen the hand of repressive governments around the world who seek to cast their attacks on political opponents and civil society as legitimate use of force against combatants.

• *Scrap the Current Military Commissions and Try Suspects in Courts Martial or Federal Courts.* While military commissions generally have long been an accepted part of our military justice system, current commissions under the Military Commissions Act bear little resemblance to these traditional fora for dispensing battlefield justice. First, military commission rules permit the admission of evidence obtained through coercion, including cruel, inhuman, and degrading treatment, if it was obtained before December 20, 2005. A coerced statement can be admitted if found to be "reliable," sufficiently probative, and its admission is "in the interest of justice." If the interrogation techniques used to obtain the information are classified, it could be extremely difficult for a defendant to show that coerced evidence should not be admitted.

Second, defendants before a military commission can be convicted for acts that were not illegal when they were committed. Basic due process requires that a person cannot be held criminally responsible for an action that was not legally prohibited at the time it was taken. But military commissions may punish individuals for offenses—including the crimes of conspiracy and "providing material support for terrorism"—that were either not illegal before the passage of the MCA, or not recognized as war crimes under the laws of war.

Third, the scope of judicial review of military commission decisions is restricted and inadequate. The review by the initial appeals court (the Court of Military Commission Review) is limited only to matters of law (not fact) that "prejudiced a substantial trial right" of the defendant. This provision would prevent the first appellate court, the U.S. Court of Appeals for the District of Columbia, and the U.S. Supreme Court from considering factual appeals, including possible appeals based on a defendant's factual innocence.

Last, the military commission rules for classified evidence are so broad that they would prevent the defense from seeing evidence that tends to show innocence or a lack of responsibility. Upon the request of the government, the judge may exclude both the defendant and his lawyer from the process in which the government argues to the judge that classified information should be withheld. The government has no duty to disclose classified information that could result in a more lenient sentence for the defendant. The judge is specifically permitted to limit the scope of examination of witnesses on the stand, which could hamper the ability of the defense to challenge a witness's testimony or basis for classification.

There is no question that the commissions are staffed by many talented, dedicated, and honorable service personnel. But the system itself is illegitimate and no amount of good will or good lawyering can change that. Even some members of Congress who voted for the Military Commissions Act did so while expressing the hope that the courts would step in to remedy its many defects. The next president should not wait for the courts to come to the rescue nor merely tinker with the machinery of military commissions. Instead, he or she should shut down the military commissions system altogether.

Terrorist suspects at Guantánamo should be tried either pursuant to the rules for courts martial under the Uniform Code of Military Justice or in regular federal courts. Such trials would satisfy the requirement of the laws of war—and of our own laws—that sentences be carried out pursuant to a "previous judgment pronounced by a regularly constituted court affording all the judicial guarantees which are recognized as indispensable by civilized peoples."[33]

As House Armed Service Committee Chairman Ike Skelton (D-Mo.) remarked recently, "The last thing that we would want is to convict an individual for terrorism and then have that conviction overturned because of fatal flaws in the Military Commissions law passed in the previous Congress."[34] That risk is quite real. Khalid Sheikh Mohammed would likely have few defenses in a fair trial. But in a military commission under the current rules, he will raise the defense that the trial is not fair. The United States can deprive him of that defense by moving his trial to a court martial or, preferably, to a regular federal criminal proceeding. That not only would guard against the risk but is smart counterterrorism policy as well. As the *Counterinsurgency* field manual points out, "to establish legitimacy, commanders transition security activities from combat operations to law enforcement as quickly as feasible. When insurgents are seen as criminals, they lose public support."[35]

Trials in federal court would also offer the advantage of a venue capable of exercising jurisdiction over a much broader spectrum of criminal conduct. The decision to treat terrorism suspects as "enemy combatants" was made in order to justify targeting, detention, and trial practices that could not be supported outside of an armed conflict paradigm. There are many reasons, legal and practical, why this decision was and continues to be a mistake. One reason is that it has led to the establishment of military commissions that have jurisdiction only over war crimes, limiting the offenses with which terrorist suspects can be charged. This limitation led the administration and Congress to try to expand the jurisdiction of military commissions to include acts such as intentionally causing serious bodily injury; mutilating or maiming; murder and destruction of property in violation of the law of war; terrorism; material support for terrorism; and conspiracy. But these actions do not constitute war crimes simply because we *call them* war crimes.

These acts are not criminal under the laws of war if the targets are legitimate military objectives. And though they are war crimes if committed "in violation of the laws of war," it appears from the charges brought so far in military commissions at Guantánamo that they are erroneously being construed to include any act of unprivileged belligerency, which is not a violation of the laws of war. Application of these new crimes to events that occurred before the passage of the law is a textbook violation of the prohibition of ex post facto prosecution, raising additional and legitimate bases for defense counsel to challenge the military commission convictions. These problems can be avoided by using civilian criminal courts and the broader spectrum of established criminal laws available in them.

Those who insist that it would be impossible to try terrorist suspects in the federal courts say that such trials would be too dangerous for judges, juries, and witnesses. But the risk of reprisals against juries, witnesses, and judges—while extremely serious—is certainly nothing new. The judiciary has long taken measures to prevent threats of violence from undermining the trial process. We protect those involved in the trial of murderous mob bosses through witness relocation, anonymous juries, and employment of the marshal service for the safety of judges. We secure courtrooms with Plexiglas shields, extra layers of security screening, metal detectors, and additional police. Our experience with prosecution of organized crime, including violent members of drug cartels throughout much of the twentieth century, indicates that terrorism cases present no unique challenge in this realm.

Those skeptical of the feasibility of moving these cases to federal court also assert that such prosecutions would force the government to reveal classified information to the defense in order to satisfy constitutional requirements for a fair trial. Leaving aside the fact that terrorist suspects *are* being tried in the federal courts, these are serious concerns that should be explored and fully addressed. But the fact that terrorism cases pose difficult challenges for the criminal justice system should not preclude trials from proceeding successfully to conviction without damage to sensitive information. Given the enormous strategic and political costs of the alternative—the status quo—it is incumbent upon those who would abandon the criminal justice system to demonstrate why the existing procedures, such as the Classified Information Procedures Act (CIPA),[36] are insufficient to protect the government's legitimate interests in these cases. Many judges believe that these procedures are adequate to meet the special challenges presented by terrorism cases. Judge Royce Lamberth recently remarked: "I have found the Classified Information Procedures Act to provide all the tools that I have needed as a district judge to successfully navigate the tricky questions presented in spy cases, as well as terrorist cases." In fact, of the hundreds of CIPA motions filed in criminal cases since the law came into effect, there have been no reversible errors found on appeal.

Time for a Clean Break

How we treat terrorist suspects—including how we try them—speaks volumes about who we are as a nation and our confidence in the institutions and values that set us apart. The distinction between the United States and its terrorist enemies has narrowed over the course of this conflict, in part because of lapses in U.S. compliance with human rights norms, but also because U.S. counterterrorism policy has unwittingly elevated Al Qaeda by treating it as a military adversary contending with the United States on a global battlefield. We can—we must—reverse this course if we are to prevail.

When Judge William Young sentenced Al Qaeda terrorist Richard Reid to life plus 110 years in federal prison in 2003, this is what he said:

> We are not afraid of any of your terrorist co-conspirators, Mr. Reid. We are Americans. We have been through the fire before. There is all too much war talk here. And I say that to everyone with the utmost respect.
>
> Here in this court where we deal with individuals as individuals, and care for individuals as individuals, as human beings we reach out for justice.
>
> You are not an enemy combatant. You are a terrorist. You are not a soldier in any war. You are a terrorist. To give you that reference, to call you a soldier gives you far too much stature. Whether it is the officers of government who do it or your attorney who does it, or that happens to be your view, you are a terrorist. . . .
>
> So war talk is way out of line in this court. You're a big fellow. But you're not that big. You're no warrior. I know warriors. You are a terrorist. A species of criminal guilty of multiple attempted murders. . . .
>
> You're no big deal.[37]

Some administration officials argue that adhering to these standards of justice and the rule of law is too great a liability. They say that these rules make for an unfair fight: we fight with one hand tied behind our backs while the enemies do as they please.[38] But while terrorists employ methods that we abhor, we too have an advantage in that asymmetrical conflict: our institutions and the values that set us apart from our enemies. The goal of terrorists, as William Taft, the former legal adviser to the State Department, described it, is the "negation of law."[39] Yet in many ways that same impulse—the "negation of law"—was the genesis of the detainee policies at Guantánamo and beyond. It is time for a clean break from these policies. The next president should set a new course, one that takes seriously the long and difficult road ahead in combating the threat of terrorism, while recognizing that adherence to our values and our system of laws is a source of strength in that struggle.

Chapter 2
National Security and the Rule of Law
Self-Inflicted Wounds

JOHN SHATTUCK

There is a remarkable paradox in the relationship today between the United States and the rest of the world. Despite economic and military assets unparalleled in history, U.S. global influence and standing have hit rock bottom.

The rapid decline in global opinion of the United States in recent years has reduced the capacity of the United States to carry out its foreign policy and protect national security. The perception of a growing gap between the values the United States professes and the way it acts—particularly on human rights and the rule of law—has eroded U.S. power and influence around the world.

As a result of both failed policies and falling world opinion, America's soft power has been diminished. In his book, *Soft Power: The Means to Success in World Politics,* Joseph Nye analyzes a nation's "ability to get what [it] wants through attraction rather than coercion." Soft power derives from "the attractiveness of a nation's culture, political ideals, and policies. When [its] policies are seen as legitimate in the eyes of others, [its] soft power is enhanced."[1] Today American political ideals have lost much of their global attraction because their appeal has been undermined by U.S. policies and actions that lack legitimacy in the eyes of the world. American foreign policy will continue to fail until the United States regains the international respect it has lost.

To restore its lost stature, the United States must once again live up to its values. Three fundamental principles, which govern the exercise of soft power through the promotion of human rights and the rule of law, are crucial guidelines for U.S. policy.

The first is practicing what you preach. The United States loses credibility when it charges others with violations it is committing itself. It reduces its ability to lead when it acts precipitously without international authority or the support of other nations. Second is obeying the law. Human rights are defined and protected by the U.S. Constitution and by conventions and treaties that have been ratified and incorporated into U.S. domestic law. The United States must adhere to these legal obligations if it is to project itself to other countries as a champion of human rights and the rule of law. Third is supporting international institutions. The United States should lead the way in reshaping existing international institutions and creating new ones, not attacking them, acting unilaterally or turning its back whenever it disagrees with what they do. Following these principles can help guide the United States back to its rightful place as a global leader.

In the Eyes of the World

In the realm of world opinion and politics, perception can quickly become reality. Although the United States may be strong economically and militarily, the rest of the world now sees it as ineffective and dangerous on the global stage. As a result, the United States has a limited capacity to deploy economic and military assets to achieve its foreign policy objectives.

Less than a decade ago the situation was quite different. International views of American leadership were favorable at the end of the 1990s. According to polling data published by the State Department Office of Research, the United States was respected across a wide spectrum of countries a decade after the end of the Cold War. A 1999 survey showed that large majorities in France (62 percent), Germany (78 percent), Indonesia (75 percent), Nigeria (61 percent), Russia (61 percent), and Turkey (52 percent), among others, held favorable opinions of the U.S.[2] This positive climate of opinion fostered an outpouring of international support immediately following the September 11 attacks. The United States was able to assemble a broad coalition in the fall of 2001 to respond with UN approval to the attacks and strike terrorist strongholds in Afghanistan.

Six years later, global support for U.S. leadership has evaporated. In poll after poll international opinion about the United States has turned sour. A January 2007 BBC survey found that 52 percent of the people polled in 25 countries around the world had a "mainly negative" view of the United States, with only 29 percent "mainly positive." In nearly all the countries where there had been strong support for the United States in 1999, a major downward shift of opinion had occurred by the end of 2006. In France it was down to 39 percent, Germany 37 percent, Indonesia 30 percent, and Turkey 12 percent.[3] A separate survey conducted in 2006 by the Pew Research Center revealed extremely hostile attitudes toward the United States throughout the Arab and Muslim world, including Egypt, 70 percent negative, Pakistan 73 percent, Jordan 85 percent, and Turkey 88 percent.[4]

A major factor driving this negative global opinion is the way the United States has projected its power in the "war on terror." Four years after the Iraq invasion, U.S. military presence in the Middle East was seen by 68 percent of those polled by the BBC "to provoke more conflict than it prevents."[5] Similarly, a poll published in April 2007 by the Chicago Council on Global Affairs showed that in 13 out of 15 countries, including Argentina, France, Russia, Indonesia, India, and Australia, "the US is playing the role of world policeman more than it should be" and, more ominously, "the US cannot be trusted to act responsibly in the world."[6]

The United States is now seen internationally to be a major violator of human rights. The BBC poll showed that 67 percent of those surveyed in 25 countries disapproved of the U.S. government's handling of detainees in Guantánamo, Abu Ghraib, and other military prisons.[7] A survey conducted in June 2006 by coordinated polling organizations in Germany, Great Britain, Poland, and India found that majorities or pluralities in each country believed that the United States has tortured terrorist detainees and disregarded international treaties on the treatment of detainees and that other governments are wrong to cooperate with the United States in the secret "rendition" of prisoners.[8] Perhaps most disturbing was the finding in 2006 that overwhelming majorities in Germany and Great Britain, our closest European allies, condemned the United States for "doing a bad job" on human rights.[9]

The Bush Record on Human Rights and the Rule of Law

The administration of President George W. Bush has repeatedly violated each of the principles governing the exercise of soft power through the promotion of human rights and the rule of law. It has opened the United States to charges of hypocrisy by criticizing other governments for acting outside the rule of law and committing human rights abuses it has committed itself. The annual country reports on human rights practices issued by the U.S. State Department cover official actions such as "torture and cruel, inhuman or degrading treatment or punishment," "detention without charge," "denial of fair and prompt public trial," and "arbitrary interference with privacy, family, home, or correspondence"—the very practices the Bush administration itself has systematically engaged in recent years.

The Bush record on these issues is abysmal and notorious. Detainees in U.S. custody have been brutally abused at Abu Ghraib and other prisons in Iraq and Afghanistan. Prisoners have been held indefinitely without charges and without access to habeas corpus or any other form of judicial review in Guantánamo. The executive branch has asserted authority to arrest U.S. citizens without charges and deny them legal counsel on the bare assertion that they are "enemy combatants." A vast warrantless electronic surveillance program was conducted inside the United States in violation of federal law. The president has claimed unprecedented authority to disregard congressional enactments by issuing statements when signing bills that claim he is not bound by their requirements—even in the case of a recent prohibition on the use of torture, which merely codified existing law. This is just a sampling of the massive and well-documented human rights abuses that have been authorized and committed by U.S. officials in recent years in the name of fighting terror.

In light of this record, international readers of the State Department country reports will conclude that the United States does not practice what it preaches on human rights and the rule of law. For example, the 2006 report on Egypt criticizes the fact that "Egyptian security forces detained hundreds of individuals without charge"; that "abuse of prisoners and detainees by police, security personnel and prison guards was persistent"; and that "the [Egyptian] Emergency Law empowers the government to place wiretaps without a judicial warrant." These same criticisms apply to the United States.

The Bush administration has diminished a second source of soft power by flaunting basic requirements of international and domestic law. These include the Geneva Conventions, the Convention Against Torture, the International Covenant on Civil and Political Rights, and the Foreign Intelligence Surveillance Act, among others. The result is the creation of "law-free zones" in which foreign detainees in U.S. custody overseas have been brutally abused; thousands of foreign citizens have been held indefinitely as "unlawful combatants" without being accorded the status of prisoners of war; and repressive regimes around the world have implicitly been given the green light to crack down on political dissidents and religious and ethnic minorities in the name of fighting terrorism. This may have contributed to what a prominent international opinion survey reported in June 2007 is "a global crisis in confidence over [President] Bush's handling of world affairs . . . most apparent among Muslims in the Middle East."[10]

The administration's history of disregard for the established framework of international law is exemplified by a 2002 memorandum prepared by White House counsel Alberto Gonzales before he became attorney general. The memorandum stated that "terrorism renders obsolete the Geneva Conventions' strict limitations on the questioning of prisoners."[11] No recent president has questioned the basic rules of international humanitarian law in times of war. The administrations of Lyndon Johnson, Richard Nixon, and Gerald Ford during the Vietnam War, and George H. W. Bush during the Gulf War, all adhered to the Geneva requirements. The reasons are clear and were spelled out in a 2002 memorandum by Secretary of State Colin Powell, challenging the Gonzales memo. Powell warned that the White House interpretation of the Geneva Conventions would "reverse over a century of US policy and practice, undermine the protections of the law for our troops, and provoke negative international reaction, with immediate adverse consequences for the conduct of our foreign policy."[12]

A third source of soft power has been undermined by the Bush administration's attacks on and disengagement from international human rights institutions. The United States has been a world leader in building these institutions since the time when Eleanor Roosevelt chaired the international committee that drafted the Universal Declaration of Human Rights. The current administration has renounced that leadership by refusing to run for a seat on the new UN Human Rights Council and by undermining efforts to shape the new International Criminal Court (ICC). Both institutions are flawed but, as a result of the administration's disengagement, the United States now has no influence over their future development. In the case of the Human Rights Council, the administration abandoned its support when it was unable to limit council membership to countries with good human rights records and then failed to mobilize diplomatic efforts to prevent the council from being taken over by violator governments. In the case of the ICC, changes may need to be made to better assure the primacy of national justice systems before the United States can become a full participant. In recent years, however, the United States has lost all leverage over the ICC by withdrawing its signature from the treaty establishing it. In addition, an active U.S. campaign to put pressure on other governments not to join the court has engendered international ill will and may have further undermined the capacity of the United States to exercise human rights leadership in situations like the genocide in Darfur.

Looking Inward

Other, less visible aspects of the current U.S. record on human rights have also had a negative impact on foreign policy. These include issues surrounding application of the death penalty, racial discrimination in the administration of justice, and pressures to restrict access to U.S. courts by those seeking to redress international human rights violations.

Death penalty practices in the United States have caused diplomatic friction in recent years. In several capital cases a number of states have failed to comply with the Vienna Convention on Consular Relations, which requires access by consular officials to foreign nationals charged with serious crimes. Allies like Mexico have been angered by such mistreatment of their citizens and the International Court of Justice ruled against the United States in one such case involving a German national.[13] While the State Department initially supported the court's position, the United States subsequently withdrew from the Optional Protocol to the convention that subjected it to the court's jurisdiction.[14] More broadly, American death penalty practice puts the United States at odds with the great majority of countries in the world that have abolished capital punishment. One result is that United States has sometimes been hampered when it has sought extradition of terror suspects from countries that do not practice capital punishment, as exemplified by a recent case involving a terrorism suspect sought by the United States for extradition from Great Britain.[15]

Racial discrimination in the administration of justice is a global problem that reaches deep into the U.S. justice system. A variety of discriminatory practices in the United States have been criticized in recent years by federal courts and extensively documented by human rights organizations and UN special rapporteurs.[16] One such practice is racial and ethnic profiling, including the use of race as the basis for traffic stops by police and the roundup and detention without charge of thousands of Arab and South Asian men following the attacks of September 11. At many stages of the criminal justice system in the United States, racial minorities are disproportionately represented and more severely treated than nonminorities. This is particularly true in death penalty cases. A 2001 Justice Department report indicated that 85 percent of the defendants on death row in federal cases were racial minorities and that 80 percent of federal cases where the death penalty could be imposed involved black or Hispanic defendants.[17] This evidence of systemic discrimination may not have a direct impact on U.S. foreign policy, but it fuels the perception in some parts of the world that the United States is a human rights violator.

Another area of domestic human rights controversy is the aggressive effort by the Bush administration to curtail the use of U.S. courts by foreign nationals to redress international human rights violations. The Alien Tort Claims Act provides a limited opportunity for foreign victims to sue their abusers in the United States. Recently the act has been interpreted by several U.S. courts to allow suits against transnational corporations, introducing a potential new instrument of corporate accountability for human rights practices. As a result, a U.S. corporation recently settled a lawsuit brought under the act and agreed to compensate human rights victims in Burma (Myanmar) in connection with the installation of an oil pipeline. Using the act in this manner to redress human rights abuses has drawn strong opposition from the Bush administration, which is now seeking a judicial ruling and legislation to sharply limit the act's scope.[18] By doing so, the administration once again has exposed the gap between the U.S. commitment to human rights and recent government actions that undermine it.

Undercutting U.S. National Security

The Bush administration's record on human rights and the rule of law has undercut the country's capacity to achieve a number of crucial national security objectives. The erosion of America's soft power has made it more difficult for the United States to succeed in preventing or containing threats of terrorism, genocide, and nuclear proliferation. The denigration of American values has made the United States ineffective—and often counterproductive—in promoting human rights and democracy.

Self-described strategic "realists" from Bismarck to former Secretary of Defense Donald Rumsfeld have downplayed human rights in their calculations of how best to promote their countries' interests in international relations. But in an age of terrorism, genocide, and nuclear proliferation, the protection of the rule of law must be a central feature of any strategy for containing threats to international security. Today's threats include failed states, political repression, authoritarian rule, religious fanaticism, racial, ethnic, and religious discrimination, and the many other breeding grounds of political violence and instability in our world today. To deny that human rights and the rule of law must be part of a strategy to address these threats is to invite international chaos.

Five frequently stated foreign policy objectives have been jeopardized by the current administration's frequent disregard of the rule of law. The first is countering the threats posed by Iraq, Iran, and Afghanistan. For more than a decade these countries have topped the U.S. list of dangers to international security. Strategies to reduce the violence and terrorism in Iraq and Afghanistan and to prevent the export of terrorism and acquisition of nuclear weapons by Iran require a mixture of hard and soft power. Soft power objectives include close cooperation by allies and tacit support by civil society elements within the countries. Against the background of its preemptive and unilateral intervention in Iraq, the U.S. record of human rights abuse has weakened its soft power to mobilize allies and appeal to civil societies. Reports of CIA and U.S. military torture and mistreatment of prisoners at Abu Ghraib in Iraq,

Afghanistan's Bagram airbase, and other secret prisons and detention centers in the region may have weakened the ability of the United States to counter the deterioration of human rights conditions in Iraq and Afghanistan. Similarly, State Department criticism of the Iranian regime's political repression has been blunted by the U.S. record of detainee abuse and illegal electronic surveillance. The U.S. military presence in the Middle East is now seen by more than two-thirds of the public in 25 countries as "provoking more conflict than it prevents." Years after the U.S. military interventions, Iraq and Afghanistan remain major exporters of terrorism and centers of human rights abuse. Iran is not only a terrorist exporter but a human rights disaster.

A second major stated objective of U.S. foreign policy is to prevent genocide. The lesson of Rwanda, where 800,000 ethnic Tutsis and moderate Hutus were slaughtered in 1994, was that the cost of failing to stop genocide is not only massive killing of innocent civilians but also ongoing humanitarian catastrophe and long-term regional instability. Following the Rwanda genocide, a doctrine of "humanitarian intervention" was developed under U.S. leadership and invoked, with broad international support and authority under the Genocide Convention, to end the genocide in Bosnia in 1995 and then to prevent a genocide in Kosovo in 1999. Today that doctrine is in shambles, undermined and discredited by the Bush administration's intervention in Iraq. As a result, the United States has been unable to mobilize support to stop the ongoing genocide in Darfur. In the four years since Secretary of State Colin Powell publicly characterized what was happening in Darfur as "genocide," more than 200,000 lives have been lost, a vast humanitarian crisis has been created and an entire region of northwest Africa has been destabilized. Weakened by its own record on human rights and the rule of law, the current administration has proven singularly ineffective in dealing with the gravest human rights crisis on its watch.

Addressing the challenges posed by geopolitical rivals such as China, Russia, and Cuba is a third longstanding preoccupation of U.S. foreign policy. Already complicated, interactions with these countries have been made more problematic by the Bush record. The administration has lost diplomatic leverage by opening itself to criticism in an area where the United States has traditionally been strong—human rights and the rule of law. China is leading the way in effectively exploiting the growing global perception that the United States is a human rights violator. For several years the Chinese government has produced and publicized its own report on U.S. human rights failings in an attempt to counter U.S. criticism of China's record. China's March 2007 report was particularly blunt: "We urge the US government to acknowledge its own human rights problems and stop interfering in other countries' internal affairs under the pretext of human rights."[19] Russian president Vladimir Putin has been similarly direct in rejecting recent U.S. criticism of the Russian government's press censorship. Cuba has been quick to point to the U.S. record of detainee abuse at Guantánamo whenever Cuban human rights practices are challenged by Washington.[20] In addition to losing diplomatic leverage, the Bush administration has provided China, Russia, and Cuba with a convenient excuse for cracking down on political dissidents and ethnic and religious minorities under the guise of fighting terrorism within their borders.

Creating and managing strategic alliances is a fourth major U.S. foreign policy objective. The Bush administration's record on human rights and the rule of law has alienated traditional democratic allies and complicated relations with authoritarian countries. As we have seen, large majorities of the public in Europe now have a negative view of U.S. leadership. The Council of Europe, a parliamentary assembly of elected representatives from across the continent, has condemned European governments for cooperating with Washington in running secret detention centers, calling for Europe to distance itself from the Bush administration's tactics in the "war on terror." Negative European opinion about U.S. human rights practices has placed a strain on Washington's relations with its closest allies, making it politically difficult for European leaders to support U.S. positions on other issues. Elsewhere in the world, America's ability to hold authoritarian governments accountable for their abuses of human rights and the rule of law has been compromised by the Bush human rights record. By condoning torture, prisoner abuse, secret detention, illegal surveillance, and other violations of human rights, the administration has undercut its ability to promote reform with authoritarian allies like Egypt, Saudi Arabia, Morocco, and Uzbekistan, implicitly endorsing the very repressive measures it has criticized in the past.

Finally, holding accountable those who commit human rights crimes has been a bedrock objective of U.S. foreign policy since the Nuremberg trials following World War II. The United States has long been in the forefront of efforts to create a system of international justice, most recently in the establishment of the international criminal tribunals for the former Yugoslavia and Rwanda. By opposing the International Criminal Court, the Bush administration has relinquished its leadership on these issues. The indispensability of international justice to U.S. foreign policy is illustrated by the administration's retreat in 2006 from outright opposition to the ICC to reluctant acceptance of the UN Security Council's referral of the Darfur genocide case to ICC jurisdiction. But this begrudging exception unfortunately proves the rule. Through repeated attacks on the ICC, failure to obtain extradition of terrorism suspects from countries that oppose capital punishment, and continuing efforts to block the use of the Alien Tort Claims Act to redress human rights violations, the administration has abandoned the longstanding U.S. objective of bringing to justice those who commit international crimes against civilization.

Repairing the Damage

Repairing the damage to American values and moral authority around the world must be a top priority of the next president. Acting within a framework of the rule of law and respect for human rights will be essential to restoring America's international leadership.

History shows that the capacity to lead can be restored when U.S. values and policies are brought into synch. During the first decade and a half of the Cold War, images of racism and segregation in the United States undercut America's ability to project moral leadership. By the mid-1960s, however, the civil rights movement and the leadership of Presidents John F. Kennedy and Lyndon Johnson had revived this vital capacity.

Similarly, following the disaster in Vietnam, a number of U.S. foreign policy successes were achieved during the last quarter of the twentieth century through bipartisan presidential leadership within a framework of human rights and the rule of law. President Gerald Ford signed the Helsinki Accords, which led to international recognition of the cause of human rights inside the Soviet bloc. President Jimmy Carter mobilized democratic governments to press for the release of political prisoners held by repressive governments. President Ronald Reagan signed the Convention Against Torture and sent it to the Senate, where it was subsequently ratified. President George H. W. Bush joined with Western European governments to nurture the fledgling democracies of post-Cold War Central and Eastern Europe. President Bill Clinton worked with NATO to end the human-rights catastrophe in Bosnia and prevent genocide in Kosovo. Each of these foreign policy successes was achieved by linking American interests and values.

The United States now must strengthen its alliances by demonstrating that it adheres to international norms in pursuing its national security objectives. Several immediate steps involving the status and treatment of terrorism suspects and detainees should be taken. An announcement that the United States will close the detention center at Guantánamo and transfer detainees to the United States or detainees' home countries will be a critical first step. In addition, the United States should announce that it is bound by the Geneva Conventions as a matter of law and policy. Restoring the practice of providing individualized status hearings to detainees would demonstrate a respect for international norms without restricting the government's capacity to conduct lawful interrogations to obtain intelligence information about terrorist activities. Fully applying the Geneva Conventions also would not preclude Washington from trying detainees in military commissions if there is evidence that they have participated in war crimes or crimes against humanity.

A second means of underscoring the U.S. commitment to address national security threats within the rule of law would be to provide assistance to other countries for counterterrorism operations that comply with basic human rights standards. "Fighting terror" has become a convenient excuse for repressive regimes to engage in further repression, often inspiring further terrorism in an increasing cycle of violence. To break this cycle, the United States should provide assistance and training to foreign military and law enforcement personnel in methods of fighting terrorism within the rule of law.

The United States should also work to strengthen international law on terrorism as a way of building global cooperation on containing and preventing acts of terror. Washington should play a leadership role in drafting a comprehensive treaty defining and condemning terrorism within a framework of human rights. Getting agreement on the definition of terrorism will be difficult, and will certainly not be a panacea, but working toward a consensus on this global issue would help counter the claim that differences in cultural values, religious beliefs, political philosophies, or justifiable ends make it impossible to define the crime of terrorism. By leading an international effort to stigmatize terrorism as a crime against humanity, the United States would work with other nations and with international institutions to isolate and combat terrorists as international outlaws and bring them to justice.

In building alliances for international security, the United States must also protect human rights at home so that it can demonstrate the values for which it stands. In times of threat and instability the rule of law may seem expendable. History tells us, however, that this is when the rule of law is most needed. Former Attorney General John Ashcroft provided a good example of why that is when he announced in a Senate hearing in 2002 that "those who scare peace-loving people with phantoms of lost liberty . . . only aid terrorists." This view suggests that a choice must be made between law and security. In a democratic society such a choice is profoundly false. Only in an open society can good policies be separated from bad and errors corrected. A nation based on the rule of law will attract other nations to stand with it against common enemies. When a nation abandons the rule of law, it isolates itself, alienates its allies, and encourages those who would destroy it.

The United States should make clear to the world that it is prepared once again to be an active participant in strengthening the system of international law it has helped create over the last half century. Important treaties drafted with U.S. leadership have lingered for years in the Senate and should now be ratified or renegotiated. Some were signed by Republican presidents and once enjoyed bipartisan support, but have been blocked for the last seven years by the current administration and its Senate supporters. The United States should also rejoin negotiations on such critical issues as human rights, international justice, climate change, and nonproliferation of weapons of mass destruction. By doing so the next president would demonstrate that globalization can be made to work within the rule of law.

The United States should support those seeking to promote the rule of law, democracy, and human rights in their own countries. Democracy and human rights activists are the shock troops in the struggle against terrorism, genocide, and nuclear proliferation. Repression breeds hate by closing off avenues for peaceful dissent and hate fuels the terrorism and genocide movements that can fester inside failed states and authoritarian countries. But democracy can never be delivered through the barrel of a gun. Assistance to those who are working to build their own democratic societies must be carefully planned and targeted, sustained over time, and based on a thorough understanding of the unique circumstances and profound differences among cultures, religions, and countries. None of these admonitions has been followed by the Bush administration in its disastrous policies toward Iraq. As a result, many of the elements of Iraqi society that should be allies in the struggle for democracy and against terrorism have instead become ardent sectarian opponents of American occupation. A new administration must work within an international framework, not unilaterally and preemptively, to assist those struggling around the world to bring the rule of law, democracy, and human rights to their own societies.

Finally, the United States should work with other countries, alliances, and international organizations to reassert America's role in working to prevent or stop genocide and crimes against humanity. The doctrine of humanitarian intervention that was applied in Bosnia and Kosovo in the 1990s should be invoked to address the genocide in Darfur. Extensive diplomatic and economic tools are available and should be used but international military intervention remains available under international law if all other avenues have been exhausted. Because the Iraq intervention was unilateral, preemptive, and conducted under a false justification, it has given humanitarian intervention a bad name and drastically reduced the credibility of the United States as a defender of human rights.

By recommitting the United States to a foreign policy conducted within a framework of human rights and the rule of law, the next president can rebuild U.S. national security and restore America's moral leadership in the world.

Chapter 3
The United States and the Future of Humanitarian Intervention

RACHEL KLEINFELD

The images appear on television: the mother's eyes wide with loss, the children's bellies distended, the corpses piled along the roadside, the stumps where once were a teenager's arms.* In some places these scenes repeat themselves year in and year out. The world takes no notice as rebel groups or government militias kill, rape, and starve tens of thousands of people. In other places, by luck, a few well-placed words or photographs of skeletal figures standing behind barbed wire garner attention. The world sits up and proclaims "Never again." Television cameras record; religious groups hold candlelight vigils; political leaders call for action.

What should the United States do in the face of extreme human misery and massive human rights violations? Do we have a responsibility to protect those facing genocide or humanitarian disaster?

As realism reasserts itself among America's foreign policy elites on the political left and right, the idea of deploying the country's military on humanitarian missions has fallen out of favor in Washington. Although many pundits assume that the American public is suffering war fatigue from the debacle in Iraq, Americans outside the Beltway draw a clear distinction between the trumped up claims of the Iraq War and dire human need: in early 2007, 65 percent of Americans favored sending U.S. troops to Darfur as part of an international force to stop the genocide there.[1]

The inclination of Americans to help those in need, even at a time when our ground forces are stretched thin, should not surprise us. America is, after all, a country based on values and ideals. We are a nation of immigrants, many of whom arrived fleeing abuses elsewhere. We are a religious nation with a sense of mission. We are a nation founded on a creed of universal rights.[2] When Americans see suffering on their television screens, when they hear homilies about mass atrocities, they believe that the United States, as the strongest and most powerful country on earth, should do something.

But "doing something" is not a strategy. Too often American politicians approach humanitarian intervention as if it were merely a political or even public relations problem rather than a military mission. They focus on doing "something" rather than on mounting the most effective force possible to achieve a realizable goal. This kind of an approach not only minimizes the good we can do for others, but can actually inflict even greater harm on victims and on our own troops because of a failure to develop realistic military plans for attainable goals.

Humanitarian intervention is about saving lives. Therefore the yardstick against which all activities should be measured is whether we *are* in fact saving lives in the short and the long term. Any policymaker considering a humanitarian intervention should begin with this concrete question: Is this an intervention we are capable of fielding, given political and military constraints, that is likely to do more good than harm?

This chapter uses this question of effectiveness rather than the traditional framework of just war theory as the primary measure by which to judge the appropriateness of intervention.[3] That does not mean eschewing the crucial question of legitimacy. Allies and global opinion can make or break an intervention's effectiveness: legitimacy is a crucial component of success and will be addressed immediately after we define what is meant by humanitarian intervention.

Defining the Problem: Consent and Intent

There is no universally agreed upon definition of "humanitarian intervention." Some wish to exclude coercive interventions entirely, arguing that force can never be "humanitarian." Others claim that "intervention" implies a lack of government consent and that the definition should be limited to nonconsensual military deployments to stop egregious human rights abuse—basically, wars to stop genocide.[4] And indeed, there seems little to connect a consensual aid mission to tsunami victims in Indonesia with a war to stop genocide in Kosovo.

This chapter will define humanitarian intervention as the deployment of military forces in a potentially hostile environment to help civilians in the face of massive and immediate humanitarian need. It includes both providing aid and ending abuse: there is no moral distinction between saving a thousand lives trapped beneath the rubble created by an earthquake or saving the same thousand innocents fleeing forces wielding AK-47s. Long-term development assistance, aid missions that do not require military forces, and predominantly strategic wars are excluded from the definition.[5]

Our definition focuses on the key problem of humanitarian intervention: deployment of military forces in hostile environments to help civilians.[6] It does not turn on government "consent"; in terms of mission danger, it is misleading to draw a hard and fast line between consensual and nonconsensual missions.[7] A government may offer consent and withdraw it mid-mission or allow troops to deploy but reject rules of engagement that would protect civilians (as occurred in the Bosnian genocide in the 1990s and now again in Darfur). A weak government's consent may mean little of practical protective value in areas where irregular and government forces from several countries are fighting for supremacy and civilians are caught in the crossfire (as in the Democratic Republic of Congo).[8] A consensual intervention may face a hostile environment the instant civilians receiving aid are threatened by a mob. Moreover, regardless of government consent, guerrilla fighters who did not give *their* approval may create a hostile environment for foreign troops.

The intent of the intervening powers is another critical issue. Many claim that for a mission to be humanitarian, intervening governments must have no strategic interest at play. Moral reasons should be sufficient to compel the international community to act since strategic interests sully an intervention, making it less "pure" and more political—little different from an invading aggressor and therefore illegitimate.[9]

Yet some strategic interest is important to sustaining the political will to field an effective humanitarian intervention. After all, committing troops to potentially die in a hostile environment is an enormous responsibility. Interveners must be willing to sustain casualties. We would not need to send troops, after all, if we did not expect danger and violence. Choosing intervention also requires spending taxpayer money on people in a far-off land when there are pressing needs at home. While less dangerous humanitarian interventions, such as earthquake aid provided by the military, may be purely altruistic, few nations, including the United States, will engage in high-risk interventions such as ending a genocide from purely disinterested motives. Since the costs in lives, livelihood, and political capital are so great and the benefits diffuse, the United States is likely to intervene in the toughest cases only when humanitarian and strategic needs coincide. Nor is it the only country to display this attitude. Morality alone has rarely been enough to force any country to act in situations where casualties were likely. In the interventions to end the massacre of civilians in East Pakistan (1971), silence Cambodia's killing fields (1975–1979), and halt Idi Amin's reign of destruction in Uganda (1979), bloodshed continued with no action from the world community. Neighboring countries finally intervened when moral compulsion coincided with strategic interest: these crises had begun to spill over into their borders.[10]

In fact, some strategic interest in an intervention is more likely to lead to mission effectiveness. If the military, a government, or the general public cannot tolerate casualties, troops may become hostages or pawns to the powers on the ground—as happened to the Dutch soldiers in Srebrenica.[11] Fighting effectively requires a willingness to sustain casualties and Americans are more willing to accept casualties if strategic interest is involved.[12] Strategic interest also allows politicians to persevere in the face of difficulty and commit adequate resources to the cause. When some strategic interest is at play, politicians look for real success, not just good public relations.[13]

This reality should not tarnish the humanitarian reputation of military interventions. An intervention should still be deemed "humanitarian" when the humanitarian goal—protecting the welfare of the population—is preponderant.[14] And while motives may be difficult to discern, this preponderant goal to protect civilian life should be reflected in cost-benefit calculations of whether to deploy, the make-up of forces deployed, the mission they are deployed to achieve, and particularly the manner in which war is conducted.[15] With this guidance in mind, a new administration should adopt the following policy recommendation:

- *We should not commit troops in a humanitarian intervention unless the American people are prepared to lose troops in battle for the cause.[16] As a check against overly precipitous or overly cautious stances, a politician should ask: "Is this a cause for which I would be willing to let my own child fight and die?"*

Do We Have the Right to Intervene?

America has undertaken nearly a dozen humanitarian interventions since the end of the Cold War, including delivering food aid to Somalia under the UN banner in 1992; working with allies to create a protected area for Kurds in northern Iraq between the two gulf wars; returning an elected leader to Haiti in 1994; and undertaking a bombing campaign with NATO in 1999 to stop forced ethnic cleansing and resettlement in Kosovo. But did we have a right to do so? Does the United States, or any other nation, have the right to send our military into another country to provide aid, stop genocide, or curtail mass human rights abuses and humanitarian catastrophe?

The first question concerns the rights of Americans, and is a version of the argument used against foreign aid: Do U.S. leaders have the right to send American troops and taxpayer dollars overseas, absent vital national interest? Realists claim that humanitarian intervention is unethical because it could weaken American strength without advancing America's strategic goals. Both the Weinberger and Powell doctrines[17]— guidelines for when the U.S. should commit troops to military engagements—implicitly rule out humanitarian intervention since both require a vital national interest of the United States or its allies to be at stake before troops are committed.[18]

This position ignores the fact that America's capacity to inspire the world and to act in ways that advance the good of others is a potent source of our own strength. After World War I President Woodrow Wilson supported Albania's right to independence from European colonial ambitions; in 1999 President Bill Clinton intervened in Kosovo to stop the forced flight and murder of ethnic Albanians. In appreciation for these largely altruistic stands, overwhelmingly Muslim Albania provided NATO with basing rights during the Kosovo conflict, has assisted the United States in fighting terrorists transiting its soil, and was one of the first countries to send troops to Afghanistan. In Indonesia, the country with the world's largest Muslim population, pro-American sentiment doubled following the dispatch of the U.S.S. *Mercy* to provide post-tsunami relief in 2005 and Indonesian support for suicide bombings dropped by two-thirds.[19] Better publicity about the U.S. protection of Muslims in Bosnia and Kosovo (largely unknown in the Muslim world) could have a potent effect on fundamentalist claims that the United States hates Islam. Cold War historian John Gaddis claims that the perception in years past that America acted for the good of others and in pursuit of world stability rather than solely for its own self-interest was a key factor in enabling the United States to hold NATO together and to attain overwhelming power without engendering the enmity or fear of our allies, in stark contrast to the Soviet Union's relations with its satellite nations.[20] America's reputation for moral and humanitarian actions directly influences its ability to persuade other nations to accept its outsized power.

The second moral question turns on nonconsensual interventions. Does any country or international organization have the right to violate the sovereignty of another country? After all, some have claimed that humanitarian intervention is simply imperialism under a different name, an updated version of the old "white man's burden," or a sop to Western conscience that avoids responsibility for deeper issues caused by the imbalance of power.[21]

Humanitarian intervention is not an idea "made in America," or even

in the West. Nations across the globe have codified the idea of a right—
even a responsibility—to protect those facing grave danger. In the wake
of the UN's failure to act in Kosovo, Secretary-General Kofi Annan asked
the General Assembly to "forge unity" around basic principles of
humanitarian intervention, saying, "If humanitarian intervention is,
indeed, an unacceptable assault on sovereignty, how should we respond
to a Rwanda, to a Srebrenica—to gross and systematic violations of
human rights that affect every precept of our common humanity?"[22]
The International Commission on Intervention and State Sovereignty,
led by Canada, took up Annan's challenge. The commission squared the
circle by concluding that national sovereignty is not an irrevocable given
but is earned by a government's upholding the basic rights of its citizens.[23] A state that fails to protect the rights of its citizens abandons its
right to claim sovereignty.

Nor was this a movement of Western nations alone. At the UN World
Summit in 2005, the General Assembly endorsed the idea that

each individual State has the responsibility to protect its populations from genocide, war crimes, ethnic cleansing and crimes against humanity. . . . [W]e are
prepared to take collective action, in a timely and decisive manner, through the
Security Council, in accordance with the Charter, including Chapter VII, on a
case-by-case basis and in cooperation with relevant regional organizations as
appropriate, should peaceful means be inadequate and national authorities are
manifestly failing to protect their populations from genocide, war crimes, ethnic
cleansing and crimes against humanity.[24]

Perhaps not surprisingly, a backlash against this concept has developed from ruling elites in repressive countries such as China, Zimbabwe,
Egypt, and Venezuela eager to retain the power they have held under
the old notion of inviolable sovereignty without responsibility.[25] But
their own citizens disagree. In a poll asking whether the UN has the
right to authorize the use of military force to prevent severe human
rights violations such as genocide, the respondents in every single state
polled answered with a resounding "yes." In the United States, 83 percent agreed, as did 73 percent in Mexico, 85 percent in France, 64 percent in Russia, 78 percent in the Palestinian territories, 69 percent in
Iran, 72 percent in China, 80 percent in Ghana, 75 percent in Kenya,
and 65 percent in Zimbabwe. When asked how they would prefer a crisis
such as Darfur to be resolved if it occurred in their own country, 64 percent of Africans endorsed the UN, the African Union, or a rich country
coming to their aid and only 11 percent rejected all foreign military
intervention.[26] Indeed, a plurality in most countries thought the U.N.
had a *responsibility* to intervene.[27] This is not a battle between the underdeveloped South against a strong, imperialist North but of repressive

elites in a few countries against both their own citizens and world opinion.

It is hard to argue that saving others from severe human rights abuse is "imperialism" when the majority of the world, including former colonies, thinks it is the right thing to do. But these polls discuss UN intervention. A final, crucial question is whether the United States (or any single country, such as Britain, France, or Nigeria) has the right to intervene. This question will be dealt with in greater detail later in the discussion of authorization and military readiness for intervention. But two centuries ago, the philosopher Immanuel Kant laid out a central ethical principal: "ought implies can"—we must be able to act in order to have an ethical imperative to do so.[28] A growing world consensus regarding the responsibility to protect means that some force in the world must be able to carry out that responsibility. The United States is by far the most able force in the world to serve this purpose now, followed by a handful of countries, NATO, and the European Union (EU). The UN is structurally unsuited for immediate intervention although it can play a crucial role in authorization and long-term stabilization. While multinational missions are by far the most likely to be effective, it makes no sense to assert that the world should do something to save innocents and then to deny the right to act to the country most suited to saving lives.

A final moral objection is that we should not violate the principle of nonintervention, even for humanitarian reasons, because the norm of sovereignty upholds world stability.[29] In other words, it "feels good" to intervene now, but we will regret it over time as we weaken international law and allow countries to violate one another's sovereignty with impunity. There is great value to upholding peace and order in the world, and to subjecting the use of force to legal control to prevent the rule of the strong. The norm of nonintervention served this purpose in the first few decades—even centuries—after Westphalia. Yet in the twentieth century, the split between what is "legal" (authorized by the UN Security Council) and what is "legitimate or ethical" (as determined by the growing norm of individual rights) has grown so wide that the principle no longer serves to uphold stability—or international law. As scholar Eileen Donahoe states: "If intervention is viewed as morally warranted, yet illegal under international law, the entire international effort to subject the use of force to the rule of law will continue to be undermined."[30] The international laws on sovereignty are already weakened from repeated breaches by states waging war for self-interest, and by the growing calls for humanitarian action in the face of brutal genocides on a scale unimaginable in previous centuries. If international law is not to be rendered completely ineffective, it must be recast to bring it closer to ethical norms once again.

What Are Our Goals?

We may, then, have the right to intervene in some circumstances. Whether we should exercise that right turns on the question of the likelihood of success. *We should only intervene if we believe that by doing so we will do more good than harm.* Despite dire need and grand hopes, we must always make sure that our mission is congruent with what is actually possible to achieve.

In his authoritative study on the subject, Taylor Seybolt has conceptualized four goals for humanitarian interventions. In ascending order of danger and the potential for violence, these are 1) assisting in the delivery of aid; 2) protecting aid operations; 3) protecting victims of abuse; and 4) defeating the perpetrators of abuse.[31]

The first element of effectiveness, then, is to focus on the right goal. Is suffering caused mainly by privation or by violence? Do we need to focus on aiding the victims or on defeating the perpetrators? Failure to choose the right goal can lead to the "well-fed dead" of Yugoslavia, the haunting phrase coined by those stuck providing food aid when what was needed was military protection for civilians.

What Are Our Means of Achieving the Goal?

Once we have chosen the goal wisely, we must determine the means to accomplish it. Delivering aid might require airdrops, as in the Berlin airlift of 1948–1949, or providing transport or rebuilding infrastructure, such as bridges and roads. Protecting aid might entail guard duty, escorting humanitarian convoys of NGOs, or creating safe areas. Saving victims could require providing safe passage through dangerous areas, securing safe zones, or fighting off attackers. Defeating the perpetrators of abuse requires war followed by peacemaking or nation-building and occupation. The means employed must be sufficient to fulfill the goal. At times that will require force deployed against the will of the government or guerrilla groups.

But war, even war to end atrocities, is hell. If the level of violence is high enough, even "humanitarian" intervention will result in innocent civilians fleeing their homes, children crushed by "friendly" bombs, and the deaths of soldiers. Any consideration of military intervention to end suffering should be tempered by the lessons of history: the first modern military interventions to stop human rights violations took place in the Middle Ages when Catholics and Protestants attempted to protect their co-religionists from abuses in Europe.[32] What followed was war so prolonged that it was known as the Thirty Years' War. Its resolution, the Peace of Westphalia, created the idea of state sovereignty because the warring parties felt that human rights abuses within states were a lesser evil than the horrors of the war they had just witnessed.

Therefore, if coercive measures short of force—such as embargoes, smart sanctions, or divestment—might serve the goal, they should be tried first for they are likely to have far fewer unintended consequences and far lower costs than military deployment. And if military intervention does become necessary, we should do everything in our power to gain the consent of all parties involved, since a consensual deployment will likely have lower costs and fewer risks than a coercive one. Coercive intervention is a "reasonable" last resort only after a serious effort has been made to attempt other options. This is the appropriate reading of just war theory's claim that force should be used only as a "last resort." There is always one more diplomatic mission or one further attempt at the United Nations that can be tried. Meanwhile, people are dying. The deaths from inaction must be weighed against the deaths that would result from forceful intervention.

To minimize the latter, just war theory says that means must be proportional to ends. This is often wrongly interpreted as meaning that intervening parties should "use as little force as possible," resulting in incomprehensibly complex or overly weak rules of engagement. But if the goal is to stop a government-sponsored genocide or to prevent mobs from massacring their neighbors, saving lives may require significant force. A truer reading of the just war principle focuses on the desired end: saving lives and leaving the situation better than before the intervention. We should deploy force in ways that cause as little harm to civilians as possible and minimize the work of rebuilding but maintain our ability to save lives in the face of violent opposition.

Finally, mission effectiveness requires military potential for success, and this will depend on the size and geography of the region of intervention and the nature of the enemy. The United States will not deploy troops to protect the entire Democratic Republic of the Congo, for example. Undertaking a such a mission would be preposterous, for it would require us to employ virtually all of our strategic resources and put our own security at risk. Nor would we intervene to halt famine in North Korea in the 1990s or in China during the Great Leap Forward— the prospect of deploying troops to provide even welcome food aid in an armed hostile country that likely harbors nuclear weapons would be foolhardy.

In the early stages when the United States is considering humanitarian intervention, it should:

- *Work in tandem with other nations to apply coercive diplomacy, including sanctions, smart sanctions, aid cutoffs, embargoes, and divestment before turning to military options. If military options become necessary, the U.S. government should work assiduously to gain consent to deploy troops. But these efforts need not continue until the last civilian is killed. The dangers to the deploying country and to civilians alike of a nonpermissive mission must be weighed against the deaths occurring each day a mission is not deployed.*

- *Ensure that the military mission to relieve the problem is achievable. Before any humanitarian intervention, a military plan must determine the area of need, the actions that must be undertaken to relieve this need, and whether those actions are militarily feasible. We should not spend taxpayer dollars or put troops into danger for public relations purposes alone. It is not enough to be in horrific human need: the mission must improve the situation on the ground, not make it worse.*
- *Create rules of engagement that allow sufficient retaliation to achieve the mission without being overly complicated for troops in the field. They must enable enough force to protect civilians, deliver aid, or otherwise meet the goal of the intervention. Any humanitarian intervention will entail rebuilding afterward, so rules of engagement should refrain from setting the stage for wide-scale destruction of infrastructure.*

Who Should Conduct the Intervention?

Once we know the goal, the strategy, and the tactical capacities needed, the next step is to determine who has the capabilities to fulfill these requirements.

This is rarely how humanitarian interventions are conducted. Countries commonly seek the authority to intervene or create a coalition to "do something" *before* a military strategy is even formulated. This risks backing into a force structure that may not be suitable for the goal and it almost guarantees the loss of valuable time.

If we actually want to do more good than harm, we must start by looking at who has the capabilities to achieve the mission. Two capabilities are crucial: first, for all humanitarian interventions, success is largely determined by how rapidly troops can be deployed on the ground.[33] Second, for any intervention that requires longer-term deployment, success requires a force that will be accepted by the local population and can occupy the territory for the long haul while maintaining peace and rebuilding the country.

PHASE ONE: RAPID DEPLOYMENT

World opinion prefers that interventions be undertaken by the United Nations. But currently only the United States, the United Kingdom, France, and NATO can deploy rapidly and with sufficient logistical support and planning capacity to halt a large-scale genocide. Australia and, to a lesser extent, Nigeria can also deploy rapidly in their neighborhoods and the European Union, while relatively untested, has recently built a rapid deployment capacity.[34] Of all of these, however, the United States has by far the greatest capacity for larger undertakings. Europeans possess only about 10 to 15 percent of the long-distance lift capacity (the ability to move troops from the home country to the theater of battle) of the United States.[35] For the rapid reaction phase of an intervention, states acting unilaterally or in coalition with other states (as opposed to the United Nations) have the greatest record of success.[36] And that means the United States, the United Kingdom, France, Australia, or Nigeria, bolstered by NATO or the EU.[37]

The United States need not always take the lead, of course. The United Kingdom, France, Australia, and Nigeria have significant and successful track records of humanitarian intervention, both alone and in coalition. In some regions their intelligence assets and historical ties may make them better suited to a mission than the United States; in others their colonial histories may carry unnecessary baggage. The United States should encourage other countries to lead coalitions where they have a comparative advantage. To ensure that world opinion does not find Washington too quick to resort to military force and to calm fears that we are acting as "the world's policeman," we should encourage other strong nations to take on the mantle of humanitarian action when they wish to and to praise them publicly for doing so.

Other than the United States, the United Kingdom, France, NATO, and the EU, the ability to deploy rapidly to far-off areas does not exist. Within Africa ECOMOG, the military arm of the Economic Community of West African States (ECOWAS), has deployed multiple times, largely for humanitarian reasons. Forces are committed on an ad hoc basis, usually under Nigerian leadership or with Nigeria committing the bulk of the troops. A new plan to create an ECOWAS Standing Force is intended to be part of the continent-wide plan for an African Standby Force (ASF), which many nations, including the United States, are working to build.[38] The African Union (AU) does not have troops on call to deploy rapidly nor does it have the headquarters management or planning capacity, logistics, airlift, ground transport, communications, or any of the other necessary components for fielding a military mission in Africa. Its current mission in Darfur is heavily reliant on the UN, the EU, and the United States.

The United Nations is probably the least prepared of any force to deploy rapidly and the most likely to fail in the early stages of a humanitarian intervention. The UN has no standby force; at each crisis it must go begging for soldiers who end up having no common training and no training standards. The UN has no capability to move troops to distant locations and must rent U.S. equipment to do so. It also lacks the communications, intelligence, logistical, and airlift capabilities that are crucial to success in difficult humanitarian missions.

The United States has played a role in making the UN so ineffective. Withholding payment of its UN dues has made fiscal management nearly impossible. American refusal to commit troops to a standing UN force is a serious roadblock to rapid reaction.[39] But U.S. intransigence is only one of many factors that render the UN unsuitable for rapid reaction. Great power interests block nearly all humanitarian action in the Security Council. Repressive states and many poor states have stymied reforms needed to improve the Department of Peacekeeping Operations (DPKO), either because they harbor memories of colonialist interventions in their own states or because they fear that improved capacity of DPKO might lead to interventions against their own violent activities. In addition, many countries that commit peacekeeping troops worry about casualties and refuse rules of engagement that call for peace enforcement. The innate problems with sharing intelligence and sensitive technologies with a multinational body are additional structural variables that impede effective action.

As a result, the UN has an abysmal success rate in rapidly deploying to meet humanitarian need. Even a high-level UN panel agrees that "collective security institutions have proved particularly poor at meeting the challenge posed by large-scale, gross human rights abuses and genocide" and then describes failure after failure.[40] And because many of these factors are inherent to the structure of the UN,[41] it is quixotic to try to make the UN something it is not, or to create capabilities when member states, NATO, and the EU have these capabilities. "The United Nations does not wage war," states the UN's Brahimi Report;[42] "where enforcement action is required, it has consistently been entrusted to coalitions of willing States, with the authorization of the Security Council, acting under Chapter VII of the Charter."[43] The United Nations has a crucial mission to play in long-term troop deployment but it should not be forced into a rapid reaction role for which it is unsuited.

PHASE TWO: MAINTAINING FORCES ON THE GROUND

In some contexts a quick influx of military force can stabilize a situation (for instance, a United States deployment achieved a peaceful transfer of power in Lebanon in 1958, after which the country's own government took over). In other cases the military phase of humanitarian intervention can rapidly evolve to the point where NGOs, who take longer to deploy but are better suited for long-term provision of aid, can swing into action. But if populations need protection, if the government is very weak, or if the government itself is the source of the problem, military forces must be ready to stay for the long haul. The no-fly zone to protect the Kurds in northern Iraq lasted a dozen years, from 1991 until the 2003 invasion of Iraq. The mission in Kosovo continues almost a decade after the conflict in the form of a UN Trusteeship. UN and EU forces remain in Bosnia-Herzegovina nearly two decades after the war there.

For long-term occupation the UN is far better suited, while the United States performs poorly. In part this is because the United States is not like other countries. While Vietnam, Uganda, and even regional powers such as Nigeria can intervene in other countries in their spheres of influence with little international backlash, the "unequaled national might of the United States is envied, feared, misunderstood, and interrogated by those who feel its impact, especially in military forms," as one observer put it.[44] That means that any U.S. military intervention is likely to bring opprobrium and international questioning, even when we are doing the right thing.

Fear of U.S. power is not a public relations problem that calls for a thick skin. It is a strategic problem that can impede mission success. By definition there are spoilers in situations that require coercive humanitarian intervention who wish to prolong war and extend harm. The world's most powerful nation acting alone can raise fears of imperialism and occupation that galvanize more recruits for these spoilers and help mobilize them against our troops.

Moreover, the United States is hostage to its own political cycles, which rarely work in tandem with the needs of poor, far-off countries. The point at which the United States ends an intervention will almost inevitably be dictated by American public opinion and political rhetoric—not by the facts on the ground. This means that violence can break out again if the United States pulls out before another power can fill the vacuum.

For long-term staying power, nothing beats a multilateral force—particularly the United Nations. Having no single home public to answer to and hence generally less in the public eye than single-country missions, multinational forces have a greater ability to stay and see a job through, even as individual countries drop in and out. Because they represent no single national interest, multinational forces, especially the UN, are more likely to be seen as legitimate and acting on behalf of the people facing oppression.[45] They are also less likely to be seen as "occupiers," making it more difficult for local rebels to summon fresh recruits to oppose UN "occupation." Even when multinational forces are disliked by a local population, it is rare to hear accusations that the UN covets Sudan's oil or wishes to "weaken" the Balkans, as might well be heard of the United States or another country acting on its own. The United Nations' peacekeeping preeminence is reflected in the numbers of forces in the field: it currently has more than 120,000 peacekeepers deployed, the second-largest international deployment of soldiers after the United States and several-fold more than NATO.[46]

Building a Better Intervention Force

Coalitions of states or states acting by themselves have the best track records when it comes to successful short-term humanitarian intervention.[47] Yet a multinational—preferably UN—force is perhaps the only force capable of long-term nation stabilization and occupation if a trusteeship situation is required. Since both capabilities are necessary, we should ensure that both are available.

Such a solution would also best fit with U.S. public opinion. While Americans favor action in Darfur, 66 percent of Republicans and 85 percent of Democrats now feel that the United States is playing the role of world policeman more than it should.[48] And though Americans rallied around President Bush's campaign declaration in 2003 that he needed no "permission slip" from a multilateral body before going to war,[49] most Americans approve of UN action when it is framed in a convincing way: in a 2006 Chicago Council on Foreign Relations poll, 72 percent favored having a standing UN peacekeeping force selected, trained, and commanded by the United Nations and 79 percent thought strengthening the UN's law enforcement authority was an important foreign policy goal.[50] In other words Americans, like the rest of the world, believe in humanitarian intervention as a moral good—but neither Americans nor other countries' publics want the United States to be the main delivery mechanism for that intervention.

America has begun building the capacity of other nations to intervene but greater political support, particularly in Congress, is essential. In April 2004 Bush approved a five-year Global Peace Operations Initiative to build the response capabilities of African nations and has since broadened it to other regions.[51] The effort envisioned putting $660 million from fiscal years 2005–2009 into training 75,000 troops—mainly in Africa, though now expanded to Central America, Europe, and Asia—for peacekeeping operations. But the 109th Congress balked at funding this program in part because it perceived there to be lax management, poor strategic planning, and weak State Department support for the project.[52] These criticisms were valid. A less ideological, more militarily focused effort is needed to build better deployment capacity for others. But in general this initiative is a step in the right direction.

When it comes to building UN capacity to undertake long-term missions, however, we are failing miserably. For decades Congress under both Republican and Democratic administrations has maligned the work of the United Nations, despite the crucial assistance that body has given to the United States when it took over the U.S. mission in Haiti, for example, or provided an alternative to a long-term American presence in Kosovo. President George H. W. Bush's secretary of state, James Baker, described UN peacekeeping as a "national security priority" and a "pretty good buy."[53] Contrast that with the firm unilateralist and anti-UN rhetoric of the current administration.[54] The UN has a role to play that neither the United States nor its allies can easily fill but it needs help to play it well. The UN requires greater logistical capabilities, planning, airlift, transport, and communications and intelligence support to fulfill a long-term peace enforcement role.[55] It needs consistent funding. It needs to improve its training programs. And it needs greater public legitimacy—particularly greater recognition from Congress and the American people that the UN Commission on Refugees, UN peacekeepers, the World Food Program, and other UN organizations play an essential role in averting humanitarian disasters and permitting the United States to share humanitarian burdens.[56]

To ensure that the world has the capabilities needed for short- and long-term deployments:

- *The United States should build the capacities of other international actors to undertake humanitarian interventions. We should abandon the dream of a UN rapid reaction force and work instead on configuring UN forces for long-term occupation, peacekeeping, and rebuilding. We should in the meantime support NATO, the EU, the AU, and ECOWAS forces to enable them to better deploy rapidly, with or without the United States.*
- *We should view the United Nations—and explain its importance to the American public—in the same spirit that Winston Churchill adopted toward democracy: it is the worst system . . . except for all the others. We should stop disparaging the United Nations and instead give it public credit for its successes and build its capacity for long-term peacekeeping and peace enforcement while improving its financial and other forms of accountability.*

Who Has the Right to Authorize Humanitarian Intervention?

When lives are in the balance, speed is of the essence. The United States is often the leader in galvanizing other countries to act for humanitarian purposes, can react the quickest and has the most robust ability to get large-scale forces on the ground anywhere in the world. Given these realities, shouldn't the United States act without authorization if necessary to save lives? Why wait for multilateral dawdling, international authorization, and the creation of coalitions when each day more people are dying?

First, because authorization from the UN or other respected international institutions like NATO is essential for the success of most missions. If there is any chance that long-term occupation is going to be necessary (and there often is), it is essential to have the imprimatur of an international body. Few forces are likely to take over a mission they did not authorize in the first place.

Second, the UN, as the "court of world opinion," provides a form of unsurpassed legitimacy. Other countries have a real fear that the United States—or another intervening country—may cloak self-interest in humanitarian garb. The United Nations is seen (whether deservedly or not) as the best means of ensuring that the goal of an intervention is truly humanitarian. If the UN authorizes action, it becomes much more difficult for unintended negative effects of intervention to boomerang against the intervening country. Without UN authorization, intervention faces far greater skepticism worldwide, is more likely to be seen as self-interested, and is therefore more likely to be questioned by frustrated groups on the ground, increasing the likelihood of insurgent action, civilian sympathy for anti-intervention activities, and threats to troops on the ground.[57] The political legitimacy of an operation should be seen as just as important a strategic asset as battlefield intelligence or night-vision goggles.

But there are some very real problems with the UN serving as the sole legitimator of humanitarian intervention, beginning with the records of powerful members of the Security Council. What gives Russia, with its *revanchist* authoritarian government and abusive war in Chechnya, or China, with its gulags full of political prisoners and history of killing millions through man-made famine, the moral authority to decide whether the UN may authorize an intervention? Of course, in light of Abu Ghraib, Japanese internment during World War II, and past US interference in Latin America, what gives the United States such authority? These failings are not equivalent, but they are equally worthy of moral pause.

Nor may the UN as a whole claim the moral high ground. Multinational bodies, after all, are not composed of angels. In the words of Michael Walzer, "If governments have mixed motives, so do coalitions of governments."[58] At times, there appears to be a presumption that the joining together of multiple interests will somehow magically cancel out individual national interest. But states generally use international bodies as one more way to work for their own self-interest. At worst, the UN Security Council is a forum for power plays that disregard the needs of the innocent; at best, it tends toward inertia—hardly what the world is looking for when it comes to a body charged with authorizing interventions.

Quite apart from morality, UN authorization can be deathly slow.[59] This is not simply the result of bureaucracy but a reality of power politics: it takes time to horse-trade to overcome great power interests. When ethnic cleansing began in Kosovo, the Security Council could not overcome Russian intransigence. In Rwanda it was the United States that vocally advocated pulling UN peacekeepers out of the region two weeks into the genocide and prevented UN action for six weeks.[60] In recent years it has been China that has stood in the way of more robust action in Darfur.

If the intervention is likely to be short term, such as the speedy delivery of aid, the United States should seek authorization from the government itself or, if the government is incapacitated, from a regional body such as the EU, NATO, the OAS, or the AU (preferably the body that serves the region where the intervention will take place, if such a body exists; if not, any regional body provides greater legitimacy than a unilateral mission).[61] If a mission may become long term because of the level of violence, the complexity of the mission, or because a government refuses to allow deployment, the UN should be the authorizing force of first resort. If the Security Council is paralyzed because of power politics, the United States can and should seek authorization from another multinational body that has the capability to carry out a long-term deployment after the rapid reaction phase. At the moment there are only two: the EU and NATO.[62]

In the long term, building a more robust Community of Democracies, a global grouping of countries that unite North and South, rich and poor, around a pillar of common democratic values—a project started under the Clinton administration and embraced by the Bush administration—could create an institution that would eventually have some of the prestige and legitimacy that now adheres to the United Nations without the UN's Achilles' heel of providing equal voice to countries that harm their citizens. To create legitimacy for such an organization, the United States would need to abide by its dictates (just as through give and take, winning some battles and losing others but always maintaining U.S. commitment to the process, President Harry Truman built the original international institutions erected after World War II). This body could augment NATO or the EU by adding a crucial non-Western dimension but, without the long-term force capabilities they bring, could not substitute for them.[63]

If we cannot gain authorization from one of these bodies, we should not proceed because the mission itself is highly unlikely to succeed.[64] The issue is not simply legitimacy. It is creating a solution that can effectively save lives. Where we fail to garner international agreement, we must seriously reconsider the wisdom of our proposed actions. While we may wish to save lives, others may understand better than we do the Pandora's Box that intervention may unleash or may have a more balanced sense of how perceptions of the United States will color our chances for success. A future course of action should include the following:

- *When the United States decides to intervene to protect human rights abroad, it should attempt to gain legitimacy by receiving the imprimatur of the country itself or, if that is not possible, then that of a multinational body— preferably the UN but, if not, then NATO, the EU, ECOWAS, or the AU, depending in part on where intervention is needed. If an intervention may require long-term occupation, this legitimizing function is crucial and the United States should not proceed without it.*
- *The United States should work to build a Community of Democracies as a worldwide body of states that adhere to a set of liberal values. Such a body could provide a global voice alongside the EU or NATO to authorize interventions when the UN is stymied. The United States should ensure broad non-Western membership and it must agree to abide by its decisions, even when it disagrees with them, so that the organization gains legitimacy and is not seen as a rubber stamp for an American agenda.*

When Should We Undertake Humanitarian Intervention?

We can now turn now to guidelines for when the United States should engage in humanitarian intervention. Faced with a people under attack or a nation sliding into chaos, policymakers should ask themselves:

- Are atrocities being committed on a scale that "shocks the conscience" of humankind?[65]
- Have coercive measures short of force been attempted and clearly failed to meet the need?
- Is intervention supported by the American people and Congress to the degree necessary to allow for the likely level of casualties?
- Is there a clear military plan to halt or significantly slow these atrocities and does this strategy have a reasonable chance of success?
- Are the benefits of an intervention likely to outweigh the risks and costs to the United States, to the civilians in the country being assisted, and to the region?
- Is the United States the most appropriate country to lead the mission or might the United Kingdom, France, Australia, or Nigeria be

more suited? Are there any multinational forces willing to participate in the intervention?

- Is there a plausible exit strategy that would allow the United States
  to quickly remove its troops? Or is there a partnership in place that
  would allow the United States to hand the mission over to an international body so that long-term U.S. occupation will be unnecessary?
- For an intervention likely to require long-term deployment, do we
  have clear authorization from the UN, NATO, or the EU?

These guidelines should enable humanitarian intervention to occur
when it has a high probability of success and should prevent interventions that are set up for failure. If we follow these guidelines, the United
States is likely to see itself engaged in future humanitarian actions. What
can we do now, in addition to the policy prescriptions already mentioned, to increase the chances of future success?

1) *Create coherent doctrine.* The United States currently lacks coherent
   military doctrine on humanitarian intervention. Developing such
   doctrine would encourage the military to acknowledge that this is
   a task it will be asked to fulfill and to begin force training for such
   missions.
2) *Build political support for preventative interventions.* An ounce of prevention is worth a pound of cure. Deploying troops to calm antago-
   nists *before* they are mobilized for war can be a good investment.
   The UN mission in Macedonia, fielded by the EU in 1992, involved
   a few hundred troops and managed to prevent violence in that former Yugoslav republic.
3) *Improve relationships between the military and aid workers.* In any
   humanitarian intervention, the military and international aid community will have to work together. Yet current relations between
   these groups are characterized by mistrust and lack of mutual
   understanding. Improving relations between these key players
   ahead of time will maximize the chances of those relationships
   being fruitful and productive on the ground when it really matters.[66]

The Ethics of Prudential Calculation

Michael Walzer, the father of modern just war theory, writes that
"humanitarian action is justified when it is a response (with reasonable
expectations of success) to acts 'that shock the moral conscience of mankind'."[67] There has been considerable debate trying to assess when

actions rise to this level. But in fact, atrocities that shock the moral conscience—or *should*—abound in multiple parts of the world at any given time. The more important criterion in humanitarian intervention is Walzer's parenthetical comment: "with reasonable expectations of success."

Calculating such expectations is a complicated business and should give pause to those who, in the face of a crisis, advocate willy-nilly that we "do something." Yet humanitarian intervention is often required of us morally. As world opinion gravitates toward accepting the "responsibility to protect,"democratic leaders must respond. Intervention can also, as we have seen, serve strategic purposes in preventing conflict spillover.

Those resisting the concept of intervention are not only battling the waves of history; they can cause great harm. By refusing to accept that humanitarian action is a call that will need to be answered, they prevent America from preparing for such interventions, increasing the odds that our troops will be sent on ill-considered missions with inadequate training and resources.

America is a global power. When a voice cries out seeking help, the people of the world look to us for rescue. We should build the rapid reaction forces of other countries and the long-term peacekeeping abilities of the United Nations in order that we may share the burden of these calls to conscience. But we must be prepared at times to answer that call ourselves.

Chapter 4

Matching Means with Intentions
Sanctions and Human Rights

GEORGE A. LOPEZ

U.S. policymakers and human rights advocacy groups alike have long embraced the use of economic sanctions by the United States to halt human rights abuses by governments and foster democratic governance to enhance the protection of rights. Depending upon how strictly one defines the primacy of the rights issue, an analysis of all the instances in which the United States participated in sanctions since 1945 shows that "rights" and "democracy protection" comprised the goals of between one-third to one-half of the cases in which sanctions were used.[1]

Of course, the type of sanctions imposed and their effectiveness have varied over time, depending upon such factors as domestic U.S. politics, the complexity of the threat to rights that the sanctions seek to redress, and the degree of economic entanglement the United States has with a target state. Sometimes the United States has employed strong, direct sanctions against governments, such as those imposed on Guatemala and Nigeria. Other times, when trying to influence the prospects for peaceful transitions to greater democracy, the United States has aimed targeted sanctions at nonstate actors in places such as Colombia, Cambodia, and Sierra Leone.

Modern U.S. sanctions in support of human rights began with strong congressional action to counter the Soviet Union's exorbitant and discriminatory educational exit taxes on Jews seeking to leave Russia for Israel or the West. The Jackson-Vanik Amendment to the 1974 Trade Authorization Act demanded that the president suspend trade with planned economy nations that placed certain restrictions on emigration. Further congressional action under the Carter presidency solidified the early trend that U.S. sanctions involved denying or withdrawing military, trade, or financial assistance packages to nations with poor human rights records. From these beginnings until now the effectiveness and impact of such actions have been hotly debated.[2]

Since the end of the Cold War, multilateral economic sanctions, sometimes complemented by congressional action but often as stand-alone measures, have occupied an increasingly prominent place in the coercive tool kit of U.S. policymakers. Ever since championing UN Security Council Resolution 661 in August 1990, which demanded that Iraq withdraw unconditionally from Kuwait after its invasion of the country, the United States has imposed multilateral trade and targeted sanctions under the UN Security Council mandate for a wide array of goals. These include ending international and civil wars, extraditing international fugitives, controlling the spread of international terrorism, and deterring the proliferation of weapons of mass destruction as well as restoring democratically elected governments and protecting human rights.[3]

Although practitioners and politicians frequently resort to sanctions to punish wrongdoers, the assessment of the utility of sanctions by the pundits continues to be mixed—something that might possibly give pause to a new administration when it comes to employing them to advance human rights or related policy objectives. Some observers caution that the limited success rate of sanctions in achieving their objectives—most analysts consider that rate to be about 33 percent but some claim it is much lower—make them a poor bet.[4] Others worry that the combination of congressional trade and aid restrictions across a broad array of issues from technology export controls to commodity embargoes and the obligations the United States incurs to participate in UN and regional sanctions create a counterproductive sanctions "epidemic" in U.S. foreign economic policy.[5] Yet other analysts applaud the results of applying coercive, targeted sanctions to attain key U.S. policy goals, especially such national security goals as denuclearizing Libya and North Korea.[6]

The entire sanctions debate becomes even more pointed when we examine the effectiveness of economic sanctions for punishing rights violators or enhancing human rights in fragile political environments. On the one hand the historical evidence shows that neither unilateral nor multilateral sanctions has ever toppled a targeted, rights-violating government. Nor have sanctions, by themselves, ever forced rights violators to desist in their actions. Sanctions have, however, had more dramatic success in safeguarding fragile democracies, thereby protecting political climates in which rights are respected.[7]

Sanctions proponents argue that whatever the poor results, they stem from the half-hearted intentions, design, or implementation of sanctions, especially by powerful nations like the United States. These supporters of sanctions cite multiple cases from the 1970s and 1980s in Latin America, as well as the premier example of South Africa, in which economic sanctions—especially in the form of aid withdrawal by the U.S.

Congress—effectively denied repressive regimes the tools to continue their harsh abuse of rights. They further argue that a close scrutiny of the Kosovo, Sudan/Darfur, and Burma (Myanmar) cases reveals that the reluctance of powerful states to enforce a full slate of coercive measures has sabotaged what otherwise might have been effective sanctions for improving human rights.[8]

A more skeptical, if not condemnatory view emerges from some ethicists and international development practitioners. They declare that economic sanctions are so fundamentally flawed that the only meaningful policy question is how to assess accurately their substantial negative impact on humanitarian conditions or human rights.[9]

Yet contemporary economic sanctions can be harnessed as an effective tool for improving human rights by a new U.S. administration. To accomplish this, new leadership must maximize the benefits of a number of mutually reinforcing trends that have developed in the past decade. First, more sharply targeted sanctions techniques—so-called smart sanctions—have replaced general trade sanctions and aid withdrawal as the tool of choice. They provide national leaders with a versatile panoply of coercive economic measures while limiting the unanticipated humanitarian damage that sanctions can bring. But as with all techniques, their implementation is not without certain difficulties.[10]

Second, U.S. policymakers must recognize that we have acquired considerable knowledge from recent cases that can help us identify those factors that lead to sanctions success. Perhaps because those insights have often come from diplomats, especially European, the Bush administration has too often considered them merely partisan opinion or idiosyncratic case examples, rather than historical generalizations that might serve as the basis for sound policy.[11]

Third, sanctions success requires astute and timely management of the complex, symbiotic relationship that has emerged between the United States and the UN Security Council. The deterioration of that relationship has been well documented, but there is little question that the future use of sanctions by the UN for rights protection needs the United States as a key and committed player.[12]

Being Smart About Sanctions

Sanctions are "smart," that is, precisely targeted, in two ways. First, they take aim at specific subnational economic actors, such as companies, asset-holding entities, or individuals, deemed most responsible for the policies or actions considered illegal or abhorrent. Second, they narrow the focus of economic coercion to a specific, microeconomic activity. Hence, luxury goods desired by elites, for example, or single high-value commodities, such as timber or diamonds, or specific armaments and related arms and security technologies may be embargoed. Financial assets of varied types are frozen and aviation and travel are restricted or denied. Recent history demonstrates that such precise mechanisms both constrain and inflict pain on their targets, which most often are key subsectors of the ruling elite.[13]

Since the mid-1990s all UN and multilateral sanctions in which the United States has participated (as well as almost all rights-focused sanctions imposed unilaterally by the United States) have been smart sanctions. Of the 19 major UN sanctions cases over the past two decades, 9 have involved financial restrictions (always in combination with other measures); 6 were commodity boycotts (most involving petroleum products, 3 involving diamonds, and 1 lumber products); 10 were travel sanctions (also in combination with other measures); and 15 cases included arms embargoes.[14] As with the larger universe of sanctions, these smart sanctions may have human rights protection or improvement as a very direct goal, as in Kosovo, or aim to improve the rights climate indirectly, as in the use of arms embargoes to end violent wars in sub-Saharan Africa.[15]

The practice of imposing financial sanctions and visa bans simultaneously on lists of designated targets was used to decrease the war-making capability of armed factions in the internal wars of Angola, Sierra Leone, Afghanistan, Liberia, the Democratic Republic of Congo, Sudan, and Ivory Coast. Ending these wars had to occur before governments that would protect human rights could emerge. In the case of Angola, the combination of selective UN sanctions along with European and U.S. embargoes and travel suspensions imposed over the years (arms and oil in 1993, travel and diplomatic in 1997, and diamonds in 1998) resulted in a nearly comprehensive embargo on territory controlled by the rebel forces of the National Union for the Total Independence of Angola (UNITA), thereby encouraging them to seek peaceful resolution of the conflict with the government. There is little question that this led to democratic elections and then legitimate government in Angola.[16]

Commodity-specific sanctions have increased in frequency and impact since the mid-1990s. Highly to moderately successful oil embargoes were imposed as part of the sanctions against Iraq, the former Yugoslavia, Haiti, UNITA in Angola, and against the military junta in Sierra Leone. As aid agencies and human rights NGOs documented the role of diamond smuggling in financing the civil wars in Angola and Sierra Leone and in the recruitment and retention of child soldiers in other conflicts, the Security Council pushed the United States and European states to take action to interdict the trade in so-called blood diamonds. Diamond embargoes were imposed against UNITA in 1998, against areas held by the Revolutionary United Front (RUF) of Sierra Leone in 2000, and against Charles Taylor's Liberian government in 2001. A log export ban also was imposed against the government of Liberia for its support of the RUF.[17]

Despite condemnation of the Khartoum regime for its actions against the citizens of the Darfur region of Sudan, a watered-down financial assets freeze as well as travel restrictions were imposed against a small number of Sudanese officials by the UN in various Security Council resolutions from 2004 through 2006. The United States, as in other selected cases of sanctions against rights abusers, has imposed stronger, smart sanctions on a wider range of Sudanese government elites and across more diverse categories of economic activity, thus increasing the coercive leverage that sanctions are designed to provide.

The Power and Perils of Sanctions as Foreign Policy Tools

One of the more frustrating aspects of the Bush administration's use of sanctions has been the administration's inconsistent recognition that there are some hard-learned lessons from the past two decades that have become truisms in the international community and have guided the sanctions policies of our Atlantic alliance partners, even while Washington has held them at arm's length. To ignore these maxims is to risk sanctions failure.[18] Whether a new administration chooses to use sanctions to bolster human rights policy or as a technique to further other policy goals that indirectly benefit human rights, such as controlling the financing of terrorist organizations, these generalizations constitute an essential checklist that should not be ignored.

1) *In this age of globalization, unilateral sanctions cannot succeed; multilateral participation and cooperation are essential to the success of sanctions.* When international (UN), regional (for example, European Union, Commonwealth of Nations), and national authorities coordinate their actions to effectively monitor and enforce sanctions, compliance by the country or entity being targeted increases.

For the United States this generalization about unilateral sanctions makes clear the sanctions on Cuba are antiquated and explains why more recent efforts to bolster rights through sanctions that had less than full international support—in Darfur and in Zimbabwe—have fallen short of their goals.

2) *Sanctions as means of punishment and isolation rarely succeed.* Sanctions form only half of the mix of mechanisms needed to alter the behavior of stubborn targets such as regimes or non-state actors engaged in human rights violations. Positive inducements—the proverbial "carrots"

of international economic and political relations—are a necessary complement to the "sticks" of a sanctions strategy.

How essential is the stick and carrot pairing? No application of sanctions for dealing with difficult policy change has succeeded in recent years without some type of incentive mix—even if the carrot entails the simple removing of the original sanctions.[19] This maxim was consistently resisted for six years by the Bush administration in using sanctions for weapons proliferation control against North Korea and Iran. But as the nuclear standoff with Pyongyang worsened, the administration gave a great deal of ground on the need to combine both sticks and carrots for North Korea or face failure.

3) *Smart sanctions, despite their precision, seldom produce immediate and full compliance from targets.* The nuances of this point often evaded and frequently angered members of the Bush administration as they used sanctions against recalcitrant targets. Smart sanctions often produce partial compliance and generate pressure on both targets and imposers to engage in more direct bargaining to achieve the objectives the sanctions are intended to achieve. The economic squeeze felt by the target comprises only the first tier of smart sanctions success. The political success of getting the target to change its behavior results less over time from the economic pain it experiences and more from gains to be made at the bargaining table.[20]

Evidence supporting this claim abounds. In Yugoslavia between 1991 and 1995, sanctions exerted leverage on the Belgrade regime that eventually brought Slobodan Milosevic to the table at the Dayton conference where the peace accords were negotiated. In Libya sanctions were a central factor in the ongoing negotiations from the mid-1990s until a decade later that brought suspected terrorists to trial and convinced the regime to reduce its support of international terrorism. In Angola sanctions that were initially ineffective but became stronger over the years combined with military and diplomatic pressures to weaken the UNITA rebel movement. In Liberia sanctions first denied resources to the Charles Taylor regime and then, after increased engagement by the United Nations with the fighting factions in the region, helped to reduce Taylor's legitimacy.[21]

4) *When sanctions become the policy or are maintained for so long that they de facto become* the *policy, they cease to be effective.* Sanctions succeed when decisionmakers remember that they are only one set of tools—and thus only one of the important means—to advance larger foreign policy goals and that multiple tools should be used to achieve those clearly specified goals. This was the trap the United States and the United Nations fell into by the mid-1990s with the sanctions on Iraq and it has been the case with Cuban sanctions for decades.

A corollary to this larger point is that sanctions that are failing to accomplish their goals after, say, two years time, should be suspended or ended in full. There may always be good reason to continue arms embargoes against repressive regimes in order to deny them tools of abuse. But if economic coercion on the target produces no change in political behavior, or compliance in a reasonable time, a new set of tools are in order. Resistance to this truth means that policy elites have become committed to sanctions for the sake of sanctions alone and have failed to reevaluate how to attain their goal.[22] This is an important maxim for U.S. officials to accept and act on, especially when dealing with rights violators who know that sanctions have not, by themselves, ever toppled a rights-abusive regime.

5) *Sanctions succeed when the target believes that the next component of the imposer's strategy is to engage in even harsher action, especially military force, should sanctions fail.* Understandably, this principle is not a favorite among those who consider sanctions an effective alternative to war and who support them because they are firmly grounded in international law and can involve UN and multilateral agency support. Nonetheless, if sanctions are to be more than just a means of "doing something" when rights violations or other illegal action is taken by another nation, they must be linked to the possibility of stronger enforcement measures else they become little more than a bet supported by a bluffing hand we hope the target does not discover or "call." The Haiti example, where the lax enforcement of UN and Organization of American States sanctions ultimately led to military intervention, stands out as the best exemplar of this maxim.[23]

6) *The more effective sanctions detail a very clear, credible, and limited number of demands.* The game plan for the use of sanctions, including the structure of the endgame desired from the target, must be clear. Both the United States and the target must be in full agreement about what constitutes compliance. Moreover, the target must be confident that if it changes its behavior in accord with actions specified in the sanctions, this will result in a timely lifting of coercive pressure and extension of the promised benefits.

This might at first appear to be a minor matter best left to the bureaucrats who implement sanctions. But it is critical for human rights sanctions that the target knows what specific behaviors are required of them and that the powerful imposer will deliver on its side of the implicit bargain that sanctions represent. U.S. decisionmakers have found the most difficulty dealing with "partial compliance" by targets ranging from the Haitian military to Saddam Hussein. Thinking through how the United States will cope with this reality is essential. Zimbabwe's president, Robert Mugabe, for example, was able to manipulate early UN sanctions resolutions and quickly show his supporters that they could be resisted because those resolutions lacked sufficient bite.[24] Such evasiveness by targets should be fully expected and constrained at the stage at which the sanctions are designed.

Effectively Managing the UN-U.S. Sanctions Relationship

As with other foreign policy tools, the use of smart sanctions and its broader stick-carrot strategy unfolds against the backdrop of complex and often competitive political environments. For the United States this includes international tensions that result from being a partner of the United Nations and a member of the UN Security Council. At a domestic level, the legislative power of the U.S. Congress poses an array of both constraints and opportunities in relation to the executive branch's sanctions authority and obligations.

The last seven years have been unduly tumultuous for the UN-U.S. relationship, with the depth of the rift varying from mutual displeasure to outright disdain.[25] Often led by members of Congress anxious to score domestic political points and sustained by presidential acquiescence, there has been a litany of U.S. accusations against the UN: it has a bloated bureaucracy; it reeks of official corruption (the oil-for-food program, for example) [26] and promotes incompetent management. Charges such as these led the Congress to withhold the payment of UN dues throughout the 1990s.

From its side, UN secretaries-general and various governments sitting on the Security Council have charged the United States with a lack of leadership (at best) and obstructionist action (at worst) when UN action was called for during the genocides in Bosnia, Rwanda, and Darfur. As the Iraq sanctions unfolded in the 1990s, various UN diplomats and professional staff criticized the United States for manipulating sanctions and weapons inspections for its own geopolitical agenda, causing innocent children and the elderly to die in large numbers because of U.S. stubbornness. The inability of the United States to build a consensus for Security Council action against Iraq in the run-up to the March 2003 invasion led both Secretary-General Kofi Annan and various council members to condemn the United States for waging an unauthorized war.

The forging of sanctions through congressional legislative power often reflects a wide range of salient domestic interests and thereby poses a complicated challenge to any administration, even if its own party controls the majority in Congress. On one level congressional sanctions legislation may be out of sync with either presidential preferences on the means and ends of foreign policy or with the obligations that fall to the United States as a permanent member of the Security Council once that body has passed sanctions.

On another level Congress permits the president to play a two-tiered strategy when it passes or renews sanctions against a target nation: the president can be tough on the target nation—seen as a U.S. foreign policy foe—by maintaining all or several aspects of a U.S. embargo but then through an executive order may declare the sanctions ended under the rubric of following UN sanctions policy. The case of Libya from 1998 through 2004 illustrates this dilemma. After six years under various UN smart sanctions, Libya agreed in 1998 to comply with UN demands to turn over suspects wanted in connection with the 1988 bombing of Pan-Am Flight 103 to an international tribunal at The Hague, where the trial was held in 1999. When the extradition was completed, the Security Council responded by suspending and—later—lifting sanctions.[27]

The U.S. Congress, however, lobbied heavily by domestic groups like the American Israel Public Affairs Committee (AIPAC), opted to maintain certain U.S. sanctions and demanded that Tripoli take further steps to compensate the families of victims of terrorist attacks and cooperate in global counterterrorism and nonproliferation efforts. These discrepancies, which the Libyans and others argued were tantamount to the United States "moving the goalposts," were not resolved until August 2003 when a final compensation package to the families of Lockerbie victims was agreed to by the Libyans.[28]

This brief history illustrates an important nuance that every president will face. In the two-tiered dimension of sanctions, either congressional agreement or dissent can be used to an executive's advantage, depending on foreign policy goals. The key is not to be caught by surprise and to maximize the policy flexibility this structure provides.

Another challenge posed by UN-imposed smart sanctions developed in the Security Council is the UN can exercise only the stick of coercive diplomacy. The carrot of economic incentives that must be added to the equation needs to be provided by powerful member states like the United States and members of the European Union. Under the Bush administration the United States has had a mixed record of linking these two elements, especially when dealing with recalcitrant regimes like Iran, Syria, and North Korea. This reluctance to offer economic inducements appears grounded in the claim that to offer carrots after—or in combination with—sticks sends an inconsistent message to a target that might misinterpret the incentive as weakness on the part of the United States.

Another tenet of the Bush administration's thinking on carrots is that they reward the bad behavior of a target. According to the administration's logic, if these incentives are part of a sanctions package, they should be offered only after the target is in full compliance with relevant law and has earned whatever privileges the incentives promise to provide.

While one might appreciate the Bush position as one among contending theoretical views about how coercion best works in international relations, or as a set of strict philosophical claims about how actors change their behavior, these claims run into serious trouble when compared to the reality of sanctions. After being coerced, embarrassed, and forced to acknowledge that their practices are unsustainable, a target needs some wiggle room to change its behavior—something that is most often provided during negotiation of an agreement to end sanctions. A new administration committed to maximizing such win-win deals through the leveraging that sanctions can provide will be an effective human rights force in global politics.

Still another problematic area in Washington's relationship with the UN involves the effective use of targeted financial sanctions, which have become the technique of choice in both the U.S.-led global war on terror and UN-led counterterrorism efforts. UN Security Council Resolution 1373 calls for sweeping and strict financial asset control and travel restriction measures against secret, transnational organizations like Al Qaeda. To implement these restrictions requires intelligence and research capacity in financial transactions and the compilation of an accurate list of targeted people and entities. Because these tasks lie beyond UN institutional capability, in practice national governmental units, such as the U.S. Office of Foreign Assets in the Treasury Department, supply these lists to relevant UN sanctions committees. Soon after September 11, concerns about the accuracy and reliability of these lists, as well as the legal and human rights of those targeted, began to emerge. A few of the individuals placed on the Al Qaeda and Taliban designation lists complained that they were wrongfully listed and that their civil and human rights had been violated. They subsequently took legal action to seek removal from the Security Council list.[29]

By 2006 the total number of individuals and entities on UN lists of targeted persons was approximately 1,000. Arriving at that number was more art than science. One thousand may seem like a relatively small number but concerns about the political and legal procedures involved in the listing process, which is driven by the technical capability of the powerful UN permanent Security Council members like the United States, has clouded UN successes in counterterrorism and made other nations less cooperative with new U.S.-UN initiatives over time. More than 50 UN member states filed concerns about the lack of due process and absence of transparency involved in the listing process. This assessment was reinforced further in the December 2004 report of the secretary-general's High-Level Panel on Threats, Challenges, and Change.[30] A new administration will need to delve into this morass with the conviction that there is no reason for a strong counterterrorism policy to compromise human rights. This conviction will also need to be conveyed by a U.S. ambassador to the UN whose credentials on rights issues are impeccable.

A final and more recent problem in U.S.-UN sanctions relations relates to a basic challenge that sanctions have faced since their inception. When nations impose sanctions, the measures they employ and the clarity about those targeted must be sufficient to have some "bite." Sanctions that are merely symbolic and are little more than scolding will never succeed. But it is also the case that UN sanctions that lack the full and active support of council members also fail. Thus the dilemma for a new U.S. administration faced with human rights crises in Zimbabwe, Burma, and other nations will be how to maximize international cooperation for a strong and relevant sanctions resolution that deals with rights violations when other states are less committed to such a course of action.

Anxious to demonstrate to Sudanese leaders the unity of the UN Security Council's permanent five nations in condemning the Sudanese government's behavior regarding Darfur, the Bush administration determined that it would be better for the Security Council to pass a watered down consensus sanctions resolution with relatively little economic coercion in it than to pass nothing at all. In sacrificing coercive leverage for great power agreement, the United States (and the UN) may ultimately find this action to have been self-defeating. Sudan and other recalcitrant targets are in the enviable position of using the imposition of the sanctions as a domestic rallying cry. This same response was mobilized by Iranian President Mahmoud Ahmadinejad when weak sanctions were passed against Iran in December 2006 in an attempt to force Iran to shut down its uranium enrichment program. A new administration will need to formulate its own balance in this emerging tension between coercion and consensus.

Some analysts suggest this is precisely when the United States should act unilaterally, imposing its own heavier penalties against these (and possibly a much expanded list of) smart sanctions targets when the UN has passed a weak resolution. But such a multilayered action is a delicate, if not dangerous, practice. It tempts states that have already agreed to a certain level of UN sanctions to cut back their full enforcement of these sanctions if they perceive the United States has exceeded the already agreed level of target sanctioning

In truth, this dynamic is new and unchartered territory. It presents a significant challenge to an incoming administration that rightfully recognizes the importance of a strong UN-U.S. relationship in imposing sanctions to protect rights but that also wants to maximize the economic pressure that robust sanctions can bring to bear on targets.

A Strategy for Success

Smart sanctions provide the United States with a form of economic coercion that is precise and effective. The blending of U.S., European, and UN efforts to sanction both brutal ruling elites and nonstate fighting forces whose actions violate international human rights has also been increasingly successful. But the prospects for failed implementation of smart sanctions always exist.

Thus key advice for a new administration on how to use smart sanctions to protect and enhance human rights can be summarized succinctly: use smart sanctions in direct and indirect ways; maximize the chances for sanctions success by learning from the recent past; and, develop and use wisely the complex and sensitive relationship the United States has with the UN Security Council.

A new U.S. administration must guard against the power politics temptation to use sanctions for punishment and isolation but instead combine these coercive tools with incentives as part of a dynamic bargaining process that eases or increases pressure in response to cooperation or defiance from a targeted regime. More than ever before, new leadership will be faced with subtle and substantial challenges in employing sanctions as a means to advance U.S. human rights policy. This requires that leaders in Washington pay more attention to the conditions of smart sanctions success than they have in the past.

To be successful in the use of economic sanctions in the rights arena, a new U.S. leadership needs to appreciate how the nation benefits greatly from collaboration with the UN. A new administration must craft a coordinated strategy that balances U.S. action with that of multilateral agencies. It should also blend sanctions with incentives as complementary tools—something evidence indicates increases the likelihood that sanctions will achieve their goal.[31]

In a sense the versatility to play both the multilateral or unilateral cards does not in and of itself make for successful sanctions policy. It is the sophisticated and subtle blending of the UN-U.S. relationship that makes for success. As the Libyan and North Korean cases illustrate (but as the Iranian case by late 2007 proves in the negative), carrot-and-stick diplomacy that blends U.S. action harmoniously with international efforts offers the best strategy for achieving success—especially in the highly charged area of human rights.

Chapter 5
Setting the Record Straight
Why Now Is Not the Time to
Abandon Democracy Promotion

JENNIFER L. WINDSOR

For almost 15 years American policymakers of all stripes have largely agreed that democracy promotion ought to be a U.S. foreign policy priority. But today Washington is awash with criticism not only of the Bush administration's specific methods and approaches, but also the value and premises of the enterprise as a whole.

Partly this has to do with global trends. The last decade has seen the pace of democratic change slow and in some cases reverse. The euphoria that was felt after the collapse of the Berlin Wall in 1989 and that reemerged with the ouster of Slobodan Milosevic in Serbia in 2000 and the "color revolutions" in Georgia in 2003 and Ukraine in 2004 has largely evaporated. In each of these three countries, politics has become messy and heroes are harder and harder to identify. Other apparent breakthrough moments, such as the "Tulip Revolution" in Kyrgyzstan and the "Cedar Revolution" in Lebanon (both in 2005), have apparently fizzled as well. Finally, the emergence of a backlash against democracy promotion among authoritarian regimes, coupled with the inability of democratic nations to present a unified front against that backlash, has also contributed to the malaise within the Washington policymaking community.

While recognizing the formidable challenges that exist, this chapter argues that it would be a grave mistake for new American leadership in Congress or the executive branch to abandon democracy promotion as a fundamental priority in U.S. foreign policy. President George W. Bush's personal embrace of the cause is unprecedented. But the goal of promoting freedom and democracy around the world has a long and distinguished parentage among twentieth-century political leaders in the United States. Franklin Delano Roosevelt, Harry S. Truman, John F.

Kennedy, Jimmy Carter, Ronald Reagan, and Bill Clinton all sought in different ways to use the influence and resources of the United States to advance the cause of freedom.

The Bush administration deserves credit for elevating attention to freedom in presidential speeches and in official documents articulating U.S. foreign policy priorities. Its commitment to reform in the Middle East—which my colleague Tom Melia has aptly described as the "abrogation of the 'Arab exception' that governed previous efforts to foster democracy abroad"—is an especially important and courageous departure.[1] Yet despite a record of achievement, this administration has also done enormous damage to the very goals it has committed itself to advance. The conflation of the invasion and military occupation of Iraq with the promotion of democracy, the inconsistent application of democracy standards to U.S. allies in the war against terror, and the failure to ban the use of torture and the cruel, inhumane, and degrading treatment of detainees have all had an unambiguously disastrous effect on the efforts of those of us who were committed to the "freedom agenda" long before that term was identified with a particular U.S. president.

The obstacles that lie in the path of restoring the "good name" of democracy promotion are vexing but not insurmountable. While critics and supporters should admit mistakes as part of a constant revisiting of the means by which the U.S. government and others are promoting democracy, the goal itself should be preserved. The U.S. government must remain actively engaged in supporting those on the ground who are working to change systems and policies that are critical to any sustained respect for fundamental human rights in their own societies. In short, the promotion of democracy cannot—and should not—be abandoned.[2]

To meet the current challenges, those both inside and outside government who are committed to programs and policies aimed at generating more respect for human rights and for progress toward democracy need to clarify what we are trying to achieve in democracy promotion; accurately assess opportunities and constraints in advancing the cause of freedom; and design and implement comprehensive, thoughtful, and flexible strategies to support the reformers within countries—the people who are, and have always been, the true engines of change within any society.

Those strategies may mean that programs and policies may best be implemented on a multilateral basis with the UN or the Organization for Security and Cooperation in Europe (OSCE); by quasi-nongovernmental organizations like the National Endowment for Democracy (NED); or by groups like Freedom House that receive a mixture of private and U.S. government grants or the Open Society Institute (OSI), which is funded completely by private sources.

While recognizing the strengths of alternative approaches, and the need to amplify them in the future, it would be a mistake to simply rule out *any* role for the U.S. government in programs and policies that promote democracy. That would be to ignore the positive contributions that the U.S. government has made in the past to assist those who successfully brought about democratic progress in their societies, as well as the negative impact the U.S. can have by simply backing the political status quo.[3]

The Best of Times Turn into the Worst of Times: The Backlash Against Democracy Promotion

What are the critical challenges facing advocates for democracy promotion?[4] The most serious is the emergence of an increasingly well-organized and in some cases, thanks to rising oil and natural gas prices, well-financed collection of authoritarian regimes—including Russia, Venezuela, Iran, Kazakhstan—that seem determined to block and delegitimize the entire democracy promotion endeavor.[5] Throughout the world, governments—including but not limited to Russia, China, Zimbabwe, Iran, Egypt, Belarus, and Uzbekistan—are asserting the right to punish their own citizens because they communicate with and in some cases receive training or material assistance from the international community. As a result, it is becoming far more difficult to provide outside assistance to beleaguered activists, even in some countries that are not categorized among the world's most repressive.[6]

These governments justify their actions as necessary to prevent their own color revolutions, which they cynically misrepresent as Western plots orchestrated by the U.S. government and implemented by outside groups such as Freedom House or the National Democratic Institute (NDI), which are portrayed as mere instruments of the CIA, the U.S. Agency for International Development (AID), or the NED. Even groups such as OSI or those that engage in academic conferences, such as the Woodrow Wilson International Center for Scholars, are not immune from these allegations: witness the Iranian government's imprisonment of representatives of both organizations on charges that they were part of a larger strategy to foment a "velvet revolution" within Iran.[7]

Nondemocratic governments also have been using the bully pulpit at the United Nations and other international forums to conflate the promotion of democracy with colonization or cultural imperialism, arguing that it is an unlawful infringement on sovereignty.[8] While not formally a coalition, it is clear that a number of authoritarian governments, including members of the Organization of the Islamic Conference (OIC), have been a unified and destructive force at the UN Human Rights Council, successfully blocking a number of country-specific resolutions and arguing that any assistance for human rights should be provided only with the explicit permission of those currently in power.[9]

While such arguments are not new, it is dismaying that they are gaining traction and that there is apparently growing acceptance of the underlying premise that it is inappropriate or harmful for the U.S. government, or any entity, whether governmentally funded or not, to assist democracy and human rights advocates across borders. Even among democratic countries, we have seen a willingness to compromise on the right to assist such advocates when the existing government is hostile to such programs.

The international community long ago recognized the right of individuals and countries to assist human rights defenders and activists across borders—if done so peacefully. In 1998 the UN General Assembly adopted, with the active support of democracies and the human rights community, a Declaration on Human Rights Defenders that in Article 13 states that "everyone has the right, individually and in association with others, to solicit, receive and utilize resources for the express purpose of promoting and protecting human rights and fundamental freedoms through peaceful means."[10]

Unfortunately, we have yet to see a unified, coordinated approach by the world's democracies designed to counter effectively the arguments put forth by Russia, Iran, and others. For example, those of us who believe that democratic governments share a common goal in advancing and protecting democracy around the world were heartened by the establishment of the Community of Democracies (CD) in 2000. However, the results to date have been disappointing. The CD, an international group of democracies that meets every two years, has yet to produce anything concrete.[11] Its members have not formed an effective democracy caucus at the UN to expand acceptance of the right to democracy and have not voted together in a coordinated fashion to protect fundamental human rights principles. The CD has only released one statement critical of repressive regimes since its inception. And at its latest meeting at Bamako, Mali, there was no mention of the crackdowns against demonstrations that had occurred in the weeks and months before in Burma (Myanmar), Pakistan, and Georgia. Instead, negotiations on the final declaration led to a reopening of some of the fundamental principles that have guided the entire initiative.

Frustration with the CD process, combined with the inability of the UN Security Council to stop ongoing atrocities in Darfur, have led to calls for the creation of a new "Concert of Democracies" constituted by a smaller, more select group of democracies that would be willing to use force to stop regimes that are committing gross violations of human rights and crimes against humanity.[12]

In order to effectively counter the pushback against democracy promotion at the international level, the United States must use its diplomatic weight at such international forums and persuade a core group of the world's democracies to join them in asserting the right of the international community to help those struggling for universally recognized human rights and freedoms. The challenge now is that the United States government is so internationally isolated that it is unable to forge coalitions with other democratic governments, even when its policy goals are worthy and important.

That the United States failed to prevent outright dictatorships from gaining membership on the new UN Human Rights Council and failed to preserve the Council's ability through special rapporteurs to report on human rights violations in such obviously repressive regimes as Belarus and Cuba should be troubling to all who support human rights.[13] Unfortunately, these failures, the consequences of which are devastating for the credibility of the new UN Human Rights Council, have initially been met with glee by some members of the international human rights community, which take them as more evidence of the overall failures of the Bush administration, without adequately taking into consideration the negative impact that such U.S. policy failures have on the larger (and shared) goal of furthering human rights in the world.

Indeed, after a decade of recognition by both the human rights and democracy promotion communities that their two sets of goals are interrelated, we have seen in the last several years indications of a reopening of the schism between the two communities that was commonplace in the debates during the 1980s about Central America.[14] Some human rights leaders advocate the abandonment of democracy promotion altogether as a goal so as not to endanger further the hard-fought gains in the protection of human rights internationally. Critics of the current U.S. policy toward Iran, including members of the human rights community and some Iranian activists, have attacked the Bush administration's publicly announced program to provide aid to promote democracy in Iran as further endangering the activists on the ground, and have called for a suspension of the program.[15]

It is of course completely understandable that some activists in Iran (or Cuba or Egypt) would disavow and distance themselves from U.S. efforts to instigate change in their societies and to refuse to accept any outside assistance for their efforts. They stand to go to jail—or worse—if they say otherwise in public. But we should not conclude that all Iranian civic activists are united in their distaste for assistance—even assistance from the U.S. government—if it is designed to support their own vision for change (as opposed to the foreign policy goals of the U.S. government) and delivered in a fashion that does not endanger them.

Such debates are not surprising given that America's human rights luster and the genuineness of its desire to support democratization have been tarnished in global (and domestic) opinion. It is easy to point out the missteps, miscalculations, and errors of judgment in the Bush administration's approaches to Iran, Iraq, Pakistan, Venezuela, and other countries. But while we should criticize, we also have to be careful not to give unwitting credence to the insidious canard that there is something inherently damaging about official American support for reform efforts (and reformers) in other countries and that such assistance should be cut off. This would give the Ahmadinejads of the world exactly what they want: to turn world opinion against the right of their own citizens to receive outside support in their efforts to achieve universally recognized freedoms.

Beyond Euphoria

A renewed American commitment to the expansion of global freedom does not mean that success will come easily. While we have yet to see a wholesale global democratic reversal, and slow, steady, undramatic progress is being made year by year in more than two dozen African countries as well as in Turkey, the Balkans, and Indonesia, it is true that we have seen a "freedom stagnation." While freedom was on the march during the 1980s and much of the 1990s, in the last decade the proportion of countries designated as "free" has remained flat. At the end of 2006, Freedom House's annual survey reported only modest increases in global freedom.[16]

The expansion of freedom has become more complicated as we more closely examine the real challenges to further democratization in China, the Middle East, and Central Asia. While most focus understandably remains on the slow pace of change within the Middle East, other regions also deserve exploration and analysis.

The downward trends in Central and Eastern Europe and the former Soviet Union are particularly worrisome. The rise of an undemocratic Russia fueled by oil wealth and reenergized to use its influence regionally and globally is perhaps the most strategically important long-term threat to the continuation of—let alone an expansion of—the positive trends seen in many countries in the Eurasia region.

In 2006, the largest backsliding occurred in Asia, where Thailand's democratic path was interrupted with a military coup to replace a corrupt, although democratically elected, government. Setbacks also occurred in Bangladesh, Sri Lanka, East Timor, and Fiji and we continue to see ongoing deterioration in the Philippines, a country earlier considered a success story in democratic achievement. In 2007, Burma and Pakistan, already considered "not free" societies, saw massive crackdowns by the state against civic groups pressuring for an opening of the political system.

Along with the freest set of elections in decades, Latin America has seen a new rise of populist leaders who circumvent democratic institutions in favor of "direct democracy" and who have taken advantage of the growing disenchantment that democracy has not "delivered" economic advances for the poor. While the implications of these elections in other parts of the region are still uncertain, the consequences for Venezuela are grave. As independent media struggle to maintain their existence, any vestige of an independent judiciary is eradicated. And as fear and intimidation are used against civil society and human rights groups, the state continues to pass and apply illiberal laws to further damage Venezuela's institutions and democratic culture, which will take years if not decades to remedy.

We are seeing stagnation in many countries that have made progress in the last 20 years. Thus continued corruption in new democracies is crippling democracy's advance across the globe from Nigeria to Ukraine to Bangladesh. The absence of an impartially applied and independent rule of law plagues much of Latin America, leading some to argue that democracy cannot truly function or should be curtailed until the centuries of inequities within those societies are addressed.[17] The crackdowns against opposition in Georgia and the unsavory political coalitions that have emerged in Ukraine are a vivid reminder that democratic gains are extremely fragile, and reversals still possible.

In the last few years, we have seen significant deterioration in freedom of expression around the world. In Russia, Mexico, and the Philippines, the murder of journalists has become almost routine. Greater, if subtler, long-term threats lie in the smothering of free media by regime-directed economic pressure (such as discouraging advertisers from doing business with independent newspaper and broadcast outlets); the denial of licenses to privately owned television stations; takeovers by the state or by state-owned enterprises; and criminal slander charges against reporters who criticize government leaders.[18]

Regimes such as those in North Korea, Burma, and Turkmenistan have been able to cut off and isolate their citizens from one another and from flows of information from the outside world. We have seen a transfer of knowledge between authoritarian regimes on techniques that can be used to block or limit citizens' use of global information technology—the Internet, text-messaging, or cell phones—in order to prevent effective citizen organizing. And the deliberate steps taken by leaders such as Russia's Vladimir Putin, Belarus's Alexander Lukashenk, Uzbekistan's Islam Karimov, Zimbabwe's Robert Mugabe, and Iran's Mahmoud Ahmadinejad to choke off connections between their own civil societies and the international community by making such connections illegal have made the environment for democracy promotion even more hostile.

A Blueprint to Strengthen U.S. Democracy Promotion Policy

We need to be mindful of all of these challenges and realize that the future will not bring easy gains in the short term. But we should not abandon democracy promotion. Nor should we stop using the term because it is somehow tainted by its association with the Bush administration. Instead, the next administration should seize the opportunity to redefine the contours of the debate and clarify what democracy promotion actually means and how it can be made more effective.[19]

Many of those who have been involved in democracy promotion have been frustrated by the continuing confusion as to what democracy itself entails. As both scholars and serious practitioners have known for years, democracy is about electoral processes and all that is necessary for elections to be fair and meaningful: free association, free speech, and an independent and professional news media. Yet democracy also involves a broader range of vital institutions: an independent judiciary, a meaningful legislature, and security forces that defer to the authority of elected civilian leaders and whose purpose is to serve and protect the people. Democracy is about laws and behavior that protect and promote individual freedom, which means respecting core human rights; protecting minority rights in addition to majority rule; and tolerating ethnic, religious, linguistic, and political diversity.[20] And it involves fundamental principles like accountability of the government to the governed, and the application of the rule of law to all citizens, including government officials.[21]

There is of course no simple "one size fits all" model of democracy. The American democratic system is quite different from those that operate in Great Britain, France, Chile, Indonesia, or India. Some countries have presidential systems while others have parliamentary systems (the relative merits of which seem to be endlessly debated in academic circles.) The possible combinations in fashioning an electoral system ("first past the post," majority rule, single-member districts, party-list systems) are enough to make a nonexpert's head spin. Societies can choose between a jury-based system or judge-based system, or a combination of both. The different institutional arrangements and processes seem end-less. But the core principles are the same: the protection of internation-ally recognized rights and freedoms and accountability of those who rule to their own citizens.

Perfection in democracy is never attained. Each society has to secure and re-secure democratic freedoms continuously. The enactment of laws must be accompanied by institutions that effectively function and implement those laws and that provide both negative and positive incentives for behavioral change in individual citizens. Every established democracy has to struggle to make progress and prevent regression—just look at our own country's history of civil rights, the continued inequalities in our judicial system, and the limitations and distortions inherent in the U.S. political process.[22]

What Democracy Promotion Is Not

We have also seen confusion or, more often, a caricaturized depiction of what democracy promotion entails. Democracy promotion is seen variously as only promoting elections, using the U.S. military to topple regimes and occupy countries to impose a political system on unwilling citizens, or as a rhetorical cover for U.S. imperialist tendencies that are really aimed at global economic dominance, control of oil, or other objectives.[23]

To help restore the credibility of democracy promotion as a goal for the United States, we need to clarify what it is not. Democracy promotion has never been—not yet at least—the principal motivation for any military action by the United States or other governments.[24] While military means can be used to remove a repressive leader, this does not automatically lead to the establishment of a functioning democratic system. The great gains for freedom in Latin America, Eastern Europe, Africa, and Asia in the last three decades have been attained through peaceful means led by civic forces within the society *itself*.[25]

Moreover, democracy promotion was certainly not the main motivation for, nor arguably the overarching strategic goal, of the Bush administration's policies toward Iraq. There is little evidence that the initial stages of the American presence in Iraq were informed by plans for establishing a democratic political system. Yet because the Bush administration has shifted the rhetorical explanation for its actions to democracy building ever since the principal rationales for the invasion evaporated, it will not be easy to disentangle democracy promotion from Iraq and the U.S. military. Still, a new administration should clearly articulate that its commitment to democracy promotion is not synonymous with—nor simply a cover for—actions taken by the U.S. military to serve other U.S. national interest objectives.

Second, a new U. S. political leadership must be careful in making the case for democracy promotion to imply that it will automatically lead to gains for other U.S. national interests.[26] While both Democratic and Republican administrations have argued (correctly) that more democracy in the world helps to advance U.S. security and economic interests in the long term, it is also true that the process of democratization will not automatically bring about governments that are sympathetic to U.S. foreign policy interests in the short term. Indeed, as newly elected governments are held to higher standards of accountability by their own citizens, they may find it more difficult in some cases to ally themselves publicly with U.S. government policy, especially given the level and depth of anti-Americanism that currently exists in the world. Moreover, linking democracy promotion programs too closely with other U.S. foreign policy goals may damage our ability to provide effective support for democracy movements on the ground in a number of countries.[27]

We should also not fall into the trap of asserting that "all good things go together," and that more democratization is a magic elixir that, when applied, can cure all global ills, whether they be terrorism, poverty, instability, or global distaste for the United States as the only remaining superpower.[28] That is not to say that democracy should be removed as a goal of U.S. foreign assistance. Some critics assert that the Bush administration's policy of democracy promotion has come at the expense of U.S. efforts to provide humanitarian and other assistance aimed at the poorest in societies, and imply that democracy promotion should be separated from U.S. policies and programs to promote development. To do so would mean effectively turning back the clock on two decades of learning the lessson that ignoring political realities within a country will undermine the long-term impact of most aid interventions. Most academics and policymakers now agree that governments in the developing world do not have to face a trade-off between political rights and poverty alleviation and that democratic countries can provide economic security and political rights and civil liberties, but that should not lead to assertions that democratization automatically leads to gains in development.[29] Policy choices still matter, no matter what the regime type. Democracies do better at avoiding the worst kinds of economic outcomes and may achieve steady acceptable rates of growth, but there are plenty of examples of bad economic policies that emerge from a democratic process. Partial democracies—which have adopted only some of the institutions and processes of democracy—are especially vulnerable to being hijacked or undermined by a dominant elite intent on using its political or economic clout to deflect attempts to address poverty eradication and social inequities. These elites can also restrict further democratic progress and undercut critical principles such as the free flow of information, government accountability, participatory mechanisms for decision making, and a predictable, impartial system of rule of law.

A similar process of policy clarification needs to be undertaken with regard to democratization and its relationship to failed or fragile states. In the long-term, a properly functioning democratic system is the best conflict-containing mechanism that exists. But we need to recognize that democratization processes can generate some instability in the short term. Progress toward a system of providing accountability of the government to the governed is ultimately about changing power relations within society. Expanding political representation or shifting political balance between groups can be destabilizing. Those who have benefited from the existing power structure or have something to gain by continuing a conflict will undoubtedly maneuver to maintain or increase their position. In turn, those pushing for more power and access can grow impatient and restive, all of which can lead to short-term instability. To be effective, the U.S. government has to increase its tolerance for some political instability in the near term and not simply drop the goal of democracy promotion in a panic when it occurs.

What Democracy Promotion Is: Demystifying the Policy and the Practice

What then is democracy promotion? The main tools include:

- Setting standards for elements of a functioning democratic system and evaluating a country's progress in putting those elements in place;[30]
- Engaging in diplomacy at both bilateral and multilateral levels to encourage adherence to those standards;[31]
- Leveraging aid or trade or membership in international organizations, such as the European Union, to provide incentives for progress toward democracy;[32] and
- Providing assistance to support those inside or outside of a government who are committed to system or policy change that will increase respect for fundamental democratic freedoms, or further strengthen democratic processes and institutions within a society.

There is a clear lack of general understanding about the last approach so it is worthwhile to explore it in more detail. First, the overall perception is that the U.S. government is spending a huge proportion of its resources on democracy promotion. That is not the case. While U.S.

resources for democracy promotion have increased in recent years—and reached $1.2 billion in 2006—most of the additional $400 million added since 2001 was due to the very large programs in Afghanistan and Iraq. Regions outside of the Middle East and South and Central Asia remained essentially at the same funding levels for democracy.[33] And in terms of the percentage of the overall international affairs budget of $31.3 billion, democracy promotion represented a scant 4 percent. (It is also worth noting that the United States is no longer the largest funder of such programs internationally, now that member states of Europe, the European Union, UN Development Program, and the World Bank, have become much more heavily engaged in the area.)

Most democracy assistance programs are geared to support at least the subcomponents of democracy, including civic participation, good governance, the rule of law, and human rights. Democracy assistance programs typically consist of the provision of training and grant support to democracy activists; facilitation of the flow of information and expertise between democracy activists inside a society or from those outside; provision of on-site advice and encouragement, as well as visible demonstrations of solidarity; and advocacy on behalf of those working to make their governments more accountable, transparent, representative, and respectful of human rights and the rule of law.

The role of responsible democracy promotion programs is to facilitate and inform the thinking and strategy development of those within countries working toward political reform, not to dictate outcomes or attempt to direct change from the outside. Decades of experience and analysis have reinforced the basic point: democracy cannot be imposed; it must be homegrown in a process owned by local actors.

But we have also seen in many cases that the provision of support—financial, technical (that is, "know-how"), and moral—from the international community can make a significant contribution in terms of increasing the capacity and effectiveness of democracy activists on the ground. While the organizations, coalitions, and individuals themselves who receive and use assistance will ultimately be the ones to determine whether change happens or not, outside nongovernmental organizations, governments, and multilateral institutions have a pivotal role to play in providing them indispensable support to help them become more skilled agents of political transformation.

While the full impact of these efforts may not be apparent in the short term, in the long run programs that combine ideas with concrete action have the power to move entire societies in new directions.[34] Among such programs are those that support human rights defenders with small grants, advocacy training, and protection strategies so that they can continue to carry out their vital work even under highly repressive political conditions. Outside assistance can help bring together activists to cata-lyze and bolster effective coalitions to educate the citizenry on funda-mental human rights and galvanize popular support for the realization of those rights. Direct government-to-government assistance can also be an important part of democracy promotion. Training government offi-cials and staff in communication and outreach, establishing complaint mechanisms, and setting up ombudsman offices can help governments weed out corruption and manage the public's expectations during always difficult transition periods.

Where Do We Go from Here?

First and most important, *the United States must work to regain the moral and political high ground that earns credibility and respect for our country to engage effectively in democracy promotion.* The next administration must unambig-uously prohibit the use of U.S. techniques against detainees that run counter to all international agreements (and U.S. law) for the protec-tion of international human rights. Any effort to promote democratic change and respect for the rule of law in other societies is undermined by continued international perceptions that the U.S. government itself refuses to abide by its own laws or ignores fundamental human rights precepts in its own policies. Adopting a posture of humility and acknowl-edging that our own democracy is also a work in progress would help strengthen the American position in this endeavor. So too would further steps to ensure that all our own citizens enjoy their democratic rights in elections, in the criminal justice system, and elsewhere.[35]

Second, *a new administration must more systematically incorporate democ-racy and human rights concerns into U.S. policies toward strategic allies whose commitment to democracy is in serious question.* The failure to do so will only hurt U.S. national interests—as the current situation in Pakistan reminds us. The United States will undoubtedly still have—or want—to pursue trade relations or make security arrangements with regimes that do not respect human rights and are not democracies. The challenge is integrating the promotion of freedom into U.S. policies toward impor-tant but politically flawed states such as Russia, Saudi Arabia, or Paki-stan.[36] As it pursues other goals, the United States should not remain silent on the need for more progress in democracy and human rights. And the United States should continue to provide diplomatic and other support—through nongovernmental organizations preferably—to those who are seeking to advance their freedoms.[37]

Third, *while the next administration should not primarily focus on elections or push them in cases where they are inappropriate, elections serve an important mechanism for accountability that should not be abandoned.* The right to choose one's own leaders is enshrined in the Universal Declaration of Human Rights; moreover, citizens around the world have come to expect the holding of elections, regardless of whether or not external actors think they are "ready." Elections did not create Hamas in Palestine or political Islam in the Middle East. Indeed, over the years the lack of open political space and meaningful ways for citizens to hold their governments accountable in the Middle East and elsewhere have fostered the growth and strength of extremist movements.[38] Opening up political competition and allowing the emergence and strengthening of a variety of political actors within societies is the only path that allows for the establishment of viable democratic options in most countries.

The challenge is to provide time to allow for the emergence of these viable options before another nondemocratic alternative—religious hardliners or militant nationalists, for example—can monopolize the opposition. Reform forces inside a country may legitimately choose to delay or defer elections or make participation in them contingent on all candidates pledging to renounce violence and agreeing to maintain a democratic system and respect for human rights. But it is critical that those calls come from *inside* the country; we know that inappropriate edicts and timetables handed down by the U.S. government (or the UN or NATO) have backfired in the past, as we have seen in the cases of Angola and Bosnia.

In addition, regardless how noxious certain candidates are, the U.S. government should also reaffirm that it is backing a process and not attempting to dictate outcomes. It is naïve to believe that support for democracy will ever be considered noninterventionist. But we have too often seen the counterproductivity of explicit U.S. statements of support for a preferred candidate. Moreover, a new administration should consider reinstating a ban on any material assistance to parties outside of a multilateral mechanism in which the rules for allocation of resources are transparent and open to the public.[39]

Fourth, *we need to put the promotion of human rights back into the promotion of democracy and not attempt to separate the two goals.* Many in the human rights community have traditionally been loath to be identified with democracy promotion and have refused to accept U.S. government funds for any purpose. An unintended side effect of that distancing is that human rights promotion has too often been left out of the panoply of democracy assistance programs funded by the U.S. government, which have focused more on civic activists and advocates, elections, political parties, and governmental support. Yet, as Article 21 of the Universal Declaration of Human Rights affirms, a human being cannot enjoy a full range of human rights in a system that denies the right of individuals to freely choose their representatives. At the same time, success in democratization must mean the establishment of effective mechanisms for the protection of fundamental human rights.

Efforts to promote democracy must include support for those who engage in systematic monitoring and documenting of human rights abuses and advocate for reforms that will limit future violations. But targeted support for the human rights defenders, who are typically viewed as thorns in the side of any government, has often been underemphasized in U.S. democracy promotion strategies. The State Department's Bureau of Democracy, Human Rights, and Labor provides short-term support for defenders and a few AID missions do fund some work, but a new administration should do more in this regard to ensure that the promotion of human rights and democracy is seen as an integrated goal, not divergent (or, worse, rival) strategies.

Finally, *the political, economic, and social structures within a society are inextricably intertwined and the transformation of all of them is necessary to achieve sustainable poverty alleviation, broad-based human development, and strong democracies. The United States should value each of these objectives equally in its foreign assistance strategies.*[40] The Bush administration's decision to link the Millennium Challenge Account to performance on democratic governance is an important contribution that has great potential for fostering such integration and should under no circumstances be abandoned. The next administration, however, must reverse the simultaneous weakening and incorporation of AID into the State Department that has occurred in the Bush administration. This has served to undermine rather than reinforce the connection between democracy and development.

Bringing an End to the Short-Term Crisis Response Mode

Keeping AID engaged in democracy promotion is also linked to the need for the U.S. government to stay engaged diplomatically and provide financial support throughout the complex and challenging period that often follows free and fair elections. This is the only way to help guarantee the creation of durable institutions of government and civil society that are the prerequisite of stable liberal democracies.

An analysis of funding patterns over the last 10 years has shown that the United States has been far too quick to declare success and to stop funding for democracy promotion after successful elections have taken place but before reformers have had time to consolidate democratic gains. Past proclamations that particular countries or entire regions have made irrevocable democratic gains and now can be "graduated" from democracy assistance have been revised when reversals occur, and the U.S. government struggles to put back in place programs and institutional relationships that arguably should never have been terminated.

These experiences tell us that we are bound to be disappointed if we expect a quick fix in such a difficult region as the Middle East. While the pace of political change in many countries may be disappointing, it would be unwise to simply retreat from the objective of promoting democratic reform in this region. And yet there is a real possibility that Bush administration programs such as the Middle East Partnership Initiative (MEPI) (which provides resources for pro-reform elements within that region) will simply be abolished in the congressional appropriation process or by a new administration. This would be a mistake. It has taken decades for the U.S. government to realize that it has not directed enough democracy assistance funds to that region and returning to the old and failed policy of ignoring the need for political change will be disastrous.

The next administration must understand that advancing democracy and freedom will take time and must recognize that some setbacks are inevitable. It must be willing to be flexible in adapting strategies and approaches but continue to address challenges of democracy's advance with appropriate resources, strategic thinking, and, especially, patience.

Who Does What, and How?

In addition to understanding what is possible to achieve in democracy promotion and what is needed to create a realistic strategic framework for providing assistance, it is also important to look at the actual nuts and bolts of how the United States goes about providing that assistance. Who implements democracy promotion programs and how they do it makes a major difference in determining potential success.

Currently a multitude of U.S. agencies and departments provide funds for democracy promotion—most of which are then channeled through competitive awards to non-U.S. government entities to actually implement programs within countries.[41] The plethora of both funders and implementers has arguably led to innovative and flexible approaches and resulted in programs that reach a broader range of local actors than would be possible with a more centralized assistance structure.[42] Nonetheless, the large number of both funding agencies and implementing organizations involved in U.S. democracy promotion has made it difficult to present a unified U.S. government assistance strategy for a particular country.[43] The disparate and fragmented nature of the effort also makes it difficult to determine that the overall strategic choices were the correct ones—and to assert with certainty that U.S. taxpayer dollars had been spent in the most effective fashion. Congressional enthusiasm for tracking quantifiable results for all federally funded programs has put U.S. government officials involved in democracy promotion under tremendous pressure to show results in unrealistic time frames. That pressure—and the embrace of democracy promotion as a core U.S. foreign policy objective—has led U.S. officials to want to become more deeply engaged in the work of implementing organizations.

The extent—and appropriateness—of U.S. government control over those programs is a matter of some considerable debate within the democracy promotion community. Some recipients of U.S. government funds are mission-driven nonprofit organizations that only accept grants from the U.S. government to further their own organizational goals to advance democracy and human rights. These groups want to receive funds but continue to be seen as separate and distinct organizations from the U.S. government. Others—including for-profit enterprises that provide expertise to the U.S. government for a wide range of areas other than democracy—have no objections to playing the role of a direct service provider to the U.S. government. Indeed, while there are many dedicated individuals in such enterprises, the goal of their companies is not to promote democracy and support local counterparts, but to satisfy their main client, the U.S. government, and to make a profit.[44]

A new administration must grapple with these organizational and operational issues as it rethinks how to improve and strengthen U.S. democracy promotion policies and assistance strategies. The policymaking community is already debating whether there should be a clearer division of labor between various elements of the U.S. government, whether some types of programs are best implemented through a quasi-governmental organization such as the National Endowment for Democracy, or whether the U.S. government should fund a separate foundation which would operate completely autonomously of U.S. foreign policy interests.[45]

That is not to say that the U.S. government should get out of the democracy promotion business entirely. Without active U.S. government involvement, international efforts to promote democracy would undoubtedly be less effective. Yet it is also clear that democracy cannot be only a U.S. goal: it requires a strong partnership between the United States and its democratic allies, which include but should not be limited to the nations of Europe. Indeed, in some cases it would be strategically wise to allow other countries to take the lead in environments where strong anti-American sentiment is a dominant force in internal politics.

Many democracy assistance programs work well when there is active coordination among donors and implementers or where international bodies such as the UN Development Program or OSCE take the lead.

On the other hand, "not made in the USA" is not an automatic brand of success either. Other actors have their own limitations—as anyone who has worked with the EU or UN Development Program or other funders can attest.

Finally, while the United States should continue to stay engaged in democracy promotion, the paucity of nongovernmental funding sources is itself deleterious to the long-term viability of on-the-ground efforts to promote change. Especially with President Bush's vigorous embrace of democracy and freedom, every democracy promotion effort or group is seen as somehow connected to U.S. policy or controlled by the U.S. government. Enhanced private resources are absolutely necessary to complement U.S. government-supported efforts by funding people-to-people exchanges and scholarly discussions, supporting human rights defenders, and providing opportunities for dialogue between like-minded democrats around the world.

There is a rich tradition of involvement by private foundations and individual donors in supporting dissidents, opposition movements, and alternative media in countries suffering under dictatorships. Unfortunately, this tradition seems to have waned along with memories of the Cold War. While George Soros broke new ground by committing considerable resources to promote open societies in the early 1990s, the intervening years have seen no one else who could be considered to be a "Bill Gates" of democracy promotion. Indeed, many of the traditional foundations involved in funding international affairs have tended to shy away from democracy promotion and have policies that prohibit funding groups that have received U.S. grants in the past. This leaves nongovernmental groups that accept government grants unable to secure private funding to continue important initiatives even when they fit a foundation's stated area of interest directly.

The incoming American leadership needs to spend time and effort not only in strengthening efforts to promote democracy within the U.S. government, but also in encouraging greater participation and pluralism in the private sphere.[46] The future may lie in inspiring new family foundations that have been established in the last decade or so and reaching out to key individuals who have made fortunes and now seek to make a difference. The spread of freedom would seem a natural cause for the relatively youthful billionaires in the information technology community, given the Internet's claim to be a force for free expression and the wide dissemination of ideas.

We should not shy away from the considerable challenges and issues facing future U.S. democracy promotion efforts. But it would be a strategic mistake for the next administration to move away from its pursuit.

Instead, we should focus on how the next U.S. president can more systemically and effectively use the full range of tools and tactics at his or her disposal to help support the efforts of those who continue to take considerable personal risks to make their own governments more accountable and responsive to the needs of their own populations.

Chapter 6
A Tale of Two Traditions
International Cooperation and American Exceptionalism in U.S. Human Rights Policy

CATHERINE POWELL

> *It was the best of times, it was the worst of times, it was the age of wisdom, it was the age of foolishness, it was the epoch of belief, it was the epoch of incredulity, it was the season of Light, it was the season of Darkness, it was the spring of hope, it was the winter of despair, we had everything before us, we had nothing before us, we were all going direct to Heaven, we were all going direct the other way.*
>
> —*Charles Dickens,* A Tale of Two Cities *(1859)*

This is a tale of two traditions in U.S. human rights policy.[1] The first tradition is one of international cooperation and multilateralism. The second is one of American exceptionalism, unilateralism, and isolationism. Both traditions run deep in American history.

Part I of this chapter explores America's seemingly contradictory commitments to international cooperation and exceptionalism, and argues that these dual commitments need not necessarily pose an inherent conflict. The United States can be an exceptional nation and play an exceptional role in the world today by asserting its historic leadership in the human rights field through regional and international legal regimes and the institutions that support them.

Part II builds on this argument by examining both the negative and positive elements of American exceptionalism. Part III, drawing on international law and international relations literature, demonstrates why it makes normative and pragmatic sense for the United States to practice international cooperation and how this cooperation may transform both our own and other governments' conceptions of national interest. To illustrate my case, I focus on the treatment of detainees taken into custody in the course of the U.S. "War on Terror."[2] I conclude with recommendations for the future.

I. Dual Commitments to International Cooperation and Exceptionalism

This tale of two traditions begins with a story of U.S. leadership in international legal regimes and organizations both in the field of human rights and in other areas of international law. In this tradition the United States has been an active participant in creating international organizations and norms, even while agreeing to be constrained by them. While internationalism is sometimes (mis)understood as un-American, the United States was the primary driver behind the establishment of the United Nations system and the development of contemporary treaties as well as the institutional regimes that enforce these treaties in both public and private international law.[3] Moreover, for several decades the United Nations enjoyed the bipartisan support of Republicans and Democrats alike.[4]

The tale continues with a story of American exceptionalism. In this tradition the United States is an exceptional nation "with an exceptional role to play in the world."[5] Historically, this concept—which is frequently attributed to Alexis de Tocqueville—has referred to "the perception that the United States differs qualitatively from other nations, because of its unique origins, national credo, historical evolution, and distinctive political and religious institutions."[6] Indeed, America's commitment to exceptionalism is deeply rooted in the notions of popular sovereignty, democratic self-governance, and republican self-rule that were integral to the revolutionary act of independence at the founding of the nation.[7]

The notion that America is exceptional, however, has often been cynically deployed to justify nonparticipation in and withdrawal from international legal regimes and institutions. Admittedly, from its founding, the United States has had isolationist and unilateralist tendencies.[8] Since World War II, these tendencies have been particularly pronounced in the area of human rights, where resistance to international law has been opportunistically framed as a way of protecting "states rights" against the federal treaty power. For example, in negotiating the United Nations Charter, the delegation representing the United States included language "reaffirming faith" in fundamental human rights, but it balanced this with language that eventually became Article 2.7: "Nothing contained in the present charter shall authorize the United Nations to intervene in matters which are essentially within the domestic jurisdiction of any state."[9] As Harvard Professor John Ruggie notes, "because the support of southern Democrats was critical to the charter's ratification by the Senate, keeping Jim Crow laws beyond international scrutiny obliged the United States to push for this Article 2.7 language."[10] Moreover, in 1954, in a backlash to attempts to ratify human rights treaties (starting with the Genocide Convention), the Senate considered a constitutional amendment—the Bricker amendment—that, had it been adopted, would have amended the Constitution's treaty clause, which states that treaties are made by the president, with the advice and consent of two-thirds of the Senate.[11] The amendment, which was ultimately defeated, would have required implementing legislation by both houses of Congress for treaties to be effective as well as approval by the legislatures of all 50 states.

Europeans, in the aftermath of World War II, were more motivated than Americans to embrace international cooperation, since the war itself and particularly the Holocaust had demonstrated the potential abuses of nationalism and democracy.[12] To the extent American leadership in the post-World War II period of internationalism was motivated by "high-minded" ideals (as opposed to economic self-interest),[13] it was often based on a conception of international law that involved the *export* of American ideals.[14] Though the *import* of international law as a means to interpret the Constitution has also been an important part of the American experience going back to the founding of the nation,[15] the inconsistent commitment to international law and international cooperation has helped sow seeds of skepticism and resentment toward U.S. leadership in human rights policy.

As many observers have noted, "in the years since September 11, 2001, international law has come under unrelenting attack" by the United States.[16] Perhaps the most prominent example of this disregard for international law and multilateral institutions has been the U.S. decision to invade Iraq without explicit authorization by the UN Security Council.[17] Also startling have been the claims from the White House that it is not bound by the Convention against Torture or the Geneva Conventions[18] in conducting its "War on Terror."[19]

But even before September 11, the United States had taken other steps reflecting disdain for multilateralism.[20] Within a year and a half of entering office, President George W. Bush "unsigned" the treaty establishing the International Criminal Court,[21] unilaterally abrogated the 1972 Anti-Ballistic Missile Treaty, and withdrew from the Kyoto global climate accord. Moreover, during the Bush years, the United States has refused to participate in the new UN Human Rights Council; withdrawn from the compulsory jurisdiction of the International Court of Justice; walked out on the World Conference against Racism in Durban; rebuffed international efforts to address the devastating humanitarian impact of small arms proliferation; suspended negotiations on strengthening the 1972 Biological Weapons Convention; and resisted raising the age of recruitment of soldiers to 18 in accordance with the Optional Protocol to the Convention on the Rights of the Child on the Involvement of Children in Armed Conflicts.[22] Since as far back as 1979, the United States has also unilaterally withheld UN dues at times.[23] Over successive administrations, the United States has also failed to ratify widely accepted human rights treaties, such as the International Covenant on Economic, Social and Cultural Rights (ICESCR), the Convention on the Elimination of Discrimination Against Women (CEDAW), the Convention on the Rights of the Child (CRC), and the Landmines Convention.[24] As for those human rights treaties to which the United States is a state party, their ratifications have been encumbered by numerous reservations, understandings, and declarations.[25]

Reflecting these trends in U.S. human rights policy, a "new sovereigntist" movement is also on the ascendancy in the academy.[26] This movement has begun to shape policy debates inside the Beltway, as prominent academics from this camp have moved in and out of the executive branch.[27] Moreover, these new sovereigntists have questioned the legitimacy of using international law in domestic courts.[28]

II. The Negative and Positive Faces of American Exceptionalism

The notion that the United States is an exceptional nation with a distinctive leadership role to play globally is not inherently counterproductive nor is it exclusively a Republican or Democratic idea.[29] Madeleine Albright, for example, President Bill Clinton's secretary of state during his second term, famously called the United States the "indispensable nation." For his part, President Ronald Reagan in his farewell address described the United States as a "shining city on a hill." The United States, he said, is "still a beacon, still a magnet for all who must have freedom, for all the pilgrims from all the lost places who are hurtling through the darkness, toward home." Indeed, Reagan proclaimed:

We cannot escape our destiny, nor should we try to do so. The leadership of the free world was thrust upon us two centuries ago in that little hall of Philadelphia. In the days following World War II, when the economic strength and power of America was all that stood between the world and the return to the dark ages. . . . We are indeed, and we are today, the last best hope of man on earth.[30]

Echoing President Reagan, Democratic presidential hopeful, Senator Barack Obama of Illinois, stated in one of his early foreign policy speeches on the campaign trail that "I still believe that America is the last, best hope of Earth."[31]

Yet, as University of Toronto historian Margaret MacMillan has astutely observed,

> American exceptionalism has always had two sides: the one eager to set the world to rights, the other ready to turn its back with contempt if its message should be ignored. . . . Faith in their own exceptionalism has sometimes led to . . . a tendency to preach at other nations rather than listen to them, a tendency as well to assume that American motives are pure where those of others are not.[32]

A positive side of American exceptionalism generally entails drawing upon the American tradition to promote the rule of law and respect for universal human rights. When the United States uses its "soft power" to persuade through principle and example, it promotes the rule of law and human rights in ways that ultimately serve U.S. interests.[33]

As the calamitous situation in Iraq demonstrates, however, the current thinking in Washington relies on an alternative, negative kind of exceptionalism, namely, unilateralism and disengagement from international cooperation. While the United States relied on hard power without UN approval to topple the authoritarian regime in Iraq, it has failed to cultivate effective diplomatic initiatives that would bring lasting peace there. Despite initial success in the military campaign that ousted Saddam Hussein in Iraq, "the greater challenge has not been winning the war, but securing the peace."[34]

The ruinous conditions in Iraq today reflect an impoverished U.S. foreign policy that relies heavily on hard power, which increases conflict and is not accompanied by sustained diplomatic engagement or international cooperation aimed at reducing conflict. Securing lasting peace, democratic reform, and human rights in many parts of the world will require, as Yale Law School Dean Harold Hongju Koh argues, "diplomatic engagement designed to create broader legal frameworks: orderly, reasonable sets of expectations rooted in mutual consent." Indeed, the broader aim of American power "should be the creation of new, constraining and facilitating legal orders," whether to support the rule of law in a democratic Iraq or elsewhere. After all, Koh continues, "American exceptionalism succeeds best when it seeks not simply to coerce, but rather, to promote sustainable solutions."[35] The promotion and creation of such solutions will generally require international cooperation to foster and maintain mutual consent.

Consider President Franklin Delano Roosevelt's response to totalitarian aggression in World War II. It was not merely military in nature but outlined an affirmative multifaceted vision of a postwar world guided by four fundamental freedoms: freedom of speech, freedom of religion, freedom from want, and freedom from fear.[36] Roosevelt's plan for winning and sustaining the peace was wrapped, says John Ruggie, "in a broader vision that tapped into America's sense of self as a nation: a promise of an international order based on rules and institutions promoting human betterment through free-trade and American-led collective security, human rights and decolonization, as well as active international involvement by the private and voluntary sectors."[37] This view was reinforced by Roosevelt's successors, for whom countering the Soviet threat strengthened a bipartisan commitment to internationalism. This aspect of American exceptionalism—which emphasized spreading human rights and democracy in ways that echoed American values—"became," says Ruggie, "the basis for a global transformational agenda whose effects are still unfolding."[38]

Since World War II, Republican and Democratic administrations have both generally advanced U.S. human rights policy through this broader vision that embraces an international order based on rules and institutions of the sort outlined by Roosevelt and his successor, President Harry Truman. Roosevelt's Four Freedoms framework provided the blueprint for the modern human rights construct, which was initially embedded in the Universal Declaration of Human Rights (drafted with the assistance of Eleanor Roosevelt)[39] and the subsequent basic international human rights covenants that protect civil and political rights (for example, freedom of speech and religion), economic, social, and cultural rights (freedom from want, for example), and freedom from persecution and other gross violations (as reflected in the Refugee Convention, the Genocide Convention, and the Torture Convention).[40] In bringing his vision to fruition, Roosevelt made a point of appointing prominent Republicans to the delegation that represented the United States at the San Francisco conference establishing the United Nations.[41] Moreover, "during the Cold War, Presidents from Harry Truman to Ronald Reagan sought to minimize the international embarrassment resulting from the exemptionalist impulse, especially in relation to civil rights, often acting through executive agreements or other such means."[42]

But with the expansion of globalization and "the end of the external disciplining effects imposed by the Cold War," the negative side of American exceptionalism came to the forefront.[43] Yale's Harold Koh, drawing upon his experience as a former Assistant Secretary of State for Democracy, Human Rights, and Labor, distinguishes among four negative faces of American exceptionalism that can have harmful repercussions for America's reputation. From the least destructive to the most, he calls these faces "distinctive rights," "different labels," the "flying buttress mentality," and "double standards."[44]

By "distinctive rights," Koh refers to those rights that grow out of our particular social, political, and economic history, such as our conception of the right to free speech, which "is far more protective than other countries' laws of hate speech, libel, commercial speech, and publication of national security information." Noting that this distinctiveness is not "too deeply unsettling to world order," Koh points out that "human rights law allows for flexibility."[45]

With regard to the "different labels" face of exceptionalism, Koh notes that America's tendency to use different words "to describe synonymous concepts [similarly] turns out to be more of an annoyance than a philosophical attack on the rest of the world."[46] For example, instead of gathering national statistics on the incidents of "torture and cruel, inhuman or degrading treatment or punishment," which is the international nomenclature for human rights crimes involving brutality, the U.S. gathers statistics on such practices under the rubrics of, for example, "cruel and unusual punishment, "police brutality," or violations of civil rights under color of state law. This is akin, Koh says, to "our continuing use of feet and inches, rather than the metric system." But, "different labels don't necessarily mean different rules." Indeed, "except for some troubling post-September 11 backsliding, the United States generally accepts the prohibition against torture, even if it calls that prohibition by a different name."[47]

To describe the third face of American exceptionalism, Koh borrows from Louis Henkin's characterization of the United States as having a "flying buttress mentality." This refers to the fact that "in the cathedral of international human rights, the United States is so often seen as a flying buttress, rather than a pillar, willing to stand outside the structure supporting it, but unwilling to subject itself to the critical examination and rules of that structure." "By supporting and following the rules of the international realm most of the time, but always out of a sense of political prudence rather than legal obligation, the United States tries to have it both ways[:] enjoy[ing] the appearance of compliance[, while] maintain[ing] the illusion of unfettered sovereignty."[48] As an example, Koh cites Washington's notorious record of tardy ratification, nonratification, or "Swiss cheese ratification" of international treaties, which he calls a "perverse practice of human rights compliance without ratification" unlike many other countries, which "adopt a strategy of ratification without compliance."[49] However, U.S. failure to ratify such major human rights treaties as CEDAW, the CRC, and the ICESCR undermines the significance of these instruments abroad as well as the ability of the United States to persuade other countries to comply with them.[50]

The fourth face of American exceptionalism, "double standards," entails America's "propos[ing] that a different rule should apply to [the U.S.] than applies to the rest of the world."[51] "Recent well-known examples," Koh notes, include such diverse issues as the International Criminal Court, the Kyoto Protocol on Climate Change, executing juvenile offenders or persons with mental disabilities, declining to implement orders of the International Court of Justice with regard to the death penalty, or claiming a Second Amendment exclusion from a proposed global ban on the illicit transfer of small arms and light weapons. In the post-9/11 environment, further examples have proliferated: America's attitudes toward the global justice system, holding Taliban detainees on Guantánamo without Geneva Convention hearings, and asserting a right to use force in preemptive self-defense.[52]

This is the most troubling face of exceptionalism. The problem with double standards exceptionalism is that "when the United States promotes double standards, it invariably ends up not on the higher rung, but on the lower rung with horrid bedfellows[.]"[53] Moreover, defending a double standard weakens the moral authority of the United States, thereby reducing our ability to persuade through the invocation of principle. How, for example, can we justify criticizing other countries that fail to meet fair trial standards for detainees when we ourselves have short-circuited those standards?[54] Furthermore, the hypocrisy evident in the application of double standards breeds resentment against the United States, making it harder to gain international support for the "War on Terror" and creating fertile ground for the recruitment of future terrorists.[55] Finally, by undermining international law, the United States erodes the legitimacy and force of international law itself, and "by doing so, the United States disempowers itself from invoking those rules at precisely the moment when it needs those rules to serve its own national purposes."[56]

In short, while the most destructive face of American exceptionalism may appear to be a result of the United States pursuing its national interests, this exceptionalist behavior is in fact destructive of and defeating for U.S. interests, both domestic and international.

III. Reconceptualizing What Is in the National Interest

Since international organizations and legal regimes influence the way all governments perceive their interests (that is, their preferences), it makes sense for the United States to participate in these institutions and regimes in order to influence those preferences. From both normative and pragmatic perspectives, taking the lead in the development of international law and institutions so that others will follow our lead is the best course of action. Even though the United States is the unquestioned global hegemon, it must exercise its military, economic, and political power within a global normative framework that it helps construct and reinforce, even as it is constrained by this framework.[57] If the United

States chooses not to play by the rules of the game, it risks creating incentives for other states to flout the rules as well.

The true measure of U.S. global power is determined, according to Joseph Nye of Harvard's Kennedy School of Government, by its "ability to set the agenda in a way that shapes the preferences of others."[58] If the United States can use its soft power to persuade other countries to do what America wants, then it will not have to use its hard military power to force or coerce others to do what it wants. "If the United States represents values that others want to follow, it will cost us less to lead."[59]

With this in mind, I offer criticism of the thinking that pervades U.S. human rights policy in Washington today. In contrast to the Bush administration's approach, I seek to demonstrate why it makes normative and pragmatic sense for the United States to cooperate with the international system and how through such international cooperation the United States may, in turn, transform other governments' conceptions of self-interest (as well as ongoing conceptions of its own self-interest). To make the normative and pragmatic case for international cooperation, I offer three accounts of international law compliance theory to describe processes though which U.S. participation in international organizations and legal regimes can influence the behavior of other states (as well as its own): 1.) interest-based accounts; 2.) norm-based accounts; and 3.) acculturation-based accounts.[60] In each case, I will focus on the treatment of terrorism suspects detained in the U.S. "War on Terror" to illustrate why participation in international institutions and legal regimes is ultimately smart policy.

INTEREST-BASED ACCOUNTS[61]

Interest-based accounts of international cooperation find their roots in the tradition of realism that pervaded American political science scholarship in the aftermath of World War II.[62] Emphasizing the role of coercion, power, and self-interest in explaining why states comply with international law, adherents of this view argue that "states create and comply with international law only when there is some clear objective reward for doing so."[63] Viewing states as rational, unitary actors that pursue their self-interest, this approach holds that "politics is the phenomenon and law is the epiphenomenon,"[64] and that law "is nothing more than one of a variety of tools used by states to enhance their own power."[65]

Some interest-based scholarship characterizes international institutions as being "based on self-interested calculations of the great powers" and therefore posits that "institutions are basically a reflection of [this] distribution of power in the world . . . and they have no independent effect on state behavior."[66] More recent scholarship in this area, however, asserts that institutions can change state behavior and facilitate cooperation.[67] While sharing the view that state behavior is based on self-interest, these scholars emphasize the role of international institutions in altering a state's conception of its self-interest[68] by minimizing one of the principal obstacles to cooperation among states with mutual interests, namely, the phenomenon of cheating.[69] Cheating occurs as a result of the classic prisoner's dilemma in which the likely short-term strategy chosen by a state faced with the choice of either cheating or cooperating will be to cheat and hope that another state will pursue a cooperative strategy.[70] While this outcome maximizes gain for the cheating state, if both states pursue this logic and cheat, both sides may be worse off than had they cooperated. Thus, in assessing the longer-term consequences, based on a comparison of costs and benefits of competition, cooperation, or defection from cooperation, self-interested states will choose cooperation.[71] On this account, law and legal institutions influence the conduct of states based on those states' self-interested assessment of the costs and benefits of engaging in particular legal regimes. According to this perspective, international law and institutions may be able to "facilitate state cooperation and coordination by reducing transaction cost and overcoming other collective action problems."[72]

Some observers have noted that accounts based on coercion are not well placed to explain why states comply with international law in the area of human rights in light of the fact that the sovereignty costs involved in entering into such arrangements often outweigh the benefits to individual states.[73] Nonetheless, a coercion-based account can help explain why the United States has incentive to comply with international law regimes in the treatment of prisoners of war. During wartime at least, states have a reciprocal interest in treating each other's prisoners humanely. Lack of cooperation leads to insecurity in that each state is not able to guarantee humane treatment for its own soldiers who may be captured by the other side during a war. By contrast, cooperation secured under the Third Geneva Convention leads states to observe standards guaranteeing humane treatment of captured enemy soldiers.[74] In taking the position that the Third Geneva Convention's prisoner of war protections do not apply to the terrorist suspects detained at the U.S. naval base at Guantánamo Bay in Cuba, the Bush administration has argued that the benefit of reciprocity that exists with regard to states does not exist vis-à-vis a terrorist organization, such as Al Qaeda. But it is important here to apply broader notions of reciprocity. "Reciprocity calculations should take into account reactions that might play out over a longer period of time than during the present conflict and, especially, reactions that might come from actors other than the current enemy."[75]

A similar example involves cooperative arrangements under the Vienna Convention on Consular Relations (VCCR) requiring that governments notify a detained or arrested foreign national of his right to consult with an official from the consulate of the foreign national's home country.[76] Lack of cooperation between two states leaves both sides worse off in the sense that it is difficult to ensure access to one's own citizens detained or arrested overseas. While the United States has been found to be in violation of the VCCR in several cases before the International Court of Justice (ICJ) involving foreign nationals on death row,[77] the U.S. Supreme Court claims that the ICJ opinions concerning the rights of foreign nationals on death row are not binding but deserve mere "respectful consideration."[78] Nonetheless, in light of the reciprocity benefits, federal government officials have begun to acknowledge the value of cooperation and compliance with the VCCR regime by providing law enforcement officials with information regarding the notification requirement.[79]

As these examples demonstrate, international organizations and legal regimes can change a state's calculations about how to maximize gain by assisting states to realize that short-term sacrifices in terms of cooperation will lead to long-term gains.[80] International rules can alter this calculation by, for example, rewarding states that develop reputations for adherence to international rules; by creating greater interdependence between states, thereby raising the cost of cheating; by increasing the amount of available information to ensure effective monitoring of adherence and early warning of cheating; and by reducing the transaction costs of individual agreements, thereby making cooperation more profitable for self-interested states.[81]

As a descriptive matter, interest-based accounts usefully explain why self-interested states cooperate and how forms of cooperation change states' conceptions of self-interest. As a normative matter, these accounts are helpful because they shed light on how reconstituted conceptions of a state's self interest that favor collaboration can, in turn, shift normative expectations toward greater compliance with human rights. Because of its hegemony and ability to impact the global normative framework, U.S. participation in international institutions can assist in reshaping self-interest both for itself and the wider world.

NORM-BASED ACCOUNTS

Norm-based accounts of international cooperation emphasize norms and ideas and the role of persuasion in influencing state behavior.[82]

According to these accounts, "governments create and comply with [international law] not only because they expect a reward for doing so, but also because of their commitment (or the commitment of transnational actors that influence and persuade them) to the norms or ideas embodied in [international law]."[83] Normative accounts—which range from liberal internationalism to neoconservatism—span the ideological spectrum. Normative scholars acknowledge that self-interest plays a role in influencing state behavior, but assert that it is "motivated by the power of principled ideas—ideas that are not given by nature but are themselves constructed through interaction among individuals, groups, and states."[84] In other words, while interest-based approaches emphasize how economic or military interests are exploited to coerce compliance, norm-based approaches emphasize the ideas and communicative processes that define which state interests are perceived as relevant in the first place.[85] Furthermore, as a response to the traditional focus of interest-based scholars on state-to-state interactions, normative scholars have broadened the paradigm to include the role of nonstate actors and substate dynamics within the state.[86]

A particularly relevant variant of the normative model is Koh's "transnational legal process" theory, which posits that state behavior is influenced through a process of persuasion involving transnational "interaction, interpretation, internalization, and obedience."[87] As Koh explains, "Instead of focusing exclusively on the issues of 'horizontal jawboning' at the state-to-state level as traditional international legal process theories do, a transnational legal process approach focuses more broadly upon the mechanisms of 'vertical domestication,' whereby international law norms 'trickle down' and become incorporated into domestic legal systems."[88] This view emphasizes, Koh argues, the role of norm entrepreneurs, including nonstate actors, in facilitating this process of persuasion. A central part of the transnational legal process is the institutionalization and habitualization of norms once they are internalized in the domestic legal system "through executive action, judicial interpretation, legislative action, or some combination of the three."[89]

Such persuasion-based accounts of how international law influences state behavior help explain Washington's episodic compliance with the international prohibition on torture in its "War on Terror."[90] As foreign governments and international bodies denounce practices used by the United States in interrogating detainees, calling them, for example, "tantamount to torture,"[91] a variety of actors can use this traditional "horizontal" state-to-state interaction at the international level to debate, interpret, internalize, and facilitate U.S. government obedience to the international prohibition on torture through mechanisms of "vertical domestication" at the national level.[92]

In analyzing the debate in Congress over the McCain Amendment's ban on cruel, inhuman, or degrading punishment, for example, Koh describes Senator John McCain (R.-Ariz.) as a classic "government norm sponsor" and the McCain Amendment as a classic "example of vertical, transnational human rights enforcement."[93] Against the backdrop of "the vigorous objections and lobbying efforts of the Bush Administration," Koh writes, "a transnational network arose, consisting of private citizens and some twenty-eight retired generals, led by former Secretary of State Colin Powell, who came forward to speak in favor of the Amendment." In the face of a White House threat to veto the entire $440 billion military budget if the amendment was not withdrawn, the Republican-controlled Senate and House voted resoundingly in support of it. This caused the president to reverse himself by accepting a compromise that had been offered earlier.[94] In "persuading" the president to sign the legislation (albeit with a signing statement), "a transnational network against torture" used the process of persuasion to "provoke an interaction, which led to an interpretation of law, which [in turn] promoted the internalization of a norm against torture and cruel, inhuman, or degrading treatment into U.S. law."[95]

From Koh's analysis, we can see that while coercion-based and persuasion-based accounts are often placed in opposition to each other, these two accounts can in fact work synergistically to explain how the debate in Congress led President Bush to reverse his initial position on the McCain Amendment. As international relations theorists Thomas Risse and Kathryn Sikkink write, "persuasion is not devoid of conflict. It often involves not just reasoning with opponents, but also pressures, arm-twisting, and sanctions."[96] In describing persuasion as a socialization process, Risse and Sikkink point out that while persuasion entails the development of argumentative consensus through moral discourse,

This is not to argue that moral discourses and discursive practices in general resemble "ideal speech" situations in the Habermasian sense, where power and hierarchies are absent and nothing but the better argument counts. In real-life situations, relationships of power and interest-based arguments are rarely completely out of the picture.[97]

But "principal beliefs carry the day when they persuade actors in potentially winning coalitions to interpret their material and political interests and preferences in light of the idea and to accept its social obligations as appropriate."[98] Thus, coalitions of norm entrepreneurs involved in the debate over torture have argued that given how morally problematic the idea of torture is, it is not in the U.S. government's interest to use torture to assist in gaining intelligence (which, in any event, may be more reliably elicited through other means).[99]

Interestingly, the coalitions that have emerged to criticize the possible use of torture in fighting the U.S. "War on Terror" have been formed "not just through the convergence of pre-existing actors' interests, but also through argumentative consensus."[100] These coalitions have thus brought together a somewhat unlikely group—military and religious leaders, human rights groups and libertarians—all of whom believe in the power of an idea: that torture is wrong.

In terms of the nature of this debate, while democratic deliberation about human rights issues often involve the exchange of logical arguments on the merits, as we have seen in the torture debate, "actors," Risse and Sikkink note, "rely on a variety of techniques to persuade, including appeals to emotion, evoking symbols, as well as the use and extension of logical arguments."[101] While a "marketplace of ideas" paradigm tends to privilege the role of logic over emotion, "psychological research suggests that both emotion and cognition operate synergistically to produce and change attitudes." Indeed, "in the area of human rights, persuasion and socialization often involve processes such as shaming and denunciations, not aimed at . . . changing minds by logic, but on changing minds by isolating or even embarrassing the target."

ACCULTURATION-BASED ACCOUNTS

Acculturation-based accounts of international cooperation focus on how a state's identification with a reference or peer group of states "generate[s] varying decrees of cognitive and social pressures—real or imagined—to conform."[102] This underexamined approach provides an additional explanation of whether and how international legal regimes influence the ways state "preferences form and the conditions under which these preferences change." In effect, acculturation is a mechanism "whereby conformity is elicited through a range of socialization processes."[103] The goal of this socialization "is for actors to internalize norms, so that external pressure is no longer needed to ensure compliance."[104]

While the notion of socialization through acculturation has been discussed by sociologists and political scientists for years, legal scholars have only hinted at this as a process for explaining how international law affects state behavior. Professors Ryan Goodman and Derek Jinks provide the first comprehensive account of acculturation and other socialization processes as mechanisms of international law compliance.[105] The account offered by Goodman and Jinks focuses on the social pressures that influence a state's behavior in its interaction with other states and with nonstate actors through international organizations, for example.[106]

As is clear from the debate over U.S. detention of terrorism suspects at Guantánamo and in secret prisons overseas, U.S. participation in international institutions performs a socialization role through acculturation. The UN High Commissioner for Human Rights and various UN special rapporteurs were early critics of U.S. detention policies at Guantánamo and helped lead the international call for the detention camp to be shut down.[107] Former UN Secretary-General Kofi Annan also recommended closure of the detention camp.[108] Furthermore, the European Union has conducted an investigation into the operation of secret CIA interrogation centers in Europe, placing additional pressure on the United States.[109]

The concerns raised within these institutions and by the network of rapporteurs affiliated with them have been indispensable tools for acculturating states to comply with international norms since "acculturation is . . . propelled by social pressures [which] include (1) the imposition of social-psychological costs through shaming or shunning and (2) conferral of social-psychological benefits through 'back-patting' and other displays of public approval."[110] The imposition of these social pressures has likely played a role in the fact that the Bush administration is considering proposals for closing the detention camp at Guantánamo.[111] Moreover, in the face of growing international pressure and faced with a Supreme Court ruling applying the Geneva Conventions to the detainees, President Bush announced that he was transferring a group of prisoners previously held in secret prisons to Guantánamo Bay in the fall of 2006.[112]

While acculturation is often characterized by precisely this type of "public conformity without private acceptance,"[113] public conformity to the norm is often the first step toward deeper compliance for two reasons. As Goodman and Jinks point out:

First, "shallow" structural reform—such as the ratification of a human rights treaty—often constitutes an important shift in the domestic political opportunity structure of the reforming state. These shifts often disproportionately empower groups and individuals committed to the cause of human rights—perhaps by imbuing human rights [NGOs] with social legitimacy or by emboldening private citizens to seek formal redress for human rights violations.

Second, acculturation triggers what Professor Jon Elster calls the "civilizing force of hypocrisy." . . . [V]arious constituencies will provide incentives for public actors to live up to their "hypocritical" endorsement of a norm. Cognitively, acculturation narrows the gap between public acts and private preferences: under certain conditions people change their beliefs to avoid the unpleasant state of cognitive dissonance between what they profess in public and what they believe in private.[114]

In the case of *torture*, we have certainly seen on the first point how ratification of the Torture and Geneva Conventions and implementation of these treaties through legislation have emboldened groups and individuals committed to human rights. While no prosecutions have been brought under the War Crimes Act (the implementing legislation for the Geneva Conventions), the threat of prosecution (perhaps under a future president) and the labeling of those who support torture as "war criminals" may provide a deterrent.[115]

On the second point, perhaps the "civilizing force of hypocrisy" might help explain why the executive branch has backed away, at least publicly, from some of the more extreme claims and practices regarding treatment of detainees. For example, following both international and domestic criticism, the Justice Department rescinded one of its notorious "torture memos" justifying brutality against detainees.[116] Moreover, former Secretary of Defense Donald Rumsfeld was forced to rescind his approval of some of the more extreme forms of coercive interrogation techniques. Further, President Bush was forced to transfer detainees from the CIA's network of secret prisons, where alleged abuse tantamount to torture had occurred, to Guantánamo Bay. Such public conformity can, in fact, have a domino effect. As Goodman and Jinks point out:

Public conformity signals to other recalcitrant actors that social opposition to the norm in question is declining (or, put differently, that social support for the norm is rising). In other words, public conformity, even without private acceptance, exerts collateral influence on other actors in the social system.[117]

Leading by Example

Future policymakers would be wise to consider that the United States would be more credible and therefore more effective in advancing respect for human rights law, rule of law, and democracy overseas if it led by example through its participation in international institutions and regimes. The credibility of U.S. human rights policy suffers as long as the United States applies a double standard, insisting that other states comply with international human rights regimes, but refusing to participate in these regimes itself. Moreover, U.S. efforts to advance human rights overseas would be more persuasive and therefore more effective if these efforts were informed by U.S. participation in international institutions and regimes.

A new administration should try to salvage the reputation of the United States by taking a number of steps to (re)engage with international institutions.

- A new president should seek ratification of CEDAW, the CRC, and the ICESCR.

- A new administration should assess the performance to date of the International Criminal Court and evaluate whether the time has come for the United States to become a state party to this important institution.
- An incoming administration should review all reservations, understandings, and declarations that have been previously submitted upon ratification of human rights treaties to which it is already a party. Some of these, such as the reservation on the ban on juvenile executions, are obsolete.[118]
- The next administration should develop a less hostile stance toward the United Nations, and should try to be elected to the new UN Human Rights Council, despite its disappointing start, so that the United States can work from within the Council to try to reform it to be more effective in Darfur and elsewhere.
- The president, with such an ambitious agenda, should re-establish the interagency working group on human rights, set up previously to coordinate U.S. compliance with human rights.
- The new administration and new Congress should consider the establishment of a nonpartisan national human rights commission, which could monitor U.S. domestic compliance with human rights in a more thorough-going and independent way than either the Justice or State Departments.

Taking the lead in the development of international law and institutions so that others will follow our lead is the best course of action from both normative and pragmatic perspectives. Despite its current status as the world hegemon, the United States must exercise its military, economic, and political power within a global normative framework. Even while the United States helps to construct and reinforce this framework, it is constrained by it. If the United States chooses not to play by the rules of the game, other states will flout the rules as well. By contrast, the United States should lead by example and make international cooperation a cornerstone of policy.

Chapter 7

Putting Economic, Social, and Cultural Rights Back on the Agenda of the United States

PHILIP ALSTON

The internationally recognized catalogue of human rights consists of two broad categories. First and, in the view of most, foremost, are the more traditional civil and political rights. Because their ancestry is most readily traceable to two eighteenth-century landmarks—the United States Bill of Rights and the French Declaration of the Rights of Man and the Citizen—their importance is almost never challenged in the United States. Second and, according to the United Nations, of equal importance, are the economic, social, and cultural rights that the sociologist T. H. Marshall famously referred to as the major contribution of the twentieth century to the evolution of human rights.[1] Because most of these have no counterpart in the U.S. Bill of Rights, they are inevitably considered more exotic within the United States.

Despite the UN's insistence that all human rights are "indivisible and interdependent and interrelated,"[2] the reality is that civil and political rights (CPR) have dominated the international agenda while economic, social, and cultural rights (ESCR) have been accorded second-class status. This is not to say that ESCR have not been the subjects of long and noisy rhetorical campaigns championed in particular by developing countries, or that the UN and other actors have not mounted a significant number of initiatives designed to promote and enhance the status of these rights. The bottom line remains, however, that ESCR continue to enjoy an inferior status and that endeavors to enhance that status have often been blocked.

While the background to this analysis is the largely negative role played by the United States in the post-World War II era in relation to economic and social rights,[3] its principal focus is forward-looking. The inauguration of a new president in January 2009 will provide an important opportunity to revisit existing policies and fashion new approaches that are more consonant both with the U.S. national interest and with the fundamental principles of human rights.

It is a fact, albeit an uncomfortable one for many non-American observers and proponents of international human rights law, that the United States has been the single most important force in shaping the international human rights regime. This is by no means the same as arguing that it has been the most positive or constructive force; only that its influence has made a very big difference for better or worse in relation to many of the more important initiatives.

This impact is important to note in the present context because the United States has played a central role in discouraging and sometimes blocking the development of the concept of ESCR. This opposition has not, however, followed a single unchanging course. As a result, one of the principal challenges in terms of exploring future policy options for the United States in this domain is to identify the precise nature of recent or current U.S. policy. This quest is not assisted by the fact that this policy has been subjected to little sustained attention from human rights groups, scholars, or policymakers.

Economic, Social, and Cultural Rights Before Bush

President Franklin Delano Roosevelt is often credited with having first launched the specific proposals that led to the inclusion of ESCR in the Universal Declaration of Human Rights.[4] In developing the notion of freedom from want into a proposed "second Bill of Rights" for the United States, Roosevelt urged the recognition of "the right of every family to a decent home; the right to adequate medical care and the opportunity to achieve and enjoy good health; the right to adequate protection from the economic fears of old age, sickness, accident, and unemployment; [and] the right to a good education."[5]

President Harry Truman supported including ESCR in the Universal Declaration and it was under his auspices that Eleanor Roosevelt participated in the early and crucial phases of the drafting of the International Covenant on Economic, Social and Cultural Rights (ICESCR). President Dwight Eisenhower, under the impetus of the debates surrounding the Bricker amendment, repudiated both that draft covenant and the draft of the International Covenant on Civil and Political Rights (ICCPR) but neither he nor other opponents of the UN's human rights aspirations expressed special animus toward the covenant that dealt with ESCR.[6]

The administration of President Lyndon Johnson not only participated in the resumed drafting of the ICESCR but also voted in favor of its adoption in 1966 by the UN General Assembly. And the same administration supported the inclusion of economic and social rights provisions in the International Convention on the Elimination of All Forms of Racial Discrimination.

In 1975, President Gerald Ford signed the Helsinki Accords, which proclaimed that the participating states would "promote and encourage the effective exercise of civil, political, economic, social, cultural and other rights and freedoms all of which derive from the inherent dignity of the human person and are essential for his free and full development."[7] By agreeing to a follow-up declaration, adopted in Vienna in January 1989 by the Conference on Security and Cooperation in Europe, the United States joined other countries in recognizing that the promotion of ESCR "is of paramount importance for human dignity and for the attainment of the legitimate aspirations of every individual."[8] Accordingly the United States said it would guarantee the "effective exercise" of economic, social, and cultural rights and consider acceding to the ICESCR.[9]

The administration of President Jimmy Carter embraced ESCR as a central part of its human rights policy; Carter signed the ICESCR in 1978 and transmitted it to the Senate for its advice and consent. Although hearings were held which included coverage of the ICESCR, the Senate took no action in relation to it.

One of the first acts of President Ronald Reagan's administration in the human rights field was to signal a clear and straightforward policy of opposition to economic and social rights.[10] The earliest and best known statement of policy was included in the introduction written in 1982 by the new assistant secretary of state for human rights and humanitarian affairs, Elliott Abrams, and published in the State Department's annual review of human rights practices around the world.[11] This report explicitly removed the treatment of economic and social rights, which had previously been included in the reports. Abrams subsequently offered several justifications for the policy change. The most significant was that the inclusion of these rights blurred "the vital core of human rights." The distinction he drew was between economic and social rights, which he portrayed as "goods [which] the government ought to encourage over the long term,"[12] and civil and political rights, which are "rights [that] the government has an absolute duty to respect at any time."[13] The second reason given was that economic and social rights are easily exploited for propaganda purposes by unscrupulous governments whose real aim is to avoid respect for civil and political rights. Because such abuses have occurred, the more prudent path was seen to be to deny the very existence of economic and social rights.

The administration of George H. W. Bush was considerably less ideologically engaged, at least overtly, in its opposition to these rights but, when it advanced (and achieved) the ratification of the Covenant on Civil and Political Rights in 1992, no thought was given to advocating concurrent action on the "other" covenant.

The administration of President Bill Clinton initially proclaimed an inclusive approach that included a commitment to support ESCR in international fora and to promote U.S. ratification of the covenant. As a result, one of its first major international acts was to participate in the consensus emerging from the 1993 Vienna World Conference on Human Rights, which proclaimed that "all human rights are universal, indivisible and interdependent and interrelated. The international community must treat human rights globally in a fair and equal manner, on the same footing, and with the same emphasis."[14] Fairly soon thereafter, however, the Clinton administration began to distance itself from its original embrace of ESCR and adopted a number of policies effectively designed to marginalize them.[15]

It reluctantly signed on to the Convention on the Rights of the Child (CRC) but the fact that this treaty contained a number of provisions giving effect to ESCR was often cited as a reason for not proceeding with ratification. This was rather ironic since most of the relevant formulations had in fact been significantly watered down at the insistence of the Reagan administration during the process of drafting the CRC in the 1980s. At the end of the day, the Clinton policy was an uneasy combination of affirming its general support, at least in principle, for ESCR[16] while creating considerable difficulties in relation to most efforts undertaken in UN forums to make progress in relation to specific rights. It also made no attempt to promote ratification of the ICESCR, insisting only that its priority was to achieve ratification of the Convention on the Elimination of All Forms of Discrimination against Women.

The Bush Administration and Economic and Social Rights

The administration of President George W. Bush has not diverged fundamentally from the policies towards ESCR that its predecessors had developed since 1982. "Goods" such as food, housing, education, and water are acknowledged to be desirable components of an adequate standard of living but they do not constitute "human rights" in the full sense of the term. Thus there can be no claim to their realization *as a matter of right* on the part of those who are being denied those "goods" even if the denial threatens the individuals' survival. Despite this, the United States regularly invokes the Universal Declaration (with its clear recognition of ESCR) in relation to other states.[17]

Because the administration has not adopted any comprehensive policy statements relating to economic and social rights, its views must be discerned from the various speeches and interventions made by U.S. officials in the context of debates and votes within the relevant international forums. The most important of these has been the UN Commission on Human Rights up until 2006, and subsequently the Human Rights Council. Close inspection reveals that the Bush administration has varied its attitude toward economic and social rights significantly in the course of its first seven years.

At least four separate concerns relating to economic, social, and cultural rights motivate the United States position, although they are usually expressed together as though they were part of a seamless whole. They are 1) a belief in the chronological priority of civil and political rights; 2) an objection to the terminological equivalence of the different sets of rights; 3) a concern over what might be termed the "internationalization of responsibility" for failures to meet economic and social rights; and 4) a concern about the justiciability of economic and social rights. Each of these warrants more detailed consideration.

CHRONOLOGICAL PRIORITY

In a general statement of human rights policy issued in 2004, Richard Williamson, U.S, ambassador to the UN Commission on Human Rights, noted that "the keys to prosperity are . . . created by economic and political freedom." This emphasis on economic freedom rather than economic rights is justified on the grounds that "nations that share a commitment to protecting human rights and fundamental freedoms and to guaranteeing political and economic freedom will be able to unleash the potential of their people and assure their future prosperity." Williamson went on to assert that "there is no doubt that societies that respect civil and political rights, practice democracy, and respect the rule of law can do a better job of allowing individuals to fully realize the needs of their citizens [sic], including education, health care, and the eradication of hunger and poverty."[18]

Later in the same session of the commission, a different speaker used very similar language, suggesting that this was a clear "message" that the United States was keen to present as the essence of its policy.[19] Marc Leland, the U.S. delegate to the commission, noted that "There is no doubt that societies that respect civil and political rights, practice democracy, and respect the rule of law can do a better job of allowing individuals to fully realize their economic, social, and cultural rights."

There is, however, a revealing difference between the statements by Williamson and Leland. Williamson spoke in terms only of meeting citizens' "needs" while the statement by Leland treated those needs as being the equivalent of economic and social "rights."

The most noteworthy common element of the two statements involves the use of the phrase "societies [that respect civil and political rights] . . . *can* do a better job" rather than the assertion that they "*do*." "Can" would appear to concede that a strong performance in civil and political rights does not automatically result in the satisfaction of the other set of rights. This is significant because the assertion of an automatic linkage or flow-on effect for economic rights once civil and political rights are respected would justify a focus only on one set of rights. But if it is conceded that a positive flow-on effect is neither inevitable nor sufficient, then it remains necessary to address economic and social rights specifically and not only as mere corollaries of efforts to ensure the operation of a democratic political system.

Rejection of Terminological Equivalence

One of the most important elements in the United States position is that, while the United Nations refers to all rights as human rights and does not contest abstract assertions of their indivisibility, the United States insists that the two sets of rights are fundamentally different from one another. Thus, for example, in a statement on the right to food, the United States emphasized that it must be seen as "a goal or aspiration to be realized progressively" and that it translates into "the opportunity to secure food; it is not a guaranteed entitlement."[20] Or as the U.S. representative to the 2003 meeting of the UN Commission on Human Rights expressed the difference, economic and social rights "are aspirational; [civil and political rights] inalienable and immediately enforceable."[21] As Marc Leland noted:

One of the elements which distinguishes the two sets of rights concerns the nature of the obligation, especially in terms of resources. Thus, [i]t is not an excuse to say that economic difficulties prevent a country from respecting civil and political rights. On the other hand, economic, social and cultural rights are to be progressively realized. While they require government action, they are not an immediate entitlement to a citizen.[22]

Ironically, it is the first part of this position that is the least sustainable. Economic realities affect the realization of civil and political rights dramatically. A lack of resources does not make it necessary or excusable to torture but it does make it much more difficult to fund some of the measures taken to train police in other law enforcement techniques, to deter the use of torture, to monitor behavior, and to punish effectively. On the other hand the proposition that economic and social rights do not necessarily give rise to immediate entitlements is certainly correct in many, but not all, contexts. That leaves open, however, the question of what the nature of the resulting entitlement is. The United States sought to clarify that issue in 2004 when it proposed a generic preambular paragraph to be included in all commission resolutions dealing with ESCR.

The proposal was prompted by a concern that "language frequently used in these resolutions . . . raises important sovereignty and legal concerns about the legal entitlements of such rights." The draft paragraph read as follows:

Bearing in mind that sovereign States must determine from time to time through open, participatory debate and democratic processes the combination of policies and programs they consider will be most effective in progressively realizing the achievement of economic, social and cultural rights and objectives; that each State must determine in accord with its own system the role of various institutions in its society in carrying out such policies and programs; and that each State must define in a manner consistent with its own legal system the administrative and legal recourse available to those seeking review of the implementation of those policies and programs.[23]

This proposal is quite revealing. It is premised first of all upon an assertion of the sovereign power of governments to determine their own policies. In the abstract this appears true but in fact if governments opt for approaches that are inconsistent with human rights obligations, they are considered to be in violation of those obligations, considerations of sovereignty notwithstanding. Caveats regarding sovereignty have never been put forward in the commission context in relation to civil and political rights because the reality is that a commitment to international human rights standards is in fact seen as providing some form of constraint upon the prerogatives of governments.

Aside from this dimension, the statement contains three propositions: 1) economic and social rights policies are matters to be decided by the democratic process; 2) institutional arrangements in relation to economic and social rights are matters for the state to decide for itself; and 3) the provision of legal and other forms of recourse are also matters for each state's own determination.

Each of these propositions is defensible, at least in formalistic terms. The problem again is to determine what constraints exist on a state's freedom of action as a consequence of the recognition of a specific set of human rights. Is a state free, for example, to decide that laissez-faire policies are the best option for promoting economic and social rights, that majority decisions in the Congress or parliament are the only appropriate institutional arrangements, and that the courts shall have no role whatsoever? If it is, then how does the designation of something as a right (a right to education, say) make any difference by comparison with the status of any other policy preference? How are we to interpret the right to a remedy in cases where human rights have been violated? Where is the element of accountability that is the foundation stone of twenty-first-century human rights law? Finally, would any of these propositions be acceptable if proposed in relation to civil and political rights?

It seems that the U.S. position of insisting that economic and social rights are merely "aspirational" is to be taken literally. These rights are not to be considered rights in any moral, legal, or administrative sense since they do not give rise to any specific obligations in those spheres. Rather, they are matters to which individuals might aspire, if they so wish. And the role of a government is to ensure that no one stands in the way—in the sense of positively obstructing—the opportunity to seek those rights,

But this interpretation is not only incompatible with the formal approach long agreed to within the UN; it also distorts the concept of a human right beyond recognition and plays into the hands of those who argue that economic and social rights are not in fact human rights at all because they have no clear content and because no tangible obligation attaches to them. It amounts to a rejection or repudiation of the approach reflected in the UDHR and the ICESCR, both of which give clear content to rights, as well as to the positions advanced by the UN Committee on ESCR, which have not only been consistently endorsed by the Commission on Human Rights but also have been extensively cited and applied by constitutional courts in a wide range of countries.

The Bush administration restated its position in September 2004 when it agreed to endorse the "Voluntary Guidelines to Support Member States' Efforts to Achieve the Progressive Realization of the Right to Adequate Food in the Context of National Food Security" that had been adopted by the Food and Agriculture Organization. In doing so, it appended a formal statement to the guidelines, noting that the United States did not thereby

recognize any change in the current state of conventional or customary international law regarding rights related to food. The United States believes that the attainment of any "right to adequate food" or "fundamental freedom to be free from hunger" is a goal or aspiration to be realized progressively that does not give rise to any international obligations nor diminish the responsibilities of national governments toward their citizens.[24]

THE "INTERNATIONALIZATION OF RESPONSIBILITY"

Another recurring theme in the Bush administration's attitude to economic and social rights is that they "will not be achieved through shifting blame from a country's government to the international community."[25] In other words such rights do "not give rise to international obligations . . . , nor [do they] diminish the responsibilities of national governments toward their citizens."[26] The concern is that an obligation to international cooperation could be interpreted as requiring wealthy countries to support poor countries that are unable from their own resources to satisfy the economic and social rights of their own citizens.

Three sources of an international obligation to cooperate are usually cited. They are the general undertaking given in the UN Charter; Article 28 of the Universal Declaration of Human Rights, which provides that "everyone is entitled to a social and international order in which the rights and freedoms set forth in this Declaration can be fully realized"; and the reference in Article 2(1) of the ICESCR to states parties' obligations "to take steps, individually and through international assistance and co-operation." Concern that the obligation to cooperate would be extremely costly for a wealthy country such as the United States has been around at least since the U.S. Senate Committee on Foreign Relations held hearings into the ICESCR in 1979. Conservative advocate Phyllis Schlafly asserted at those hearing that, if ratified, the covenant "would obligate us to take steps by all measures, including legislation, to distribute food all over the world and to finance a rising standard of living" for other nations.[27]

Despite these concerns, it must be emphasized that no UN body has yet accepted the proposition that any given country is obligated to provide any specific assistance to any other country. The nature of any obligation posited as emerging from these provisions is, at best, a generic one that attaches to the international community.

The Justiciability of Economic and Social Rights

To say that a right is justiciable is to posit that it raises issues that can be, and appropriately are, dealt with by the courts. The claim that ESCR are justiciable does not imply that every issue arising in relation to the implementation of these rights is best determined by a court nor even that individuals should be able to bring a legal claim in respect of every single dimension of a particular right. Nonetheless, as the Committee on Economic, Social and Cultural Rights has observed, "While the general approach of each legal system needs to be taken into account, there is no Covenant right which could not, in the great majority of systems, be considered to possess at least some significant justiciable dimensions."[28]

In 2003 the United States decided to throw down a strong challenge to this notion. "By agreeing to [justiciability]," the U.S. delegate to the UN Commission on Human Rights said,

You—as governments—agree to provide housing for the millions who claim their present housing is not "adequate." You agree to provide food for each and every one of your citizens. And, even where not possible, you agree to provide the best available medical care for each and every citizen. If you fail to provide these "rights," you agree to provide monetary compensation. A claim that these "rights" are justiciable is a false promise because it cannot be fulfilled.[29]

The following year the U.S. representative returned to the same issue by insisting that the progressive realization of ESCR "will not be achieved through . . . efforts to make these rights the basis for an individual legal cause of action against a government by persons who differ with that government's policy approaches or priorities."[30]

Both of these statements betray a failure to understand the concept of justiciability or the ways in which it has been applied by a variety of constitutional courts, including those following a common law system similar to that of the United States. The latter comment is off-target because, where a government chooses not to make a right justiciable, any court challenge taken by those who oppose the government's policy will need to be launched under another concern, such as equal protection, due process, or anti-discrimination. Where the government has opted to make the right in question justiciable, the claim will generally not be brought by those opposed to the government's policies in general but by those who feel that they personally have been wrongly excluded from the reach of a particular program.

The former statement also entirely misrepresents the consequences of justiciability. If we take the example of the application of the justiciability clauses of the South African constitution by the Constitutional Court, there is no sustainable claim that can be made by the millions of citizens who consider their housing inadequate. The claims that have been entertained are those that demonstrate that government policies have irrationally failed to address an issue of urgency and magnitude; the absence of resources can be an entirely adequate justification for the inability to resolve a particular problem.

The same applies in relation to the right to food. The Indian Supreme Court has had the issue under consideration for several years in the context of public interest litigation brought in 2001 by the People's Union for Civil Liberties (Rajasthan). In this case the court has devised a range of affordable measures that governments have subsequently implemented.[31] Nevertheless, a number of right-to-food proponents are not necessarily in favor of full justiciability for the right. As Jean Drèze has noted, many of the issues that arise in relation to the right to food ultimately belong "to the domain of democratic politics rather than of legal enforcement." Moreover, in his view "even if the right to food is deemed fully justiciable, it will remain necessary to spell out the constructive interventions through which this right is to be protected."[32]

The limited nature of claims to the justiciability of ESCR has been underscored in a general comment on the subject by the UN Committee on Economic, Social and Cultural Rights:

It is sometimes suggested that matters involving the allocation of resources should be left to the political authorities rather than the courts. While the respective competences of the different branches of government must be respected, it is appropriate to acknowledge that courts are generally already involved in a considerable range of matters which have important resource implications. The adoption of a rigid classification of economic, social and cultural rights which puts them, by definition, beyond the reach of the courts would thus be arbitrary and incompatible with the principle that the two sets of human rights are indivisible and interdependent. It would also drastically curtail the capacity of the courts to protect the rights of the most vulnerable and disadvantaged groups in society.[33]

The United States has also invoked the justiciability argument as one of the main grounds for its opposition to the drafting of an optional protocol to the ICESCR by which states that have ratified the covenant (of which the United States is not one) would have the option of also ratifying a protocol that would provide for a complaints procedure. Under such procedures, which are now common in the human rights field, individual citizens or groups within the country concerned could allege violations of the rights recognized in the covenant. Perhaps the most puzzling element in seeking to understand U.S. opposition to this initiative is that comparable optional procedures that permit matters relating to ESCR to be contested already exist in relation to both the International Convention on the Elimination of All Forms of Racial Discrimination and the International Convention on the Elimination of All Forms of Discrimination against Women.

The U.S. government's official position with regard to the protocol conflated several different elements, including the question of justiciability—which by definition applies to judicial application of these rights (whereas the committee does not exercise judicial functions), the technical expertise available to the committee, and the type of powers to be given to, and functions to be performed by the committee.[34] Nevertheless, the basic thrust of the argument is that ESCR are simply not susceptible, in any respect, of effective treatment by the courts.[35]

Curiously, this argument flies in the face of very extensive practice in the United States in relation to a range of matters that would fall within the purview of an optional protocol. They include issues surrounding the right to education, going well beyond questions of discriminatory practices and rights to exemption for religious or other reasons (including home-schooling). Indeed, they embrace the most wide-ranging dimension of economic and social rights review, which is the question of whether the state has provided sufficient resources to ensure that each child covered by a given school system is able to receive an adequate education.[36]

One of the most enduring laments of those who oppose economic and social rights is that the introduction of rights beyond those contained in, for example, the U.S. Bill of Rights, dilutes or devalues the catalogue of "real" rights and constitutes a distraction from the main challenge that is defined solely in terms of civil and political rights. This position was expressed in surprisingly blunt terms by the U.S. ambassador in his address in 2003 to the UN Commission on Human Rights:

The future effectiveness of the Commission . . . requires prioritization: in other words, a return to the time-honored basics such as freedom of speech, thought, assembly, worship, and the press; the equal protection of the law; and of governments limited in power, subject to the will of the people expressed through competitive, regularly-held elections.[37]

One implication seemed to be that the commission should not devote any of its time and resources to other issues, perhaps including the rights of women, children, minorities, indigenous peoples, and other groups. But the main targets were economic and social rights, as was made clear when the ambassador went on to express concern about the "recent proliferation of special rapporteurs who dissipate the Commission's limited resources, and whose mandates stray from the Commission's core mission."[38]

In the end, no single clear and comprehensive policy statement outlines the Bush administration's approach to economic and social rights. On the basis of the various elements reviewed above we can, however, discern the key elements of the policy. First, the United States has moved from some early statements denying that ESR are rights to a stance that acknowledges them as rights but proceeds to distinguish them in fundamental ways from civil and political rights. Second, the United States has been consistently negative in debates on economic and social rights and has used characterizations of the quality and status of those rights that no other countries feel constrained to make and that rarely garner support from any others. Third, this underlying negativism has resulted in long and intense struggles within the UN over any initiative designed to improve the status of economic and social rights, illustrated by efforts to promote the right to health and to establish an optional protocol to the ICESCR.

None of these considerations have, however, prevented the United States from manifesting formal support for economic and social rights.

This indicates that the administration is confident that it has succeeded in defining economic and social rights in such a way that they are now considered harmless and toothless, at least for all practical purposes. Under such circumstances there is no reason not to seek the high ground and engage in rhetorical support. This policy reached its high point in President Bush's address to the UN General Assembly in September 2007. He chose to devote almost his entire speech to human rights, based on the fact that the drafting of the Universal Declaration on Human Rights had begun 60 years earlier (an anniversary that no other government saw fit to comment upon). His speech was built around what he termed the four great "missions of the United Nations": "liberating people from tyranny and violence"; "liberating people from hunger and disease"; "liberating people from the chains of illiteracy and ignorance"; and "liberating people from poverty and despair."[39]

The Domestic Side of the Debate

Before considering how the Bush administration's policy towards ESR could be changed by a new administration, it is essential to acknowledge one key dimension of that policy which is all too rarely addressed. It concerns the domestic policy constraints on support for economic and social rights in international forums. Many of the issues human rights proponents would characterize as economic and social rights are debated domestically by politicians and commentators within the United States not as human rights issues but in terms of the appropriate role played by the state in social policy matters. In stark terms Democrats tend to support an active role in various domains while Republicans advocate only minimalist state involvement in matters of private welfare.

In the lead-up to the 2008 presidential elections, the contrast has been most clearly played out in relation to health care. Most Democratic Party contenders have advocated plans to achieve comprehensive health insurance coverage. President Bush on the other hand issued only the fourth veto of his presidency in October 2007 when he rejected the State Children's Health Insurance Program (SCHIP) on the grounds that it was a move toward a socialist-style health care system, involved excessive state intervention, undermined private insurance schemes, and cost too much.[40]

It might reasonably be expected that this intense and important clash of ideological perspectives would be enough to prevent any possibility that the United States might adopt a more open and progressive stance on economic and social rights at the international level. The irony, however, is that the United States has succeeded in defining economic and social rights in such minimalist terms that the domestic policy stance of the Bush administration has not prevented it from proclaiming that its domestic policies are in fact fully in line with the requirements that would flow from the recognition of economic and social rights. Thus, for example, the U.S. representative told the UN Commission on Human Rights in 2003:

Let there be no misconception about the position of the United States on this issue. As a nation, we are committed to providing the conditions for individuals to achieve economic, social and cultural well-being, both at home and abroad. Our citizens enjoy access to free public education. Those Americans unable to find employment have access to state and federal welfare programs. Health care is provided through state and federal programs for individuals with no means to pay for it themselves. And, in the United States, an active charity community, both religious and secular, provides myriad social services covering a broad range of needs for neglected communities.[41]

The resulting situation is somewhat paradoxical. A Republican administration is prepared to assert that U.S. domestic policies are consistent with respect for economic and social rights and President Bush takes the extraordinary step of describing the principal missions of the UN in economic and social rights terms. Yet Democrats are promoting concrete policy initiatives that are economic and social rights-based but are keen not to characterize those initiatives in terms of human rights for fear of provoking additional resistance.

The purpose of this analysis is not to seek to resolve the inevitable inconsistencies and contradictions that permeate domestic policy in this area. In terms of human rights, the legal and policy question that arises is how far should domestic policy considerations restrain international policy options. In other words, if the Bush administration's policies are seen to be inconsistent with what would be required by accepted international understandings of economic and social rights or if a new administration's policies are determinedly cast in terms which eschew the label of economic and social rights, can the United States in good faith nonetheless support these rights internationally?

It is clear that for a variety of reasons it will be a long time, if ever, before the United States adopts a set of social policies explicitly premised upon recognition of individual economic and social rights for the purposes of the domestic legal system. But the crucial point here is that all too few nations have taken steps such as according constitutional recognition to specific economic and social rights, putting comprehensive legislative frameworks in place, or making many of the rights fully justiciable. That has not prevented them from supporting and facilitating the work of the UN in the field of these rights and it has not prevented some 155 states from ratifying the ICESCR.

This is not to suggest that the United States can or should fraudulently embrace the notion of economic and social rights internationally while pursuing inconsistent policies domestically. But there is considerable space for a state to determine for itself the ways in which it will seek to give effect to economic and social rights. While ratification of the ICESCR is a step that should not lightly be undertaken and certainly not until there is a basic preparedness to address systematically and openly all of the obligations addressed in the covenant, it is important not to confuse the issue of ratification with that of international support for initiatives designed to promote respect for economic and social rights.

The Costs and Consequences of U.S. Opposition to Economic and Social Rights

For the past 25 years, a succession of U.S. administrations has tended to assume that there were no costs attached to their rejection of, or reticence about, economic and social rights.

Because of its aversion to codifying these rights, the United States has insisted in recent years that the human rights dimensions of efforts to tackle poverty or to improve the plight of women should consist essentially of a focus on establishing democracy and ensuring the rights of the relevant groups to participate fairly in the domestic political process. The problematic nature of this approach is well illustrated in remarks made by the under secretary of state for democracy and global affairs in April 2007 in launching a report on democracy:

In many countries that we reported on, ensuring women have equal access to the legal system is a fundamental part of our efforts. In Africa we supported initiatives to combat sexual violence and abuse against women and improved the ability of governments to investigate and prosecute these cases. And political participation is key. In Egypt a U.S.-funded program helped thousands of women obtain national identity and voter registration cards, allowing them to participate fully in the civic and political life of their country for the first time.[42]

Yet there is strong evidence to show that the empowerment of women must go beyond the formalities of access to legal and political institutions. The Grameen Bank experiment in microfinancing, for example, was all about strengthening the economic roles of women, thereby empowering them across a wide range of other contexts.[43] A recent systematic global study of the gender gap between men and women focuses on four categories: economic participation and opportunity; educational attainment; health and survival; and political empowerment. The strong assumption is that political empowerment on its own will not serve to close the gender gap.[44] While programs designed to empower educated female elites are increasingly common, and are often supported by the U.S. government,[45] it is now widely recognized that some dimension of comprehensive economic and social empowerment, such as that implicit in the fulfillment of women's basic economic and social rights, is a necessary complement to political rights-based initiatives. As long as the substance of economic and social rights remains off the U.S. agenda, however, there will be resistance to moving in this direction.

A statement by the U.S. representative to the Third Committee of the UN General Assembly in November 2006 on the issue of extreme poverty and human rights could be interpreted as representing a slight change in perspective: "Sound economic policies unleash the enterprise and creativity necessary for development. With the world's help, and the right policies, citizens in the developing world can and should live under governments that deliver basic services and protect basic rights. There is no better way to address extreme poverty."[46] While the reference to "governments that deliver basic services and protect basic rights" could reasonably be taken as a recognition of the need to ensure basic economic and social rights, there is no indication in subsequent statements of such a change in policy.

Another cost of the artificial exclusion of economic and social rights from the overall human rights equation is that in at least some situations involving gross violations, the most egregious aspects of the abuse are overlooked. Two examples. The first concerns North Korea, where problems of hunger and starvation and denial of medical care have been particularly acute. The U.S. statement to the Human Rights Council blocked out those dimensions and focused solely on civil and political rights issues: The North Korean "regime controls many aspects of its citizens' lives, denying freedom of speech, religion, the press, assembly, and association. An estimated 150,000 to 200,000 persons are believed to be held in detention camps in remote areas, many for political reasons."[47]

Similarly in an impassioned attack on the human rights situation in Zimbabwe, the U.S. representative focused exclusively on political developments and related government-sponsored violence to the exclusion of the dramatic plight of Zimbabweans in relation to virtually all economic and social rights.[48]

A related consequence of America's failure to engage substantively with economic and social rights is its inability to challenge those nations that profess to place a higher priority on economic and social rights than on civil and political rights. Thus, in lamenting the architecture of the new UN Human Rights Council, Deputy Assistant Secretary of State Mark Lagon suggested that the high number of developing country members was unfortunate "because many African and Asian countries tend to favor economic, social, and cultural rights over civil and political rights."[49] In reality, the majority of those countries are far more deeply attached to the rhetoric of ESCR than to the practice and the United States would be ideally placed to make an issue of this hypocrisy if it were not for the fact that it cannot bring itself to dignify any sustained discussion of those issues. The result is that a country such as China can get great mileage out of the priority that it claims to accord to ESCR without being called to account for the fact that it does remarkably little by way of treating issues such as housing, food, and health care in terms of rights.

The Bush administration's misgivings about economic and social rights, notwithstanding its selective rhetorical embrace of them, have had a major negative impact on its attitude toward key international treaties other than ICESCR. The most notable casualties are the Convention on the Rights of the Child and the Convention on the Elimination of All Forms of Discrimination against Women. One of the administration's first international statements, in February 2001, focused on the dangers of the Convention of the Rights of the Child because of its inclusion of ESCR:

The Convention on the Rights of the Child may be a positive tool in promoting child welfare for those countries that have adopted it. But we believe the text goes too far when it asserts entitlements based on the economic, social and cultural rights contained in the Convention and other instruments. The human rights-based approach, while laudable in its objectives, poses significant problems.[50]

The Bush administration has continued to object systematically to the inclusion of references to the Convention on the Rights of the Child in the annual resolutions of the General Assembly and the Human Rights Council on children's rights. The *administration's* line has changed slightly, however, so that the objection to ESCR is no longer quite as explicit but is instead phrased in terms of respect for states' rights. Thus, for example, in explaining the U.S. "no" vote on the annual resolution dealing with children's rights in the General Assembly in 2006, the U.S. representative stated:

The U.S. has repeatedly made clear that the Convention raises a number of concerns. In particular, the Convention conflicts with the authority of parents, and the provisions of state and local law in the United States. Many of the activities covered by the Convention in areas such as education, health and criminal justice are primarily the responsibility of state and local governments in the U.S.[51]

While the problems raised by the Bush administration and other actors in relation to the child rights convention go well beyond the economic and social rights dimension,[52] it is clear that they remain an important stumbling block.

Policies for a New Administration

What should the approach of a new administration be with regard to economic and social rights? The following are the main components of any such policy:

- State clearly that the United States supports the indivisibility of the two sets of rights;[53]
- Affirm that it will be supportive of efforts within the UN to promote respect for economic and social rights;
- Amend the policy that defines economic and social rights as being fundamentally different in nature from civil and political rights so as to recognize not that the two sets of rights are identical but that substantive obligations do in fact attach to the recognition of economic and social rights;
- Drop the position that insists that there is no freestanding right to housing and that it is merely a component of the right to an adequate standard of living;
- Engage seriously and constructively with the debates on the right to health and the right to food;
- Focus systematically on the economic and social rights components of the debates over the right to development;
- Engage actively with those civil society actors, such as Amnesty International and Human Rights Watch, which have now developed serious programs designed to promote and defend economic and social rights.

These guidelines for the new administration rest on a series of conclusions drawn from the preceding discussion in this essay. First, rather than representing a fundamental break with the past, the authentic embrace of economic and social rights would involve reverting to a policy that was more or less accepted by a succession of American administrations from Truman through Carter. Second, given the superficial or rhetorical support for these rights that characterizes current U.S. policy, the required change in policy in order to take them seriously at the international level is not nearly as dramatic as it might seem.

Third, the adoption of a more affirmative and supportive attitude to international efforts to promote economic and social rights need not await a dramatic change in domestic policy. The United States would be acting consistently with the approach adopted by many other free market economies that firmly espouse and support economic and social rights internationally but have not implemented formal structures for the promotion of these rights per se at the domestic level. And fourth, there are powerful instrumentalist arguments in favor of constructive engagement by the United States in this rights debate. It will give the United States the credibility needed to expose the hypocrisy of those states that pretend to prioritize economic and social rights while in fact ignoring both sets of rights. It will make the domestic debate over ratification of the Convention on the Elimination of All Forms of Discrimination Against Women and the Convention on the Rights of the Child much more manageable. Moreover, it will enable the United States to promote a more rounded and compelling notion of human rights both in terms of its own approaches to issues such as democracy and women's rights and in exposing the shortcomings of chronic human rights violators whose assaults affect economic and social rights every bit as much as civil and political rights.

Chapter 8

Strange Bedfellows
U.S. Corporations and the Pursuit of Human Rights

Debora L. Spar

Corporations are hardly obvious candidates to advance the cause of human rights. Indeed, the modern multinational firm, motivated as it must be by the drive to maximize profits, is an improbable agent for any kind of normative social change. Why would a multinational compromise its financial interests for the vague, if lofty, causes of labor rights or protection of children? Why would a corporation even care about human rights, much less do anything to advance them? And why would any government think to involve corporate actors in the pursuit of non-commercial policy objectives?

It isn't a logical fit. Yet, as this chapter will demonstrate, U.S. multinational corporations can actually be a powerful channel to advance human rights. They can promote labor rights in their factories and supply chains; they can protect children and vulnerable groups by providing educational opportunities rather than sweatshop jobs; and they can advance basic human rights by allowing for incomes to rise and mouths to be fed. At a political level U.S. corporations may prove in many cases to have greater leverage with abusive governments than the U.S. State Department. They have more money at their collective disposal than the U.S. Agency for International Development and more "weapons" than the U.S. armed services, though admittedly of a different sort. U.S. firms also have webs of influence that penetrate deep into the core of most nations, affecting some of their most basic economic and development choices. If the U.S. government can harness the incipient power of these firms, and if it can draw U.S. multinationals more deeply into the pursuit of international human rights, it will be able to develop an innovative and inclusive means of advancing some key foreign policy objectives.

Before embarking on this course, however, it will be critical for the

U.S. government to realize that U.S. multinationals will not—and indeed probably cannot—pursue human rights out of any sort of normative obligation. Instead, they will remain primarily devoted to profit maximization, the objective that defines their operation and determines their course of action. The policy challenge, therefore, is to craft strategies that pair the commercial interests of multinationals with the political and normative interests of the United States in expanding human rights. This is actually easier than it might initially appear.

Despite the gap that might seem to divide the spheres of human rights and international business, there are at least four distinct areas in which these actions overlap—areas in which firms, simply by virtue of pursuing their commercial objectives, have the potential to improve human rights as well. Two of these areas, as described below, involve little more than the firms' self-conscious search for profits among the poor. The other two involve a search for profit combined with a growing awareness of how these profits can be shaped by distinctive kinds of interaction with both wealthy consumers and vulnerable populations. None of these paths, either singly or in combination, can substitute for state sponsorship of a human rights agenda since the normative realm of rights remains tightly wedded to the political sphere. Yet states, like firms, are not destined to act in isolation. By following any of the four paths discussed in this chapter, government leaders can work with and through corporations to add another line of attack to the fight for human rights.

Of Firms and Foreign Objectives[1]

Many supporters of a human rights agenda would no doubt cringe at the thought of bringing multinational firms into a process long dominated by international institutions and nongovernmental organizations (NGOs). Indeed, most of these groups have traditionally viewed multinationals not only as improbable allies in the campaign for human rights but as direct contributors to the human rights problem. Starting with Lenin's early work on imperialism, impassioned critics have charged multinationals, especially U.S. multinationals, with being a direct source of abuse in the developing world—the reason why the rich got richer and the powerful more powerful in regions marked by poverty and inequality.[2] According to Lenin, imperial expansion and the exploitation of foreign markets were a necessary stage in the development of advanced capitalism. As profits flattened in their home markets, firms would be forced abroad, exploiting foreign populations and seizing foreign resources to maintain their own rates of growth. In the process the increased concentration of capital and resources in corporate hands would relentlessly widen the gap between the capitalists and the exploited classes, the controllers and the controlled.

In 1971 Stephen Hymer expanded upon these ideas in an influential article.[3] Inherent in corporate capitalism, Hymer argued, is a pattern of dual development that leads to a deterioration of human rights in the host countries of the developing world. To maintain their system of financial dominance, multinationals must keep the poorest segments of the world's population "under control," unable to rise up against the inequities of this system.[4] To do so, they turn to and support the repressive mechanisms of their host countries. An unholy alliance soon emerges as multinationals support repressive regimes in the developing world and those repressive regimes actively solicit the capital and connections associated with foreign direct investment. As a result, human rights are decimated and the masses of the developing world become a source of cheap labor for multinational factories.

Hymer's thesis is both persuasive and neat. It completely separates commercial and normative objectives and casts multinationals into an inevitably evil role: forced to cooperate with repressive regimes, they are simultaneously destined to support them. Any riches that the firms might bring are siphoned off to rapacious government leaders and any employment they offer is of an abusive kind. In this analysis—and indeed in the dominant stream of analysis that followed Hymer—the only way corporations can affect human rights is by making them worse. In pursuit of their commercial interests, firms trounce individual freedoms.[5]

Since Hymer's time, however, the theory and practice of multinational corporations have both undergone significant shifts. Firms are investing outside their home countries at record levels ($873.1 billion in private portfolio flows in 2006; $1.2 trillion in direct investment)[6] and in configurations unimaginable just 40 years ago: 10.7 percent of total U.S. investment in 2006 went into the information technology sector, and roughly 5 percent went to formerly Communist countries, primarily China.[7] While the stereotypical firm of Hymer's analysis—a wholly U.S.- or European-owned company, buying an oil field or banana plantation in a small repressive Asian nation—undoubtedly still exists, it represents an increasingly small piece of the overall international corporate landscape. Most of today's firms are cosmopolitan hybrids, owned by shareholders spread across the globe and managed from multiple headquarters. Many of the fastest growing companies are emerging from what was once the developing world (think of Russia's Gazprom, for example, China's Lenovo, or India's Wipro) and most of the West's most prominent firms no longer focus on the extraction of resources—the economic activity that is arguably most likely to lead to physical and economic exploitation. New demands for transparency have forced even the most reclusive of Western firms to be more forthcoming with their internal information; new modes of social networking have pushed corporations toward a more frequent, if still occasionally awkward, relationship with international institutions like the World Bank and NGOs such as Oxfam and the WWF (formerly the World Wildlife Fund). In response, scholars who might once have spent their careers lambasting the global reach of corporate capitalism are instead crafting frameworks to analyze patterns of interaction between firms and their erstwhile critics.[8] While shifts in the global economy could yet bring back the intellectual specters of Lenin and Hymer, their shadows have retreated at least for now, giving way to a consensus—in both policy and academic circles—that multinational firms will play a disproportionate role in shaping the lives and livelihoods of distant peoples but that the bulk of that interaction is likely to be positive.

What remains to be probed is how firms can be yoked to a specific agenda of human rights and what role they can play in an administration dedicated to human rights as a foreign policy goal. How can corporations simultaneously pursue commercial and normative objectives? How can they structure their relations with repressive regimes or vulnerable populations? And how could a U.S. administration engage corporate energies without compromising the autonomy of either state or firm and without unleashing the deleterious effects that critics of multinationals have long feared? The sections that follow outline four possible paths towards this elusive but vital policy goal.

Doing What Comes Naturally: Profit Maximization as Development Strategy

Despite the complexity that appears to surround them, despite the stock options and share prices and employee retention schemes, multinational corporations are at their very cores rather simple entities. They take capital and labor, transform them into a good or service, and then sell the resulting product for a profit substantial enough to compensate the firm for its time and energy. The more successful the firm is in crafting products and strategies, the larger its profits and the more capital it has to invest in new goods and services and new ways of earning profit. Normatively, the firm has no clear function. Although social critics and internal reformers periodically call on corporations to "be responsible" or "give back to society," it is difficult to define what these responsibilities would look like or how a firm—even one truly dedicated to societal causes—would calculate the configurations of its giving back. Instead, firms are structured to do only what economist Milton Friedman so pithily described: to maximize profits and thus returns to shareholders. Asking firms to shoulder any burden beyond that is essentially asking them to perform a task for which they were never intended and to which they have no apparent connection.

Left to their own profit-making devices, however, firms do have a substantial opportunity to create social welfare and even in some cases to advance human rights. Consider, for example, the chain of events that typically surrounds foreign direct investment. When a Western multinational firm invests in a poor developing country, it by definition brings capital along with it. Sometimes when the state is corrupt (think of Burma or Chad) and the investment narrow in scope (think of oil extraction or gold), the incoming capital is liable to flow directly to the overseas coffers of the country's elite, helping to perpetuate a regime that represses human rights. In other cases the capital will flow more widely, seeping into neighboring areas of the domestic economy and pushing income levels up. When Mattel builds toys in China, for instance, it creates thousands of low-level assembly jobs and dozens of managerial positions; when Intel builds a semiconductor assembly facility in Costa Rica, it attracts hundreds of suppliers, each of whom brings more investment capital and hires more Costa Rican workers; and when General Electric opens a credit card operation in Indonesia, it allows thousands of cash-strapped Indonesians to buy household items on credit, spurring increased consumption across the economy. None of these spillover effects, admittedly, has a direct impact on social and political rights. But insofar as foreign investment increases aggregate income levels, it will also tend to increase the standard of living of local populations: the Chinese worker will be able to purchase more food for her family; the Indonesian shopkeeper will sell more bowls. Empirical studies bear out this anecdotal relationship: in general, the growth spurred by foreign investment reaches all strata of the population in recipient countries with average incomes among the poorest in those countries increasing in proportion to aggregate income levels.[9]

Having more bowls or even more rice does not necessarily constitute an improvement in human rights. Our fictitious Chinese worker, for instance, could be earning higher wages but still be condemned to work excessively long hours in an unventilated factory without the possibility of union representation. Our Indonesian shopkeeper could be watching her income rise while still being unable to express her political views or religious beliefs without fear of reprisal. Such is the gap between economic welfare and social or political rights.

Just because this gap exists, however—that is, just because social and political rights do not necessarily accompany economic improvement—does not, or at least should not, negate the benefits of increases in economic welfare. Let's take again our young Chinese employee and imagine that, since the arrival of the foreign toy-making multinational, she has been able to leave her poverty-stricken village in western China and earn wages that are at least twice as high as those she could have earned in other occupations. She sends most of her money back home, providing for some rudimentary health care for her aging parents and some basic schooling for a young niece. Even if the worker is toiling in an unsanitary or unventilated factory or even if she is being denied the right to unionize, it is hard to argue that her human rights are necessarily worse than they would have been had the multinational never come to China. In some cases, of course, they could be: if the work in the factory kills her, for example, or maims her or causes her to become targeted by hostile authorities. But in the absence of such deleterious effects, the multinational's contribution to this woman's life will have been mostly positive: she is eating better; her family has access to some health care, albeit probably basic; and she has cash that will provide at least some hope for a more prosperous future. Even if her social and political rights have not improved—and in this situation, they probably would not—her economic rights have almost certainly been pushed in a positive direction.

Note that in this case the investing multinational presumably paid no attention to human rights concerns. It came; it invested; it hired (or subcontracted) local workers and paid prevailing wages. Had it chosen consciously to seek to improve human rights, the firm could undeniably have had a substantially bigger effect. Had it been investing in sectors that involve higher-skilled jobs or more local sourcing, its impact would probably have been wider and more deep-seated. Contrarily, had it been investing in capital-intensive resource extraction, its impact would likely have been worse.[10] The critical point, however, is that simply by investing in poor countries—bringing capital, technology, and know-how to countries where these attributes are scarce—multinational firms will in many cases tend to advance at least *segments* of a human rights agenda. All that Western governments need to do to harness this power is to acknowledge it; celebrate it as appropriate; and, as described in subsequent sections, find ways to push the multinationals beyond their natural course of business and toward a more conscious concern for advancing human rights.

"Bebop": Business at the Base of the Pyramid[11]

For decades most of the literature on multinational corporations—both the literature that critiqued these firms and that which advised them—presumed that firms investing in poor regions were motivated primarily by cost. They ventured to places like India or Vietnam or Nigeria either to get access to low-cost resources in the country (oil, for example, or gold) or to use low-cost labor. Selling products to local populations was rarely mentioned in theory and rarely a consideration in practice.

More recently, firms and those scholars that study them have recognized the vast commercial potential that exists inside even desperately poor countries.[12] Motivated in part by the high-profile commercial emergence of India and China (with a combined population of 2.45 billion), businesses have realized that selling large quantities of inexpensive goods and services to poor people can be just as profitable as selling more expensive products to wealthier but often smaller or sated populations. Take, for instance, the case of Unilever, which uses a network of some 27,000 micro-entrepreneurs to sell soap and other personal-care products to 93 million consumers in India's remote and impoverished rural regions.[13] Similarly, Nokia estimates that, with the technology becoming more and more affordable, 80 percent of the 1 billion new mobile phone customers expected by 2010 will come from emerging economies.[14] In financial markets as well, global firms are discovering that small (and poor) really can be beautiful. GE's consumer finance arm sees the bulk of its revenue growth in the next decade coming from the underbanked regions of emerging Europe and Asia,[15] while microlending organizations and, increasingly, microfinance divisions at some of the world's major banks are providing credit to small-scale entrepreneurs across the developing world.

How do these developments affect human rights? Again the connection is through entirely commercial channels with firms doing little more than pursuing what might be considered "enlightened self interest." In all of the examples described above, firms are selling to the poor not because they conceive these sales primarily as contributing to the advancement of humanity but because they have found ways to profit from this long-neglected segment of the global marketplace. The impact of their commercial activity, however, is undoubtedly to raise the living standards of their customers and to contribute in some small but significant way to their well-being. It is not just that people in India, for example, realize the psychic benefits of purchasing packaged goods. Instead, the goods that appeal to people at the pyramid's base are, for the most part, also goods that contribute to their physical well-being: small sachets of soap, for example, improve basic sanitation and thus health.[16] The spread of mobile telephony helps to facilitate the free exchange of information and political opposition under repressive regimes.[17] Drugs targeted at the rural poor—like Novartis's Coartem for malaria or GlaxoSmithKline's HIV drug Combivir – are often the first or only line of health care for affected populations while low-cost supermarkets in rural areas or squatter communities can provide a vital channel for basic affordable foodstuffs.[18]

Similarly, the awarding of the 2006 Nobel Peace Prize to Muhammad Yunus, founder of Grameen Bank, stands now as a tangible symbol of the importance of microcredit—finance directed squarely at the pyramid's base. Microcredit, as a growing number of surveys has demonstrated, can be extremely profitable.[19] Indeed, in many cases it is more profitable than typical retail banking, generating returns on equity that can be well over 30 percent.[20] The pursuit of these returns, however, has also generated equally massive benefits—both economic and social—for the loan recipients: the woman in Bangladesh, for instance, who started 10 years ago with an initial loan of about $30 from Grameen to buy a rickshaw and now owns a fleet of 27, a poultry firm of 3,000 chickens and a pond for raising fish; or the villagers in Cambodia who pooled their loans to buy irrigation equipment and seed and now turn a profit selling vegetables to exporters.[21] Again one must be careful not to conflate economic gain with social and political rights: the Bangladeshi woman may still be repressed by her husband or father; the Cambodian villagers may still fear attack from a local despot or authoritarian state. But successful microfinancing at least pushes its recipients in the direction of greater freedoms: a woman who earns a reasonable income from her own enterprise will be able to afford health care and medicines that would otherwise be unobtainable for her; she may be able to send her children, including her daughters, to school; she can exert greater control over her children's destiny; and, anecdotal evidence indicates, she will have some greater means to defend herself against violence perpetrated by male relatives or local elites. Because the structure of microcredit rests with individual responsibility, it also tends to foster a sense of confidence in its recipients and an enhanced willingness to take risks that might once have been considered impossible.[22] In cases where extreme poverty meets extreme powerlessness, therefore, there is reason to believe that money can indeed buy some measure of protection and some advance in basic human rights. Again, the role for government in this realm is small but powerful: to celebrate and promote microcredit initiatives and businesses aimed at serving the poor.

Competition and Codes of Conduct

When firms engage at the bottom of the pyramid, as when they invest more generally in the developing world, they are essentially doing what business considerations alone demand. They are delving into new markets, exploring new opportunities, and searching, always, for greater profits. Even if these profits are consciously linked to a social agenda that includes human rights, as is typically the case with private microfinance, the firms involved are not departing radically, if at all, from standard business practice.

The third corporate path toward human rights, by contrast, depends distinctly on firms pursuing new ways of business. Indeed, it asks firms to monitor their activity and *change* their activity, if need be, so that it enhances whatever aspect of human rights it encounters. Not surprisingly, this is a path that has only recently been paved, largely at the urging of human rights activists. It has proved remarkably powerful over the past two decades, however, and shows strong signs of becoming more deeply engrained in corporate behavior.

The archetypal case is well known but still bears repeating. In the 1970s U.S. shoe manufacturers like Nike and Reebok were rapidly expanding across Asia, using the region's low wages and productive labor to produce athletic footwear for a fraction of what it would cost to do so in the United States. Rather than investing directly in Asian factories, the companies were contracting nearly all of their production to local manufacturers, lowering their costs even further by encouraging these manufacturers to compete aggressively for each round of the multinationals' business. For Nike and Reebok it was a model that nearly guaranteed profit: between 1972 and 1982 Nike's revenues soared from $60,000 to $49 million.[23] But for labor and human rights activists, it was exploitation that bordered on abuse. According to critics such as labor activist Jeff Ballinger, Nike's contract labor system meant that thousands of (mostly female) Asian workers were condemned to work excessively long hours without breaks or benefits for wages that were little more than slavery. Indeed, Ballinger argues, this is very much the point: "They're [corporations] on a search for cheap labor. When labor becomes not so cheap, they're on their way out."[24] Initially Nike responded to its critics by echoing the argument laid out above: simply by investing in poor countries like Vietnam or Indonesia, the company's executives argued, they were supporting the local economy and improving the population's living standards. Or as Phil Knight, the company's CEO, explained, corporations like Nike "are the ones that lead these countries out of poverty."[25]

Under the intense scrutiny that faced the company, however, Knight's argument failed to convince. Instead, activists tirelessly attacked Nike (and, to a lesser extent, Reebok), insisting that the companies take responsibility for the human rights of their workers—even if those workers were not directly on the company's payroll.

In the end the companies capitulated, launching (enthusiastically in the case of Reebok, more begrudgingly for Nike) a series of initiatives that over time have reshaped the landscape of relations between multi-

national firms and their overseas workforces. At the core of this new connection are codes of conduct, formal standards to which companies like
Nike and Reebok now pledge themselves. Nike's code of conduct, for
example, sets a minimum age of 16 for all employees hired by subcontractors, limits their workweek to 60 hours, and requires compensation
to match the minimum wage or prevailing industry standards. Reebok's
code contains similar provisions as well as guarantees of employees'
rights to organize and express grievances without fear of retribution.[26]
Although these codes are not legally binding, companies (for reasons
described below) are increasingly diligent in enforcing them. Nike conducts routine inspections of its subcontractors' factories—it performed
some 810 over the last three years—and makes public the detailed auditing tools it uses to gauge factory performance in such areas as hiring
practices, working hours, and safety conditions.[27]

As these policies and procedures have proliferated, they have also
engendered a series of industry initiatives and overarching codes.
Groups like the Fair Labor Association and Council for Responsible
Jewelry Practices, consortia of related firms, establish industry-wide standards to which all their members adhere. They are matched, increasingly, by nonprofit organizations such as Social Accountability
International and the Business Social Compliance Initiative, which help
firms to create and adhere to appropriate codes of conduct. A cottage
industry of for-profit certification firms has also arisen, offering, for a
fee, to monitor corporate behavior and supply chains, attesting to compliance when it occurs and drawing attention to any gaps.

All this activity has led to a fundamental rethinking of how firms operate and what responsibilities they have with regard to human rights.
Whereas the Nike of the 1970s felt no compunction even to address the
human rights of its workforce, the Nike of today must bring a concern
for human rights into the core of its business operations, spending
money, time, and energy to ensure that the lives of those it affects—its
employees, subcontractors, suppliers, and consumers—are improved in
the process. The firm (along with hundreds of other high-profile multinationals) explicitly pledges to care about working conditions, to limit
working hours, to provide for adequate health and safety measures and,
in some but not all cases, to permit its workers the right of association
and organization. To critics these steps still do not go far enough since
most corporations do not undertake to guarantee either a "living wage"
or unionization.[28] Yet the codes nevertheless push multinational firms
farther than they have ever gone before: toward an explicit, formal, and
accountable promise to enhance human rights.

Admittedly, the rights affected are not complete. Corporate codes
rarely address political rights (such as free speech) and vary in their

commitment to workplace freedoms. Indeed, according to a major study completed for the United Nations in 2007 by John Ruggie, the bulk of corporate codes focus on labor rights such as nondiscrimination and the right to a safe and healthy work environment.[29] But this relatively narrow focus is both vital and sensible, concentrating as it does—and arguably should—on the aspects of human rights that touch most directly on the terrain of business firms: the right to benefit from one's own toil; the right to work in a safe environment; and the right to labor with dignity.

Harnessing the Spotlight Effect[30]

A final path toward corporate involvement with human rights follows directly upon the codes of conduct just described and on the obligations they so publicly establish. It also shifts from the arena of corporate initiative to that of outside pressure.

When firms go abroad—particularly if they are large, wealthy U.S. firms that sell a brand-name product—they rarely go in silence or in secret. Instead, they trumpet their expansion to investors and analysts and often to the media. Wal-Mart's entry into China, for example, attracts widespread attention as does Shell's development of a new oil field in Nigeria or the Gap's venture into Bangladesh. Generally firms regard this attention as a benefit: evidence of their commercial prowess and the interest it warrants. In a world of corporate codes and concern for human rights, however, such attention also means that firms are publicly held to the standards they have set—and to which others would like to hold them. For example, if Wal-Mart has promised not to hire underage workers and if an enterprising reporter suspects that 12-year-olds might well find employment at a new Chinese Wal-Mart, the reporter will be particularly diligent in tracking down any child workers at Wal-Mart and publicizing their existence. Similarly, if Shell has pledged to respect indigenous rights or the Gap to maintain healthful factory conditions, their public pronouncements stand as a spotlight that follows them closely abroad, focusing media attention on any departure from their self-established norms and causing firms to be particularly careful about compliance. As a result corporations will tend to operate in a way that fosters at least some consideration for human rights and human rights, in turn, will tend improve. It may be a cynical dynamic, it may not be adopted for the purest of motives, but it works nevertheless.

In some cases concern for the spotlight's glare can even prompt firms to embrace a proactive agenda of human rights, distinguishing themselves from their competitors along this dimension and winning the loyalty of consumers who care. Reebok, for example, broke early from Nike's model and undertook a wide (and well-publicized) campaign for human and labor rights. Shaken by reports that 12-year-old Pakistani workers were stitching its popular soccer balls, Reebok pledged not to employ child labor and moved in 1995 to create a central production facility in Pakistan monitored by independent observers. It also promulgated a rigid internal code of conduct and affixed new "Manufactured without Child Labor" labels to its soccer balls. The Body Shop grabbed headlines (and apparently customers) in 1996 when for the first time it included in its annual report a comprehensive and independently verified "social audit" assessing the company's impact on the environment, animal protection, and what it termed "human relationships."[31] And more recently DeBeers, the world's largest producer of rough gem diamonds, spearheaded a major international campaign against "blood" or "conflict" diamonds.[32] In all of these instances, the spotlight effectively shone in two directions, pushing firms to demonstrate their concern for human rights and then, with even greater brilliance, threatening to punish them should they back away from their now very public commitments. Or to put it more crudely: once DeBeers has run ad campaigns denouncing blood diamonds or Reebok has promised only to produce "child-labor free" soccer balls, the ante is upped. If they are caught, respectively, with blood diamonds or child labor, the public backlash will be especially harsh—and expensive. This is the threat that keeps the spotlight burning and that tends, once again, to push corporations to pursue policies that protect and even advance human rights.

Of course, it is easy to dismiss such operations as pure corporate marketing (as critics would have it) or as pure corporate altruism (as some executives might opine.) Yet the truth, as in most things, probably lies somewhere in the middle. Not even the most altruistic of firms are embracing human rights simply because they care. Corporations can't "care" in a real sense; they aren't structurally equipped to do so. Indeed, they are not structurally equipped and probably are not structurally well suited to do anything other than earn returns and maximize profits. Thus any steps they take to tie themselves to human rights commitments are driven, as they must be, by a desire to maintain their reputation or to woo customers or compete on the basis of intangible appeal. By the same token, many of the high-level executives who have committed their firms to the pursuit of human rights do, personally, care a great deal. They are simultaneously trying to juggle what should be a contradictory set of objectives: satisfying their shareholders, satisfying the media, and pursuing a normative agenda that often flies in the face of commercial considerations. Moreover, they are juggling those agendas under the increasingly relentless glare of the spotlight, which both tempts and threatens them at the same time. Under these conditions any steps that they manage to take toward human rights, no matter how cynical or self-interested their motives, are almost certainly steps in the right direction.

Bringing the State Back In: Policies to Link U.S. Firms to a Human Rights Agenda

What can the U.S. government do to harness the power of U.S. firms to the pursuit of human rights? How should the state insert itself into the fragile connections between private corporations, foreign governments, and vulnerable populations?

In the section that follows, I describe five distinct policies for a new administration. I conclude by discussing the political conversation that should surround these policies and the conditions that will make them most likely to succeed.

• *Actively and explicitly involve corporations in discussions of human rights.* If one accepts the proposition that U.S. corporations can be powerful tools in the fight to expand human rights, then it follows logically that corporations and their executives should be included in the human rights community, a group that has not typically welcomed their presence. A new administration should reverse this practice, identifying those firms that have taken a particular interest in the social impact of their commercial activities and including them in policy forums and debates. The more specific the conversation, the more likely it is to prove both instructive and fruitful. Recent policy initiatives directed at malaria treatments for Africa, for instance, have benefited greatly from the participation of executives such as Daniel Vasella, CEO of Novartis, whose company makes one of the most potent and inexpensive antimalarial drugs available.[33] Ongoing discussions of labor rights in China have included, as they must, executives from those U.S. firms that manufacture and source from this labor pool. Expanding similar conversations beyond the confines of those pursued in the Bush administration should be a key priority for those charged with overseeing human rights policy in a newly elected U.S. government.

• *Foster and support industry-wide codes of conduct.* As noted above, corporate codes of conduct have been one of the most powerful ways of harnessing corporate power to a human rights agenda. With codes, private firms commit themselves to preserving the environment (usually, both physical and social) in which they operate and to acting in a way that, like the original Hippocratic code, at least does no harm and ideally helps as well. Because codes are written, they tend to be long-lived.

Because they are public, they create an enforcement mechanism of sorts that binds the firm to its own standards.

The problem with individual codes, though, is that they can vary so widely, becoming in the process elements of competition between firms. If Company A binds itself to paying the prevailing local wage but Company B pledges to pay a "living wage," then either A or B (depending on how B interprets "living") could find itself at a competitive disadvantage, bound by its own code to paying a higher wage than its competitor. Industry-wide codes, by comparison, eliminate this potential for competitive code setting. If A and B are bound by their industry code to pay, say, the prevailing wage plus vacation and overtime, then neither firm can compete on the basis of their wage codes. Instead, they will each pay what they, and, critically, outside observers, view as a "fair" wage and they will have to compete on other, less dangerous, grounds.

More subtly, perhaps, it turns out that industry-wide codes are good for business. And industry-wide codes that are sanctioned by the U.S. government are especially good. The reason for this counterintuitive outcome rests, again, with the dynamic of competition. If all firms have their own codes, and if some firms have no codes, then the "better" firms—those most interested in protecting human rights and social welfare—can easily find themselves at a competitive disadvantage, chased down by the regulatory scramble known colloquially as a "race to the bottom."[34] But if all firms in an industry are pushed, both by public pressure and statute, to adhere to a common standard, then the proverbial playing field is level again. The stronger and wider the code, the smaller the probability that any individual firm will try to gain advantage by deviating from it. And in the process human rights will be advanced. In this realm, therefore, the role of government is clear: to sanction industry-wide codes of conduct; to create forums in which these codes can be promulgated and promoted; and to make the circle of membership in these codes or code-making forums as wide and inclusive as possible.

• *Embed codified practices in statute and international organization.* Once U.S. firms have created industry-wide standards, the next step is to entrench these standards in both U.S. statute and international organization. The policy here need not be absolute. It just needs to progress, slowly but surely, toward greater legal recognition of private firms' own industry standards.

Once again, the motive is competition. If all U.S. firms agree, for example, to uphold a common labor standard in the electronics industry but all Chinese (or Thai or Brazilian) firms adhere to no standard, then the U.S. firms (along with their foreign subsidiaries) will find themselves competing at a disadvantage. It is in their interest, therefore, as well as in the interest of the affected workers, to push the non-U.S. firms to the U.S. standard—even if that standard itself does not have the force of law. Instead, it can be vested in international codes or in the criteria attached to contracts falling under the auspices of major international institutions like the World Bank or its affiliate, the International Finance Corporation (IFC), or major financial entities (like any of the global banks). Already movement along these lines is under way. In February 2006, the IFC updated the standards it applies to all of the private-sector projects it finances in developing nations to include new guidelines on labor rights, local health and safety, and the projects' environmental impact.[35] Based on these changes, in July of the same year 41 of the world's largest financial institutions revised the Equator Principles, their own set of voluntary environmental and social responsibility guidelines for developing-nation project finance.[36] Pushing the process farther along, however, and using the power of the U.S. government to convince other major players in the international financial sector to adopt similar criteria would simultaneously help U.S. corporations and global human rights. Whenever possible, the U.S. government should work to convince international financial institutions to adopt human rights criteria in their own evaluations and to hold their partners, both firms and governments, to corresponding levels of concern.

• *Engage firms in country-specific trade negotiations.* Over the past decade the U.S. government has signed several bilateral trade agreements with specific provisions for human (mostly labor) rights. In two of the most notable cases, Cambodia and Jordan, labor rights were central to the conclusion of each treaty, essentially offering the foreign nation enhanced trading relations with the United States in exchange for guaranteed protection of workers' rights.[37] If similar agreements are signed in the future, a new administration should be diligent in ensuring that the firms most likely to invest or trade in these nations are actively engaged in the negotiating process and fully aware of its implications both at home and abroad. The objective of course is not to hand these firms a competitive advantage or to guarantee them market access. Rather, it is to convince the target countries that trade and investment will follow on the completion of the treaty and to educate firms about how their investment can generate social as well as financial returns. The earlier in the process that these discussions occur, the easier it will be for all parties—government, labor, and business—to identify where their interests overlap and how they can plot a common path toward economic prosperity and individual rights.

• *Make firms' involvement as high profile and public as possible.* One of the strengths of corporate codes of conduct are the spotlights they put in place. Once firms have committed publicly to certain modes of operation, it becomes harder and harder for them to permit themselves any departure from these standards. Accordingly, a final policy prescription for a new administration is relatively straightforward: engage firms in discussions of human rights as much as possible and publicize the extent and intent of their engagement. The calculus here runs in two directions: first, as corporate executives become more deeply involved at the highest level with human rights issues, they will tend to adopt these issues as their own and fight for them with greater enthusiasm. Second, as their involvement becomes recognized more widely, they will also feel compelled to deliver on their commitment as fully as possible and to put their money truly where their mouths are.

A New Politics of Corporate Involvement

Because using corporations to advance human rights is not an obvious policy, it is also not a particularly easy policy to sell. Bringing corporate executives into high-level discussions of labor rights or freedom of association will always engender suspicion on the part of some critics who will see corporate involvement as merely a disguise for increasing corporate profits.

Yet the politics here are far from insurmountable. The key lies with creating real success stories based on human interactions on both sides of the equation.

For better or worse most Americans are either uncomfortable or unfamiliar with abstract concepts like trade, foreign investment, and human rights. They want "their rights" but don't typically worry much about the rights of others—especially when the rights are vague and the people distant. Instead, concern for international human rights has typically been the province in the United States of a small but intensely committed group of lawyers, academics, some students, and activists. For most Americans, therefore, any possible fear of corporate involvement will be mitigated by tales of corporate success: by true stories of companies that bring jobs to the unemployed, loans to the impoverished, and vital products—medicine, food, tools, soap—to those long accustomed to doing without. Even if people do not necessarily see these successes in terms of human rights and even if the role of the government is not paramount, the politics of Americans bringing good will and good things to foreign lands is deeply and perpetually appealing. After several years of bad news from Iraq, it will also be particularly welcome.

Meanwhile, even some of the most vocal proponents of human rights have increasingly seen the value of including corporations as part of the equation. The Fair Labor Association, now one of the most well-established groups concerned with labor rights, brings some 20 major clothing and apparel manufacturers, including Nike and Adidas, together with more than 200 university affiliates and many prominent NGOs and trade unions. The Joint Initiative on Corporate Accountability and Workers' Rights, a pilot project in Turkey devoted to improving working conditions in that country's garment industry, has members from European and U.S. companies, local suppliers, trade unions, and NGOs. And the ambitious United Nations Global Compact, conceived by former UN Secretary General Kofi Annan as a social and environmental initiative, is composed of corporate members pledged to implement and advocate the Compact's 10 human rights, labor, environmental, and anticorruption principles. The idea of corporations working together with their former critics is no longer new or radical. Yet such cooperation has occurred largely outside the realm of the state, conceived, one might even argue, as a way of advancing a policy agenda that no longer had sufficient prominence within the U.S. government.

A new administration has the potential to change that perception and to employ U.S. corporations as a powerful ally in a reinvigorated battle to advance human rights. Presented as a model for societal collaboration, joining labor, business, and government and publicized in terms of its real, on-the-ground, successes, such a strategy would almost certainly prove politically attractive both to those who prize free enterprise and to those who concern themselves with social causes. More important, it is also a strategy that can work: improving the lives and rights of the world's most vulnerable citizens while also advancing U.S. political and commercial interests.

Chapter 9

Prioritizing Workers' Rights in a Global Economy

CAROL PIER AND ELIZABETH DRAKE

Workers' rights are often omitted from human rights discussions and misunderstood as inferior to other human rights norms. But workers' rights are human rights. They are protected in the same international instruments that enshrine more traditional human rights, such as the right not to be subjected to torture, and they should be understood as an important part of any human rights policy agenda.

The Universal Declaration of Human Rights (UDHR), which all United Nations members, including the United States, have pledged to uphold, and the International Covenant on Civil and Political Rights (ICCPR), to which the United States is party, establish a worker's right to form and join trade unions, ban slavery and servitude in all its forms, and prohibit employment and workplace discrimination. The International Labor Organization (ILO) fleshes out these and other workers' rights in its conventions and interpretive jurisprudence. In 1998, responding to the call to establish a set of core workers' rights, the ILO adopted its Declaration on Fundamental Principles and Rights at Work (ILO Declaration), listing four fundamental rights: freedom of association and the effective recognition of the right to collective bargaining; the elimination of all forms of forced or compulsory labor; the effective abolition of child labor; and the elimination of discrimination in respect of employment and occupation. Even ILO members like the United States that have not ratified all of the eight core ILO conventions defining these rights are obligated "to respect, to promote and to realize . . . the principles concerning the fundamental rights."[1]

Facilitating respect for these core rights should be a key component of the U.S. government's international human rights strategy. It is often argued that the realization of such rights may help offset pressure on working conditions in the United States resulting from global competition. But it is also that true that when these fundamental rights are respected, workers around the world are empowered to join together to advocate for their interests, in the workplace and beyond, and thereby generate change that can help fulfill important U.S. international economic and foreign policy goals.

Workers' exercise of their right to form and join trade unions and bargain collectively, for instance, can support economic development by lifting wages and benefits, reducing income inequality, and increasing productivity.[2] It can also lead to the creation of powerful, independent workers' organizations that give workers a voice in the broader society, support and strengthen emerging democracies, and demand transparency and accountability from governments. Trade unions played a central role in the transitions to democracy in Poland and South Africa, for example.

The United States has historically voiced support for workers' rights around the world. Yet the persistence of weak democracies, underdeveloped civil societies, and inequitable distribution of globalization's benefits are a few of the many signs that existing infrastructures and policies to safeguard global workers' rights still fall short. The United States should take the lead in seeking innovative and bold solutions.

These solutions should offer much-needed funding, training, legal expertise, and other assistance to countries wishing to improve their workers' rights records. And they should provide concrete incentives to change the behavior of those nations that simply lack the political will to respect workers' rights or that tolerate their violation in an attempt to win the proverbial "race to the bottom." Thus, the solutions should also reform, at all levels, the rules governing global economic integration to reward respect for labor rights and penalize their abuse.

U.S. Labor Law and International Workers' Rights

If the United States is to take the lead in advocating for workers' rights abroad, it must first get its own house in order. Any such advocacy is undermined by weak U.S. labor laws that fall far short of U.S. international obligations and leave workers in the United States vulnerable to abuse.

The Fair Labor Standards Act (FLSA), for example, allows child farm workers as young as 12 to work *unlimited* hours outside of school and, if they are over 16, to work in hazardous conditions. As a party to the ILO Worst Forms of Child Labor Convention, however, the United States is required to prevent children under 18 from engaging in harmful labor, which includes long hours, work with dangerous implements, and exposure to high temperatures and unhealthy substances like pesticides—all of which are typical of U.S. agricultural labor.[3]

U.S. laws also fail to fully prevent employment and occupation discrimination, defined in the ILO Equal Remuneration Convention as including the principle of equal remuneration for men and women for work of equal value.[4] This principle, similar to the doctrine of comparable worth, requires the value of work, even very dissimilar work, to be assessed based on job content, without regard to gender.[5] Yet comparable worth has generally been rejected by U.S. courts as a basis for relief under U.S. pay equity laws.[6] Instead, the Equal Pay Act of 1963 and Title VII of the Civil Rights Act of 1964 require equal pay for men and women doing equal work only on substantially equal jobs.[7]

Nowhere, however, do U.S. labor laws and practice stray further from international norms than on a worker's right to freedom of association and collective bargaining. This basic right is systematically violated in the United States.[8] Union membership is at historic lows at 12 percent in the overall U.S. workforce,[9] though surveys suggest that if allowed to freely exercise their right to organize, roughly 58 percent of the U.S. workforce would select union representation.[10]

The National Labor Relations Act (NLRA), the set of U.S. laws governing the fundamental right to freedom of association and collective bargaining, fails even to cover significant segments of the U.S. workforce: agricultural and domestic workers, independent contractors, and supervisors. Judicial and administrative decisions have increasingly expanded the ranks of workers falling under these exclusions, most recently extending the category of "supervisors" to include low-level workers with only incidental oversight authority, such as staff nurses.[11] As a result, tens of thousands of workers fall outside the NLRA, in violation of international law, which requires countries to guarantee that "everyone" has the right to form and join trade unions.[12]

Even those workers covered by the NLRA face an uphill battle if they wish to organize. U.S. employers can reject workers' request for union recognition based on majority sign-up, known as "card check," and force a union election. Employers often use the pre-election period to mount aggressive anti-union campaigns, during which they hold workplace "captive audience" meetings to deliver impassioned anti-union messages. They do so knowing that they can legally keep union representatives at bay by denying them an opportunity to respond to the anti-union meetings and even banning them entirely from company property, including publicly accessible sidewalks and parking lots. As a result, the campaign periods leading up to union elections are often acrimonious and coercive, making a mockery of basic standards for a free, fair, and democratic political election in which both sides have an equal opportunity to be heard by the electorate.

The ILO Committee on Freedom of Association, charged with reviewing and ruling on complaints alleging ILO members' violations of workers' right to organize, has rejected these one-sided union election campaign rules, requesting the United States "to guarantee access of trade union representatives to workplaces . . . so that trade unions can communicate with workers, in order to apprise them of the potential advantages of unionisation."[13]

The ILO Committee on Freedom of Association has also decried U.S. law permitting permanent strike replacements during economic strikes, a legal provision that employers also regularly cite during anti-union campaigns to link union formation to possible job loss. Specifically, in a case against the United States, the committee held that the right to strike, an integral component of freedom of association, "is not really guaranteed when a worker who exercises it legally runs the risk of seeing his or her job taken up permanently by another worker, just as legally."[14]

Even NLRA provisions that substantively comport with international standards, such as the ban on anti-union firings, are rendered impotent by the law's weak penalties. The NLRA does not provide for fines or other punitive sanctions—only a "make-whole" remedy that requires a violating employer to cease and desist from illegal conduct, post workplace notices promising not to repeat violations, and restore the status quo before the illegal activity by, for example, reinstating fired workers with payment of lost earnings.

Undocumented migrant workers fired for union activity are not even entitled to a make-whole remedy, according to the Supreme Court, which ruled in *Hoffman Plastics* that they are not due lost wages.[15] Since undocumented workers are also not due reinstatement because their employment is inherently unlawful, the decision allows U.S. employers to fire such workers with virtual impunity.

Under international law, the United States is obligated to ensure "an effective remedy" for all workers whose right to organize is violated and provide "sufficiently dissuasive sanctions" to deter such violations.[16] The negligible consequences of NLRA violation, combined with long National Labor Relations Board (NLRB) enforcement delays,[17] however, do neither. In particular, according to the ILO Committee on Freedom of Association, "the remedial measures left to the NLRB in cases of illegal dismissals of undocumented workers . . . are inadequate to ensure effective protection against acts of anti-union discrimination."[18]

Despite these significant obstacles, a small percentage of U.S. workers have organized. Yet even *they* are not guaranteed a collective contract. Although the NLRA requires employers to bargain collectively with workers' representatives, many employers engage in "surface bargaining"—negotiating, often for years, with no intention of reaching an agreement. The remedy for such illegal bad-faith bargaining is more bargaining, perpetuating the cycle. This loophole opens the door to the de facto denial of workers' right to bargain collectively, again violating international standards. And some workers cannot even enjoy surface bargaining. A number of states, such as North Carolina, ban government employees from collective bargaining, in violation of international standards that permit such restrictions only for high-level "public servants engaged in the administration of the State."[19] The ILO Committee on Freedom of Association has urged the United States to ensure the repeal of the North Carolina ban.[20]

To protect U.S. workers' fundamental rights and ensure that a call by the United States for greater respect for labor rights around the world is not increasingly dismissed as the height of hypocrisy, the United States should bring its labor laws and practice more in line with international standards by, at a minimum, adopting the following recommendations:

- Amend the FLSA to provide child farm workers with at least the same protections as other child workers;
- Amend the Equal Pay Act of 1963 and Title VII of the Civil Rights Act of 1964 to require equal pay for work of "equal value" or of "comparable worth";
- Repeal the NLRA exclusions of agricultural and domestic workers and independent contractors and redefine "supervisors" narrowly to include only those workers genuinely representing management interests;
- Redefine "employer" under the NLRA to include state and local governments, thereby prohibiting state-law bans on public sector collective bargaining;
- Protect workers' right to receive information from union representatives, including by requiring employers to permit union representatives to respond in kind to any workplace captive audience meetings and to communicate with workers on company property in non-work areas during non-work time;
- Permit only temporary, not permanent, replacement workers during all strikes;
- Reverse the *Hoffman Plastics* decision; and
- Enact the Employee Free Choice Act of 2007 to require employers to grant union recognition based on NLRB-validated card check, eliminating the often coercive pre-election campaign periods; increase employer penalties for NLRA violations and require the NLRB to seek injunctions against employers accused of significant

illegal anti-union conduct, giving affected workers temporary relief while they await final legal rulings; and allow workers negotiating their first collective contract to seek mediation after 90 days and, if mediation is unsuccessful, to refer the dispute to arbitration, leading to a binding contract.[21]

Workers' Rights and Trade

As the United States improves its labor laws and practice to comply with ILO standards, it should work to strengthen international trade rules so other countries have the incentive to do the same. Over the years, the United States has come to recognize the inherent link between labor rights and trade. The United States has yet to find a winning formula, however, for ensuring that more trade goes hand in hand with greater respect for the rights of workers whose labors make such trade possible. Despite important intermittent attempts over the years, the country has also proved incapable of convincing a critical mass of trading partners to similarly acknowledge and respect this important link. The World Trade Organization's (WTO) rules are largely silent on labor rights. U.S. free trade agreements (FTAs) and preference programs contain labor provisions with some positive elements, but they also fall far short of effectively protecting workers' rights.

The United States should embrace the challenge of addressing these shortcomings. The country should vigorously strive for consensus among WTO members to address workers' rights in global trade rules and should simultaneously ensure that U.S. FTAs and preference programs providing additional market access contain strong, enforceable labor rights protections worth emulating.

The WTO and the Challenge for Workers' Rights

The WTO governs the vast majority of trade occurring between nations; therefore, any comprehensive, global solution to protecting workers' rights in the context of trade must involve that organization. As far back as the Havana Charter establishing the International Trade Organization (a predecessor to the WTO that was envisioned after World War II at the Bretton Woods Conference but never realized), it was acknowledged that "unfair labour conditions, particularly . . . for export, create difficulties in international trade." "Each member," the charter went on to say, "shall take whatever action may be appropriate and feasible to eliminate such conditions within its territory."[22]

The WTO has yet to show any similar recognition. At the WTO's Singapore Ministerial in 1996, ministers declared their commitment to observing core labor standards but stated that the ILO was the competent body to set and deal with such standards.[23] Ministers could not agree to proposals to establish a working group or other formal mechanism to discuss workers' rights within the WTO, noting only that the WTO and ILO Secretariats would continue their existing collaboration. And although the ILO and WTO have worked together to some extent since the Singapore Ministerial Declaration, there have been no meaningful elaborations on the declaration from WTO ministers or other steps towards integrating WTO rules and ILO labor standards since 1996.

Just as WTO members have resisted proposals to address workers' rights, ILO members have been hesitant to allow their organization to authorize trade measures. Although the ILO Constitution suggests that its founding members understood the link between workers' rights and trade and allows the organization to authorize "wise and expedient" actions "to secure compliance" by recalcitrant labor rights violators, there is no express authority for the ILO to impose trade remedies or authorize members to violate other international trade obligations in response to workers' rights violations.[24] In 2000, the ILO took an important step when, for the first time, it recommended that members review their bilateral relationships with a member country—Burma (Myanmar)—and take all appropriate steps to ensure those relationships do not perpetuate the country's repeated and egregious violations of basic workers' rights.[25] While the United States has imposed trade sanctions on Burma, it is unclear whether the decision was linked to the ILO recommendation or to broader concerns regarding other serious human rights violations perpetrated by the country's military rulers.

Thus, more work is needed to establish a predictable and universal regime that links trade benefits to compliance with core workers' rights. Several approaches could be pursued,[26] yet each must begin with a change in current WTO rules under which a member country that denies another access to its market on workers' rights grounds could face a WTO challenge alleging violation of some of the organization's most basic rules.[27] If the challenge were successful, that country could lose its own market access rights.[28]

One approach to such WTO rule modification is to amend Article XX of the General Agreement on Tariffs and Trade (GATT)—the primary WTO agreement governing trade in goods—to provide that a country may maintain a measure otherwise inconsistent with the GATT (such as a quota, a tariff increase, or other trade measure) in response to violations of ILO-defined core workers' rights. Such a solution would expand upon the existing general exceptions to WTO rules already permitted by Article XX for measures related to prison labor and to protect public morals. Moreover, it would fit neatly within the existing structure of the GATT, building upon Article XX precedent, and would allow countries to develop their own procedures for conditioning market access on workers' rights compliance.

However, unilateral restrictions invoking this exception would no doubt be challenged at the WTO, creating a need for WTO expertise on workers' rights. WTO dispute settlement bodies would eventually have to determine not only whether the restrictions were truly "related to" or "necessary to protect" core workers' rights but whether those rights had even been violated. Without WTO labor rights expertise, WTO and ILO interpretations of core workers' rights could diverge.

One way to avoid competing WTO and ILO labor standards is to specify that trade measures related to core workers' rights shall only fall within the WTO's general exceptions if they are in furtherance of specific ILO recommendations and to simultaneously create an ILO mechanism to issue such recommendations. The ILO mechanism would be similar to the ILO Committee on Freedom of Association and charged with receiving and reviewing public and member-state complaints alleging countries' violations of core labor standards. The ILO would then authorize ILO members to invoke the WTO general exceptions clause if violations were found. As a result, the norm-interpreting and labor-related dispute settlement work would be left to the ILO and the WTO would be restricted to its traditional role of determining the appropriate level of trade retaliation under WTO rules.

Another approach to WTO rule change is to develop a new WTO agreement on workers' rights similar to the agreements on Trade-Related Aspects of Intellectual Property Rights and Trade-Related Investment Measures. The agreement would oblige WTO member countries to respect ILO-defined core workers' rights, subject disputes regarding violations of these obligations to formal WTO dispute settlement, and authorize the withdrawal of trade concessions if a violation is found. As an affirmative requirement applicable equally to all WTO members, rather than an exception likely invoked by only a few members against a handful of others, this approach could enjoy broader political legitimacy and motivate more widespread compliance with ILO standards than amending WTO Article XX. Existing WTO dispute settlement mechanisms may be ill-suited for many workers' rights disputes, however, since they provide for little public participation, can be somewhat slow, and offer very limited remedial options. In addition, such an approach would again require either WTO workers' rights expertise or closer WTO-ILO collaboration. Establishing the ILO mechanism proposed above, however, could help prevent many of these potential problems.

Whether WTO rules are changed to include a general exception for measures related to core workers' rights or to establish affirmative obligations to respect those rights and whether the primary responsibility for adjudicating disputes regarding these rules rests with the WTO, the ILO, or is shared, the fundamental challenge remains to create the political will among ILO and WTO members to consider such changes. The following recommendations outline an approach the United States can take to start building the necessary consensus for reform.

- Make integration of core workers' rights into the international trading regime a top priority and communicate that priority publicly and consistently to trading partners. Since the Singapore Ministerial Declaration, the United States has at times sent mixed signals about the importance of workers' rights relative to its other trade policy goals. Real progress will not be possible until other countries understand that the United States is serious about effectively addressing workers' rights in global trade rules. The United States should not agree to new WTO trade concessions until there is also an agreement to incorporate workers' rights into WTO rules. The United States can begin using existing WTO mechanisms to signal its commitment by including workers' rights issues in discussions with newly acceding countries, raising workers' rights problems in Trade Policy Reviews of individual countries, and advocating expansive interpretations of the existing prison labor and public morals exceptions in WTO rules.
- Cultivate developed and developing country allies. The United States should have some natural allies in its existing FTA partners and others that are already subject to trade-related workers' rights commitments and stand to gain if these commitments are universalized. In addition, a coherent global regime linking trade and workers' rights would provide a needed trade advantage to those developing countries striving to protect core workers' rights and becoming increasingly concerned about competition from China and other countries that fail to do so.
- Emphasize reciprocity and accept criticism. It should not be assumed that rules linking trade and workers' rights will uniformly advantage developed countries over developing countries. As detailed earlier, the United States falls far short of upholding core workers' rights in a number of key areas.
- Build in public participation and transparency. Fears about the abuse of labor rights-related trade measures for protectionist purposes may be assuaged if the enforcement mechanism guarantees an opportunity for workers' representatives in the country where

violations have been alleged to participate in the process. While participation by workers' representatives globally as well as by the public at large should also be welcome, the system will enjoy greater legitimacy if complaints are received from or at least verified by the workers directly affected.

- Ensure countries have the resources to comply. The United States should boost labor-related development aid to ensure that countries that want to respect workers' rights have the means to do so and that trade measures are focused on those nations which lack the political will to protect these basic rights.
- Think creatively about trade-offs. The United States should engage key developing countries in a broader discussion about the reform and revitalization of WTO rules, examining their concerns about shortcomings in international economic policy in exchange for their consideration of strong WTO workers' rights requirements. Given the current shaky state of the Doha Round trade negotiations, there may be significant room to consider innovative approaches that address developing country concerns, including declining terms of trade, preference erosion, need for reform in agriculture and other markets, supply management arrangements, domestic policy space for development, currency and tax practices, debt relief, and international financial regulation.

Bringing Workers' Rights into U.S. Free Trade Accords

In contrast to the WTO, U.S. FTAs, beginning with the North American Free Trade Agreement (NAFTA), have included a variety of labor rights provisions. In May 2007, congressional leaders and the United States Trade Representative (USTR) unveiled yet another proposal: a new trade policy template that has since been applied to pending U.S. agreements with Peru, Panama, Colombia, and Korea. At this writing, the U.S.–Peru FTA is the only one of these FTAs to have been approved by Congress.

The new template-based workers' rights provisions are an important step forward, but they also will almost certainly be inadequate. They fail to fully remedy important shortcomings plaguing existing U.S. FTA labor rights provisions and leave intact a fundamentally flawed enforcement model.

The United States should fix the substantive weaknesses remaining in the template-based labor provisions and forge a new mechanism to guarantee their enforcement. If Congress grants the president trade negotiating authority in exchange for meeting certain negotiating objectives, that authority should include binding requirements that mandate this new approach as well as threshold workers' rights criteria for selecting potential FTA partners, ensuring that workers' rights are finally protected in the context of U.S. trade agreements.

All FTAs should, at a minimum, categorically require that parties' national laws uphold at least the core labor rights in the ILO Declaration and that those laws, as well as any laws addressing acceptable conditions of work, be effectively enforced in trade- and investment-related sectors. No caveats or qualifiers should undermine these basic obligations, and serious consideration should be given to extending them as well to cover state and local laws and their enforcement.

The new template-based workers' rights provisions come closer to this standard than those in any prior U.S. FTA, but they still fall well short. They finally eliminate the escape clause that permits parties to allocate grossly insufficient resources for labor law enforcement so long as the resource allocation decision is "bona fide" and reflects a "reasonable exercise of . . . discretion."[29] But the new provisions retain a loophole establishing that a breach of FTA labor provisions only violates the accord if it occurs in a manner "affecting trade or investment between the Parties."[30] And a confusing footnote may yet undermine the language in the main text that for the first time purports to require that parties not only effectively enforce their national labor laws but also "adopt and maintain," in both law and practice, the "rights" listed in the ILO Declaration.[31]

Adopting and Maintaining Fundamental Workers' "Rights"

The new template-based FTA labor provision that finally requires parties to "adopt and maintain" in their national laws and "practice thereunder" the workers' "rights" listed in the ILO Declaration is qualified by a footnote clarifying that these obligations, "as they relate to the ILO, refer only to the ILO Declaration."[32] The footnote is confusing, potentially makes the provision internally contradictory, and should be eliminated.

Unlike the plain language of the new template-based provision, the ILO Declaration obligates members to respect, promote, and realize "*the principles* concerning the fundamental rights" (emphasis added) in the declaration, not the rights themselves. Rights are defined in international instruments and interpretative jurisprudence. In contrast, while the declaration clarifies that "principles . . . have been expressed and developed in the form of specific rights and obligations" in ILO conventions, there is no international consensus on the extent to which the principles incorporate these "specific rights and obligations." As a result, the principles' meaning is unclear and heavily debated.

An FTA arbitral panel hearing a dispute under this new template-based FTA provision could interpret the footnote as benign and meaningless and rely fully and faithfully on the ILO conventions and jurisprudence to interpret FTA parties' ILO-related obligations. It could also find, however, that as a result of the footnote, parties are obligated to "adopt and maintain" only the principles concerning fundamental workers' rights, incorporating the ILO Declaration's ambiguity. Under such a scenario, the panel could conclude that it has broad discretion regarding whether to rely heavily or lightly on relevant ILO conventions and jurisprudence to interpret this obligation or even that it is confined by the footnote's plain language to "refer only to" the four corners of "the ILO Declaration." Such a narrow interpretation of the arcane footnote could significantly weaken FTA parties' ILO-related obligations and render them largely unjusticiable, subverting the clear intent of the accord's main text.

Coverage for All Workers in Trade- and Investment-Related Sectors

If the application of FTA workers' rights provisions is to be limited to certain sectors, the limitation should be narrowly drafted to ensure the requirements extend at least to all trade- and investment-related matters. Restricting their application only to conduct "*affecting* trade or investment between the Parties" (emphasis added) could potentially overreach. This limitation might be interpreted, for example, as requiring the difficult showing that anti-union discrimination in a U.S. trading partner leads directly to lower labor costs, correspondingly cheaper exports, and a resulting increase in that country's trade with the United States.

This loophole should be closed, building on the example of NAFTA, which makes any "trade-related" breach of a workers' rights provision sanctionable. U.S. FTAs should clarify that workers' rights protections extend to workers in at least all "trade- or investment-related sectors," regardless of whether the violation of their rights can be shown to "affect" trade or investment with the United States.

In addition, the United States should consider establishing an incentive structure based loosely on the U.S.-Cambodia Bilateral Textile Agreement, which linked increased U.S. market access for Cambodian textiles to increased respect for Cambodian textile workers' rights. The new incentive could, for example, accelerate FTA benefit phase-in for parties that fulfill FTA workers' rights requirements not only in trade- and investment-related sectors but throughout their economies. Under this model, parties could apply for the incentive to an independent body—such as that proposed below for the effective enforcement of FTA labor provisions—and gain additional duty-free access for each year they demonstrate such widespread respect for workers' rights.

No Free-Rider Countries

There should also be no exceptions to the requirement that countries exporting goods under U.S. FTAs meet FTA labor obligations. Unfortunately, the U.S.-Singapore FTA and the proposed U.S.-South Korea FTA create the possibility that the accords' benefits could be extended to nonparty countries that, by definition, are not bound by any of the agreements' obligations, including those on workers' rights. As a result, goods produced under abusive labor conditions in these nonparty countries could legally enter the United States under the accords.

The U.S.-Singapore FTA includes an integrated sourcing initiative (ISI) listing electronic and high-tech goods to be treated as originating in the United States and Singapore, despite being produced in nonparty countries, so long as they pass through one FTA party on the way to the other. For example, cell phones manufactured in the Indonesian islands of Bintan and Batam—frequently cited as ISI beneficiaries—could pass through Singapore and enter the United States under the FTA.[33] Yet according to the State Department, Indonesia fails to effectively protect any of the fundamental labor rights listed in the ILO Declaration.[34] And the same could be true of the many other nonparty countries that could potentially enjoy FTA benefits with no strings attached under the ISI.

Similarly, Annex 22-B of the pending U.S.-South Korea FTA mandates the creation of a committee to recommend North Korean "outward processing zones" for potential accord coverage. Although Annex 22-B establishes workers' rights criteria for the committee to consider, they fall far short of the new template-based labor provisions in the main accord, including only "labor standards and practices" prevailing in the zone, with "due reference" to be given to an undefined set of "relevant international norms" and the egregious workers' rights situation "elsewhere in the local economy."[35] And once the FTA is legislatively amended to cover a zone that fulfills this low workers' rights threshold, that zone is under no further labor-related obligations, which is particularly troubling given North Korea's record as one of the world's most closed countries and worst human rights violators.[36]

This free-rider problem should be remedied in the U.S.-Singapore and U.S.-South Korea FTAs and prevented in all future accords. If any FTA is to allow for coverage of nonparty goods, the agreement should require nonparty countries to meet the main accord's labor rights requirements and require immediate termination of benefits upon a credible showing of violation. The accords should also establish meaningful procedures to ensure such compliance, including a public complaints process and an annual compliance assessment that includes in-country worksite monitoring visits.

Adequate Enforcement Mechanisms

Even if the myriad weaknesses afflicting existing U.S. FTA labor rights provisions are remedied, workers' rights will not be effectively protected without a strong enforcement mechanism. With the notable exception of the U.S.-Jordan FTA, all U.S. FTAs in force at this writing establish mechanisms for enforcing labor rights provisions that are different from and inferior to those available to enforce commercial requirements. The new template-based FTA language remedies this shortcoming in agreements negotiated with Peru, Panama, Colombia, and South Korea by returning to the U.S.-Jordan FTA model, creating one enforcement procedure for most FTA provisions.[37]

This remedy, however, will not be sufficient to protect workers' rights in the context of U.S. free trade accords. A new enforcement mechanism is needed that is independent of FTA parties' political whims. Under the current model, in most cases, only parties can move complaints of noncompliance with FTA provisions through dispute settlement procedures and, ultimately, to an arbitral panel empowered to impose penalties. As a result, enforcement of most FTA provisions is more dependent on geopolitical and other strategic considerations than levels of actual accord compliance. Workers' rights considerations generally rank near the bottom of issues on which countries are willing to strain diplomatic relations, however, and largely as a result, no case alleging violation of FTA labor rights commitments has ever come close to reaching an arbitral panel for final dispute resolution.

A new FTA model should create a well-funded, nonpolitical body, independent of the parties and with exclusive jurisdiction over complaints, submitted by interested members of the public or accord parties, alleging violation of FTA workers' rights requirements.[38] The decision whether to proceed with an investigation, consultation, or arbitration or to authorize penalties should rest solely with this body and be made after careful consideration of any relevant interventions from complainants or other interested parties throughout the process. In the event that penalties are authorized, the body should recommend concrete measures to remedy violations identified and annually authorize penalties until full remediation is confirmed.

The body should be composed following procedures similar to those for convening arbitral panels under NAFTA's labor side agreement and other recently concluded FTAs, which provide for the selection of panel-ists from a large roster of experts, who are chosen by the parties "strictly on the basis of objectivity, reliability and sound judgment" and who must be "independent of, and not be affiliated with or take instructions from, any Party."[39] Relying on this model, the independence and objec-tivity currently reserved for FTA arbitral panel deliberations initiated by governments would be extended throughout the workers' rights-related enforcement process and apply to complaints from the public, as well.

Strengthening U.S. Trade Preference Programs' Workers' Rights Criteria

The United States has maintained unilateral trade preferences for devel-oping countries for decades and first added workers' rights to the eligi-bility criteria in 1984. Today, the United States has two basic levels of preference programs—a broad program for all developing countries (the Generalized System of Preferences, or GSP) and supplemental pro-grams for the Caribbean, Andean, and African regions that provide additional market access and contain slightly different eligibility criteria.

The workers' rights requirements in the programs vary slightly, from mandating that beneficiaries take steps toward affording "internation-ally recognized worker rights" to requiring that they make continual progress toward their protection.[40] No program, however, demands absolute respect for these rights in both law and practice. And no pro-gram defines "internationally recognized worker rights" to include, at a minimum, all four fundamental labor rights; they all omit the elimina-tion of employment and occupation discrimination.

While members of the public may petition for the withdrawal of trade preferences on workers' rights grounds, the president decides whether or not to accept these petitions and withdraw trade benefits, a decision not subject to judicial review. In addition, the programs do not create monitoring mechanisms to track violations and set benchmarks for improvements. As a result, the administration of the programs has been uneven. While the credible threat of the withdrawal of trade preferences has in some cases provided a powerful incentive for countries to improve respect for workers' rights, the programs' vague standards and inconsis-tent enforcement have frustrated more sustained progress.[41]

Following, in part, the new FTA model recommended above, the United States should remedy the shortcomings that have historically prevented U.S. trade preference programs from adequately protecting workers' rights.[42] All programs should categorically require that benefi-ciaries' laws uphold at least the core labor rights in the ILO Declaration and that those laws and any addressing acceptable conditions of work be effectively enforced in trade-related sectors. The programs should also encourage respect for workers' rights throughout each beneficiary, not solely in traded sectors, with incentive structures awarding increased market access to those countries that can demonstrate nationwide respect for labor rights. For countries violating programs' workers' rights requirements, loss of beneficiary status, in whole or in carefully targeted part, should be mandatory, with reinstatement only upon an affirmative showing of compliance.[43]

An effective mechanism should be created to monitor and enforce compliance and to administer the special incentive program, drawing heavily from proposals in the New Partnership for Development Act of 2007.[44] The legislation would create a new preference program with a special oversight office, staffed in part by experienced jurists and labor inspectors. The office would be charged with receiving and evaluating public petitions submitted throughout the year alleging violation of the program's workers' rights requirements and issuing decisions and remediation recommendations.[45] It would also be responsible for monitoring beneficiaries' compliance with the labor rights criteria, gathering information from the ILO, civil society, and in-country workplace visits, and preparing reports on those findings. An annual report assessing, among other issues, countries' compliance with workers' rights requirements would be submitted annually to Congress and considered in the president's annual evaluation of beneficiary status eligibility.

International Financial Assistance and the Protection of Workers' Rights

In addition to using trade benefits to promote respect for core workers' rights, the United States should also ensure that financial assistance provided to foreign countries or companies through international financial institutions (IFIs) and domestic entities such as the Overseas Private Investment Corporation (OPIC) encourage labor rights compliance.

The IFIs lack comprehensive policies to ensure that their programs uphold core workers' rights, to guarantee the effectiveness of their labor-related promotional efforts, or to link countries' financing to their workers' rights records.[46] Such policies are urgently needed to address workers' rights issues that arise in the context of IFI policy lending and in IFI-backed public and private-sector projects.

In the policy lending arena, the International Monetary Fund (IMF) and World Bank in particular have often been criticized for requiring or recommending that borrowing countries adopt policies such as labor market flexibility reforms, privatization, and reductions in public employment that can, absent the appropriate safeguards that the IFIs are sorely lacking, undermine core workers' rights.[47] In addition, while there have been some IFI efforts to fund labor rights promotion activities, there is little detailed policy to guide and increase such efforts.

In contrast, there has been some important progress on workers' rights in IFI project financing.[48] In May 2006, the World Bank's International Finance Corporation (IFC) adopted a policy requiring its private-sector projects to comply with core workers' rights and a number of other labor standards,[49] with a few notable caveats, including that a company may take only partial steps toward meeting its obligations on freedom of association when operating in a country that bars independent trade unions. In December 2006, the bank announced it would also require all public infrastructure projects it finances to comply with the ILO's core labor standards.[50]

Similarly, OPIC also lacks an adequate workers' rights policy. U.S. law allows OPIC to support private-sector projects in any GSP beneficiary country, largely incorporating the weak GSP workers' rights criteria discussed earlier.[51] Although OPIC includes workers' rights guarantees in its individual funding contracts, it lacks consistent, transparent, and effective monitoring and compliance procedures to apply them, rendering enforcement efforts ad hoc at best. Most oversight occurs through inherently unreliable, confidential project self-reporting. OPIC selects only a handful of its projects for on-site monitoring and, even then, workers' rights is only one of many issues addressed and results are not publicly disclosed, producing superficial and unverifiable labor reviews. And although OPIC will investigate workers' rights-related complaints as they arise, the narrow scope of violations reviewable by OPIC's formal compliance mechanism leaves the resolution of many labor-related complaints entirely at the discretion of OPIC management.[52]

To remedy these deficiencies and begin to ensure that financial assistance for foreign countries and companies encourages rather than undermines respect for workers' rights, the United States should implement the following recommendations:

- Establish a coherent policy position on workers' rights at the IFIs that is strongly advocated at all levels—in funding authorizations, replenishment negotiations, U.S. Executive Director (USED) interventions, and votes and policy discussions.[53] The United States should oppose any IFI program that is not subject to binding safeguard policies to ensure that core workers' rights are upheld within that program. The United States should work with the IFIs to identify priority countries for promotion of workers' rights and set funding goals for those programs. The United States should also begin discussions on how IFI funding might be affected for countries that repeatedly and seriously violate core workers' rights, exploring possible threshold eligibility criteria for IFI assistance or the attachment of conditions to IFI loans to require improvements in countries' labor laws and practice.

• Require that all projects funded by OPIC or other bilateral financing vehicles fully comply with core workers' rights and require public disclosure of all such projects. To facilitate compliance, monitoring and reporting procedures, as well as complaint and other compliance mechanisms, should consistently apply to all projects, be fully transparent, and be easily accessible to workers' representatives.

Development Aid Targeted on Workers' Rights

The United States should also ensure that its development aid programs play a central role in the promotion of core workers' rights abroad. Development aid can provide countries with the financial means, technical expertise, and incentive to improve compliance with core workers' rights. Unfortunately, U.S. general development aid currently fails to prioritize workers' rights, and assistance specifically intended to encourage respect for labor rights abroad is sorely inadequate.

For example, the Millennium Challenge Corporation (MCC), which directs general development assistance to countries that score well on 17 different performance indicators, has no indicator specifically dedicated to measuring countries' compliance with core workers' rights.[54] Instead, partial workers' rights indicia are subsumed within other MCC indicators, allowing violators of workers' rights to still score well on overall performance benchmarks. Thus, countries seeking aid from the MCC face little incentive to prioritize labor rights compliance.

In addition, the Department of Labor's Bureau of International Labor Affairs (ILAB), the U.S. agency charged specifically with providing international labor-related technical assistance, has seen its budget fall by more than 50 percent from 2004 to 2006. And the Bush administration's most recent funding request would again cut the department's budget by more than 80 percent from 2007 appropriations.[55]

Although contributions reported from other U.S. agencies with far less labor expertise than ILAB make it appear that the overall funding for workers' rights-related development assistance has remained relatively stable under the Bush administration, the reporting is misleading. Funding tagged as labor-related trade capacity building assistance has increasingly gone not to programs that promote core workers' rights but to unrelated programs, such as those that develop small businesses or create new export opportunities.[56] Furthermore, trade capacity building labor-related assistance has been disproportionately awarded to FTA partner countries, at the expense of countries participating in U.S. trade preference programs, which as discussed earlier, also include labor rights eligibility criteria.

To address these shortcomings and revitalize and refocus development aid to promote fundamental workers' rights abroad effectively, the United States should adopt the following recommendations:

- Increase labor-related development aid to reflect the severe needs in developing countries and ensure that the aid is clearly focused on core workers' rights, targeting priorities identified by workers' organizations in particular. The proposed New Partnership for Development Act of 2007 provides an instructive model, requiring the creation of a Workforce Competitiveness Program to, among other goals, provide assistance to workers' organizations to increase their capacity to promote core labor rights and, in coordination with such organizations, develop workers' rights programs and projects.
- The United States should coordinate its aid efforts with its trade and investment policies so that aid programs help countries meet eligibility criteria for trade and financing benefits, drawing from the proposed Workforce Competitiveness Program, designed in part to help facilitate compliance with the labor rights criteria of the New Partnership for Development Act of 2007.
- The United States should better coordinate its aid efforts internationally and make maximum use of the ILO. The ILO has launched important programs on core workers' rights, such as the Decent Work Campaign, that deserve sustained and vigorous U.S. support. The proposed New Partnership for Development Act of 2007 again provides a useful model, requiring that the Workforce Competitiveness Program develop projects and programs with the ILO to help promote compliance with core workers' rights.
- To the extent that the United States conditions aid on meeting certain performance benchmarks, as under the MCC program, the United States should include a separate indicator specifically dedicated to core workers' rights.

Taking the Lead on Workers' Rights

As part of its human rights policy agenda, the United States should develop and implement a coherent, well-funded, and multifaceted strategy for promoting workers' rights around the world. The strategy should integrate promotional tools, such as labor rights-related aid and development finance, with concrete compliance incentives, such as trade conditionality. It should also include amendment of weak U.S. labor laws to comply fully with ILO core workers' rights, ensuring that U.S. advocacy for such change of global rules is credible. Such a strategy should be directed by the highest levels of government to maximize resource leveraging, facilitate interagency information sharing and collaboration, and ensure that all available policy tools are used to promote the same priorities. Only with such a coordinated, comprehensive, and committed strategy at home can the United States effectively advocate abroad for greater coherence in global rulemaking on workers' rights and finally take the lead in ensuring that respect for core workers' rights becomes an international priority.

Chapter 10

Back to the Basics
*Making a Commitment to Women's
Human Rights*

REGAN E. RALPH

In one form or another, human rights have been linked explicitly to U.S. foreign policy since the 1970s. From one perspective the increased emphasis on human rights was revolutionary—challenging the long-held belief that national interest and human rights are largely incompatible. But looked at another way, the idea of promoting justice and dignity around the world was simply consistent with America's tradition of exceptionalism—the idea that this nation is uniquely situated to promote democracy and liberty in other countries because it is a nation founded on values (life, liberty, and the pursuit of happiness) that could and should benefit people regardless of where they live. From this exceptionalist belief in the unique moral role of the United States two assumptions have followed: first, that the country must lead the way, by force if necessary, so that others might benefit from similar values and a similar form of government; and, second, that because the United States *is* exceptional and powerful, it need not conform to the human rights standards it urges upon others nor play by the same rules because it can be trusted to police itself. Sometimes the United States even goes so far as to ignore some of those human rights norms that are widely accepted by others, including, for example, the prohibition against the death penalty.

At first glance it might seem that the first of these assumptions serves the interests of human rights well. Isn't it desirable to have the world's most powerful nation touting the importance of liberty, equality, and justice and integrating an emphasis on these values into its dealings with other countries? The answer is "not necessarily." U.S. leadership matters but its effectiveness is too often compromised by inconsistency and hypocrisy. As we know all too well from the recent experience in Iraq, the United States can do more harm to the cause of human rights than good when it invokes the language of freedom and human rights but fails to carry out those principles in practice.

It is the second assumption upon which I want to focus, for the case of women's human rights illustrates how damaging an exceptionalist approach that indulges in the selective embrace and application of human rights protections can be. To take just one example: the United States remains the only industrialized nation that has not ratified the Convention on the Elimination of Discrimination Against Women, the signal women's human rights treaty that would set standards of equality for women both in the United States and abroad. The harm done to women's human rights by this failure reveals dramatically both the U. S. government's hypocrisy when it claims to be a leader on human rights in general and the insincerity of its commitment to women's human rights in particular. The United States cannot credibly claim to be a leader on human rights while subverting women's human rights; it cannot claim to promote women's human rights while failing to ratify or respect the international frameworks that protect those rights; and it cannot claim to promote freedom and democracy around the world while curtailing women's freedoms in order to satisfy a domestic political constituency.[1]

Far from being a leader on women's human rights, the United States has worked systematically to dismantle protections for such rights at the international level, undermined women's rights in the United States, and cynically deployed the language of women's human rights to provide unconvincing cover for everything from war to health policies that put women's lives at risk (the Bush administration, for example, has defended the invasions of Afghanistan and Iraq on the grounds that they have improved women's status and ability to enjoy their rights).[2] It has claimed to be actively defending women's rights around the globe while at the same time placing restrictions on U.S. funding of international efforts to improve women's reproductive health, to fight the spread of HIV/AIDS, and to combat trafficking—all actions that have resulted in women, especially poor women, losing access to vital services. While the recent U.S. track record reveals progress on some women's human rights concerns, that tentative progress is overshadowed by the selective approach to women's human rights displayed in Bush administration policies and statements and by the damage that has been done to international standards designed to promote and protect women's human rights in the first place. This administration has promoted women's rights only narrowly and on limited issues while crippling women's ability to act and be recognized as human beings in other areas.

Ultimately, policymakers know what needs to be done on key women's human rights concerns. Human rights standards offer clear benchmarks and popular opinion supports improving women's status as a part of U.S. foreign policy.[3] Moreover, ample evidence supports the conclusion that great benefits result from policies that meaningfully promote women's equality, women's access to health and education, economic participation and opportunity. Yet no U.S. administration has taken the steps to implement a policy that would begin to dismantle the structures that keep women poor, subordinate, and powerless.

Stalled Momentum

More than 10 years ago women and governments from around the world gathered in Beijing at the Fourth World Conference on Women to proclaim that "women's rights are human rights." The 1990s were heady days for women's human rights advocates. At the 1993 United Nations World Conference on Human Rights in Vienna, women won recognition that their rights and status are entitled to human rights protections. World leaders decried violence and discrimination against women and pledged to respond to violations of women's rights. In Cairo in 1994, at the International Conference on Population and Development, the revolution continued when advocates upended the traditional paradigm on population and development to demand that women no longer be treated as objects to be manipulated in the pursuit of slowing population growth but actors whose control over their bodies and reproductive choices should be recognized and protected. And finally in Beijing in 1995, governments acknowledged their complicity in violations of women's human rights. They pledged to promote women's education, health, and economic and political participation with resources, programs, and policies and to change their laws and practices to guarantee women's equality.

Today it is commonplace not just for advocates but also for academic researchers and political leaders to acknowledge the central role that women play in economic and political development. Where women are well educated and healthy, communities thrive. On a larger scale, women's well-being and status are critical to economic development, active civil society, and good governance. According to Council on Foreign Relations scholar Isobel Coleman, "those [countries] that suppress women are likely to stagnate economically, fail to develop democratic institutions, and become more prone to extremism."[4] The U.S. government has declared that women's rights are key to promoting strategic goals, such as fostering democracy and promoting development.[5] International institutions such as the World Bank reinforce this message.[6]

The evidence clearly establishes that not only is promoting women's rights the right thing to do; it is the smart thing to do as well.

All this does not mean, however, that the promotion of women's human rights is a "done deal" or even lacking in controversy. To the contrary, the momentum of the 1990s has slowed, if not stagnated. Some governments and conservative political forces have grown more vociferous in their efforts to paint women's rights as a societal ill rather than a boon. Women's rights advocates in countries from Guatemala and Uganda to Pakistan find themselves fighting battles over basic issues like the right of women to inherit property, to live free from violence, and to make decisions affecting their own bodily integrity. It is as if the gains of the 1990s had evaporated with nary a trace and the research about the importance of women's rights meant nothing. Under the Bush administration the United States has contributed to the stagnation on women's human rights by deciding selectively which rights will be respected (and when and where) rather than supporting the basic building blocks of women's equality. The consequences of this failure in leadership are devastating for women—in the United States and in countries around the world.

The price paid by women and their communities is profound. The denial of women's rights is a constant in every society. In all societies violence against women is routine and often condoned by official action or indifference. A 2005 report by the World Economic Forum reveals that in not one of the 58 countries studied had women achieved equality in five critical areas: economic participation, economic opportunity, political empowerment, educational attainment, and health and well-being.[7] Two-thirds of the world's estimated 771 million illiterate adults are women. In three regions of the world—South Asia, sub-Saharan Africa, and the Arab states—only half of all women are literate. Every year an estimated 500,000 women die in childbirth and millions more are maimed for life. In most cases maternal mortality and morbidity would be preventable if women had access to a minimum level of reproductive and sexual health services. Two-thirds of the world's poorest people are women; a considerable part of women's economic exclusion and poor pay is attributable to sex discrimination. The majority of the 1.5 billion people living on one dollar a day are women, and research suggests that the gap between the number of men living in poverty compared to that of women has widened over the past 10 years.

In the face of such statistics and given the social and legal obstacles to change, it is clear that achieving women's equality and respect for women's rights will be an agonizingly slow process. With such a long way to go, we cannot afford for policymakers in the world's most powerful country—especially with millions of aid dollars in play—to indulge in backward steps, hollow statements, and counterproductive policies. When international standards are undermined, when support for women's rights is compromised, the impact is felt not in the halls of the United Nations but in the everyday lives of women around the world.

Do We Understand the Problem?

One of the givens among human rights advocates is that it is essential to understand the nature of the human rights problem or abuse being tackled, as well as who is responsible for it, in order to craft appropriate remedies and effective solutions. When women's rights advocates around the globe began using human rights tools to challenge abuses against them, they started with the starkest example of women's subordination: violence. Violence against women occurs in prison cells and police stations and when warring factions raid villages; it also takes place at the hands of family members, employers, and community leaders. Initially advocates called for a better response to individual acts of violence but they soon realized that violence against women would be prevented only if the problem of women's second-class status, which makes them vulnerable to most gender-based violence in the first place, was also addressed.

One of the major accomplishments of women's rights advocacy, then, has been to win the recognition that violence in women's lives—and not only that which takes place in a prison cell or interrogation room—is indulged, condoned, and tolerated by societies and officials the world over. Violence and the threat of violence perpetuate women's subordination to men and marginalization in the economic and political lives of their countries. Women are subject to violence because they are women and because their abusers do not fear any consequences. And with such violence—whether at home or on the fields of war—women's subordination is reinforced; their capacity to change their circumstances—to increase their income, to protect their physical integrity, to guard their health—becomes less and less. The challenge for the next U.S. administration will be to craft a policy on women's human rights that recognizes and responds to the comprehensive nature of women's oppression.

Media coverage and policymaker attention tend to focus on isolated outrages against women or the most extreme cases—like rape in war or trafficking into forced prostitution. These abuses, however, almost always take place in a context in which women's relative lack of power and autonomy make them a target for abuse and also make it harder to find successful solutions. In a July 2007 statement, for example, the United Nations special rapporteur on violence against women observed that rampant sexual violence carried out by armed groups in eastern Congo—where an estimated four million have been killed and hundreds of thousands displaced in a conflict that has raged off and on since the late 1990s—is less a horrifying departure from the norm than just one more manifestation of the violence women in the area experience in all aspects of their lives. "Violence against women seems to be perceived by large sectors of society to be normal," the rapporteur observed. Women in the Democratic Republic of Congo, she noted further, disproportionately bear the burdens of poverty; preventing violence and remedying discrimination against women are thus essential to the country's future. "Empowerment and equality of women, socio-economic development and change of mentalities on gender must be prioritized as integral components of the reconstruction process if sustainable and just peace is to be achieved in the Democratic Republic of Congo," she said. Moreover, "the widespread use of sexual violence in the armed conflict seems to have become a generalized aspect of the overall oppression of women in Congo. Such behavioral norms will therefore remain a serious problem in the future—regardless of the security situation, unless Government and society are willing to make a serious effort to fundamentally change the prevailing gender relations that subordinate and devalue women."[8]

Beyond the price that women pay in terms of physical harm, lack of education, inescapable poverty, and ill health, women's inequality also retards a society's economic and political development. Denying women's rights worsens gender disparities that in turn make it difficult for women to play constructive roles in the economic and political life of their countries. This case is made compellingly in a groundbreaking series of reports prepared for the United Nations Development Program that identify the deficit in women's rights as one of three main reasons—the others being deficits in knowledge and political freedom—that development has been stunted in the Arab region despite its natural wealth and potential for economic and social progress. Women in the region suffer unacceptably poor health indicators and high illiteracy rates; economic participation by Arab women is the lowest in the world; violence against women is widespread and remains largely a hidden problem. Without a doubt these depressing statistics tell a story of women's inferior status and of legal and social discrimination. Countries throughout the region have paid a staggering price to keep women subordinate and now everyone suffers the consequences in the form of stagnant economies, authoritarian political structures, and limited personal freedoms.

The point of these reports, however, is not simply to catalog the ills affecting women in the Arab region but more importantly to illustrate the potential of the region to transform its fortunes, were it to tap the full participation of women. For Arab societies to develop and progress consistent with their potential, the authors maintain, there must be:

- Complete equality of opportunity between women and men in the acquisition and employment of human capabilities;
- Guaranteed rights of citizenship for all women on equal footing with men;
- Acknowledgement of and respect for differences between the sexes. Women are different from men but that in no way implies they are deficient. Under no conditions is it acceptable to use gender differences to support theories of inequality between the sexes or any form of sexual discrimination.[9]

That these discussions are taking place with the participation of civil society and academics and the support of governments and international institutions is a sign of progress in the long-term struggle to change women's status. The message of such conversations is available to U.S. policymakers if they are serious about supporting women's rights and economic and political development: support women's efforts to be educated and to work; protect women from subordination and vulnerability to violence by enshrining and enforcing women's legal rights; recognize that women's well-being is valuable—not threatening—to society; and back the national and international structures and standards that support women's rights.

These messages have been largely ignored until now by those setting the human rights agenda in the United States. The approach to high-profile women's rights issues such as trafficking is atomized and ineffective. And, as noted, it is difficult for the United States to promote the importance of women's legal rights outside its borders when it has not ratified the most important human rights treaty dealing with women's status—the Convention on the Elimination of Discrimination Against Women (CEDAW). Often described as an international bill of rights for women, CEDAW defines discrimination against women and sets a framework for national action to end such discrimination. It is the first international treaty to comprehensively elaborate fundamental rights for women in politics, health care, education, economics, employment, law, property, and marriage and family relations. The United States finds itself in the company of countries like Iran, Sudan, and Somalia in being one of the few countries that has not ratified CEDAW.

U.S. recalcitrance on CEDAW has been justified in both exceptionalist terms—the rights of women in the United States are firmly established and therefore the United States would not benefit from endorsing and agreeing to respect international standards of women's equality—and cultural relativist terms: embracing women's equality through an international treaty forces other countries to adopt standards particular to Western culture. The latter argument does not stand up to a moment's scrutiny given that almost every other country in the world has ratified the treaty and that women's rights activists in countries from Saudi Arabia to Peru to Israel to Mongolia have used the treaty's provisions to support their calls for legal and social reforms, access to education, and improved health care for women. Nor is women's equality an unassailable fact of life in the United States. Just ask the advocates who are fighting now to restore teeth to the country's anti-discrimination laws or trying to ensure that women's reproductive health is not compromised by judges who trust their own judgment over that of women and their doctors. Moreover, the United States has ratified human rights treaties protecting civil and political rights and prohibiting torture—all rights that are presumably "firmly established" in American law.

Denounce and Ignore

U.S. policymakers know (and should not pretend otherwise) that their decision not to support an international human rights treaty has consequences in large part because the United States has carved out a leadership role for itself in promoting human rights and dignity. International human rights standards gain enhanced credibility when they are endorsed and respected by a powerful country. Conversely, when the United States refuses to endorse a set of standards, it calls their legitimacy into question. Thus in the case of CEDAW, the two strains of exceptionalism cut against each other. By asserting that its record on women's equality exempts it from participating in international structures to promote women's rights, the United States undermines those standards and thus loses its credibility as an international advocate for women. This loss of credibility and thus effectiveness is compounded by the tendency of U.S. administrations to act as if rhetoric were policy enough, regardless of implementation. Put another way, to date U.S. efforts in support of women's human rights have started and stopped with denunciation of bad practices and with praise of women's contributions to society.

Although many of the world's women are deeply skeptical now that U.S. support has become something of a poison apple because of the country's association with human rights abuses and authoritarian regimes as well as its invocation of human rights to justify the invasion of Iraq, how the United States meets its obligations to protect, respect, and promote human rights at home and internationally matters. By claiming the mantle of leadership, by conceiving of an exceptional role for itself, by using its authority and influence to place women's human rights onto the international agenda, the United States has taken on a responsibility to women everywhere. When the United States acts, whether for or against women's human rights, other governments respond.

In the past the United States has been better able to hold others to account because it supported international human rights standards and showed through actions that it took them seriously. U.S. leadership played a significant role in the 1990s in promoting the notion that women's rights are human rights. During the Clinton administration, First Lady Hillary Rodham Clinton and Secretary of State Madeleine Albright spoke consistently and forcefully about the importance of women's human rights. After years of work by women's human rights activists, the U.S. Congress mandated that the State Department appoint a senior coordinator on international women's issues, an office that worked closely with the secretary of state to integrate women's human rights concerns into U.S. statements and policies on issues such as trafficking and women's political participation. Never before had women's human rights issues been so visible. As human rights advocates of every stripe know, visibility is the first step toward action. As such, these efforts represented signs of progress.

But U.S. policy seems to be stuck at the "acknowledge and denounce" stage. Moving forward, there are at least two obstacles that must be removed to allow for U.S. leadership on women's human rights. The first is a failure of implementation. Democratic and Republican administrations both have produced high-level rhetoric proclaiming the centrality of women's human rights to U.S. foreign policy. In March 2003, Ambassador Ellen Sauerbrey, then U.S. representative to the United Nations Commission on the Status of Women, asserted, "Respect for women is an imperative of U.S. foreign policy and an integral part of the U.S. National Security Strategy. As President George W. Bush said in his January 2002 State of the Union Address: 'America will always stand firm for the non-negotiable demands of human dignity: the rule of law; limits on the power of the state; respect for women; private property; free speech; equal justice; and religious tolerance.'"[10]

In 2005, on the tenth anniversary of the Beijing Conference on women, Secretary of State Rice offered:

In the decade since the 1995 Fourth World Conference on Women, the United States has worked in cooperation with many nations on improving the lives of women and girls throughout the world. We can be proud of the progress we have achieved together on advancing educational and economic opportunities, greater access to health care, protection from violence, assistance to refugees and protection in conflict situations, and increasing political participation. In many Muslim countries, while there is much that remains to be done to improve the situation for women, the bigger picture is one of freedom expanding and surmounting the forces of tyranny, including those that hold women in second-class status. From Jordan and Bahrain, to Iraq and Afghanistan, the world has witnessed elections and expanding roles for women. In the Near East and all around the world, the United States is committed to working in partnerships with other nations to enlarge the freedom and empowerment of women.[11]

The Bush administration can point to some markers to argue that it has not completely abandoned women and girls but the story is more one of unfulfilled promises than realized successes. The quotes from senior policymakers such as Sauerbrey and Rice are the strongest part of current U.S. policy on women's human rights. But as we shall see below, on some of the core women's human rights issues, a far greater investment of political will and resources needs to be made to give life to the rhetoric.

The second obstacle to future success that must be addressed is the serious harm the Bush administration has done to women's human rights by allowing a partisan political ideology focused on controlling women's lives to set the administration's agenda. This cynicism is nowhere more evident than in the case of U.S. refusal to reinstate funding for the United Nations Population Fund. UNFPA is the largest source in the world of funding for family planning and reproductive health services. It supports programs in 140 countries that help women plan their families, avoid unwanted pregnancies, and safely experience pregnancy and childbirth. UNFPA also works to help men and women protect themselves from sexually transmitted infections, including HIV/AIDS. Given that 350 million couples worldwide lack access to modern contraceptives, these can be life or death interventions.

In 2002 the Bush administration cut all UNFPA funding, claiming that the agency supported forced abortion and sterilization in China. Four separate investigative teams, including one sent by the Department of State, refuted these claims and recommended that the United States resume funding for UNFPA.[12] Advocates have worked tirelessly to bring U.S. resources back to UNFPA and offered various compromises, including one that would limit the application of the U.S. monies to combat problems like obstetric fistula, but to no avail.[13] The only possible rationale for the Bush administration's refusal to reinstate funding is politics—the anti-abortion components of the administration's political base are pleased with the decision to cut funding for an international organization providing reproductive health services and the women most affected do not have the right to vote in the United States.

As we look to the future, the United States must reclaim its credibility on human rights and craft a women's human rights agenda that reflects a commitment to women's equality in a comprehensive fashion, both in terms of practices at home and in standard-setting, development promotion, and respect for the rule of law worldwide.

Women's Human Rights? Here's How

When he was secretary of state, Colin Powell wrote, "Women's issues affect not only women; they have profound implications for all humankind. Women's issues are human rights issues. They are health and education issues. They are development issues. They are ingredients of good government and sound economic practice. They go to the heart of what makes for successful, stable societies and global growth . . . We . . . cannot even begin to tackle the array of problems and challenges confronting us without the full and equal participation of women in all aspects of life. Women's contributions are essential, whether it's stemming the HIV/AIDS pandemic, lifting populations out of poverty, or helping regions recover from the ravages of conflict. That is why President Bush is committed and I am committed to ensuring that women's issues are fully integrated into American foreign policy."[14]

Powell's sentiment was worthy, but the world's women are tired of empty promises. For women to reap the benefits of U.S. leadership on women's human rights, we need to start with the basics. What are the greatest barriers to women's equality? First, poverty and lack of access to or control over financial resources. And second, legal status—in many countries women are officially minors, officially relegated to secondary status and denied access to justice. U.S. policies must recognize women's full humanity. Women do not just need "respect"; they need rights and status and control over the decisions fundamental to their well-being.

With the advent of a new administration, there will be an opportunity for the U.S. to play its most important role ever on women's human rights—a role in which it recognizes the interplay of violence, poverty, and discrimination in undermining women's status and devotes resources and political will to attacking the root causes of women's subordination.

Migration, Trafficking, and Labor Rights

One of the highest profile women's human rights concerns during both the Clinton and Bush administrations has been the trafficking of women. The emphasis has been largely on the trafficking of (mostly) women and children into the sex industry. The landmark passage of the Trafficking Victims Protection Act in 2000 created new protections for individuals trafficked into the United States, required the State Department to monitor and evaluate countries' efforts to prevent and combat trafficking, and increased attention to and resources for prosecuting traffickers.

While it is heartening to see legislation and executive action focused on a women's human rights concern, the approach to trafficking reflected in U.S. policies and programs to date has been incomplete. It has been hampered by ideological dueling over whether all prostitution is, by definition, a human rights abuse and whether the focus of anti-trafficking efforts should be primarily on trafficking into the sex industry or on broader issues. The United Nations defines trafficking as

the recruitment, transportation, transfer, harbouring or receipt of persons, by means of the threat or use of force or other means of coercion, of abduction, of fraud, of deception, of the abuse of power or of a position of vulnerability or of the giving or receiving of payments or benefits to achieve the consent of a person having control over another person, for the purpose of exploitation. Exploitation shall include, at a minimum, the exploitation of the prostitution of others or other forms of sexual exploitation, forced labor or services, slavery or practices similar to slavery, servitude or the removal of organs.[15]

This serious human rights abuse occurs in the context of a much larger phenomenon—migration for work—that brings with it a broad array of other human rights concerns. To the extent that U.S. policy, as it applies both inside the country and beyond, treats trafficking in isolation from those broader concerns, it misses a chance to meaningfully address one of the fundamental human rights issues in this age of globalization: how to protect the rights of the millions of women who migrate to work in unregulated sectors because it is their best chance at improving the incomes and lives of their families. Some of those women are caught up in the trafficking stream but many more work in other low-wage and often exploitative arenas, such as harvesting or domestic work.[16]

Numbers are difficult to pin down but the World Bank suggests that nearly 200 million people live outside the country of their birth.[17] Globalization has led to increased levels of labor migration and unskilled workers are heading toward markets with more jobs and less regulation of the labor market. The growing opportunities in informal sectors—such as domestic work—combine with inadequate regulation of recruitment and working conditions to create new opportunities for exploitation and abuse. Compounding the problem are immigration laws that are not keeping pace with labor flows. Although there is greater integration of global markets for goods, services, and capital, movement across borders by those seeking labor opportunities remains restricted by immigration laws that drive migrants underground and into the hands of unscrupulous recruiters, brokers, employers and, in some cases, traffickers.

The large number of people migrating for work has significant implications for the economies of their home countries. In 2004 recorded remittances from migrants were larger than private and public capital inflows in 36 developing countries. Remittances can and do reduce the percentage of poor people in a country's population and many governments see remittances as essential to the development of their economies. Although the International Labor Organization cautions that remittances are private cash transfers and not a substitute for development aid, countries in need of foreign currency encourage the export of their labor force. Migration thus is part and parcel of globalization and a major issue for international development. Not surprisingly, the numbers of women migrating for work are on the rise.[18]

Why do women migrate for work? And why are the "opportunities" available to them so often in unregulated sectors? Women typically leave their families behind and risk the unknown to improve the economic well-being of their families. They face such harsh choices because, as girls and women, their educational and economic opportunities are severely limited.

While successful migration increases the wealth and resources of a woman and/or her family, migration can also place women at risk of having their rights violated. Some women who want to migrate get caught up in horrifying cycles of trafficking, forced prostitution, and debt bondage. Many more women pay exorbitant fees to often shady employment agencies to secure placement in unskilled positions—often as domestic workers—far from home. Domestic workers, most of whom are women and girls, lack basic labor protections, may begin work deeply indebted for recruitment and transportation "fees" and are vulnerable to abuse by employers. Employers may keep domestic workers trapped in the home, take their passports, lie to them about their immigration status, and then take advantage of their isolation by physically and sexually assaulting them, forcing them to work endless hours and refusing to pay them. Because most migrant domestic workers have gone into debt to secure their jobs, they are afraid to leave before they pay off their debt. Moreover, many fear that reporting abuse to authorities will result in harsh penalties, given their uncertain immigration status.[19]

Women are vulnerable to trafficking for the same reasons that they take the risks inherent in migration: they are desperate for economic opportunity and have been denied education and employment opportunities at home. Few women would choose to leave their families and communities behind if viable alternatives were close at hand. Those who do choose to migrate for work require opportunities that turn out as promised and allow them to increase their economic fortunes without suffering abuse and degradation to do so.

What difference could U.S. policy make to the millions of women migrants spread across the globe? Even the most shameless abusers of human rights work hard to avoid that label. When the United States increased its attention to trafficking as a human rights abuse in the 1990s, other countries noticed. And when the United States started ranking countries based on their efforts to eradicate trafficking in its annual report on trafficking in persons, it made a difference. To date, however, the United States has focused its efforts primarily on the prosecution of traffickers. It needs to parlay its leadership into a broader effort to tackle the causes of women's vulnerability to trafficking and other abuses related to migration. As one policymaker deeply involved with the fight against trafficking has pointed out, the prosecution of traffickers is a popular response to this human rights abuse but prevention of trafficking has to be about providing women and girls with economic opportunity closer to home. Accountability for human rights abuse remains a priority but if the goal is to end or prevent trafficking in the first place, a more comprehensive approach is needed.

To a large extent trafficking will be fought most effectively with the same tools needed to remedy abuses against migrant workers more generally. Migration for work is, as former United Nations High Commissioner for Human Rights Mary Robinson put it, "the human face of globalization." As such it requires international cooperation and standard-setting to deal with women's poverty, low status, and lack of opportunities in their home countries and the restrictive immigration policies in their host countries that increase their vulnerability to abuse. The United States could start by articulating and funding programs designed to increase women's educational and employment opportunities in their home communities. Understanding, however, that demand for labor will keep migrant streams flowing, the United States should also play a role in strengthening standards and monitoring mechanisms for international labor recruitment with the goal of reducing unsafe migration. At the same time, it is important for the United States to deal with the shortcomings of its own labor laws in protecting migrants, especially those who toil in typically unregulated sectors such as domestic work, and extend labor law protections to those who suffer abuse for lack of them. The United States also will need to confront the role that restrictive immigration policies play in creating underground networks for moving migrants and trafficking others into forced labor. The United States could play a leadership role by reviewing its own immigration policies and reforming those that drive migrants underground into the hands of unlicensed recruiters and smugglers. Because the problems of migration and trafficking are complex and intertwined, they will require coordinated responses that implicate various U.S. agencies and decision-makers. Interagency efforts—involving the Departments of Justice, Treasury, and State, and the Office of the U.S. Trade Representative, for example—can, with high-level political backing, help orchestrate the responses most likely to increase women's local work opportunities, minimize the risks in labor recruitment, and reform labor and immigration laws to reduce women's vulnerability to trafficking and other human rights abuses.

Women's Rights, Lives, and Bodies

U.S. leadership on women's human rights has a credibility problem: women's rights advocates around the world see U.S. policy as counter-productive and hypocritical. Advocates express frustration that U.S. doublespeak on women's rights undermines efforts to engage their own governments on these issues. Instead, other governments are far less concerned that the United States will look askance at their failures to protect women's rights and improve women's status. Washington's poor reputation rests largely on recent efforts to undermine international agreements on women's reproductive rights and health at the United Nations as well as several policy initiatives that are understood to be motivated by the need to satisfy the domestic anti-abortion constituency. Further, with two of these policies—the so-called global gag rule[20] and the anti-prostitution pledge[21]—the administration is actually restricting the free speech rights of individuals and organizations in other countries in ways that would be unconstitutional if attempted in the United States.[22] So much for the U.S. commitment to promoting democracy and its freedoms across the globe. With policies like these the Bush administration instead sends the message that women's rights—whether to freedom of expression or to reproductive health care—are expendable.[23]

It is impossible to promote women's rights and well-being by separating out the different parts of their lives, protecting their rights in some areas and restricting them in others. The links between women's poverty, bodily integrity, and legal status are well established. In the words of women's rights advocates at Human Rights Watch,

We live in a world in which women do not have basic control over what happens to their bodies. Millions of women and girls are forced to marry and have sex with men they do not desire. Women are unable to depend on the government to protect them from physical violence in the home, with sometimes fatal consequences, including increased risk of HIV/AIDS infection. Women in state custody face sexual assault by their jailers. Women are punished for having sex outside of marriage or with a person of their choosing (rather than of their family's choosing). Husbands and other male family members obstruct or dictate women's access to reproductive health care. Doctors and government officials disproportionately target women from disadvantaged or marginalized communities for coercive family planning policies.

In such a world, how will women achieve equality? How will they contribute to the economic betterment of themselves, their families, and their communities? How will they run for office? How will they make sure their communities have potable water, medical care, and textbooks? Quite simply, they won't. And we won't change the basic facts of women's lives proceeding as we have.

The Bush administration's record on these issues has placed politics over substance with the result that money that could have supported women's health and rights was spent elsewhere. The United States is by far the largest donor to international family planning and reproductive health programs in the world. Its decisions about the use of its funds affect the well-being of women and men around the world because of the implications for the scope and nature of services and care provided. Further, the magnitude of its financial contributions to these programs gives the United States significant policy clout in international fora and multilateral agency decision making. Women have lost access to contraception and medical care that they needed, and programs designed to reach marginalized populations with HIV/AIDS prevention strategies have been hampered. In a world in which women die in childbirth every day, in which HIV infection rates among girls and women in Africa are soaring, no administration can call itself a champion of women and women's rights if it so cavalierly dismisses the real-life international consequences of its domestic politicking.

The next administration will have the chance both to make a difference in women's lives and to begin to resurrect America's credibility as an advocate for women's human rights. To do both will require a long-term commitment but there are a few actions a new administration can do at the start. It can:

- Ratify CEDAW and support international and regional efforts to articulate human rights standards that promote the full panoply of women's human rights;
- Direct resources to the programs and policies that promote women's rights and improve women's status by, for example,
  - Reinstating funding for UNFPA and supporting legislative efforts—currently via the Global Democracy Promotion Act—to protect women's access to the full range of reproductive health

services as well as women's right to advocate with their own money for policies they believe to be in their best interests.

- Supporting approaches such as that embodied in the proposed International Violence Against Women Act that aim to reduce women's vulnerability to violence by improving women's economic status, economic security and educational opportunity.
- Work with Congress to undo harmful restrictions on anti-trafficking and HIV prevention programs; and
- Invigorate interagency efforts to protect the rights of women trafficked into forced labor by bringing relevant policymakers to the table, focusing on prevention, and redefining the problem to encompass the human rights of trafficked women as well as those migrating across national borders for work.

All of these steps should be informed by a comprehensive understanding of the many fronts on which it is necessary to fight widespread human rights abuses against women and build respect for women's human rights around the globe. Beyond such first steps, the next administration faces the challenge of articulating a vision for the place of women's human rights in its foreign policy. Even when the world's attention is seized by the "war on terror" and the torture and other abuses carried out as a consequence, it would be a mistake to view women's human rights as a second-tier or less pressing concern. Human rights crises like the vicious and widespread use of sexual violence in Congo are fueled by a systemic failure to remedy women's unequal status. As former Secretary of State Colin Powell reminded us earlier, women are entitled to justice, equality, and physical security. With those basic protections, women will help create a more prosperous, stable, and secure world.

Chapter 11

Echoes of the Future?
Religious Repression as a Challenge to U.S. Human Rights Policy

FELICE D. GAER

To Americans few rights seem as natural and beyond dispute as the rights to freedom of thought, conscience, and religion. The search for freedom from religious persecution was, after all, a vital part of America's founding history. Yet introducing measures into U.S. foreign policy to stop violations of freedom of religion abroad was controversial when first proposed in the 1990s.

Madeleine Albright, the secretary of state when Congress passed the International Religious Freedom Act (IRFA) in 1998, recalled that her own education in statecraft taught that "no subject seemed more inherently treacherous than religion." She viewed religious rivalries, such as between Hindus and Muslims, as "echoes of earlier, less enlightened times" but wrote in 2006 that she realized the post-9/11 world signaled that religious factors in world affairs need more, not less attention.[1] Indeed, the destruction of the World Trade Center has brought the linkage of religion to extremist violence into sharper focus, revealing that abuses of freedom of thought, conscience, religion, or belief intersect with numerous U.S. foreign policy concerns, including American political and national security interests as well as political stability worldwide. New mechanisms created by IRFA—including annual reports, an ambassador-at-large, and an independent commission—have raised the profile of religiously linked human rights abuse. How has this legislation affected U.S. human rights policy and what are the ways in which it might be further developed to be more effective?

Religion and Universal Human Rights

Following World War II, freedom of thought, conscience, and religion, one of President Franklin Delano Roosevelt's four freedoms, was enshrined in the Universal Declaration of Human Rights (1948). In a century that had already seen militant atheism in the Soviet Union, the horrors of the Holocaust, and the partition of India and Pakistan essentially along religious lines, the Universal Declaration promised freedom to believe and freedom to manifest that belief. It was followed by the 1966 International Covenant on Civil and Political Rights, a treaty that made these guarantees of religious freedom a binding norm of law but also specified limitations on the freedom to manifest belief.[2]

When the UN General Assembly adopted by consensus the 1981 Declaration on the Elimination of Religious Intolerance, the U.S. representative to the UN Commission on Human Rights, Michael Novak, articulated a view held by many natural law advocates: that religious freedom is the first freedom. "The United States of America," he said, "recognized that all human rights *began* in freedom of thought, conscience, religion and belief" (emphasis added).[3] The adoption of the 1981 UN declaration was itself a remarkable achievement for the Cold War years.

In the United Nations, the Soviet Union was the most vocal and effective opponent of individual human rights guarantees and the machinery that might provide citizens with such protections. Domestically, Soviet authorities had instituted myriad controls and restrictions, in law and fact, to repress religion and its adherents. During 18 years of negotiations in the UN, the Soviet Union had repeatedly delayed consideration of the draft declaration and tried to delete or neutralize its guarantees. Its efforts centered on Article 6, which spells out nine specific rights that comprise its substantive advances, including explicit affirmation of the right to establish and maintain places of worship and charitable institutions, and the rights to make, acquire, and use religious articles for prayer, to publish prayer books, teach, select leaders, and maintain and establish communications with other coreligionists nationally and internationally. All these rights were denied to Soviet religious communities and religious believers were excluded from positions of public authority.

During these years, the Jewish minority in the Soviet Union had begun to publicize just how severe these policies were, and to seek emigration from the country as the only antidote to pervasive state repression. Although the 1981 declaration was initiated following swastika-smearing incidents in Europe, the Soviet Union repeatedly and effectively kept all proposed references to anti-Semitism and the Jewish religion out of the new UN instrument. To assist the Soviet Jewish minority, the U.S. Congress in 1974 adopted the Jackson-Vanik amendment, which denied most-favored-nation status to nonmarket economy countries that restricted the rights of their citizens to emigrate, and helped free hundreds of thousands of Jews. Jackson-Vanik thus placed human rights abuses of a minority religious community squarely onto the U.S. foreign policy agenda as a supplement to generic human rights legislation in Section 502b of the Foreign Assistance Act of 1961, which called for annual human rights reports and an aid cutoff for gross violators.

After the Cold War's end human rights advocacy expanded, with new institutions created ranging from international criminal courts to an office of a UN High Commissioner. Organizations in the United States receiving reports of increased religious persecution of Christians throughout the world began to complain about being left out of Washington's growing human rights agenda. If the State Department's Human Rights Bureau could be concerned with such new topics as democratization, child labor, refugee and asylum policy, and violence against women, why could it not focus on those being targeted for their religious affiliations?[4] The Jackson-Vanik model was explicitly invoked: If Jews could be rescued, why not Christians?

Indeed, Congress enacted the International Religious Freedom Act in 1998 in part because of pressure catalyzed by a revival of religion worldwide.[5] Preachers in American churches told their congregations about increasing religious repression around the globe, much of it against Christians. Advocates claimed that Christianity had encountered a demographic shift from a European and U.S.-centered world to the third world, and that the collapse of the militantly atheistic Soviet Union and its satellites now opened "far corners of the world to scrutiny by a growing array of religious groups."[6] After the Republican Party gained control of both houses of Congress in 1994, the movement seized upon what Allen D. Hertzke called "a shift toward a more faith-friendly intellectual environment in the United States."[7]

The Content of Freedom of Thought, Conscience, and Religion or Belief

When Congress adopted IRFA, it noted that "the right to freedom of religion undergirds the very origin and existence of the United States."[8] The legislation also refers to the UN Charter and the European Convention on Human Rights and cites three key instruments: the Universal Declaration of Human Rights, the International Covenant on Civil and Political Rights, and the 1981 Declaration on the Elimination of All Forms of Discrimination Based on Religious Intolerance. The three are mutually reinforcing in articulating the elements of freedom of thought, conscience, religion, or belief which constitute an inherent, indeed inalienable, human right of every individual and require protection from the state.

Two dimensions of the freedom of thought, conscience, and religion are set forth in the Universal Declaration of Human Rights: the right to believe and the right to manifest that belief, whether individually or together with others, in the areas of worship, observance, practice, and teaching. Discrimination in law and in practice due to religion is declared impermissible. Individuals are also promised equality before the law and equal protection under the law.[9]

The Universal Declaration also affirms the right to change one's religion. The International Covenant on Civil and Political Rights makes reference to an individual's right to "have or adopt" a religion or belief—that is, to maintain, alter, drop, or choose it. After the approval of IRFA, some argued that addressing abuses against religious adherents was merely a disguise for opening up other societies to missionary activity by foreign religious groups. But the ICCPR also forbids any coercion that would impair the right to have or adopt a religion, "including the use or threat of physical force . . . to compel believers or non-believers" to adhere to their religion or recant it.[10] Thus freedom of religion also explicitly protects individuals from forced conversion, proselytization, and similar measures.

The ICCPR does not define what constitutes "religion" or "freedom of thought" or "conscience." Freedom of religion may be limited but only by conditions "necessary to protect public safety, order, health or morals, or the fundamental rights and freedoms of others." No limits can be placed on the right to believe, even in time of public emergency.[11]

The third instrument cited, the 1981 Declaration on the Elimination of All Forms of Discrimination Based on Religious Intolerance, prohibits both state-imposed and private discrimination and articulates the freedom to manifest a religion or belief without unwarranted government interference. It also sets out a government's obligations to take legal and educational measures to eliminate discrimination and intolerance and identifies freedoms that comprise the right, including the right to worship and assemble, to establish and maintain places of worship, and to establish and maintain charitable and humanitarian institutions. Individuals can make, acquire, and use the materials necessary for religious rites. They have the right to communicate with individuals and communities of coreligionists at the national and international level.

IRFA explains that it is often governments that actively abuse or "severely restrict or prohibit the freedom of their citizens to study, believe, observe, and freely practice the religious faith of their choice." Sometimes, however, the government may not actively sponsor the violations of the religious freedom rights, but simply engage in a pattern of tolerating the abuses, making it complicit by its inaction. In IRFA, the Congress explains that the United States has long been "offering refuge to those suffering religious persecution" and that, as a matter of policy, the new bill will offer protection against further violations overseas of the elements of freedom of religion, as set forth in the various international instruments cited.

Religious freedom, IRFA notes, "is under renewed and . . . increasing assault" worldwide, evidenced by "severe and violent forms of religious persecution [such] as detention, torture beatings, forced marriage, rape, imprisonment, enslavement, mass resettlement and death." The act makes clear that it shall be the policy of the United States "to condemn violations of religious freedom."

Questions Raised

The charged political climate in the United States saw a number of criticisms raised regarding IRFA's appropriateness and potential effectiveness. It was frequently claimed that IRFA would destroy the credibility of U.S. human rights policy by creating a "hierarchy" of rights (placing freedom of religion above other rights, such as due process and freedom of expression, in policy considerations) and by focusing most or all attention on one religion—Christianity—and, more specifically, on evangelical Protestantism. Others said that the congressional legislation would impose automatic punitive sanctions on countries that failed to meet "Western" standards of religious freedom—an approach at odds with the conciliation model of inter-religious discourse customary worldwide. It was argued that IRFA would harm multilateral norms and institutions, reinforcing America's preference to "go it alone."[12] Some complained that IRFA was simply a backdoor way to break down the "wall of separation" between church and state within the United States government.

IRFA addressed most of these complaints, emphasizing the importance of protecting freedom of religion and belief for everyone, everywhere. It provided a flexible list of "presidential actions" to be invoked for the most severe violators of freedom of religion so that sanctions would not be the sole option for a U.S. policy response. IRFA also established a religious freedom office within the Bureau of Human Rights to avoid placing religious freedom in opposition to other rights. Finally, multilateral universal human rights standards were explicitly referenced.

To those concerned about breaking the "wall of separation," supporters of IRFA have pointed out that the act takes a human rights approach and addresses violations of *freedom* of religion, not the content of religious belief or the role of religion in society or government affairs more generally. Stopping torture, disappearances, arbitrary arrest, and detention is at the core of human rights policy for the United States and other countries. Could anyone object to the importance of combating such acts, or holding the perpetrators accountable for them?

IRFA's distinctly human rights methodology avoids any "hierarchy" of rights: the U.S. government must first report accurately about freedom of religion worldwide. By spotlighting abuses, IRFA can mobilize attention and shame offenders into changing behavior. The legislation acknowledges that severe violations of religious freedom cannot always be eliminated by a country's leader—much abuse results from conflicts between religious communities. However, countries that tolerate such actions without trying to ameliorate the abuses and/or hold people accountable for them can also be deemed responsible under IRFA. Once the president designates a country as a severe violator of religious freedom, consultations must ensue, followed by presidential actions.

New Institutions and Requirements

In an effort to be effective in ending abuses in ways that other U.S. human rights legislation had not been, particularly by designating specific countries for policy action including specific sanctions, IRFA's supporters proposed the establishment of specific new machinery. IRFA thus calls for an institutional structure with many new components for addressing severe violations of religious freedom:

- It requires a separate annual report from the State Department ("IRF Report") on religious freedom in all 198 countries in the world, including a discussion of what U.S. policy and activity has been with regard to each country. This report provides the basic information on which subsequent policy actions are to be based.
- It created both a position of ambassador at large for religious freedom (who reports to the secretary of state through the assistant secretary for democracy, human rights, and labor and serves as a principal adviser on religious freedom to the secretary of state and the president) and an Office of International Religious Freedom (OIRF) at the Department of State.
- The legislation requires the administration to designate "countries of particular concern" (CPCs) annually and determine the agency or specific official in those countries responsible for particularly severe violations of religious freedom. The act outlines 15 different actions that can be taken, beginning with a private diplomatic démarche, and including the postponement of a cultural exchange or the cancellation of a state visit. For a foreign state designated as

a "country of particular concern," the United States could select any of seven actions, denying economic or security aid and more.

- IRFA requires the president to take action regarding CPCs (such as denying economic assistance to export licenses or any "commensurate" action), but the secretary of state can waive action against a country on the CPC list if doing so "would further the purpose" of IRFA or was required by "an important national interest" of the United States. The secretary can also negotiate a "binding agreement" or invoke an exception for existing sanctions.
- The legislation creates a nine-member independent bipartisan oversight body, the U.S. Commission on International Religious Freedom, made up of private citizens, which has as its primary responsibilities:
    1) reviewing annually the facts and circumstances of violations of religious freedom as presented in the Department of State's Country Reports on Human Rights Practices as well as information from other sources, as appropriate; and
    2) making policy recommendations to the president, the secretary of state, and Congress on matters involving international religious freedom.
- Finally, IRFA amends existing U.S. laws by adding the words "religious freedom" to nearly every provision in other legislation addressing human rights. IRFA thus emphasizes the need to apply existing laws to address religious freedom violations as well as other violations.

IRFA is distinguished from other human rights legislation by requiring annual country reports on religious freedom outlining policy actions and the designation of "countries of particular concern."

Eight reports on the status of religious freedom in over 190 countries have been issued by the State Department since Secretary of State Madeleine Albright released the first compilation in this series in September 1999. Preparation of the annual report requires U.S. embassy personnel to contact sources that can advise on and assess violations of religious freedom, including desk officers and high-ranking officials. Documenting the facts and reporting publicly on the status of religious freedom worldwide provides the informational basis for the policy process of determining whether countries qualify for CPC status as particularly serious violators of religious freedom and enables officials to appraise U.S. efforts to integrate religious freedom into its foreign policy.

In fact, the most distinctive element of IRFA is the requirement to designate the most egregious violators of religious freedom every year and to take further actions toward those violators. The designation of CPC calls for the president to take into account "any finding or recommen-dations" of the independent Commission on International Religious Freedom. Since IRFA's establishment, every president has directed that the secretary of state address IRFA's requirements. IRFA does, however, direct the president to act flexibly and to take whichever of any number of actions will give the greatest leverage to the determination procedure. The president can also waive action, based on national interest.

Despite the importance of the CPC designation and the broad termi-nology under which many countries might qualify as CPCs, only 10 have merited designation in the entire history of IRFA. In 1999 Burma (Myanmar), China, Iran, Iraq, and Sudan were named CPCs, along with Serbia under President Slobodan Milosevic and the Taliban regime in Afghanistan, the latter both named "severe violators." North Korea was added in 2001; Saudi Arabia, Eritrea, and Vietnam in 2004, and Uzbekis-tan in 2006.[13]

IRFA names 15 presidential actions that can be taken to "oppose" religious freedom violations and "promote the right to freedom of reli-gion." In addition to 8 specified symbolic or policy actions, these include 7 economic and political sanctions as well as the option of tak-ing a "commensurate" action or "negotiating a binding agreement." (Significantly, no additional action is technically required if the presi-dent substitutes an existing legislative sanction that is "commensurate in effect." Thus, if a country is already subject to multiple economic sanctions for reasons other than religious freedom violations, the same sanction may be designated a second time as a sanction under IRFA.[14])

For most CPC-designated countries, presidential actions have com-monly been duplicative of already existing sanctions. While duplication technically may be in accord with the provisions of IRFA, as permitted by Section 402(c)(5) of IRFA, as a matter of policy such duplication has served as a way to avoid taking action under IRFA against violator states. The three countries the Bush administration designated as CPCs in 2004—Vietnam, Eritrea, and Saudi Arabia—did not have any pre-exist-ing sanctions. The measures taken in these three cases involved more proactive efforts of policymaking than in previous cases, where officials had merely designated pre-existing sanctions. The new actions included reaching a binding bilateral agreement with Vietnam, conducting dis-cussions leading to issuance of a "confirmation of policies" with Saudi Arabia, and denial of commercial export licenses for some defense items for Eritrea, which was the first unique presidential action under IRFA.[15]

Countries can also be taken off the list. Serbia was removed from the list of severe violators of religious freedom following the NATO invasion of Kosovo in October 2000 and after the election of a new president to follow Slobodan Milosevic in January 2001. Afghanistan and Iraq were dropped after U.S.-led invasions. Vietnam was dropped from the CPC list in November 2006 and is the only country where actual diplomacy, a "binding agreement" with benchmarks (rather than the entry of U.S. troops), played a role in the decision to revoke CPC status. The status of Saudi Arabia may also be in play. In July 2006 the United States announced it had received "confirmation of policies" of reforms in Saudi Arabia and at a September 2007 press conference Ambassador-at-Large for Religious Freedom John Hanford repeatedly referred to "progress" in Saudi Arabia.

How Vietnam and Saudi Arabia have fared under IRFA provides some key insights into the difficulties in applying the CPC designation to countries not already subject to U.S. sanctions, and some of the adjustments to U.S. human rights concerns made when a focus on religious freedom was added.

Is Religious Freedom Separate from Political Freedom? The Case of Vietnam

After it was named a CPC in September 2004, Vietnam concluded a "binding agreement" with the United States in May 2005 promising a wide array of changes in human rights practices dealing with religious communities. In November 2006, one week before a visit by President George W. Bush, Vietnam was dropped from the CPC list reportedly because of "enormous progress."[16] Since then a wave of arrests and other steps that fly in the face of the bilateral agreement's promises have led to congressional resolutions demanding reinstatement of CPC status.

When Vietnam was designated a CPC, "U.S. officials consistently urged the release of religious prisoners, a ban on forced renunciations of faith, an end to physical abuse of religious believers, and the reopening of hundreds of churches closed in the Central Highlands."[17] Details of the 2005 binding agreement were kept secret, reportedly at Vietnam's request, but the 2006 IRF report stated that Vietnam had agreed to give special consideration to amnesties for prisoner cases raised by the United States and to instruct local authorities "strictly and completely" to comply with a new ordinance opening local houses of worship. Thereafter, Vietnamese Catholics and Buddhists from the Vietnam Buddhist Sangha (VBS) reportedly encountered eased restrictions. Forced renunciations of faith were declared illegal and imprisonment and torture reportedly declined. Local officials were instructed to follow a procedure for legal recognition of religious communities and many were registered, including Bahai's, Seventh Day Adventists, and various other

Christian churches. Authorities quietly permitted reopening of previously closed house churches—independent places for assembly, discussion, and prayer. used when churches are not registered or are persecuted, or when the congregants want to return to the simplicity of the early Christian church. Specific prisoners were released, but U.S. officials remained concerned about "difficulties Protestants face in the Central Highlands and northern Vietnam."[18]

The decision to announce the end of CPC status in November 2006, on the eve of President Bush's visit, indicated that the bilateral agreement's benchmarks had been met. A few months later, however, an extensive crackdown targeted human rights, legal reform, and advocates of free speech and democracy, many of whom were either religious leaders themselves or motivated by religion in their public activities. A decline in other prisoner releases and legal registrations followed. A video showing a security officer silencing a Catholic priest, Father Nguyen Van Ly, when he shouted "Down with communism!" in court, was distributed worldwide on YouTube, spotlighting official brutality.[19] A monk from the United Buddhist Church of Vietnam (UBCV) was arrested for distributing relief aid to peasant protesters.[20] A Protestant convert, beaten in police custody and asked to renounce his faith, later died of his injuries. Proof that Montagnard children from "religious families" were denied access to public schools was reported. Taken together, these measures raise questions about "progress" and whether the United States used its leverage effectively before lifting CPC status and granting both Permanent Normal Trade Relations (PNTR) and World Trade Organization membership.[21]

Congressional resolutions criticized the crackdown. The Bush administration argued that its religious freedom benchmarks had been met and the practice of religion had improved. Drawing a line between religious freedom and political expression, the 2006 IRF report claimed in its executive summary regarding Vietnam that the "U.S. Government has regularly worked for the release of prisoners deemed to be detained *primarily for religious reasons.*"[22] A year later the IRF report continued: "Although the international media highlighted arrests and detentions of several political dissidents in early 2007, all individuals raised by the United States as prisoners of concern for reasons *connected to their faith* have been freed by the Government"[23] (emphasis added). By apparently accepting Vietnam's argument that Father Ly, prominent UBCV Buddhist leaders, and others were detained for "political" reasons not "connected to their faith," the State Department saw human rights progress where others did not. It determined that the reported crackdown would not merit any redesignation of Vietnam as a CPC.

The Bush administration's claim that religious freedom concerns and activists can be considered separately from general dissent has been contested. Many religious leaders in Vietnam are themselves convinced that legal reforms addressing freedom of expression, assembly, and association are necessary to protect freedom of thought, conscience, and religion from the arbitrary power of the state. Because freedom of religion or belief is "intimately connected to other human rights," they contend that "religious freedom cannot be fully protected without legal or some political reform."[24] Indeed, together with religiously motivated dissidents, religious leaders have often been at the forefront of peaceful struggles for reform. In June 2007 President Bush acknowledged that both religious freedom and political reform were of concern, stating that the "arrest of political and religious prisoners" in Vietnam was unacceptable. He later raised the issue with Vietnamese President Nguyen Minh Triet in Washington.

The effort to adopt a binding agreement with Vietnam rather than impose sanctions to address religious freedom violations has both positive and negative aspects. It showed that CPC status can be dropped without regime change and that flexible diplomacy backed by the force of human rights law can produce some results. It offers insights into the way specific economic and political interests—especially such issues as PNTR and World Trade Organization membership—can be used to leverage an important human rights review process, encouraging a country to promise specific actions to end specific abuses. The speed and timing of the decision to drop Vietnam from the CPC list, however, demonstrates that economic and political pressures can skew U.S. policy by encouraging an end to scrutiny at politically advantageous moments regardless of the long–term consequences for religious freedom.

The crackdown in Vietnam that followed the lifting of CPC status highlights in particular the importance of who decides when conditions are met, by what process, and whether independent monitoring is needed to reach impartial and valid decisions. It emphasizes the importance of the human rights criteria being applied under IRFA and raises the question of whether one can successfully distinguish and separate violations of "freedom of religion" from the abuse of other related human rights. The Department of State narrowed the interpretation of violations of religious freedom so much that basic human rights norms and conditions were overlooked. It made dubious determinations such as that UBCV members were primarily "political" prisoners, not religious ones. As a result, only a small number of prominent prisoners were "in play" in connection with CPC status. Once they were released and a few other items in the agreement were achieved, the status was lifted. Some U.S. officials felt the conditions established for the binding agreement were too low and, while it was easy for Vietnam to meet them, it was also easy to reverse them later. The case of Vietnam offers a warning about the potentially counterproductive results of lifting CPC status too soon without verifiable indicators of long-term change or proper monitoring mechanisms.

Monitoring, Transparency, and Measuring Progress: The Case of Saudi Arabia

The United States designated Saudi Arabia a CPC in 2004, but U.S. willingness to speak critically or publicly about repression of religious freedom in that country had been and remained muted. The CPC designation was delayed for years, despite repeated conclusions from 1999 to 2005 by IRF reports that "freedom of religion does not exist" in Saudi Arabia. Religious repression in Saudi Arabia became a mainstream concern in the United States after September 11, 2001, but only in 2003, after bombings in Riyadh that killed dozens and wounded hundreds, did the U.S. focus serious attention on the interrelationship of religion and the promotion of extremism and on the importance of naming Saudi Arabia a CPC.

Momentum built around the need to examine more closely how extremism—and terrorist bombings inside and outside the kingdom—was linked to formal teaching in schools inside and outside Saudi Arabia. In a February 2004 congressional hearing, Ambassador-at-Large John Hanford emphasized the department's goal to "highlight the connections between religious intolerance and religious-based terrorism."[25]

Even after identifying Saudi Arabia as a CPC in September 2004, the administration invoked all the provisions built into the IRFA legislation to delay other action. Secretary of State Colin Powell signaled that the naming and shaming involved in the CPC designation was enough of a presidential action. Interviewed by Al Arabiya, the Arabic-language news channel, Powell explained U.S. thinking: "This is not to punish them or in any way show displeasure, but to state a fact. . . . One should not see this as anything but two friends talking to one another about a problem of mutual concern."[26] Reform in Saudi Arabia would take place by understanding the "nature" of Saudi society and proceeding at a pace it can sustain. Ambassador Hanford explained that a long process of diplomatic discussions behind closed doors had been pursued in an effort to bring about change rather than a CPC designation but "ultimately . . . standards were not being lived up to."[27]

The IRF reports on Saudi Arabia had raised issues such as harassment and arrest of non-Muslims, particularly among the 7 million foreign workers, sometimes solely for participating in private prayer ceremonies; beatings and other abusive treatment, including torture by the religious police; and discrimination against Shi'a Muslims. But the Department of State's analysis now focused far more on the exportation and propagation of extremism. In September 2005, a year after the CPC designation of Saudi Arabia, Secretary of State Condoleezza Rice formally approved a "temporary" 180-day waiver of further action to allow continuing discussions. Two months later she inaugurated a strategic dialogue with the Saudis to "raise the level of discussion" on bilateral issues to a "senior level" and maintain a "sustained" focus on key issues. Religious freedom was not part of this discussion but counterterrorism, military affairs, education, and human development were.[28] The CPC 180-day waiver expired in March 2006 but it was not until July 2006 that it was announced that the secretary had decided to leave the waiver in place.

On July 19, 2006 the State Department announced that Ambassador Hanford had briefed Congress about the "results" of discussions between the U.S. and Saudi officials through which the United States had been able to "identify and confirm a number of key policies" of the Saudi government to improve freedom of "religious practice" and promote tolerance. These would "halt the dissemination of intolerant literature and extremist ideology, both within Saudi Arabia and around the world . . . protect the right to private worship, and . . . curb harassment of religious practice." Hanford also stated that the Saudis were engaged in "a comprehensive revision of textbooks and educational curricula" and were "retraining teachers and the religious police to ensure that the rights of Muslims and non-Muslims are protected" and to "combat extremism."[29]

Accountability about these promises has been anything but precise. The list of Saudi policies "confirmed" by the US reflected various previous promises but nothing concrete in the form of laws, decrees, advisories, or instructions to relevant parties was made available. The list of "confirmed" policies look like a substantial program of reform. But are they what they seemed or merely empty promises?

The United States claims that the Saudi government is pursuing policies that address major U.S. concerns: revising textbooks and retraining teachers, combating extremism in sermons, retraining or reassigning extremist imams, and protecting the "right to private worship." All people, including non-Muslims, may reportedly "gather in homes for religious practice." Saudi officials would "ensure that customs inspectors at borders will not confiscate personal religious materials." Harassment by the religious police (the mutawa'im) would be curtailed—they would not be permitted to "detain or conduct investigations of suspects, implement punishment, violate the sanctity of private homes, conduct surveillance, or confiscate private religious materials." Only "authorized individuals" could work for the religious police; its members would be retrained and "held accountable" for overstepping their role. A government Human Rights Commission would address complaints, including those of foreigners "whose religious rights have been violated by any public or private agency or individual." (Discrimination against Shiites was notably missing from the list.)[30]

When Ambassador Hanford announced CPC designations in November 2006, he cited both progress and some regression but not enough of the former to change Saudi Arabia's CPC status. The U.S. Commission on International Religious Freedom remarked that past Saudi commitments had "not resulted in specific actions, nor . . . in measurable improvements."[31] Persistent repression affected both public and private religious practices of Muslims and non-Muslims. Saudi financing worldwide continued to support religious intolerance, hatred, and, in some cases, violence.

How the State Department holds governments accountable was not clarified. Saudi officials claim they created committees under the Ministries of Islamic Affairs and Information to examine textbooks and religious publications that promote hostility to other religious traditions. The U.S. Commission on International Religious Freedom asked about the results of these efforts but Saudi officials only told them about changes in general. Commission members asked repeatedly for copies of the textbooks used in courses with thousands and even millions of students. But Saudi officials had not supplied a single textbook many months after commission members had visited Saudi Arabia and following numerous oral and written requests.

Teacher retraining was also promised but no one could cite any consequences for teachers who failed to teach the reformed curriculum. Asked whether the government was still paying stipends to the extremist imams reportedly fired or suspended, officials explained that the state still paid the clerics to keep them from becoming employed by extremists. While statements at the highest levels of the Saudi government claim that people are free to worship privately, this policy has been implemented unevenly and people live in fear of disruption of services or arrest. No guidelines explain when a home worship ceremony is no longer considered private.

Public criticism of the religious police emerged in a series of mid-2007 press articles but trials of the mutawa'im for deaths in custody have been dismissed and due process rights of the complainants abrogated. In short, there has not yet been appropriate monitoring of the alleged reform policies.[32]

IRFA at Ten: Problems Remain

As the International Religious Freedom Act approaches its tenth anniversary, Congressman Tom Lantos (D.-Calif.), House Foreign Affairs Committee chairman, remarked recently that "our decade-long effort to promote this most fundamental human right has not yet yielded the results we were seeking."[33] Unlike earlier human rights legislation, IRFA requires the administration to actually respond to the voluminous reporting that it has carried out by designating severe violators and taking action against them. How can this process become more effective?

* *Continue using a human rights lens to address ongoing religious freedom violations.*

It is clear that IRFA needs to remain focused on ending violations of religious freedom, not on promoting religion or religious activities per se.[34] To end severe abuses, a human rights approach is needed, involving fact-finding, public reporting, taking action, and demanding accountability of those responsible. However valuable inter-religious dialogue and reconciliation efforts among religious communities may be, those are the tools of a peacemaking approach, not a human rights methodology, which emphasizes "telling the truth" and putting facts about compliance and violations of norms into the public record.[35]

* *Stay the course: Assess religious freedom conditions accurately and maintain universal standards.*

The annual reporting required by IRFA has demonstrated that violations of religious freedom are extensive and have grown since 1998. Accurate information is as essential with regard to religious freedom as it is in any other area of human rights. Accuracy not only produces good annual reports but leads to better decisions that are more likely to have the desired policy impact.

The *quality* of reporting in the IRF reports varies considerably from embassy to embassy. To ensure consistency, report editing and production should be assigned, as it was originally, to the unit in Democracy, Human Rights, and Labor at the State Department that also prepares the annual country human rights report.

Consistent standards are essential to the reports' credibility and utility yet new thresholds and definitions have been established without adequate reflection. In dealing with Vietnam, for example, the IRF office established new distinctions between "religious prisoners" and "political prisoners." U.S. policy on Saudi Arabia has prioritized the "private practice" of religion—a concept without any legal basis and one that leaves people unprotected in fact and in law and deviates from the international instruments cited in IRFA. Permitting only "private practice" is not what freedom of religion is all about.

IRF reports, like those on general human rights, are routinely updated each year and many have become formulaic. A system to systematically update and review each country report to ensure that it reflects emerging and changing trends is needed. Policy makers may wish to invite the U.S. Commission on International Religious Freedom or a panel of independent experts to conduct independent updates of perhaps five to ten country reports annually to ensure they reflect the current rights situation in each country.

• *Designate gross violators fairly and continue scrutiny of severe abuses.*

After nearly a decade, only a dozen countries or entities have been identified as severe violators under IRFA. The criteria used to determine CPC status merit renewed attention. Physical abuse associated with religious freedom violations should not necessarily be the decisive factor in determining CPC status. Since severe repression can be achieved through totalitarian legal strictures with their rigid, comprehensive, and unfair disregard of universal norms, countries that maintain such strictures merit close scrutiny too.

Because the State Department emphasizes abuses involving violence, Saudi Arabia long evaded citation as a CPC. A government's willingness to make some improvements does not in and of itself constitute an adequate criterion for dropping a country from the CPC list altogether. In such cases the CPC process should acknowledge progress without prematurely removing "severe violator" status. The system of "tiers" used in U.S. legislation against trafficking in persons ranks countries according to a government's *efforts* to eliminate relevant abuses. The CPC process has focused on results, not intentions. If a government's *efforts* rather than results are to become the criterion for being removed from the CPC list, IRFA will need major revisions.

A lack of transparency enabled the administration to remove Vietnam from the CPC list without visible means of assessing whether changes were effective or lasting. The absence of genuine monitoring and public reporting on the CPC conditions and the Saudi government's claimed policy responses to abuses is similarly problematic.

Whether IRFA continues with a CPC style or a "tier"-type process, the annual country reports play a key role as a policy tool in assessing reality as well as the actions of the country under review. The IRF reports must include a section explaining U.S. policy actions and results. But actual U.S. policies on religious freedom toward a country are commonly the most abbreviated section in the IRF reports. Various activities are chronicled but there is scant information on how they are linked to policy and what consequences followed the actions listed. The reports should clarify country strategies and how policies like foreign aid, public diplomacy, and participation in multilateral organizations may have advanced freedom of thought, conscience, religion, belief, and related human rights.

- *Enforce rights better by using consistent criteria.*

In U.S. foreign policy, human rights, including religious freedom, need to be on the table and part of the discussions of each problem country addressed. In raising rights issues with regional bureaus of the State Department, it is vital to avoid revising definitions and criteria of human rights performance in each instance. Universal standards must be maintained.

The attempt to separate and narrowly define violations of religious freedom as distinct from other human rights violations has introduced distortions into religious freedom policy determinations, raising concern over consistency in applying norms. The 2007 IRF Report's executive summary explains that one cannot accept all government claims justifying repression on political grounds: "It is important to distinguish between groups of religious believers who express legitimate political grievances and those that misuse religion to advocate violence against other religious groups or the state. This report categorizes as an abuse a government's broad repression of religious expression among a peacefully practicing population on the grounds of security concerns."[36] In accordance with this principle, the IRF Report describes abuses involving imprisoned Tibetan Buddhist monks, many of whom, in addition to voicing concerns about religious practice, also support separatist territorial claims. The department also cites abuses in the detention and harassment of religious minorities (and majorities—the Buddhist monks) in Burma who also peacefully advocate democracy.

Ironically, the State Department's treatment of Vietnam's CPC status seemed to introduce standards enabling the United States to justify Vietnam's crackdown as not encompassing significant violations of religious freedom. Claiming a difference between religious and political prisoners based on how connected the offending actions were to the victim's faith seems to miss the point: IRFA was created to oppose religious freedom violations, not to provide an opportunity to recategorize as political those abuses motivated by religion but affecting external life.

Despite criticism that Congress was giving religious freedom top priority in a human rights hierarchy, IRFA as adopted is a flexible, broad-based foreign policy instrument with a global focus on *all* individuals and groups subjected to human rights abuses abroad because of religion or belief. It amends existing human rights laws to include explicit references to religious freedom when U.S. policymakers examine human rights. It creates special mechanisms for taking action, such as the ambassador-at-large. Consistent use of IRFA's tools can thus strengthen the State Department's human rights work.

• *Lead the effort effectively: Use a team effort to mainstream human rights, including religious freedom.*
The relationship of the ambassador-at-large to the assistant secretary for democracy, human rights, and labor and other special envoys should be strengthened. The ambassador-at-large is responsible for advancing freedom of religion abroad, denouncing violations, and recommending government responses. The ambassador also heads the IRF office, acts as a principal adviser to the president and secretary of state, and, "with advice from" the U.S. Commission on International Religious Freedom, "shall make recommendations" regarding policies of the U.S. government "towards governments that violate freedom of religion."[37] The ambassador-at-large also represents the United States in contacts with foreign governments and at international organizations. These are extensive and high-level responsibilities.

Since the 1970s, Congress has created machinery to protect international human rights globally, including a human rights bureau headed by an assistant secretary and other supporting legislation. The protection of freedom of thought, conscience, and religion or belief is directly intertwined with many other human rights, such as freedom of expression and association, and can only be realized when due process guarantees are functioning. The norms, procedures, and interpretations used by the human rights bureau and the IRF office should be integrated with one another. Many foreign service personnel report that the IRF office has been marginalized within the bureaucracy.

To correct this and promote religious freedom abroad more effectively, the ambassador should work closely with a team of other top officials concerned about human rights, including the assistant secretary for democracy, human rights, and labor, the undersecretary for global affairs, other special envoys, and a new high-level team of field-based experts worldwide, especially in high-priority countries.

Congress has created several officials to focus on issues or areas with particular human rights problems, often addressing religious freedom violations as well, with special envoys on Tibet, North Korea, Sudan, and anti-Semitism. Their status helps focus attention on an issue, emphasize its importance, devote resources to it, and engage other political actors regarding it. The special envoy on Anti-Semitism was created because neither the IRF office nor the assistant secretary for democracy, human rights, and labor has adequately addressed the human rights aspects of the growing number of violent anti-Semitic incidents and government-sponsored anti-Semitism worldwide. Nor have they developed effective policy responses. Envoys addressing North Korea, Sudan, and anti-Semitism should work together with the assistant secretary and the ambassador-at-large, forming a senior leadership team in headquarters and not in isolation from one another. Together they constitute a considerable bank of talent and potential advocacy on ways to combat religious freedom violations.

Another tool with which to counter violations of religious freedom and related human rights would be the creation of a number of high-level human rights envoys to whom the ambassador-at-large for religious freedom and the assistant secretary for democracy, human rights, and labor could turn for information, assessments, and immediate action. A small number of high-level human rights envoys at the rank of ambassador could be appointed to serve at important posts overseas, such as Afghanistan and Iraq, where there are major programs and U.S. interests to combat human rights abuses, including religious freedom. Such envoys, reporting directly to the country ambassador and the assistant secretary, could help ensure that multimillion dollar U.S. and international aid programs to rebuild these countries are used in ways that advance human rights on the ground. The human rights ambassadors would help ensure implementation of U.S. human rights and religious freedom policies in places vital to U.S. diplomacy; they would be positioned also to offer independent warnings when there are rights abuses at places like Iraq's Abu Ghraib or Afghanistan's Bagram. The assistant secretary for democracy, human rights, and labor should be given the decisive authority in the naming of such envoys. Adding five to ten such senior posts to the U.S. diplomatic corps would demonstrably advance the effectiveness of both U.S. human rights and religious freedom policy and strengthen the hands of both the ambassador-at-large and the assistant secretary.

According to IRFA, the ambassador-at-large makes recommendations on policies of the U.S. government to advance religious freedom "with advice" from the U.S. Commission on International Religious Freedom. The ambassador-at -large can suffer, however, from the mistaken impression abroad that pronouncements made by the Commission on International Religious Freedom are also those of his office, since he or she is an ex officio, nonvoting member of the commission. Two legislative approaches could be taken to address this tension: 1) require the ambassador to consult more closely with the commission to try to influence its activities and recommendations. Congress could formally require the ambassador-at-large to present his or her recommendations to the commission *before* actions are taken and to consider the commission's recommendations rather than merely receive its advice without any requirement to incorporate it in his or her work; or 2) sever the ambassador's membership in the Commission for International Religious Freedom and assign the independent commission expanded powers of oversight and monitoring of the department's work in religious freedom and other areas of human rights policy.

- *Use the tools in IRFA more robustly.*

IRFA was explicitly designed to take into account the lessons of U.S. human rights policy and legislation developed and in place since the 1970s. It literally tried to reform all this legislation by adding the words "religious freedom" to every existing law. Yet little of this legislation has been used in connection with IRFA. For example, under IRFA authorities can designate individuals responsible for religious freedom violations and prohibit them from receiving visas to enter the United States. This has been used only once in IRFA's nine years. IRFA provisions like these could be employed more creatively.

Other legislation that was amended to include explicit reference to religious freedom includes the following: the Foreign Assistance Act of 1961 (sec. 116(c); 502(b) which restricts economic and security assistance to gross violators); the International Financial Institutions Act (sec 701), regarding U.S. votes at the International Monetary Fund, World Bank and other institutions; the Export Administration Act regarding limits on crime control and similar equipment; the International Broadcasting Act of 1964 (sec. 303); the Mutual Education and Cultural Exchange Act of 1961 (sec. 102(b), on international visitors programs); and the Foreign Service Act of 1980 (sec. 405(d), regarding awards to Foreign Service Officers). With very few exceptions these legislative provisions have not been used.

IRFA requires training of a variety of U.S. diplomatic, immigration, and other personnel on religious freedom. Because reporting is commonly assigned to the youngest and newest staff at embassies, this training is particularly important. Currently only one half-day session on human rights is included in the three-week statecraft course at the Foreign Service Institute for political officers. Only one two-hour session is devoted to religious freedom issues. Congress has expressed concern regarding training "at all levels," encouraging closer cooperation with IRF and the Commission on International Religious Freedom. Training by the Commission on International Religious Freedom of immigration judges on relevant standards may serve as a model for diplomatic and other personnel.

- *Strengthen international mechanisms on freedom of religion and belief.*

U.S. capacity to uphold religious freedom worldwide has been immeasurably enhanced by the presence of experts and mechanisms in multinational organizations capable of investigating violations of this key right worldwide. Through U.S. efforts the United Nations established in 1986 a special rapporteur on religious freedom and the Office of Democratic Institutions and Human Rights of the Organization for Security and Cooperation in Europe formed an Advisory Panel of Experts on Religious Freedom in 1997. These independent actors with global and regional reach bring expertise and legitimacy to efforts to end religious freedom violations and promote universal adherence to laws and policies to remedy those violations.

These mechanisms are in peril today as efforts to eliminate them have arisen. Some governments counter international efforts by claiming that they constitute "defamation of religions." Although individuals, not religions, are rights-bearers, this formulation, which restricts freedom of expression, has been gaining ground. Two such resolutions have already been adopted in June 2006 and March 2007 by the new UN Human Rights Council with another approved in the General Assembly. Furthermore, the annual omnibus religious intolerance resolution is also being delayed at the Human Rights Council because some states want to add scrutiny of "defamation of religions" to the mandate of the special rapporteur on religious freedom.[38] The United States cannot implement universal human rights norms alone, as it clearly understood when creating these international mechanisms.

Greater U.S. presence and participation in these multilateral organizations at higher diplomatic and expert levels can protect and strengthen the mechanisms, bringing U.S. ideas, actors, proposals, and resources more effectively into play to enforce religious freedom and related rights worldwide. IRFA gives the ambassador-at-large the task of being the chief actor on these issues at multilateral organizations and his or her active presence in advocating for the maintenance and strengthening of these expert bodies would substantially enhance U.S. policy efforts to implement freedom of religion worldwide.

A Clear Focus

Nearly ten years since the adoption of the International Religious Freedom Act, the effort to combat violations of freedom of thought, conscience, religion, or belief abroad has focused valuable attention on this dimension of human rights. IRFA has not created a hierarchy of rights, but rather has ensured that U.S. human rights policy includes a lens that acknowledges and tries to address violations of freedom of religion. If anything, the attacks of September 11, 2001 brought this dimension of global discord into sharper focus. But the lens used needs to be clear and focused on human rights: policy has suffered in cases when U.S. officials have tried to reshape and redefine human rights to establish new and separate categories declaring various abuses and victims as primarily "political" as opposed to "religious." Those using egregious abuses—such as torture, arbitrary imprisonment, and similar measures of repression—do not make such distinctions. When severe violations of freedom of religion are made visible through monitoring and reporting, they can and should be addressed using the many tools of U.S. human rights diplomacy. These tools are not and should not be limited to sanctions. Better and fuller use should be made of the diverse policy instruments available, including the talents of American diplomats, and the opportunities provided through international human rights institutions.

Chapter 12

U.S. Asylum and Refugee Policy

The "Culture of No"

Bill Frelick

Although America has a tradition dating to the Pilgrims as a safe haven for the persecuted, today the so-called war on terror creates new, often insurmountable obstacles for refugees seeking protection. Refugees are people with well-founded fears of being persecuted if returned to their homelands; asylum seekers are people who claim to be refugees and ask for protection. With respect to noncitizens generally—and asylum seekers and refugees in particular—the U.S. bureaucracy has become a "culture of no" where an official risks his or her job security by saying "yes" to a noncitizen. U.S. immigration authorities preoccupied with protecting the homeland from terrorist threats and petrified of being the person who signs off on permission for a single terrorist to enter or remain in the country are under enormous pressure to make the easier, risk-free decision to deny, reject, and push away. But when this is done to a refugee, it means a return to persecution, torture, or death.

Until 2003 the government bureaucracy most involved in asylum within the United States and in overseas refugee status determinations was the Immigration and Naturalization Service (INS) within the Department of Justice. In March 2003 the INS was swallowed up by the newly created Department of Homeland Security (DHS). The Executive Office of Immigration Review (EOIR), within which immigration courts and the Board of Immigration Appeals (BIA) operate, remained within the Justice Department. The transfer of immigration services and enforcement functions to DHS has had enormous implications for the way refugees and asylum seekers are perceived and treated by the U.S. government as well as by the broader American public.

The mission of DHS is primarily counterterrorism. As a result, it displays an institutional culture that regards "aliens" as potential threats and hazards to the nation. As DHS goes on its search for terrorists, it often finds instead asylum seekers, refugees, and other noncitizens with no connection to the war on terror. They are easy targets, however, and represent lots of bodies that can be denied entry, detained in custody, or deported, thereby providing the nation with a false sense of security.

The "Culture of No": Its Impact on Asylum

Multiple measures designed to block access to asylum have had a decided impact on the ability of people to seek asylum. In 1996, the Congress passed the Illegal Immigration Reform and Immigrant Responsibility Act (IIRAIRA), the first in a series of laws that used the threat of terrorism to narrow noncitizen access to asylum procedures. In the five years prior to the IIRAIRA, from 1992 through 1996, the yearly average of asylum applicants to the INS was 106,200. In the five years after IIRAIRA, 1997 through 2001, the average yearly number of asylum applicants dropped to 46,900, a decrease of 56 percent.[1] The next drop occurred in the aftermath of the September 11, 2001 attacks. Statistics compiled by the United Nations High Commissioner for Refugees (UNHCR) that combine asylum applications filed with DHS's Bureau of Citizenship and Immigration Services (USCIS) and EOIR show that asylum applications dropped from a high of 100,270 in 2002 to 73,780 in 2003 and continued dropping to 53,360 in 2004 and 48,770 in 2005, at which point it seemed to reach a plateau. The next year, 2006, saw a slight increase to 51,510.[2] In the broadest terms it appears as if asylum applications prior to IIRAIRA averaged more than 100,000 per year, counting only affirmative applications before INS asylum officers (that is, those who come forward voluntarily and not as a defense against removal), while asylum applications in the past several years have averaged half that—around 50,000.

The rates at which asylum seekers are granted asylum have also been declining, particularly since the 9/11 attacks in 2001. Among affirmative asylum applicants who voluntarily appear before USCIS asylum officers, approval rates fell from 54 percent in 1999 to 53 percent in 2000 to 41 percent in 2001 to 35 percent in 2002.[3] A similar decline is evident among asylum seekers in expedited removal: 20 percent in 2000 to 16 percent in 2001 and then a drop to 8.7 percent in 2002.[4] In the most recently available *Yearbook of Immigration Statistics, 2004*, DHS provides a different set of statistics but similarly shows a 27 percent drop in asylum approval rates by USCIS asylum officers in the five-year period from fiscal years 2000 through 2004 decreasing from 44 percent granted asylum in 2000 to 32 percent in 2004.[5]

Statistics on defensive asylum claimants (that is, noncitizens in removal proceedings who raise their fear of persecution or torture if returned as a defense against removal) coming before EOIR immigration judges present a less evident pattern of decline prior to 2001 but a similar drop in the year after 9/11: 17.5 percent in 1999 rising to 21 percent in 2000, then decreasing to 19.5 percent in 2001 and dropping more dramatically to 12 percent in 2002.[6] The approval rates overall for all types of asylum seekers before immigration judges (defensive and affirmative), however, are remarkably consistent between 2000 and 2005, averaging 38 percent.[7]

Expedited Removal

Although noncitizens who *are* involved in "terrorist activities" were already subject to exclusion or deportation under U.S. immigration law,[8] IIRAIRA created an expedited removal procedure for arriving noncitizens who are undocumented, have fraudulent documents, or who have a valid passport and nonimmigrant visa but appear to be intending to enter for some reason other than what is specified on their visa (for example, because they wanted to ask for asylum and not just visit Disney World).[9] IIRAIRA authorized low-level immigration inspectors in DHS's Bureau for Customs and Border Protection (CBP) to order the removal of such allegedly improperly documented noncitizens without review by an immigration judge and mandated the detention of noncitizens subject to expedited removal, including asylum seekers.

People who flee persecution, particularly at the hands of their own governments, usually have difficulty obtaining valid travel documents (they need, after all, to procure them from the same authorities who are seeking to harm them) and often have to rely on forged documents to make their escape.[10] IIRAIRA made an exception to summary removal for a noncitizen able to convince an immigration inspector at the port of entry that he or she has a fear of return. But people who actually have fled persecution and fear return are often torture victims or otherwise traumatized; they generally arrive tired, afraid, confused, and ignorant of the applicable law and procedures. The expectation that they should be able to articulate to uniformed authorities in a strange land a convincing fear of return immediately upon arrival is inconsistent with the refugee reality—a reality filled with trepidation, uncertainty, and mistrust.

Nevertheless, immigration inspectors are supposed to recognize such people and refer them to asylum officers—officials in Homeland Security's USCIS who conduct interviews to determine if the asylum seeker has a "credible fear." Those found not to have a credible fear are subject to removal though they may appeal the negative credible fear determination to an immigration judge, who operates out of EOIR in the Department of Justice. An immigration judge's decision on the appeal of a negative credible fear finding is not subject to further review.[11]

If the asylum officer determines that the person has "credible fear," the asylum seeker then has the opportunity to raise his or her fear of return as a defense against removal in an adversarial hearing before an immigration judge. The government is represented by a trial attorney from DHS's Bureau of Immigration and Customs Enforcement (ICE). The asylum seeker may have counsel present but only at his or her own expense.

ICE has discretion as to whether or not to release asylum seekers who have passed their credible fear tests. Many remain in detention while they wait—often for months—for their immigration court hearings. Detention, often in remote locations, increases the difficulty for the asylum seeker to find legal representation or even the support and advice of friends and relatives, and detention, particularly when prolonged and in prison conditions, also takes a psychological toll, which is often harder to bear for those who have experienced torture and abuse.[12]

Several studies have examined the impact of expedited removal on the right to seek asylum.[13] The most comprehensive study has been that of the U.S. Commission on International Religious Freedom (USCRIF), which had unprecedented access to data, ports of entry, and detention centers.[14] The study found that the greatest risk of error was not at the "credible fear" determination stage but rather in the arriving noncitizen's encounter with an immigration inspector in "secondary inspection." If an immigration inspector at passport controls thinks that the arriving noncitizen might be subject to expedited removal, the first inspector sends him or her to secondary inspection.

In 15 percent of cases observed, the USCIRF found that immigration inspectors in secondary inspection did not refer noncitizens who expressed a fear of return to asylum officers for credible fear interviews. Among those not referred for credible fear interviews were "aliens who expressed fear of political, religious, or ethnic persecution, which are clearly related to the grounds for asylum."[15] The USCIRF observed newly arrived noncitizens expressing a fear of return and found that in the majority of cases in which referrals were not made, "the inspector incorrectly indicated on the sworn statement that the applicant stated he had no fear of return."[16]

The USCRIF researchers provided detailed reports of their observations of CBP officers interviewing arriving noncitizens in expedited removal. Some of the officers used pressure tactics and intimidation (by, for example, telling the arriving noncitizen that he or she would be detained) to discourage potential asylum seekers from expressing a fear of return. The researchers were particularly struck that they observed so much aggressive and inappropriate behavior on the part of CPB inspectors who knew they were being observed. The study commented:

> Our observers noted that on more than one occasion aliens were refused interpreters at Houston, even when they requested them. The report that aliens who claimed to have expressed a fear of persecution were initially turned away at San Ysidro border crossing is an additional concern. In addition, aggressive or hostile interview techniques, sarcasm and ridicule of aliens, and verbal threats or accusations, while not common, were not infrequent in our sample. The fact that these behaviors occurred *while observers were present* suggests that such behavior may not even be perceived as problematic by some CBP officers.[17]

Although IIRAIRA only mandated expedited removal for improperly documented noncitizens identified by immigration inspectors at ports of entry (such as airports and border crossing points), it was expanded in November 2002 to apply to all undocumented boat arrivals (except Cubans) landing anywhere on the coast. It was expanded again in August 2004 to authorize Border Patrol agents to remove undocumented noncitizens for up to two weeks after arrival who have not proceeded more than 100 miles from the border.[18]

Even while independent studies of expedited removal were showing that immigration inspectors at ports of entry were insufficiently trained or supervised to recognize arriving noncitizens with asylum claims, the Bush administration expanded expedited removal well beyond ports of entry and empowered Border Patrol agents who operate along the border between land ports of entry to summarily remove noncitizens as well. In announcing the expansion of expedited removal, the administration said that Border Patrol agents would receive a mere eight hours of training to teach them how to recognize a protection claim and refer it to an asylum officer.[19]

The mission statement of the armed and uniformed Border Patrol is focused heavily on interdicting terrorists, which discourages Border Patrol agents from recognizing refugees who enter the United States illegally in order to seek asylum from persecution:

> We are the guardians of our Nation's borders. We are America's frontline. We safeguard the American homeland at and beyond our borders. We protect the American public against terrorists and the instruments of terror. We steadfastly enforce the laws of the United States while fostering our Nation's economic security through lawful international trade and travel.[20]

Given this focus, as well as their superficial training on expedited removal, Border Patrol agents may well not be correctly identifying asylum seekers among the 1.1 million undocumented noncitizens they apprehend each year[21] and properly referring them for credible fear interviews. That possibility is reinforced by Homeland Security Secretary Michael Chertoff's August 2006 announcement that DHS had managed during the course of the previous year to "eliminate the previous policy of catch-and-release whereby most non-Mexicans who were caught at the border were released, and to reverse that and impose catch-and-remove—100 percent catch-and-remove for everybody caught at the border."[22] Is it conceivable that *none* of those people had protection claims?

Refugees and asylum seekers represent a small fraction of total immigrants: according to the non-partisan Migration Policy Institute, total immigration to the United States between 2002 and 2006 averaged 1.8 million per year, including about 500,000 unauthorized migrants.[23] Annual refugee admissions during that period averaged 40,700 per year[24] and annual asylum applications averaged 65,400,[25] which means that refugees and asylum seekers, on average, represent less than 6 percent of the total immigrant pool. Although the contours of immigration reform are not yet known, it is clear that trying to make the U.S.-Mexican border impregnable for unauthorized migrants will be a prominent feature. Chertoff is already moving forward with Operation Jump Start, a plan that doubles the number of Border Patrol agents from about 9,000 in 2001 to nearly 18,000 in 2008. He has announced the deterrent impact of "the end of 'catch and release,' the implementation of Operation Jump Start, and the expanded use of expedited removal procedures" as already resulting in "a marked decrease" in undocumented border crossers.[26] Meanwhile, the immigration debate has become increasingly xenophobic and demagogic, too often reducing noncitizens to an undifferentiated mass of "illegals" prone to criminality and terrorism.

"Material Support"

The first major post-9/11 anti-terror legislation, the USA Patriot Act of 2001,[27]and another anti-terrorism measure, the Real ID Act of 2005, amended U.S. immigration law by defining terrorism and support for terrorism so broadly that many refugees and asylum seekers, including people who fled terrorist threats and extortion, faced the prospect of return to persecution.

Terrorism is generally understood as acts of wanton violence directed against civilians in order to instill coercive fear among a general target population. But, strangely, "terrorist activity" in U.S. immigration law is defined as "any activity which is unlawful under the laws of the place where it is committed" that uses any weapon or "dangerous device" with the intent "to endanger, directly or indirectly, the safety of one or more individuals or to cause substantial damage to property."[28] That definition is so broad that George Washington's activities during the Revolutionary War would have been considered terrorist activities under it.

Moreover, the definition of a terrorist "organization" is an oxymoron: "a group of two or more individuals, whether organized or not," which engages in the terrorist activities defined above.[29] It is hard to fathom how two people who are specifically *not* organized could constitute an organization but words are frequently stripped of their common meaning in immigration law. Thus two kids who had never previously met but who join together to throw rocks (a "dangerous device") to break the windows of an abandoned building ("substantial damage to property") could be found to be an "organization" engaged in "terrorist activities."

The law defines "engaging" in terrorist activities to include providing "material support" to a terrorist activity.[30] It does not say how much support counts; it does not even specify explicitly that the support need be voluntary. Although the word "material" modifies the word "support" in the law, suggesting that the support given must be substantial or relevant to the carrying out of a terrorist activity, the term has been interpreted to mean "any" support. In oral arguments before the Board of Immigration Appeals in *Matter of S-K-*, a case involving a Baptist woman from the Chin minority in Burma (Myanmar), a member of the BIA posed a hypothetical question to the Department of Homeland Security lawyer: "So, if someone provides a pocket full of change knowing that the organization might be a terrorist organization, that's sufficient in your view?" The government lawyer replied, "That's correct, your Honor."[31]

Both the immigration judge and the BIA expressed sympathy for S-K-, finding her to be credible and to have a well-founded fear of persecution. The judge and the BIA both recognized that the Chin National Front, the group to which she provided modest material support, was not in any way a threat to the security of the United States and that it had not engaged in activities that are commonly understood as terrorism. In fact, the Chin National Front was engaged in armed resistance to a government the United States does not support. Yet given the way that the statute is written, with its overly broad definition of "terrorist organization," the judge felt bound not to grant the woman asylum. The BIA, observing that the statute was "breathtaking in its scope," said that it could not overturn the judge.[32] As a result of this peculiar definition of terrorism, the immigration judge and the BIA both felt bound to deny asylum to a woman whom they recognized as having a well-founded fear of persecution.

The Department of Homeland Security has since issued a waiver for the Chin and other Burmese minority groups but has not extended that waiver to S-K-, whose case at the moment is on the attorney general's desk. Material support waivers have helped some Burmese refugees in camps in Southeast Asia seeking admission to the United States but have been far less helpful for asylum seekers inside the United States, only a handful of whom had been granted them as of mid-2007. In any case waivers are a clumsy and imperfect backstop for a law that is so deeply flawed.

Finally, the law lacks a clear exception for support provided under duress. If a terrorist puts a gun to someone's head and robs him, the United States now denies asylum to the robbery victim because he provided "material support" to the terrorist by handing over his wallet—however unwillingly. For this reason the resettlement of Colombian refugees to the United States has ground to a halt. The vast majority of refugees have fled that country because armed groups threatened or abused them. "Alberto," who fled from Caldas, Colombia, told Human Rights Watch his story: "I had to pay a *vacuna* [a levy or bribe] to the *paracos* [paramilitaries]. Then the guerrillas came and saw that I had paid the *vacuna*, so they came to kill me. I had to pay the paramilitaries, and then I was afraid. It was 3,000 pesos [$1.20] that I paid."[33] The tragic irony is that the reason Alberto fled for his life—the basis for his well-founded fear of persecution, namely, mistreatment by the paramilitaries—is the very same reason that would be used to deny him admission as a refugee or asylum seeker if he managed to enter the United States on his own.

Deporting Refugees

The granting of asylum is a matter of discretion but the prohibition on returning refugees to places where their lives or freedom would be threatened is mandated as a fundamental principle of international law. This principle, *nonrefoulement*, is established in Article 33 of the Refugee Convention and is reiterated in the "withholding of removal" section of the Immigration and Nationality Act, which prohibits the United States from returning a refugee to persecution.[34] But under the "culture of no," this principle, too, has eroded in practice.

Article 33.2 of the Refugee Convention makes an exception to the principle of *nonrefoulement* for a refugee "who, having been convicted by a final judgment of a particularly serious crime, constitutes a danger to the community of that country." U.S. immigration law followed this exception with similar language.[35] UNHCR's Executive Committee interprets the "particularly serious crime" exception to *nonrefoulement* to apply only in "exceptional cases and after due consideration of the circumstances."[36] The UNHCR *Handbook on Procedures and Criteria for*

Determining Refugee Status further elucidates this point, saying that Article 33.2 should be applied only in "extreme cases."[37] In reference to another exclusion clause in the Refugee Convention,[38] the *Handbook* says that "a 'serious' crime must be a capital crime or a very grave punishable act. Minor offenses punishable by moderate sentences are not grounds for exclusion."[39]

UNHCR wrote an advisory opinion on Article 33.2, saying "It must . . . be shown that the danger posed by the refugee is sufficient to justify *refoulement*. The danger posed must be to the country of refuge itself; the danger must be very serious; and the finding of dangerousness must be based on reasonable grounds and therefore supported by credible and reliable evidence."[40]

Until 1990 judges had the discretion to decide what constituted "a particularly serious crime" and to weigh the seriousness of the crime against the likelihood and severity of persecution expected upon return. Beginning with the Immigration Act of 1990, however, which defined a particularly serious crime as an aggravated felony, Congress has dictated to judges the crimes that would exempt refugees from protection. Successive amendments to the Immigration and Nationality Act have expanded the definition and list of crimes that qualify as aggravated felonies for purposes of deportation until today the list includes what are in fact misdemeanors under criminal law.[41]

Mark McAllister, for example, a native of Northern Ireland, came to the United States as a juvenile with his parents in 1996 after his home had been repeatedly shot at by unknown persons and his father regularly arrested, beaten, and jailed by the Royal Ulster Constabulary. McAllister was convicted on three counts of possession with intent to distribute the drug known as ecstasy. After his conviction the immigration judge, BIA, and district court all ruled that his crime was an aggravated felony and a particularly serious one, barring him from withholding of removal.[42]

In addition the courts have ruled that people who have been recognized by the United States as refugees but who subsequently adjust their status to that of permanent residents lose their protection as refugees and can be deported for even more minor crimes. Suwan, a Cambodian refugee living in Houston, Texas with a wife and two young children was deported to Cambodia for two counts of indecent exposure. He committed these offenses, he said, because there was no toilet at the construction site where he was working and he was forced to urinate outdoors.[43] In another case involving a Bosnian refugee, Sejid Smriko, the BIA held that a person "admitted to the United States as a refugee [who] adjusted his status to that of a lawful permanent resident, is subject to removal on the basis of his crimes involving moral turpitude, even though his refugee status was never terminated."[44] Smriko's crimes involved two minor shoplifting offenses for which he was sentenced to a fine and a five-day suspended sentence, respectively, and a third conviction for receiving stolen property, which resulted in a year's probation. He was ordered deported to Bosnia.

Other refugees have been denied withholding of removal on vague national security grounds. B-Y-, a young man from Uzbekistan, applied for withholding of removal after the Uzbek government issued an Interpol warrant for his arrest based on trumped up charges that in fact stemmed from the Uzbek authorities' intent to persecute him for his religious beliefs and imputed political opinions. The immigration judge found his testimony to be credible and that "the extradition request by the Uzbek government will be given no weight . . . coming from a government . . . with a history of engaging in persecution and using torture as a sovereign tool."[45] Though the immigration judge denied B-Y- asylum because he had failed to apply for asylum within one year of entering the country, he was granted withholding of removal on the grounds that he had "established a clear probability of future persecution should he return to Uzbekistan."[46]

B-Y- gave permission to Immigration and Customs Enforcement agents searching his apartment to confiscate a computer that he shared with his two roommates. He said he had nothing to hide. The ICE agents discovered temporary Internet files on the computer indicating that someone had viewed film clips of Osama bin Laden and the war in Chechnya. The immigration judge said that neither the video clip on the shared computer nor any of his other activities showed B-Y- to "exhibit any propensity of violence or violent intention" and that "any risk of security to the United States by respondent in these regards is highly dubious, at best."

Nevertheless, ICE appealed the case to the Board of Immigration Appeals on the grounds that there was good reason to regard B-Y- as "a danger to the security of the United States"—another basis, in addition to "a particularly serious crime," for denying withholding of removal.[47] Citing a precedent ruling by the attorney general, *Matter of A-H-*,[48] the BIA ruled that "any nontrivial level of danger to national security is sufficient to trigger this statutory bar"[49] and denied withholding but noted that the Convention Against Torture, incorporated in U.S. law (and which prohibits the United States from returning any person who would more likely than not be tortured by agents of his government upon return) would prevent his return to his home country.[50] "Because the respondent in this case would almost certainly be arrested upon his return to Uzbekistan," the BIA said, "we conclude that he also would more likely than not be tortured in detention," and was therefore eligible for CAT protection.[51]

Subsequently, as B-Y- sat in the Pike County Prison in Pennsylvania, he received a letter from ICE that said "ICE is pursuing assurances from the Government of Uzbekistan that you will not be tortured upon your return." ICE advised B-Y- that any efforts he might take to prevent or obstruct his removal might subject him to criminal prosecution.[52]

At the time of this writing, B-Y- is still detained and faces the prospect of return to near certain persecution and torture in Uzbekistan. The BIA denied him refugee protection based not on the international standard of a very serious danger to the United States for which there is credible evidence but rather on the attorney general's contrived standard of a "nontrivial" danger and despite the fact that the immigration judge who first heard the case had proclaimed it "wholly lacking in any persuasive evidence that there are reasonable grounds to believe that respondent is a danger to the security of the United States."[53]

Lack of Legal Representation for Asylum Seekers

Unlike the right to counsel that is guaranteed to those charged with crimes in the criminal justice system, noncitizens in removal proceedings have access to counsel only insofar as it is "at no expense to the government."[54] The director of Law and Policy Studies at Georgetown University's Institute for the Study of International Migration, Andrew Schoenholz, has found that a represented asylum seeker in U.S. immigration courts is six times more likely to be granted asylum than an asylum seeker who appears *pro se*.[55]

Given the potentially serious consequences of deportation, particularly for a person claiming a fear of persecution upon return, and in view of the complexity of immigration and asylum law, the lack of legal counsel can be a matter of life or death for those who cannot afford counsel or for whom a pro bono representative is unavailable (and that is often the case, especially for noncitizens detained in remote locations).

In the landmark *Gideon v. Wainwright* case, the Supreme Court held that indigent criminal defendants had the right to a court-appointed attorney because they could not otherwise be assured their Sixth Amendment right to a fair trial,[56] and subsequent rulings have expanded this right to certain civil proceedings as well.[57] In the context of removal proceedings, however, the Supreme Court held in *Ardestani v. INS* that noncitizens do not have a right under current U.S. law to a court-appointed attorney, but that the "broad purposes" of the law "would be served by making the statute applicable to deportation proceedings."[58] The court added, "We are mindful that the complexity of immigration procedures, and the enormity of the interests at stake, make legal representation in deportation especially important."[59]

Employment Bars on Asylum Seekers

Asylum seekers are expected not only to pay for their own legal representation but also to do it without earning money. IIRAIRA bars work authorizations for the first 180 days after a person lodges an asylum application. The 180-day time period does not include days lost if a continuance or some other delay is deemed to be at the initiative of the asylum seeker so the actual time an asylum seeker is not allowed to work can be much longer. During the time applicants are barred from working legally, they are also not eligible for public assistance and are not provided with any type of government-funded shelter or other accommodation.

Either members of Congress were deluded and thought that most asylum seekers can afford to pay for legal counsel (at an estimated cost in New York City of $1,500 to $2,000 for an asylum claim)[60] as well as support themselves while their asylum claims are pending or they were trying to deter people without significant financial resources from seeking asylum at all. Or they were being disingenuous by creating an additional legal obstacle to force asylum seekers who are seeking legal status to work illegally while their claims are pending, thus making them even more likely to be subjected to exploitation and to be perceived by the public as "illegals."

Detention of Asylum Seekers

Under IIRAIRA all asylum seekers in the expedited removal process must be detained at least until the conclusion of their credible fear interviews.[61] Almost all of the detention facilities used for asylum seekers are no different from prisons used to incarcerate criminals. "Indeed, in some instances," said the USCIRF report, "actual criminal justice institutions—in this case, county jails—are operated as dual-use facilities that simultaneously house asylum seekers and criminal offenders, side by side."[62] The report further found that "whether they were county jails, DHS-run facilities, or private contract facilities, they were operated in more or less the same way."[63] This included secure barriers, strip searches, 24-hour surveillance lighting, and the use of segregation or solitary confinement for disciplinary reasons. The report included interviews with asylum seekers in detention. One said:

The whole detention system is there to break you down further. The time you spend there prolongs your trauma. And you are not even allowed to cry. If you do, they take you to isolation.[64]

Another said:

I felt really isolated and humiliated. I felt like a person who had no value. At any time, the security guards made us do whatever they wanted. I felt traumatized by my treatment. My blood pressure went higher and my medical problems worsened there.[65]

ICE parole decisions cannot be appealed; review is possible only through a habeas corpus petition. Immigration judges in turn have seen their discretion to grant eligible asylum seekers release on bond (as opposed to DHS release through parole) increasingly curtailed. In October 2002, for example, an immigration judge ruled that Haitian teenager David Joseph, who had recently arrived on a wooden boat, should be released to his uncle, a legal resident living in Brooklyn, N.Y., who was willing to post a $ 2,500 bond. The judge found that David posed no threat if released. Finding his asylum claim to be credible, the judge said he was unlikely to abscond. The government appealed but the BIA affirmed the judge's ruling to release David. It found that the judge correctly applied the rules regarding release on bond to avoid unnecessary, prolonged detention.[66]

At that point Attorney General John Ashcroft stepped in. Using David Joseph as a precedent-setting ruling, Ashcroft decreed that all Haitian boat arrivals should be jailed. He invoked "national security" as his rationale, not because David Joseph himself ever harmed or threatened anyone but in order that a surge of other boat people from Haiti not "injure national security by diverting valuable Coast Guard and DOD [Department of Defense] resources from (their) counter-terrorism and homeland security responsibilities."[67] After his long detention at the Krome facility in Florida, David was deported to Haiti.

Interdiction and Interception of Asylum Seekers

While the Border Patrol's mission statement calls itself "America's frontline," the anti-immigration frontline has moved well beyond America's borders. The Department of Homeland Security not only absorbed the INS from the Justice Department but also took the Coast Guard from the Department of Transportation. In the narrative accompanying its fiscal year 2008 budget, DHS says, "The Coast Guard evaluates its migrant interdiction effectiveness by counting the number of undocumented migrants from four primary source countries (Cuba, Haiti, the

Dominican Republic, and the People's Republic of China) against the combined estimated yearly migration threat from these countries. There were 5,552 successful migrant arrivals out of an estimated threat of 51,134 migrants in FY [fiscal year] 2006, yielding a deterrence and interdiction rate of 89 percent."[68] DHS openly declares that the Coast Guard regards these boat people as a "threat." It fails to acknowledge that two of the four primary source countries for interdicted migrants in fiscal year 2006, China and Haiti, were also the two leading nationalities granted asylum in the United States in that year.[69] There is in other words a complete disconnect between the enforcement-driven interdiction of migrants and even minimal notions of refugee protection.

Only a tiny number of Haitians interdicted on the high seas have ever had asylum claims heard. Upon interdiction U.S. officials provide no information to the people taken aboard U.S. Coast Guard cutters about their right to seek protection. Only those who wave their hands, jump up and down, and shout the loudest—and are recognized as having done so—are even afforded, in theory, a shipboard refugee pre-screening interview. We will never know how many people failed the "shout test" over the years. Between 1981 and 1990 the INS allowed only 11 Haitians out of 22,940 interdicted to pursue asylum claims.[70]

Today the very few Haitians who pass the "shout test" and then a shipboard "credible fear" interview are taken to Guantánamo for a full refugee interview (though without the benefit of legal assistance). In 2005 only 9 of the 1,850 interdicted Haitians received a credible fear interview and only 1 person was recognized as a refugee.[71] But Haitians whom the United States recognizes as refugees at Guantánamo are still not admitted to the United States. Some have been compelled to wait for years pending the agreement of a third country to admit them.[72]

United States Policy Toward Overseas Refugees

Only a tiny fraction of the world's refugees ever reach American shores. Nearly all of the world's 14 million refugees and 24 million internally displaced persons remain in overcrowded camps or slums, often for years and years, before they are able to return to whatever might be left of their homes and lands.[73] They do not have the capacity to travel across continents to seek asylum in the increasingly inaccessible industrialized North. Most remain nearly invisible, their suffering barely registering between the North American and European publics. Millions of refugees are stuck in protracted situations of a decade or longer. These include more than 3 million Afghans, more than 3 million Palestinians, and hundreds of thousands of Burmese, Sudanese, Congolese, Somalis, Burundians, and Eritreans.[74] And new violence and persecution churn out more people every day to join the ranks of the uprooted. Among the newly displaced, the most vulnerable are those who remain inside their own countries where the situations are so dangerous that international humanitarians are often unable to reach them to provide life-sustaining food and aid or the minimal protection their presence might provide. These include recently displaced people in Darfur, Iraq, Sri Lanka, and Somalia.

Off the refugee protection radar entirely are millions of people who are forced from their homes by hunger and economic deprivation. Their numbers are likely to grow as a result of climate change, environmental degradation, mismanagement of resources, and lack of family planning. These are not mere economic migrants voluntarily seeking opportunities, but rather people who are forced to flee because of threats to their very existence. Their numbers are staggering. The last comprehensive attempt to quantify them—in 1995—estimated 25 million, almost all from sub-Saharan Africa.[75] The Intergovernmental Panel on Climate Change estimates that by 2050, the numbers of "environmental refugees" could reach 150 million.[76] Despite the cause of their flight being the deprivation of rights as fundamental as the right to be free from hunger, international refugee law has been slow to recognize this as a basis for protection. Governments, including the United States, are prone to reject all "economic migrants" presumptively without bothering to consider whether their migration was voluntary, whether they may, in fact, have fundamental economic and social rights, and whether they have the right not to be returned to face serious harm from deprivation of those rights.

The preamble to the Refugee Convention notes the heavy burden refugees place on host countries and says that satisfactory solutions cannot be achieved without international cooperation. But international law does not mandate such cooperation; so when wealthy, faraway states exercise their discretion to relieve the refugee burden on poorer, frontline states, their actions are often highly politicized and selective, if they happen at all.

U.S. overseas refugee assistance has always reflected U.S. foreign policy priorities, notwithstanding the worthy humanitarian impact such assistance has often made.[77] This has often resulted in disparities of assistance that have nothing to do with relative need, but rather with domestic political agendas. Most recently, when the United States belatedly began to provide modest humanitarian assistance for Iraqi refugees in the Middle East, bilateral assistance was heavily weighted in favor of Jordan over Syria despite the fact that Syria hosted nearly double the estimated number of refugees (an estimated 750,000 in Jordan; 1.2 million in Syria). The United States lists Syria as a state sponsor of terrorism, making it ineligible for foreign aid. U.S. policy has, in effect, punished Iraqi refugees who went to the only country in the region willing to accept them, as Syria kept its doors open long after Jordan and others had closed theirs to all but a select few. The U.S. approach of "all stick and no carrot" not only deprived refugees of needed assistance, but also robbed Washington of the flexibility to support Damascus when it was doing the right thing by allowing refugees in. Isolated as it was from international support, Syria in September 2007 also closed its doors to Iraqis. "No one in the international community is helping us," a Syrian government spokesman told the *Financial Times*. "The Syrian government can no longer shoulder the responsibility alone."[78]

The "culture of no" extends to how the fortunate few among the millions of overseas are chosen for admission under the U.S. refugee resettlement program. The chances of recognized refugees being resettled in the United States are diminishing steadily. Indeed, overseas refugee admissions to the United States have been in an 18-year decline: in the six-year period from 1989 to 1994, the United States admitted an average of 114,000 refugees per year; in the six-year period from 1995 to 1999, the annual average of refugee admissions fell to 79,000; and in the most recent six years, 2001 to 2006, the average has fallen to 45,000, a 60 percent decrease during this time.[79]

Like other facets of U.S. refugee and asylum policy, the war on terror has had an impact on how refugees are chosen for U.S. resettlement. In 2001, the United States admitted 12,060 refugees from the Middle East. The year following the 9/11 attacks, the number fell to 3,700. In other regions, U.S. resettlement slowly picked up after 2002. However, during the next four years, resettlement from the Middle East remained at a yearly average of 3,500, despite the fact that during this time, fueled by the war in Iraq, the number of refugees in the Middle East continued to climb.[80] The pitiful U.S. response to large numbers of Iraqi refugees in need of resettlement, including those who had served the U.S. cause in Iraq and hence became particularly vulnerable to retribution—831 refugees admitted from fiscal year 2003 through the first nine months of fiscal year 2007[81]—demonstrates that a combination of foreign policy objectives and heightened security concerns have sent a resounding "no" that has trumped our obvious moral responsibilities.

Beyond Fear and Mistrust

Institutional and societal cultures are resistant to change. Real progress in the United States for refugees and immigrants is unlikely as long as fear predominates and the United States remains preoccupied with homeland security. Until this changes, it will be difficult for the United

States to be welcoming toward strangers asking for help. Prudent steps need to be taken to ensure safety against real threats. But fear can also lead to stereotyping, paranoid suspiciousness, and broad guilt by association based on characteristics such as a person's religion or national origin. The likely result is the creation of barriers—physical, legal, psychological—that simply keep out those who are "other than us" without distinguishing among them.

Making those distinctions among people claiming a need for protection is an important first step toward recognizing our common global humanity. It is a process that requires fairness and deliberation. At the end of the process, not everyone will be found to meet the standards for protection. People who are not otherwise authorized to stay and who are not in need of protection can certainly be compelled to go home. But asylum seekers should at least have access to refugee determination procedures; those procedures should be fair; and the standards people are expected to meet and the burden of proof for meeting them should be reasonable. A new administration could take the first steps in that direction by implementing the following recommendations:

- Create a system of government-funded, public-defender-like representation for noncitizens in removal proceedings.
- Restore to immigration judges the authority to order the removal of arriving noncitizens so that such life-and-death decisions are taken out of the hands of low-level immigration inspectors and Border Patrol agents. If expedited removal is retained, authorize asylum officers to grant asylum at the time of the credible fear interview to arriving noncitizens who clearly meet the well-founded fear of persecution standard.
- Allow asylum seekers who lodge nonfrivolous applications for asylum to work while their claims are pending.
- Amend the Immigration and Nationality Act to ensure that individuals whose lives or freedom would be threatened if returned to their home countries are provided protection from return to persecution unless they can reasonably be regarded as posing a genuine danger to the security of the United States or have been convicted of a crime that truly is serious within the meaning of the Refugee Convention and Protocol.
- Detain asylum seekers only when necessary; subject them to review by an immigration judge or an independent authority; and promulgate regulations to establish uniform criteria for release so that ICE officials exercise parole authority more consistently.
- When detention of noncriminal asylum seekers is necessary, make it as humane as possible in non-prison-like facilities with access to

legal assistance and separation of asylum seekers from criminal offenders.

- Change the definition of "terrorist activities" in U.S. law to reflect one that recognizably relates to the actual meaning of the word "terrorism" and amend the "material support" provision to include an exception for people who provided such support under duress and for support that was trivial, minimal, and not material to the commission of terrorist activities.
- Make a good-faith effort to identify refugees and others in need of protection when interdicting migrants on the high seas and give them a fair opportunity to make asylum claims. Provide boat people in need of protection with appropriate protection in the United States.
- Work to fix the root causes of forced migration by promoting both economic and social rights as well as civil and political rights, in part by providing more generous humanitarian and development assistance for refugees, internally displaced people, war-affected populations, and returnees, as well as victims of famine and other severe economic and social deprivations.
- Regain world leadership in refugee protection through a renewed resettlement program that not only saves the lives of the most vulnerable refugees but that also encourages other prosperous and stable countries to share the responsibility of providing durable solutions for the world's refugees, thus relieving the burden on host countries in regions of conflict that are often ill-equipped to provide asylum on their own.

These 10 "fixes" would go a long way toward repairing a system that has been paralyzed by fear and mistrust.

Chapter 13
Building Human Rights into the Government Infrastructure

Eric P. Schwartz

A coherent, well-functioning bureaucratic structure is no substitute for lack of political will.* Conversely, a president determined to ensure that human rights play a critical role in foreign policy can prevail under a wide variety of organizational arrangements. But organizational structure and decisions on appointments to key roles are hardly irrelevant to effective policy and often reflect political priorities. Whether the issue is U.S. foreign assistance, homeland security, arms control, or human rights and democracy promotion, the questions that arise about bureaucratic organization are very similar: Do arrangements (and possible reforms) help to highlight and provide appropriate focus for critical issue areas among senior officials and the President? And do they facilitate policy integration—that is, coherent policy approaches that make best use of all relevant agencies and individuals in government? These are the two principal questions this chapter is designed to address.

Integrating Human Rights Policy

A new administration must promote a "Whole of Government Approach" toward promotion of human rights, strengthen the policy development process for human rights and democracy, and ensure it is aligned with the deliberative process for foreign assistance funding.

To examine how best to approach the making of human rights policy, it is important first to consider the structure of policymaking in the area of national security and foreign policy. The National Security Council (NSC), established in 1947 by the National Security Act,[1] is the key foreign policy and national security decision-making body for the United States government. It includes the president as chair, the vice president, the secretary of state and the secretary of defense, as well as the chairman of the Joint Chiefs of Staff and the director of central intelligence as advisers. Moreover, pursuant to the decision of the president, other cabinet officials often are included in the National Security Council.[2]

A critical objective for the National Security Council is the coordination and integration of the activities of the many agencies of government involved in issues affecting national security, with a particular focus on those policy issues that are not within the domain of just one agency of government. By presidential directives issued at the outset of each new administration, the NSC has in recent history functioned with a subordinate NSC Principals Committee, which is essentially the NSC without the president and vice president.[3] It is chaired by the president's national security adviser and includes cabinet-level officials. Subordinate to the Principals Committee is the NSC Deputies Committee, chaired by the president's deputy national security adviser and composed generally of the second-ranking policy official at each of the cabinet agencies with national security responsibilities. Finally, one level further down the bureaucratic ladder, there are policy coordination committees (called interagency working groups in the Clinton administration), chaired in most cases by either NSC senior directors or assistant secretaries at the State Department.[4] Traditionally, these interagency committees operate with different degrees of formality. Some are established by presidential directive and operate effectively; others operate more on paper than in reality and still others operate informally or on a temporary basis but without explicit presidential authorization.

The staff of the NSC is located primarily in the Eisenhower Executive Office Building next door to the White House, and is composed largely of foreign policy specialists from academia and think tanks, as well as those detailed from the national security agencies of government. All NSC staff work for the national security adviser and function as both the in-house foreign policy staff for the president and the secretariat for the national security decision-making process. As a practical matter, this decision-making structure operates on the premise that decisions should be made at the lowest possible levels and should be elevated to the president only when they are of signal importance or when there are critically important disagreements between agencies that require presidential resolution.

If human rights policy is to be a priority for the United States government, it must be the subject of active consideration in the National Security Council decision-making process, including the president and his or her senior advisers. The programs and actions of many agencies—the Departments of State, Defense, Labor, Justice and Treasury, as well as the U.S. Agency for International Development (AID)—have serious implications for human rights, and integrated and coherent policy approaches will emerge only through a well-coordinated interagency process. Moreover, the president and his or her senior advisers must be involved to ensure that key decisions are made; to promote agency compliance and discipline in the execution of policy; and, most importantly, to communicate to the public, the international community, and the bureaucracy the administration's seriousness of purpose on these issues.

National Security Presidential Directive 1 (NSPD 1), issued by President George W. Bush on February 13, 2001, establishes an NSC policy coordination committee on democracy, human rights, and international operations chaired by the National Security Council staff. The Bush administration has at times used this mechanism to develop policy on human rights and democracy, but much more must be done.

Beginning in 2005, for example, the NSC staff began an interagency priority setting and strategic planning exercise for promotion of democracy, starting with policy coordination meetings for each of the regions of the world. Participants were reportedly asked to "identify the countries in which the lack of democracy or an imminent threat to democracy presented a strategic problem for the region" in question.[5] Following those meetings, NSC staff, as well as staff from the Bureau of Democracy, Human Rights, and Labor and from AID, considered the kinds of strategy and support that would be necessary to promote positive policy developments. The group drafted a democracy strategy for 49 priority countries and attached notional dollar figures to the strategy. The NSC Deputies Committee then met to approve the approach in early 2006. While these developments are significant, it is unclear whether this policy development process was well integrated into the administration's deliberative process for foreign assistance funding. The administration has apparently made efforts to improve such integration, but serious challenges remain. In this regard, the 2008 budget request envisioned overall decreases in funding for human rights and civil society as well as cuts in programs relating to countries such as Russia, Uzbekistan, and Burma (Myanmar), each of which would seem to have merited high-priority consideration.[6]

NSPD 1 indicates that the democracy, human rights, and international organizations policy coordination committee would assume the duties of a human rights treaties interagency working group established by Executive Order 13107, which was issued by President Bill Clinton in 1998. As a practical matter, however, the Bush administration does not appear to have implemented the program of action contemplated in that executive order. The order declares that the United States will promote respect for human rights in relationships with all other countries and will strengthen international institutions for human rights promotion; that all U.S. agencies shall seek to implement human rights obligations that are relevant to their functions; that each agency shall designate a single contact officer responsible for implementation of the executive order; and that agency heads will be accountable for implementation of human rights obligations that fall within their areas of responsibility.[7] The order also specifies that each agency will take responsibility, in coordination with other appropriate agencies, for responding to inquiries, requests for information, and complaints about human rights violations in areas that fall within its areas of competence and that an interagency working group on human rights treaties will provide guidance, oversight, and coordination on questions concerning adherence to and implementation of human rights obligations.

The tasks assigned to the interagency group by the executive order were many and varied. They included coordinating review of treaties for possible submission to the Senate for consent to ratification, as well as coordinating reports submitted in compliance with treaty obligations and responses to complaints concerning alleged violations submitted to various international organizations. Other tasks included development of mechanisms to ensure conformity of proposed legislation and practices with international human rights obligations, planning for public education on provisions of human rights treaties, coordinating and directing annual reviews of U.S. reservations, declarations, and understandings to human rights treaties, making recommendations to the president on U.S. adherence to or implementation of human rights treaties and related matters, and overseeing other significant tasks in connection with human rights treaties or international human rights institutions.

This executive order, which by its terms applies to the Departments of State, Justice, Labor, and Defense and the Joint Chiefs of Staff, as well as other agencies as appropriate, was never formally rescinded by President Bush but it has not been implemented in the manner suggested by its terms. Any serious United States policy on human rights and democracy must include a dedicated, disciplined interagency effort, endorsed at the highest level, that includes commitments to engagement with international human rights institutions and the active participation of all relevant agencies. These measures are a critical complement to the regionally focused human rights and democracy strategy as elaborated in the NSC-led process described earlier in this section. Moreover, the increased involvement of the Department of Defense in operations other than war, or stability operations,[8] underscores the importance of Defense Department and Joint Chiefs of Staff involvement in these kinds of interagency exercises. A new administration should reaffirm the terms of Executive Order 13107 as well as the role of the NSC process in developing overall country strategies in the area of human rights and democracy, and link both to the foreign affairs funding functions.

The Role of the National Security Council Staff

A new administration should retain an NSC staff office with a strong focus on human rights; the office should be led by a senior figure with human rights expertise and should have a broad mandate.

National Security Council staff members serve as the "in-house" foreign policy advisers to the president. They also organize senior-level interagency meetings, prepare agendas, and largely define issues for decision. NSC staff members can ensure that human rights issues are fairly considered by senior policymakers and the president, and can advocate for human rights-friendly options even when those options do not reflect consensus positions of the State or Defense Departments. Similarly, in articulating and promoting the human rights perspectives of the president, NSC staff can (and should) influence the implementation actions of government agencies.

Over the course of eight years, the Clinton administration progressively strengthened NSC staff and organizational capacity on human rights issues. At the outset of the administration in 1993, the author was appointed as director for human rights, refugees, and humanitarian affairs in a much larger Office of Global Issues and Multilateral Affairs. The office was led by a senior director, Richard Clarke, who had many years of very senior government experience in foreign affairs and defense policy, focused largely on political-military affairs. In addition to human rights, democracy promotion, and United Nations issues, this office was responsible for counterterrorism, counternarcotics, and other international crime issues. The proliferation of subject areas under its purview meant that human rights promotion could not be its highest priority.

In late 1993, the Clinton NSC added an Office for Democracy led by a senior director, Morton Halperin, who had many years of experience relating to both national security and human rights. From that point until March 1996, human rights issues were managed both in the Office of Global Issues and Multilateral Affairs and in the Democracy Office. In March of 1996, the author succeeded Morton Halperin, and the Office for Democracy incorporated the human rights, refugee, and humanitarian affairs functions and was renamed the Office of Democracy, Human Rights, and Humanitarian Affairs. In June 1998, the office was further expanded, and took on United Nations affairs, international peacekeeping, and sanctions policy—issues with very strong links to human rights. The new office was renamed "Multilateral and Humanitarian Affairs."

The Bush administration initially kept this basic structure but renamed the relevant NSC office Democracy, Human Rights, and International Operations, also led by a senior director, reporting to the Office of the National Security Adviser. The initial appointee was Elliott Abrams. In the second Bush administration, the overall NSC staff structure was altered with the creation of several new deputy assistant to the president for national security affairs adviser positions—essentially a new, senior level layer of authority subordinate to both the national security adviser and a principal deputy national security adviser. Each of these new deputies is responsible for one or more NSC offices run by senior directors. Among these new deputy positions is deputy national security adviser for global democracy strategy. Elliott Abrams was promoted to this position in the second Bush term. He has responsibilities for both the Office of Democracy, Human Rights, and International Operations (led by senior director Mike Kosak) and the Office of Near East and North Africa.[9]

The approaches of both the Clinton and Bush administrations on NSC staff organization for human rights were significant in three respects, each of which should be replicated by a future administration. First, both administrations established an NSC office in which a major focus of concern was human rights. Both appointed to NSC human rights and democracy leadership positions officials who had broad experience in and commitment to this general area. And both administrations ensured that the office maintained responsibilities for other functional issue areas. Whether it was international organization affairs, peacekeeping, or humanitarian assistance, these additional functions expanded the scope of the office for engagement in policymaking. Each of these three factors played a role in important NSC interventions to promote human rights.

For example, during the Clinton administration, the White House review that resulted in President Clinton's decision to sign the Rome Statute on the International Criminal Court was initiated and managed not by the NSC Legal Office, but rather by the NSC office dealing with human rights. The author of this essay, who was then serving as the senior NSC human rights official, determined that working through the interagency process at the working level would have resulted in deadlock and a failure to transmit to the president a decision memorandum on U.S. signature. The human rights expertise of the NSC office probably helped to ensure that its leadership in managing this process was not challenged either within the NSC or among the agencies of government.

Similarly, the NSC office responsible for human rights during the

Clinton administration played key roles in promoting safe haven and resettlement of Kurds from northern Iraq in 1996, and in ensuring strong U.S. support for the peacekeeping deployments in East Timor in response to widespread attacks on civilians in 1999. In each of these cases, the capacity of the office to play such a role was enhanced by the breadth of its mandate and, in particular, its responsibility for humanitarian and refugee issues in the northern Iraq case, and for peacekeeping in the case of East Timor.

In the Bush NSC, the staff focus on human rights and, in particular, democracy promotion, along with the commitment and expertise of senior officials, has also played an important role in moving the human rights and democracy agenda on specific issues. The NSC was deeply involved in ensuring the continuation of aid to human rights defenders in Central Asia in 2006, at a time when agency officials were questioning such assistance,[10] and the NSC role was also critical in the decision to press Egypt on human rights issues in both 2002 and 2005. In 2002 the administration withheld more than $100 million in planned assistance to Egypt to protest the conviction of human rights activist Saad Eddin Ibrahim. In 2006 the administration called off free trade talks to protest the conviction of Egyptian opposition leader Ayman Nour.[11]

The Role of the Undersecretary of State for Democracy and Global Affairs

A new administration should enhance the role of the undersecretary for democracy and global affairs by streamlining the undersecretary's operation and ensuring sufficient democracy and human rights staff.

The senior State Department official with significant responsibility for human rights and democracy is the undersecretary of state for democracy and global affairs. The democracy and global affairs undersecretary is one of six undersecretaries of state and has a widely disparate grouping of State Department bureaus and offices under her area of responsibility. These include the Bureaus for Democracy, Human Rights, and Labor; Oceans and International Environmental and Scientific Affairs; and Population, Refugees, and Migration; as well as offices relating to science and technology, women's rights, human rights in North Korea, trafficking, and Asian influenza. This democracy and global affairs position has been effectively subordinate to the undersecretary for political affairs, the State Department position that incorporates all of the regional bureaus at the department. The growing importance of global affairs issues—such as climate change—has not significantly altered this bureaucratic dynamic, and some might reasonably suggest that policy integration on global affairs issues requires that the functions (and, therefore, the influence) of this undersecretary position be expanded to include arms control and nonproliferation as well as international economic affairs, each of which is now served by a separate undersecretary.[12]

Such a recommendation is beyond the scope of this study, but whatever the mandate of the undersecretary, this official will be effective only if he or she focuses on the most critical issues of the brief—which currently includes human rights and democracy; population, refugees, and migration; and the environment and scientific affairs. Frankly, accomplishing that objective is inconsistent with the direct management of a range of offices that could easily be placed within functional bureaus for which the undersecretary has responsibility. Thus a new administration should ensure that several offices now under the direct authority of the undersecretary and dealing with issues such as women's rights, human rights in North Korea, trafficking, and Asian influenza are incorporated into the operations of appropriate bureaus.[13] This action would not be designed to diminish the importance of such issues or prevent the undersecretary from addressing them. Rather, it would enable the undersecretary to work more effectively with assistant secretaries to identify priorities for high-level engagement in policy.

In addition, given the wide range of democracy and human rights issues with which the undersecretary has to be familiar, a new administration should consider increasing the size of the undersecretary's staff involved in human rights and democracy, which now numbers only four professionals.[14]

The Choice of an Assistant Secretary of State to Promote Human Rights

Human rights expertise, national prominence in the field, and prior experience in government are all valuable qualities for an incoming assistant secretary of state for democracy, human rights, and labor.

Among the most important human-rights-related decisions confronting a new president and secretary of state is the choice of assistant secretary for democracy, human rights, and labor (DRL). This individual is the principal diplomat and policy spokesperson on the full range of issues relating to international promotion of human rights and democracy. Moreover, if the assistant secretary does not drive much of the policy development process within government on these issues, it is unlikely that any other official will do so.

Interviews with former assistant secretaries and other current and former officials, as well as the personal experience of the author, suggest that the most important asset for an assistant secretary of state for democracy, human rights, and labor is the personal confidence of the secretary of state. More specifically, the secretary must regard the assistant secretary as a force with whom to be reckoned—one whose views must be solicited regularly and advice considered seriously. During the Clinton administration, for example, the Bureau for Democracy, Human Rights, and Labor found itself at odds with others at the State Department on a number of issues, including the extradition of former Chilean President Augusto Pinochet from the United Kingdom and policy approaches toward China that were to be reflected in congressional testimony and the U.S. position at what was then the UN Commission on Human Rights. On each of these issues and more, the assistant secretary of state was able to influence or determine the position of the Department of State largely as a result of his influence with the secretary of state. Even when the secretary was not personally involved in a decision, the department-wide perception that the assistant secretary "had the ear" of the secretary of state substantially strengthened the hand of the assistant secretary. An assistant secretary for democracy, human rights, and labor who does not enjoy the confidence of the secretary will be isolated and not be in position to play a serious role in key policy debates.

This observation is almost self-evident, but it hardly means that an administration that cares about human rights must appoint as the DRL assistant secretary a friend of the secretary of state. A close personal relationship may be beneficial, but it is not necessarily the factor most likely to cause an incoming secretary to feel compelled to give the DRL assistant secretary a seat at the decision-making table or to credit his or her opinions. Several other factors will enhance the capacity for this kind of influence with the secretary.

First, the assistant secretary should be a prominent human rights advocate who does not need the job; that is, an individual with a national reputation for a commitment to human rights and democracy who possesses institutional affiliations that go far beyond government. In making such an appointment, the president and the administration's senior officials associate themselves with the values espoused by the appointee. They also send a powerful signal about the administration's determination to make human rights issues a priority, and, perhaps most importantly, to resist bureaucratic efforts to scale back commitments in this area.

The Clinton administration's decision to appoint William Gray as special envoy to Haiti in 1994 illustrates the value of this kind of approach. The appointment of Gray, a prominent former member of Congress who was a leader in the anti-apartheid movement while serving in the House, was designed to help signal a significant change of policy in May 1994. A key element of this shift was the administration's decision to end the practice of forcible return to Haiti of Haitians fleeing the island by boat. In the weeks following implementation of the policy change, the boat exodus from Haiti increased dramatically, and there were many pressures from within the administration to reverse policy and resume the practice of summary return to Haiti. That option was not chosen, however, and the administration adopted instead a more humane temporary safe haven policy for fleeing Haitians. Gray's opposition to forced return, his stature, and the awareness among administration officials that his commitment to service as special envoy was not unconditional almost certainly played key roles in this important decision.[15] By appointing Gray, the administration effectively bound itself to a more humane approach, and his integrity and stature helped the administration to stay the course.

A second important requirement is experience in or knowledge of government. While the DRL assistant secretary must be prepared to do battle with other bureaus in particular cases, he or she must also be able to work effectively with colleagues day in and day out. Knowledge of the interagency process, policy planning, budgets, and personnel are all critical. Thus a prominent figure who has logged considerable time in government will come to the office with a very valuable skill set. In this respect, the Bush administration's substantial increase in funding for the Human Rights and Democracy Fund over several years was not unrelated to the legislative and bureaucratic experience of Lorne Craner, who served for many years as the assistant secretary for democracy, human rights, and labor, and who came to the position with considerable background in government.

These two qualifications are in some tension with one another. An individual with national prominence is not likely to have spent most of his or her career toiling in the bureaucracy. At the same time, the careers of an increasing number of very senior professionals have been characterized by great diversity and easy movement between the public, private, and NGO sectors. Thus identifying candidates who clearly meet these requirements is hardly an insurmountable challenge.

Beyond Balkanization: Promoting Coherence Among the State Department's Human Rights Advocates

A new administration should integrate into the DRL management structure the work of special ambassadors and special offices dealing with human rights issues, and appoint a special envoy for multilateral human rights issues.

There has been a proliferation of special offices and special envoys on human rights-related issues at the Department of State, including an Office of International Religious Freedom, an Office to Monitor and

Combat Anti-Semitism, an Office of International Women's Issues, a special envoy for human rights in North Korea, and an ambassador for war crimes issues. One former assistant secretary for democracy, human rights, and labor who was interviewed for this chapter complained of the "Balkanization" of human rights, and his view is shared by many not only in government but also within the NGO community.

Defenders of these special initiatives argue that they help to bring prominence to important issues that would otherwise not be the focus of attention and concern. Critics argue that these very narrowly focused and single-issue initiatives often lack influence in the policymaking process and diminish the potential for an integrated and coherent policy approach across the range of human rights concerns. The same former assistant secretary indicated that he often neglected issues that were the focus of special initiatives due to his assumption that the issue was being taken care of by the relevant office or envoy.

Whatever their drawbacks, most of these offices have been created by legislation and they are not likely to disappear anytime soon. The key to resolving this dilemma may be to ensure that a new administration puts the assistant secretary for democracy, human rights, and labor clearly in charge of as many of these special processes and procedures as possible, including the work of the State Department's Office of War Crimes Issues.

Notwithstanding these concerns about proliferation of new operations, there is one additional position that the secretary of state should establish at the outset of a new administration: special envoy for multilateral human rights issues, with the rank of ambassador. In essence, this position would expand the role of the former U.S. ambassador to the Human Rights Commission, turning it into a full-time position, with the ambassador serving as the senior U.S. representative with responsibilities for engagement with the UN Human Rights Council (whether or not the United States becomes a member), the Third (Human Rights) Committee of the UN, and international human rights treaty negotiations, among other related matters. It has become clear that the assistant secretary of state for democracy, human rights, and labor does not have the time to manage ongoing relations with the institutions responsible for establishing and implementing international norms—while also overseeing the work of his or her bureau, serving as the administration's chief spokesperson on human rights and engaging in bilateral and regional human rights diplomacy. Moreover, the absence of consistent and very senior representation in international institutions has put the United States at a serious disadvantage.

The individual who occupies this position would in effect work for the Bureau of Democracy, Human Rights, and Labor but would also coordinate his or her work very closely with the Bureaus of International Organization Affairs, the Office of the Legal Adviser, and other relevant agencies of government.

Forging a Pro-Human Rights Incentive Structure at State

A new administration should improve the status, training, and career prospects of foreign service officers willing to serve in the Bureau of Democracy, Human Rights, and Labor.

The incentive structures at the Department of State work against the development of a powerful Bureau of Democracy, Human Rights, and Labor. The six regional bureaus in the department, covering specific geographic regions such as Europe and Asia, generally have the greatest influence in determining the pace of advancement for a young foreign service officer. Conventional wisdom dictates that officers must spend a substantial amount of time overseas to reach the upper ranks and need to tackle a range of assignments with increased responsibilities over time to impress promotion boards. Regional bureaus control the vast majority of overseas postings, including most of the prestigious ones. Because foreign service officers serve for limited periods in each assignment and must apply (or "bid") for new ones every few years, the disincentives to challenging regional bureau perspectives on policy issues are obvious. And while there is substantial concern about human rights among U.S. ambassadors and regional bureau staff—and many human rights champions within these groups—the regional bureaus and embassies are less enthusiastic than the DRL bureau about the promotion of human rights. In addition, they are more likely to argue that human rights issues must be subordinated to other concerns, such as trade, even when such trade-offs result in the neglect of human rights.

These career concerns are exacerbated because advancement within the Department of State is very competitive and, for those seeking promotion into the most senior ranks, there is an "up or out" system that requires that officers advance within a certain time period (a so-called window) or leave the service. The cumulative impact of these elements is a general sense that zealous pursuit of human rights goals and confrontation with powerful regional bureaus can be hazardous to one's career health. As one State Department official reportedly responded to a junior officer during a human rights crisis in Burundi, "Do you know of any official whose career has been advanced because he spoke out for human rights?"[16] In one manner or another, that decades-old query is still being asked far too often in informal conversations among officials.

It is a tribute to the commitment of many fine foreign service officers that they seek positions in the DRL bureau, notwithstanding these concerns. However, for DRL, these overall dynamics have had several dysfunctional effects. First, the bureau continues to struggle to attract foreign service officers in general; a large majority of its staff are from the civil service—and such officers do not generally serve abroad or rise to the most senior policymaking positions within the Department of State. There are enormously capable individuals in the civil service. But to be most effective, DRL must complement their talents with an adequate mix of foreign service officers who have experience in the field and contacts in the regional bureaus, and who will occupy most of the senior positions in the department. Thus the presence of a critical mass of foreign service officers in the DRL bureau is important for effective human rights policymaking.

Moreover, while many foreign service officers seek positions in DRL because of their deep commitment to human rights, there are bureaucratic incentives that draw officers to that bureau but that have little to do with the bureau's core mission—or with the applicant's commitment to human rights. Due to DRL's difficulty in attracting foreign service officers, it is relatively easy at DRL to obtain a "stretch assignment"— that is, a posting at a rank higher than the applicant would be able to secure in another bureau. Moreover, some foreign service officers find themselves working on human rights because they were simply unable to secure more competitive assignments. Despite these obstacles, there are highly talented and motivated officers at DRL who could work elsewhere but choose to stay in human rights because they care deeply about the cause. Nonetheless, the bureaucratic dynamics serve to limit the overall effectiveness of DRL.

In recent years Congress has provided to the DRL bureau a variety of tools to enhance the organizational incentives for work by foreign service officers in human rights.[17] For example, the Freedom Investment Act expresses the sense of the Congress that

any assignment of an individual to a political officer position at a United States mission abroad that has the primary responsibility for monitoring human rights developments in a foreign country should be made upon the recommendation of the Assistant Secretary of State for Democracy, Human Rights and Labor in conjunction with the head of the Department's regional bureau having primary responsibility for that country.[18]

This provision gives DRL an effective tool to secure valuable and career-enhancing assignments for personnel coming into and out of human rights positions, and also gives the bureau a valuable bargaining chip in its relations with other personnel offices within the department. But this tool has not been systematically and consistently used by the bureau since enactment of the Freedom Investment Act in 2002. A new administration should commit to its implementation and to ensuring adequate administrative capacity within DRL to get the job done. In addition, a new secretary of state should instruct the director general of the foreign service to issue guidelines making promotion to senior foreign service positions conditional on having at least one posting in which the major focus of the candidate's work has been in human rights.

A new administration should also create new training programs for effective promotion of human rights. In particular, it should call for the creation of a practical course in human rights tradecraft, covering a minimum of two weeks of intensive training and using both theoretical materials and cases. Officers should be exposed to examples of successful U.S. diplomacy in support of human rights, such as the efforts of U.S. Ambassador Philip Habib in helping to rescue future South Korean President Kim Dae Jung, or the activities of U.S. Ambassador Harry Barnes during the Chilean plebiscite on General Pinochet's regime. Completion of this course should be considered an important factor, as should service in the DRL bureau, in selecting officers for key positions where human rights issues are high on the U.S. agenda.

Funding for Human Rights and Democracy

A new administration should improve agency coordination on human rights funding and sustain a major human rights role for AID, but also augment funding and capacity at the Department of State and the National Endowment for Democracy.

As noted earlier, overall management of U.S. human rights and democracy assistance should come out of an NSC-managed policy development process closely linked to the annual budget formulation exercise. Although some efforts to this end have been made in the current administration, progress has been uneven at best and much more must be done.

At well over $1 billion in annual funding for democratization and human rights programs, AID resources far outstrip those provided to State/DRL and directly to NED for these kinds of activities. Some have argued that the culture at AID does not make it an appropriate recipient of democracy funding—that funding for human rights and democracy and, in particular, funding for civil society in countries where there are authoritarian governments creates inevitable conflicts with the recipient governments—with which AID must cooperate on development issues. It is argued that this dynamic makes the agency reticent to pursue democracy promotion aggressively unless it is the kind of government capacity building that is not controversial.

At the same time, a recent major study identifies a correlation between AID democracy assistance programs and positive movement toward democracy among aid recipients,[19] and it is difficult to imagine the Department of State taking on management responsibility for an overseas program of the magnitude of AID's human rights and democracy effort. Nonetheless, when it comes to advocacy in countries with severe restrictions on civil rights and civil liberties, AID may be in a relatively weak position to act effectively, at least compared to the Department of State and the National Endowment for Democracy.

In recent years, the Department of State has augmented its capacity to promote human rights through direct funding of human rights advocacy. DRL's Human Rights and Democracy Fund (HRDF), established in 1998, has grown from just under $8 million annually to over $70 million in 2007.[20] DRL refers to this fund as its "flagship program, used to fulfill the Bureau's mandate," enabling the United States to "respond rapidly and decisively to democratization and human rights crises and deficits" through programs that "are often politically sensitive [and] have a dramatic effect on democracy promotion and personal liberties." Although a large percentage of these monies are earmarked, considerable funds remain for discretionary use.

In addition to enhancing the bureau's capacity to aid the cause of human rights, these monies have augmented DRL's effectiveness within the department. One former assistant secretary noted that in the early days of his tenure before the fund had increased its resources, personnel in other bureaus would close their doors when he walked down the hall. Referring to how others perceived him, he said, "you were [seen as] a nag." But if he could have said that he had both an idea and the money to execute it, the reception he received would have been quite different.

A modest increase in the size of the HRDF would enhance the capacity of State to act in support of human rights and democratization as well as DRL's influence within the State Department and the administration. Such increases, however, should not be subject to rigid budget programming requirements that force bureaus to predict allocations more than a year in advance. It is also important that the DRL bureau develop the institutional capacities to implement increases effectively—with a priority on moving promptly to provide support.

Although State/DRL may generally be in a stronger position than AID to support aggressive human rights advocacy, it too operates within political constraints—especially when considering assistance to authoritarian governments with which the United States has a broad range of interests. In such circumstances, there will be strong sentiment in other parts of the government against antagonizing foreign officials. In addition, programs that operate with direct U.S. government assistance can often create risks or other complications for overseas human rights organizations. The National Endowment for Democracy and its affiliated institutions—the National Democratic Institute for International Affairs, the International Republican Institute, the Center for International Private Enterprise, and the American Center for International Labor Solidarity—provide alternative sources of support and have played an important supporting role in promoting democracy and human rights overseas.[21] To be sure, NED's core funding comes from a congressional appropriation, and both NED and NED affiliates receive other funds from Congress. Nonetheless, these institutions operate as private, nonprofit organizations accountable to independent boards, thus giving them (and their grantees) a degree of autonomy.

The Bush administration requested $80 million in general support for the NED for 2008,[22] and funds for the organization have increased substantially over the past six years. As a relative percentage of overall U.S. government financial support for human rights and democracy, however, the level is still modest—especially given NED's capacity to support more robust advocacy efforts that may be more difficult for AID and State. A new administration should propose further increases in the NED budget linked to the capacity of the institution to absorb such monies effectively. A new administration should also consider means to expand the range of affiliated U.S. regranting institutions that might benefit from NED funds. This is not to suggest deficiencies in the work of the four democracy promotion entities currently affiliated with the NED, but rather reflects recognition of the value of expanding the sources of institutional support in this area.

The additional monies suggested for both State/DRL and the NED would be modest—probably on the order of less than $100 million in the near term. If new budgetary resources cannot be identified, then a new administration should consider reallocating a small percentage of AID democracy monies for these purposes. In considering the source of savings at AID, a new administration should focus on those authoritarian countries where programming for more assertive human rights advocacy through AID may have proven problematic.

Promoting a Human Rights Focus at AID

A new administration should upgrade AID's Office of Democracy and Governance by creating a new Bureau for Democracy, Human Rights, and Governance.

There was some logic in the placement of AID's former Democracy Center, renamed by the Bush administration the Office for Democracy and Governance, in the AID bureau that deals with conflict and humanitarian assistance. Democratic development is a critical challenge for societies emerging from conflict or other disasters and democracy-building efforts must be a priority in such societies. The crisis response function of the Bureau for Democracy, Conflict, and Humanitarian Assistance, however, necessarily means that the democracy promotion function will get bureaucratic short shrift. For this reason, a new administration should separate the democracy and governance office from the crisis response bureau. Moreover, the importance of democracy and human rights and the magnitude of programs in this area certainly justify the creation of a new Bureau for Democracy, Human Rights, and Governance.

Titles Matter: Communicating a Commitment to Democracy *and* *to* Human Rights

A new administration should reattach "human rights" to democracy.

In several instances, the Bush administration has added "democracy" to the title of prominent positions and offices without including the term "human rights."[23] There are long-standing debates about whether the former word incorporates the latter term or vice versa. Whatever one's perspective on these debates, two observations are worth noting: first, use of the term "democracy" to the exclusion of "human rights" creates the perception among U.S. NGOs, foreign governments, and foreign advocates that the administration is concerned primarily about elections, rather than the building blocks of a healthy polity, including respect for civil rights and civil liberties. It is also the case that the body of international law relating to human rights is far more developed than international norms relating to democracy; therefore, diplomacy and advocacy associated with human rights has a relatively high degree of credibility and legitimacy worldwide.

These observations suggest the joining of "human rights" to "democracy" whenever the latter appears in an office or position title. Where such a change might make a title unwieldy, the appropriate solution may be to find an alternative phrase that uses neither term but incorporates both concepts.

Sending the Right Signals

Bureaucratic coherence is no substitute for political will, but organizational issues do matter. Decisions on appointments, policy development processes, and executive branch structures will send signals about a new administration's intentions to promote human rights and either facilitate or obstruct efforts to realize the rhetorical expressions of commitment to human rights that any incoming president is likely to make. The human rights bureaucracy has not traditionally received the careful attention it deserves during political transitions. But a new administration must do better, both to enhance the effectiveness of U.S. policy and to promote the basic rights and well-being of citizens around the world.

Chapter 14
International Human Rights
A Legislative Agenda

ALEXANDRA ARRIAGA

A new administration and a new Congress have an opportunity to redefine and reposition the United States as a champion of human rights. While many of the essays in this book offer explicit recommendations for change that are needed in policy and legislation, what follows is a comprehensive legislative agenda that would reestablish the United States as a global leader on human rights.

I. Restore Confidence in U.S. Detention Practices and Commitment to the Rule of Law

Guantánamo has become a global symbol for injustice, inhumane treatment, and a U.S. double standard. The president and Congress should set a clear timetable to close Guantánamo and end the use of secret prisons. The plan will require working with third countries to release detainees who have not been charged with a crime and accept detainees when they cannot be returned to their home country for fear of torture or other serious human rights abuses. The plan must include a fair process for individuals to present a claim on their fear of torture or persecution if returned to their home country. Any detainees who are charged with a crime should be brought to trial in either federal court or, where appropriate, by court martial within the United States. Anyone in U.S. custody or under effective U.S. control must be registered and the International Committee of the Red Cross must be provided access to them.

The new administration should put an end to "extraordinary renditions" and remove the possibility of suspects being picked up without the chance to challenge their detention and rendered to a third country where a substantial risk of torture exists.

II. Oppose Torture and Seek Prosecution of War Crimes

The new administration and Congress should demonstrate U.S. leadership in setting the standard for humane treatment and acting as an opponent of torture. Congress should amend the Military Commissions Act to restore provisions of the War Crimes Act that criminalize all violations of Common Article 3 of the Geneva Conventions and ensure that all U.S. personnel are bound by the same restrictions on interrogations as the U.S. military. In addition, the new administration should urge Congress not to limit the administration's options for pursuing accountability for war crimes and crimes against humanity by lifting restrictions on cooperating with or supporting the International Criminal Court (ICC). The new administration should participate in the ICC seven-year review conference in 2009 and consider resubmitting the ICC treaty to Congress for ratification.

III. Ratify Important Human Rights Treaties

The new administration and Congress should embrace international human rights standards and move quickly to ratify outstanding treaties. To demonstrate U.S. commitment to the most basic principles of human rights, the Senate should ratify the Treaty for the Rights of Women (officially the UN Convention on the Elimination of All Forms of Discrimination Against Women, or CEDAW). The Treaty for the Rights of Women addresses the basic human rights of women and can help to reduce violence against women and girls. The United States played an important role in drafting the treaty but, as one of only eight countries yet to ratify this treaty, has allowed it to languish.

The new president should sign and urge the Senate to ratify the International Convention for the Protection of All Persons from Enforced Disappearance and the Convention on the Rights of Persons with Disabilities. The Congress should also hold hearings and the Senate should move toward ratification of the Convention on the Rights of the Child and the International Covenant on Economic, Social and Cultural Rights.

IV. Adopt a Compassionate and Responsible Approach to U.S. Refugee and Asylum Policy

Recent anti-terrorism laws are so broad that they have inadvertently blocked bona fide refugees who have been harmed by terrorists from entering the United States by labeling them "material supporters" of terrorism. Survivors of rape in Darfur or child soldiers in Burma

(Myanmar) who have been forced to feed and tend their enemies are categorized as having provided material support to terrorists. Under current law, material support of terrorism is the provision of goods or services to a group of two or more people engaged in armed conflict. There is no distinction made for a person who was forced to provide the support, no matter how minimal; all are currently barred from entering the United States as refugees or asylum seekers. Forced labor, sexual slavery, and even small amounts of money paid under duress to save lives qualify as material support for violent groups, preventing victims from receiving the protection they desperately need. Attempts by the Department of Homeland Security to create exceptions to address worthy candidates have been insufficient. The unintended consequences of this policy are devastating. Congress should amend the definition of terrorist activities and the material support provision to provide an exception for those who performed activities under duress or whose support was either minimal or unknowing.

In addition, the new administration should urge Congress to set guidelines that have the force of law with regard to the detention of refugees, asylum seekers, and migrants. The guidelines should be consistent with standards for international protections and apply across the board to facilities that are run by the U.S. government or private contractors. Refugees, asylum seekers, and migrants are increasingly being held in private contract facilities that are not subject to government guidelines; many are confined for a year and some for up to five years. Since the adoption of the Military Commissions Act and the Real ID Act, there are no means of challenging their detention in these facilities. The law should make clear that all potential refugees, asylum seekers, and migrants must have access to a full and fair hearing before an impartial tribunal. It should also determine steps that must be taken to prevent the indefinite detention of these populations

V. Create Effective Foreign Assistance Programs

U.S. foreign assistance is one of the primary means of promoting human rights, responding to humanitarian crises, and supporting democratic reforms. The available funds continue to shrink and force hard decisions to be made about whether to fund projects assisting child survival, alleviating HIV/AIDS, stopping violence against women, or promoting the rule of law since there is not enough money to support them all. The reduction is due in part to the growth in nondiscretionary spending and national security and military operations. With limited funding available, it is essential to track programs and objectives for their effectiveness. The Department of State underwent a restructuring in 2006 intended to streamline policy work and make it possible to track U.S. investments for specific initiatives and goals. Congress should work with the administration to increase and improve accountability for foreign assistance available for human rights and humanitarian programs. The initiative should include tracking total investments for specific thematic goals and country recipients and monitoring the impact of such assistance over five and ten years to assess long-term outcomes.

In addition, the administration and Congress should examine current foreign assistance programs dedicated to promoting the human rights of women and, in particular, to stopping violence against women around the world. Congress should act quickly to support a comprehensive approach to stopping violence against women globally by fully funding the International Violence against Women Act. This legislation can help eliminate violence against women and girls globally by integrating antiviolence work across U.S. foreign assistance programs, creating more accountability in tracking the effectiveness of the initiatives, making prevention of violence a greater priority, and investing in nongovernmental and community-based organizations working overseas to end violence against women and girls.

Congress should also remove counterproductive restrictions that are having a potentially harmful effect on current U.S. foreign assistance programs. The United States is making important contributions to curb the HIV/AIDS pandemic by providing the largest contributions to the Global Fund to Fight AIDS, Tuberculosis, and Malaria and by offering the President's Emergency Plan for AIDS Relief (PEPFAR), which provides bilateral assistance to stem the AIDS pandemic. Many governments with few resources or with overwhelming epidemics are in dire need of the considerable funding offered through PEPFAR. To qualify for PEPFAR funds, however, recipient governments are required to abide by a number of U.S. restrictions with regard to abstinence, prostitution, and syringe exchange. These restrictions are widely understood to be ineffective or even counterproductive and can deter or prevent those who are most vulnerable from seeking testing and services. Congress should lift the overly restrictive conditions for receiving PEPFAR and other U.S. funds and facilitate the distribution of essential services.

VI. Facilitate Rapid Response to Crisis and International Peacekeeping

The international community's failure to stop the violence in Darfur demonstrates the need for a more flexible and reliable rapid response force in Africa. The United States should commit to work with the international community to develop, fund, and implement a comprehensive regional strategy in Africa to protect civilians, facilitate humanitarian operations, contain and reduce violence, and contribute to conditions for sustainable peace in eastern Chad, northern Central African Republic, and Darfur. Congress should also provide funds to back the UN Peacebuilding Commission, which was created to devise strategies for postconflict situations and has the public support of the United States. Congress should also support U.S. efforts to engage with the commission to ensure adequate attention to human rights and the inclusion of women in peacebuilding. The United States should pay its dues to UN peacekeeping operations in full, including arrears that have accumulated since January 2006.

The new administration should work with Congress to ensure that international forces serving in UN peacekeeping operations undergo vetting for human rights violations, similar to the Leahy law process for vetting U.S. assistance to foreign security forces to ensure that U.S. security assistant does not go to foreign security forces responsible for human rights violations. There should be restrictions to deny participation of military personnel from countries in which the military has overthrown a democratically elected government on missions intended to bolster democratic transitions and to supervise free and fair elections.

VII. Regulate Arms Transfers and U.S. Training and Equipping of Foreign Forces

According to an October 2007 Congressional Research Service report, the United States has reclaimed its position as the top arms supplier to the developing world, including to dozens of countries with grave human rights records. Previously Russia and France had topped the list in supplying conventional arms to the developing world. In addition, the Department of Defense has, since 2003, provided arms and training to foreign security forces under a new program called "train and equip," which bypasses most U.S. arms export control laws and standards, including human rights restrictions. Under the train and equip program, the U.S. government funded an air cargo company that had trafficked weapons to Liberia to transport weapons to Iraq. It appears the weapons never reached Iraq. As of early 2007, potential beneficiaries of this program included Afghanistan, Algeria, Chad, the Dominican Republic, Indonesia, Iraq, Lebanon, Morocco, Nigeria, Pakistan, Panama, Senegal, Sri Lanka, Thailand, Tunisia, and Yemen. Congress should exercise oversight and examine current regulations and practices to export and track weapons. It should ensure that the human rights criteria that apply to U.S. training and assistance programs managed by the Department of State extend to other U. S. government agencies. Congress should also bolster efforts to implement the Leahy law.

VIII. Account for Activities by Private Military Contractors

The U.S. government has increasingly relied on private military contractors to conduct operations traditionally carried out by military personnel. These contractors have been linked to serious human rights violations, particularly in Iraq and Afghanistan. Congress should pass legislation to clarify the U.S. laws that apply to private military contractors and to ensure the Department of Justice fully investigates and prosecutes these cases. In addition, the new administration should work with Congress to develop standard contract provisions for use by all U.S. agencies that clarify the obligations under U.S. law, ensure proper vetting of contracting employees, and provide effective training on international human rights standards.

IX. Support Human Rights Defenders

In the new millennium the focus of human rights advocacy is changing. The Internet increasingly is a tool for gathering information about political conditions, disseminating information about human rights, and organizing to bring about reforms. Several countries have adopted highly restrictive policies to stifle dissent by harassing, arresting, and imprisoning those who use the Internet to exchange ideas and transmit information and by blocking certain terms like "human rights" and "democracy." In China journalist Shi Tao was sentenced to ten years in prison for his peaceful work because of his pro-human rights Internet activity. The Chinese police traced his identity through information provided by Yahoo!, his email provider. Congress should adopt legislation to protect freedom of expression and privacy and prevent the Internet from becoming a tool for repression.

To stengthen the hand of the administration, Congress should adopt a Political Prisoners Act aimed at improving U.S. efforts on behalf of political prisoners detained by foreign governments. It should also increase funding available to human rights defenders.

X. Defend Vulnerable Populations

In recent years there has been some progress to improve U.S. policy promoting the rights of certain vulnerable groups, including religious minorities and victims of trafficking and slavery. The past decade has seen new laws and dedicated staffing in the U.S. government to promote religious freedom internationally and end trafficking and slavery. There should be an equal attempt to address human rights violations against other vulnerable groups, including individuals who are lesbian, gay, bisexual, or trangendered, as well as people with disabilities. These communities are frequently targets of harassment, persecution, and serious human rights abuses around the world. The president and Congress should work together to end abuses against these communities by ensuring adequate diplomatic attention to the issues in bilateral and multilateral forums, reporting on the abuses in the annual country reports on human rights practices, and instructing U.S. embassies to meet with and support local organizations defending the rights of these communities.

Notes

Introduction

1. That criticism has come from the left with Peter Beinart, *The Good Fight: Why Liberals—and Only Liberals—Can Win the War on Terror and Make America Great Again* (New York: HarperCollins, 2006); the right with Stefan Halper and Jonathan Clarke, *America Alone: The Neoconservatives and the Global Order* (New York: Cambridge University Press, 2004); and from the center with Zbigniew Brzezinski, *Second Chance: Three Presidents and the Crisis of American Superpower* (New York: Basic Books, 2007).

2. Michael Ignatieff, *Human Rights as Politics and Idolatry* (Princeton: Princeton University Press, 2001), p. 53.

3. Remarks by Assistant Foreign Minister He Yafei at the conclusion of the latest Australia-China Human Rights Dialogue, July 30, 2007 <http://www.australia-online.net.cn/servlet/Display?Locale = en&Id = 919>.

4. Sudanese representative to the 2006 UN Human Rights Council, October 4, 2006.

5. Thomas Friedman, "Swift-Boated by Bin Laden," *New York Times*, August 26, 2007.

6. Drawing upon his 1996 book, *Running in Place: How Bill Clinton Disappointed America*, Richard Reeves recounted in an interview with PBS's *Frontline* Clinton's comment that "My wife read this [*Balkan Ghosts*] and I read some of it too. And it says that we can't succeed in doing anything in that society. They've been killing each other for thousands of years and they're going to keep doing it" http://www.pbs.org/wgbh/pages/frontline/shows/choice/bill/reeves.html>.

7. <http://archive.salon.com/people/bc/2001/04/17/kaplan/print.html>.

8. Robert D. Kaplan, *The Coming Anarchy: Shattering the Dreams of the Post-Cold War* (New York: Random House, 2000).

9. Robert Kaplan, *Warrior Politics: Why Leadership Demands a Pagan Ethos* (New York: Random House, 2002), pp. 146–47.

10. Kaplan, *Warrior Politics*, p. 148.

11. A more sophisticated taxonomy of present-day conservatism than can be provided in this essay would distinguish between the neoconservatives such as William Kristol and Paul Wolfowitz and the so-called paleoconservatives epitomized by Vice President Dick Cheney and former Defense Secretary Donald Rumsfeld. But inasmuch as both "neo" and "paleo" were part of the Project for a New American Century, the post-Bush I organization that took the lead in conceptualizing foreign policy principles now widely associated with Bush II, signed the January 1997 letter to President Clinton urging the removal of Saddam Hussein and jointly executed policy in Bush II, it is sufficient for our purposes here to lump them all under the label "neoconservatives." (For the letter to Clinton, see <http://www.newamericancentury.org/iraqclintonletter.htm>.

12. Perry Miller, ed., *The American Puritans: Their Prose and Poetry* (Garden City, N.Y.: Doubleday and Co., 1956), p. 36.

13. Perry Miller, *Errand into the Wilderness* (New York: Harper and Row, 1956), p. 5; pp. 11–12.

14. Martin Marty, *Righteous Empire: The Protestant Experience in America* (New York: Dial Press, 1970), p. 6.

15. Robert Kagan, *Dangerous Nation* (New York: Random House, 2006). The quote is from an article based on the book: Robert Kagan, "Cowboy Nation," *The New Republic*, October 23, 2006.

16. Which is, presumably, to demonstrate that the invasion of Iraq was consistent with long American practice.

17. Marty, *Righteous Empire*, p. 48.

18. Even in places such as the Philippines that had been Christian for hundreds of years. (Many thanks to Jeff Laurenti of the Century Foundation for making this ironic point.)

19. Quoted in Forrest Church, *The American Creed: A Spiritual and Patriotic Primer* (New York: St. Martin's Press, 2002), pp. 73–74.

20. Friedrich Nietzsche, "On the Genealogy of Morals," in *Basic Writings of Nietzsche*, ed. Walter Kaufman (New York: The Modern Library, 1968), pp. 480–81.

21. Allan Bloom, *The Closing of the American Mind* (New York: Simon and Schuster, 1987).

22. Anne Norton, *Leo Strauss and the Politics of American Empire* (New Haven: Yale University Press, 2004).

23. Leo Strauss, *Natural Right and History* (Chicago: University of Chicago Press, 1999), pp. 1–3.

24. Quoted in John G. Mason, "Leo Strauss and the Noble Lie: The Neo-Cons at War," *Logos* (Spring 2004), pp. 6–7 <http://www.logosjournal.com/issue_3.2mason.htm>.

25. Kaplan, *The Coming Anarchy*, p. 172.

26. Gary Dorrien, *The Neoconservative Mind: Politics, Culture and the War of Ideology* (Philadelphia: Temple University Press, 1993), pp. 134, 340.

27. Speech given by George W. Bush at the West Point graduation, June 1, 2002 <http://www.whitehouse.gov/news/releases/2002/06/20020601-3.html>.

28. Quoted in David Brooks, "The Culture of Nations," *New York Times*, August 15, 2006.

29. Francis Fukuyama, *America at the Crossroads: Democracy, Power, and the Neoconservative Legacy* (New Haven: Yale University Press, 2006), p. 48.

30. Steven Shapin, "Man with a Plan: Herbert Spencer's Theory of Everything," *New Yorker*, August 13, 2007, p. 76.

31. See, for example, Robin Fox, "Human Nature and Human Rights," *National Interest* 62 (Winter 2000–2001); Francis Fukuyama, "Natural Rights and Human History," *National Interest* 64 (Summer 2001); and Francis Fukuyama, *Our Posthuman Future: Consequences of the Biotechnology Revolution* (New York: Farrar, Strauss and Giroux, 2002).

32. It is paradoxical that human rights advocates, who have such a well-developed sense of the tragedy that can plague individual victims of human rights crimes, resist seeing the sweep of history in tragic terms. But that may not be so peculiar. Such a faith in progress and perfectionism may be a sine qua non of "keeping the faith" in the face of all those individual tragedies.

33. David Rieff, *At the Point of a Gun: Democratic Dreams and Armed Intervention* (New York: Simon and Schuster, 2005).

34. Shirin Ebadi and Hadi Ghaemi, "The Human Rights Case Against Attacking Iran," *New York Times*, February 8, 2005.

35. Negar Azimi, "Hard Realities of Soft Power," *New York Times Magazine*, June 24, 2007.

36. "Arabs Bristle at Bush's Agenda for Region," *New York Times*, February 4, 2005.

37. Shortly after he took office, George W. Bush was presented with a letter ("Idealism without Illusions: A Statement of Principles for a 21st Century American Foreign Policy") from two dozen leading conservatives, many, like Elliot Abrams, Midge Decter, Michael Novak, and Norman Podhoretz, identified with neoconservatism, urging him to make human rights, religious freedom, and democracy a priority of his administration. The specific concerns the letter cited were sex trafficking, genocide in Sudan, and religious persecution in China—all important issues but all reflective of a very traditional American understanding of what constitute violations of human rights. See "Bush Urged to Champion Human Rights," *Washington Post*, January 26, 2001. The letter did, interestingly enough, warn against "promiscuous resort to military action" and "imposing democracy on unwilling partners."

38. Fukuyama, *America at the Crossroads,* p. 49.

39. The third, "a distrust of ambitious social engineering projects," is arguably a characteristic of only some versions of neoconservative philosophy, given the ardor with which neoconservatism has tried to reshape the world, and may or may not be attributable to human rights activists, depending upon the context. No human rights supporter, for example, would countenance the ways in which totalizing regimes seek to remake societies in uncompromising ways that often end up in forced conformity, repression, and death. On the other hand, if full social and economic rights are to be realized, it may require more than a totally laissez-faire approach to social and economic life.

40. Woodrow Wilson School of Public and International Affairs, "Forging a World of Liberty Under Law," *The Princeton Project Papers* (Princeton University, September 27, 2006), p. 20.

41. Condoleezza Rice, "Promoting the National Interest," *Foreign Affairs* (January/February 2000), p. 62.

42. The statistic is quoted in Juan Cole, "9/11," *Foreign Policy* (September/October 2006), p. 28 <http://www.worldvaluessurvey.org/statistics/index.html>.

43. UN General Assembly, "Responsibility to Protect Populations from Genocide, War Crimes, Ethnic Cleansing and Crimes Against Humanity," from the Outcome Document of the High-Level Plenary Meeting of the UN General Assembly (September 15, 2005).

44. "Americans Believe US International Strategy Has Backfired," World Public Opinion.org, January 29, 2007.

45. "Public Wants to Know More About Darfur and Many Favor US Involvement," Pew Research Center, June 7, 2007.

46. See, for example, Jack L. Goldsmith and Neal Katyal, "A New Court for Terror Suspects?" *New York Times*, July 16, 2007; and Kelly Anne Moore, "Take Al Qaeda to Court," *New York Times*, August 21, 2007.

47. See, for example, the speech given by Ruth Bader Ginsburg, "A Decent Respect for the Opinions of [Human]kind: The Value of a Comparative Perspective in International Adjudication," before the American Society for International Law, April 1, 2005.

48. Samantha Power, "Our War on Terror," *New York Times Magazine*, July 29, 2007.

49. A panel appointed by Kofi Annan has suggested as a definition: "Any action intended to cause death or serious bodily harm to civilians or non-combatants, when the purpose of such act, by its nature or context, is to intimidate a population, or to compel a Government or international organization to do or abstain from doing any act." From the Secretary General's High-Level Panel on Threats, Challenges, and Change, *A More Secure World: Our Shared Responsibility* (New York: United Nations, December 2004), p. 51.

50. For a sample of this debate, see Wesley K. Clark and Kal Raustiala, "Why Terrorists Aren't Soldiers," *New York Times*, August 8, 2007.

51. Opinion of J. O'Connor, *Hamdi v. Rumsfeld* (03–6696) 542 US507 (2004) <http://www.law.cornell.edu/supct/html/03–6696.ZO.html>.

52. Jared Diamond, *Collapse: How Societies Choose to Fail or Succeed* (New York: Viking Books, 2005).

53. Worldwatch Institute, "Desertification Is Important Factor in Darfur Crisis" <http://www.worldwatch.org/node/4087>. See also Boston University Center for Remote Sensing, "Space Data Unveils Evidence of Ancient Mega-lake in Northern Darfur" <http://www.eurekalert.org/pub_releases/2007–04/bu-sdu041007.php>.

54. Alan Dupont and Graeme Pearman, "Heating Up the Planet," Working Paper 12, Lowy Institute for International Policy, 2006, p. 56.

55. Stephan Faris, "Containment Strategy," *Atlantic Monthly* (December 2006), p. 34.

56. Charles C. Krulak and Joseph P. Hoar, "It's Our Cage Too: Torture Betrays Us and Breeds New Enemies," *Washington Post*, May 17, 2007. See also David W. Barno, "Challenges in Fighting Global Insurgency," *Parameters* (Summer 2006).

57. For a comprehensive look at how human rights impinge upon American interests, see William F. Schulz, *In Our Own Best Interests: How Defending Human Rights Benefits Us All* (Boston: Beacon Press, 2001).

58. It is one of the great ironies of history that the Soviet Union in effect accepted civil and political freedom when it signed the Helsinki Final Accord in 1976 but the United States has never accepted social and economic rights—a point made by Michael Ignatieff in *American Exceptionalism and Human Rights*, ed. Ignatieff (Princeton: Princeton University Press, 2005, p. 16.

59. Sarah Sewall at the Kennedy School's Carr Center for Human Rights Policy has spearheaded work in this area, as has Human Rights First, but they are more the exception than the rule in the human rights community.

60. Transcript from "Governing America in a Global Era," Miller Center of Public Affairs, University of Virginia, panel 3, June 8, 2007.

61. "Myanmar's Descent, Seen from 150 Miles Up," *New York Times*, September 29, 2007.

62. "Space Data Unveils Evidence of Ancient Mega-lake in Northern Darfur," *Eurekalert!* (April 11, 2007) <http://www.eurekalert.org/pub_releases/2007–04/bu-sdu041007.php>.

63. Miller, *The American Puritans*, pp. 83–84.

64. See, for example, Stephen Kinzer, *Overthrow: America's Century of Regime Change from Hawaii to Iraq* (New York: Henry Holt, 2006).

65. Dwight Eisenhower, State of the Union address, 1958 <http://www.presidency.ucsb.edu/ws/index.php?pid=11162>.

66. Paul Collier, *The Bottom Billion: Why the Poorest Countries Are Failing and What Can Be Done About It* (Oxford: Oxford University Press, 2007), pp. 3–4.

67. "W.H.O. Urges Effort to Fight Fast-Spreading New Diseases," *New York Times*, August 27, 2007.

68. Goldman Sachs, "Dreaming with BRICs: The Path to 2050," Global Economics Paper No. 99, October 1, 2003 <http://www2.goldmansachs.com/insight/research/reports/99.pdf>.

69. Charles Kupchan, "The Roots of Liberal Internationalism: Lessons from the Past" in *Power and Superpower: Global Leadership and Exceptionalism in the 21st Century*, eds. Morton H. Halperin, et. al. (New York: Century Foundation Press, 2007), pp. 23–48.

70. Brzezinski, *Second Chance*.

71. "US Role in the World," World Public Opinion.org <http://www.americans-world.org/digest/overview/us_role/general_principl es.cfm>. By a 63 to 32 percent margin, Americans told the American Security Project that they want the United States to "cooperate with other countries [and] compromise" rather than "put American interests first at all times" <http://www.americansecurity project.org/files/America%20and%20the%20World.pdf>.

72. Reinhold Niebuhr, *The Irony of American History* (New York: Charles Scribner's Sons, 1952), p. 133.

73. *Public Papers of the Presidents of the United States: Harry S. Truman, 1945* (Washington, D.C.: U.S. Government Printing Office, 1961), p. 141.

74. Second presidential debate, October 11, 2000 <http://www.debates.org/pages/trans2000b.html>.

75. See, for example, "Is the US Financing Homophobia in Africa?" International Gay and Lesbian Human Rights Commission, October 10, 2007 <http://www.iglhrc.org/site/iglhrc/section.php?id=5&detail=787>.

76. William F. Schulz, "Make the World Safe for LGBT People," in *50 Ways to Support Lesbian and Gay Equality*, ed. Meredith Maran (Maui, Hawaii: Inter Ocean Publishing, 2005), pp. 126–128.

Chapter 1

1. The views in this chapter are those of the author and not necessarily those of Human Rights First.

2. Remarks of Attorney General John Ashcroft at the Eighth Circuit Judges Conference, Duluth, Minnesota, August 7, 2002 <http://www.usdoj.gov/archive/ag/speeches/2002/080702eighthcircuitjudgesagre marks.htm>.

3. For a discussion of the benefits—and limitations—of the war metaphor, see Kenneth Anderson and Elisa Massimino, *The Cost of Confusion: Resolving Ambiguities in Detainee Treatment* (Muscatine, Iowa: Stanley Foundation, March 2007) <http://www.routledge.com/9780415962278>.

4. U.S. Constitution, Preamble.

5. Memorandum for Alberto R. Gonzales, Counsel to the President, regarding Legal Standards Applicable under 18 U.S.C. §§ 2340–2340A, August 1, 2002.

6. Detainee Treatment Act of 2006, 42 U.S.C. §2000cc (2006).

7. The signing statement relating to the McCain Amendment provisions stated, "The executive branch shall construe (the section of the Act), relating to detainees, in a manner consistent with the constitutional authority of the President to supervise the unitary executive branch and as Commander in Chief and consistent with the constitutional limitations on the judicial power, which will assist in achieving the shared objective of the Congress and the President . . . of protecting the American people from further terrorist attacks."

8. Vice President Dick Cheney appearing on ABC's *Nightline* <http://abc news.go.com/Nightline/IraqCoverage/story?id=1419206>.

9. *Hamdan v. Rumsfeld*, 548 U.S. _____ (2006).

10. "Waterboarding" is a form of near drowning in which a prisoner is immobilized, often by being tied to a board with feet elevated above the head, and water is poured over the face to create the sensation of asphyxiation or drowning, inducing a belief that death is imminent.

11. Human Rights First, "Command's Responsibility: Detainee Deaths in U.S. Custody in Afghanistan and Iraq" (February 2006).

12. National Defense Intelligence College, Intelligence Science Board, "Educing Information—Interrogation: Science and Art—Foundations for the Future" (Washington, D.C., December 2006) <http://www.fas.org/irp/dni/educing.pdf>.

13. Department of the Army, "Human Intelligence Collector Operations, FM 2–22.3" (Washington, D.C., September 2006) <http://www.fas.org/irp/dod dir/army/fm2-22-3.pdf>.

14. News transcript, "DoD News Briefing with Deputy Assistant Secretary Stimson and Lt. Gen. Kimmons from the Pentagon," U.S. Department of Defense, September 6, 2006 <http://www.defenselink.mil/Transcripts/Tran script.aspx?TranscriptID=3712>.

15. <http://www.washingtonpost.com/wp-srv/nation/documents/petraeus _values_0 51007.pdf>.

16. Address by General Michael V. Hayden, director of the Central Intelligence Agency, at the Duquesne University Commencement Ceremony, May 4, 2007 <https://www.cia.gov/news-information/speeches-testimony/cia-directors-address-at-duquesne-university-commencement.html>.

17. Memorandum to Inspector General of the Navy Vice Admiral Albert Church, "Statement for the Record: Office of General Counsel Involvement in Interrogation Issues," July 7, 2004.

18. For a legal and medical analysis of the CIA's enhanced interrogation techniques, see Human Rights First and Physicians for Human Rights, "Leave No Marks: Enhanced Interrogation Techniques and the Risk of Criminality" (August 2007).

19. "Brief of the Military Attorneys Assigned to the Defense in the Office of Military Commissions as Amicus Curiae in Support of Neither Party," *Fawzi Al Odah, et al., v. United States, et al.,* January 14, 2004 <http://www.law.george town.edu/faculty/nkk/documents/gtmo.pdf.pdf>, p. 5.

20. Among the examples of abuse on display in the photos were techniques sanctioned by Secretary of Defense Donald Rumsfeld for use on "unlawful enemy combatants" in the "war on terror." These include forced nudity, the use of dogs to terrorize prisoners, keeping prisoners in stress positions—physically uncomfortable poses of various types—for many hours, and varieties of sleep deprivation. Some of these techniques migrated from Guantánamo and Afghanistan to Iraq in 2003.
From "Final Report of the Independent Panel to Review DoD Detention Operations (the Schlesinger Report)," The Abu Ghraib Files <http://www .salon.com/news/abu_ghraib/2006/03/14/introduction/>, p. 14; also "Newly Released Reports Show Early Concern on Prison Abuse," *New York Times,* January 6, 2005.

21. National Commission on Terrorist Attacks Upon the United States, "The Taguba Report: Article 15–6: Investigation of the 800th Military Police Brigade" (Washington, D.C., 2004).

22. "Verbatim Transcript of Combatant Status Review Tribunal Hearing

for ISN 10024," March 10, 2007 <http://www.defenselink.mil/news/tran script_ISN10024.pdf>.

23. U.S. Department of the Army, "Counterinsurgency," FM 3–24/MCWP 3–33.5 (Washington, D.C., December 2006), pp. 1–23.

24. "Guantánamo Prison Likely to Stay Open Through Bush Term," *Washington Post*, March 24, 2007.

25. "New to Job, Gates Argued for Closing Guantánamo Prison," *New York Times*, March 23, 2007.

26. "Setbacks Mark Turning Point on Bush's War Powers," *International Herald Tribune*, July 15, 2006.

27. "Guantánamo Prison Likely to Stay Open."

28. U.S. Department of the Army, "Counterinsurgency."

29. While world attention has been fixated on Guantánamo as the embodiment of U.S. misconduct in counterterrorism policy, the camp is not the only prison with which we should be concerned. The continued assertion by the president, most recently in Executive Order 13440, of the authority to seize individuals anywhere in the world and hold them in secret prisons without access to the Red Cross or notification to their families is every bit as, if not more, troubling than the prolonged detentions at Guantánamo. These forced disappearances are a clear violation of international law. The next president should put an end to the practice of holding ghost prisoners and close any place of detention in which the United States incarcerates prisoners in violation of international human rights and humanitarian law.

30. Press Conference of President George W. Bush, June 14, 2006 <http://www.whitehouse.gov/news/releases/2006/06/20060614.html>.

31. U.S. Constitution, Art. 1, Sec. 9, Cl. 2.

32. "New Jersey Man Who Fled Somalia Ends Up in an Ethiopian Jail," *New York Times*, March 23, 2007.

33. See "Geneva Convention for the Amelioration of the Condition of the Wounded and the Sick in Armed Forces in the Field," *6 U.S.T. 3217*, 75 U.N.T.S. 31 (Geneva, August 12, 1949, *entered into force* October 21, 1950) <http://www.icrc.org/ihl.nsf/7c4d08d9b287a42141256739003e636b/fe20c3d903ce27e 3c125641e004a92f3>; "Geneva Convention for the Amelioration of the Condition of Wounded, Sick, and Shipwrecked Members of Armed Forces at Sea," *6 U.S.T. 3217*, 75 U.N.T.S. 85 (Geneva, August 12, 1949, *entered into force* October 21, 1950) <http://www.icrc.org/ihl.nsf/7c4d08d9b287a42141256739 003e636b/44072487ec4c2131c125641e004a9977>; "Geneva Convention Relative to the Treatment of Prisoners of War," *6 U.S.T. 3316*, 75 U.N.T.S. 135 (Geneva, August 12, 1949, *entered into force* October 21, 1950) <http://www.icrc. org/ihl.nsf/7c4d08d9b287a42141256739003e636b/6fef854a3517b75ac12564 1e004a9e68>; "Geneva Convention Relative to the Protection of Civilian Persons in Times of War," *6 U.S.T. 3516*, 75 U.N.T.S. 287 (Geneva, August 12, 1949, *entered into force* October 21, 1950) <http://www.icrc.org/ihl.nsf/7c4d08d9 b287a42141256739003e636b/6756482d86146898c125641e00aa3c5>.

34. <http://thinkprogress.org/2007/06/22/habeas-reform/>.

35. U.S. Department of the Army, "Counterinsurgency."

36. CIPA is a federal statute designed to balance the constitutional right of defendants to see the evidence against them with the legitimate interest of government to protect against such disclosures of classified information.

37. "Reid: 'I Am at War with Your Country,'" CNN.com, January 31, 2003 <http://www.cnn.com/2003/LAW/01/31/reid.transcript/>.

38. See generally *Hamdan v. Rumsfeld,* 126 S. Ct. 2749 (2006); *Hamdi v. Rumsfeld,* 542 U.S. 507 (2004); and *Rasul v. Bush,* 542 U.S. 466 (2004).

39. William H. Taft, "The Law of Armed Conflict After 9/11: Some Salient Features," *Yale Journal of International Law* 28 (2003).

Chapter 2

1. Joseph S. Nye, Jr., "Soft Power," *International Herald Tribune,* January 10, 2003.

2. Office of Research, U.S. Department of State. The 1999/2000 trends are quoted by the Pew Global Attitudes Project, June 26, 2006.

3. BC International Opinion Poll, BBC News, January 23, 2007.

4. Pew Global Attitudes Project, June 13, 2006.

5. BBC International Opinion Poll.

6. Chicago Council on Global Affairs and WorldPublicOpinion.org, April 17, 2007 <http://www.thechicagocouncil.org/media_press_room_detail.php?press_release_id=62>.

7. BBC International Opinion Poll.

8. Global Public Opinion on International Affairs, WorldPublicOpinion.org, July 17, 2006 .

9. Global Public Opinion on International Affairs.

10. Pew Institute Survey, June 28, 2007, reported by the *London Times* <http://www.timesonline.co.uk/tol/news/world/us_and_americas/article1996629.ece>.

11. Alberto J. Gonzales, Counsel to the President, Memorandum for the President, January 25, 2002.

12. Colin L. Powell, Secretary of State, Memorandum for the White House Counsel, January 26, 2002.

13. See <http://www.asil.org/insights/insigh95.htm>; <http://www.asil.org/insights/insigh75.htm>; <http://www.icj-cij.org/docket/files/104/7738.pdf>.

14. "US Quits Pact Used in Capital Cases," *Washington Post,* March 10, 2005.

15. See <http://www.telegraph.co.uk/news/main.jhtml?xml=/news/2004/05/28/nhamza228.xml>.

16. See, e.g., the UN special rapporteur's report on racism and racial discrimination in the United States, January 1995. See also Submission of the Open Society Justice Initiative to the UN Committee on the Elimination of Racial Discrimination, 65th Session, August 2004.

17. United States Department of Justice, *The Federal Death Penalty System: Supplementary Data, Analysis and Revised Protocols for Capital Case Review* (June 6, 2001).

18. See <http://www.globalpolicy.org/intljustice/atca/arcatcaindx.htm>.

19. "China Fires Back at U.S. on its Human Rights Record," *International Herald Tribune,* March 8, 2007.

20. "Cuba Abandons Vote on Detainees Held by U.S. at Guantánamo," *New York Times,* April 23, 2004.

Chapter 3

*This chapter owes thanks to Lauryn Bruck and Jessica Tacka, who provided invaluable research assistance throughout its preparation.

1. "Darfur at a Crossroads: Global Public Opinion and the Responsibility to Protect," Proceedings of a Brookings Institution's panel held in Washington, D.C. on April 5, 2007 (Alexandria, Va.: Anderson Court Reporting, 2007), p. 5.

2. Robert Kaplan, "Interventionism's Realistic Future," *Washington Post*, November 22, 2006.

3. Of course, many see just war theory as implicitly addressing the question of effectiveness.

4. See "The Humanitarian Intervention Debate" in *Humanitarian Intervention: Ethical, Legal, and Political Dilemmas*, eds. Jeff L. Holzgrefe and Robert O. Keohane (Cambridge University Press: Cambridge, 2003), p. 18. Also see Tony Coady, "The Ethics of Armed Humanitarian Intervention" (Washington, D.C.: United States Institute of Peace, July 2002), pp. 4–10; and "Introduction," in *Ethics and Foreign Intervention*, eds. Deen K. Chatterjee and Don E. Sheid (Cambridge: Cambridge University Press, 2003), pp. 1–4.

5. The United States also regularly engages in humanitarian actions that are not included under this humanitarian intervention label, such as military efforts to rescue its own citizens and coercive measures short of using force, including embargoes, divestment, and other crucial diplomatic and aid missions undertaken for humanitarian ends.

6. The U.S. military defines nonpermissive environments—and more recently "hostile environments"—as areas where "hostile forces have control as well as the intent and capability to effectively oppose or react to the operations a unit intends to conduct." Department of Defense, *Department of Defense Dictionary of Military and Associated Terms* (Joint Publication 1–02, as amended through April 14, 2006), p. 390. The term "coercive protection" was coined by the International Commission on Intervention and State Sovereignty in International Commission on Intervention and State Sovereignty, *The Responsibility to Protect* (Ottawa, Canada: International Development Research Center, 2001).

7. Consent does affect issues of legitimacy and legality, which are discussed later. The growing disconnect between legality and legitimacy (or morality) in humanitarian intervention is brilliantly discussed in Eileen Chamberlain Donahoe, "Humanitarian Military Intervention: An Obscene Oxymoron?" Unpublished working paper, CISAC. Stanford University, May 2007.

8. For instance, Muhammad Farah Aidid, the main warlord in the Somali capital of Mogadishu, grudgingly accepted aid delivery but revoked his consent when the UN mission began to move from delivering aid to trying to secure a peace that would have harmed his power base. The Indonesian government fought the arrival of an Australian-led force in East Timor until the United States increased the pressure of its military embargo and joined many European countries in urging international financial institutions to suspend aid. Indonesian consent made the Australian-led, UN-authorized mission far less dangerous but the grudging nature of the consent meant that nongovernmental militias that had been encouraged by military forces were given fairly free rein by the Indonesian government.

9. See, for instance, Thomas G. Weiss, "Principles, Politics, and Humanitarian Action," *Ethics and International Affairs* 13 (1999), pp. 1–22; James O. Jonah, "Humanitarian intervention," in *Humanitarianism Across Borders: Sustaining Civilians in Times of War*, ed. Thomas G. Weiss and Larry Minear (Boulder, Colo.: Lynne Rienner, 1993), pp. 69–83.

10. India pushed the West Pakistan army out of East Pakistan after tens of thousands of refugees spilled across its own borders. Vietnam routed the Khmer

Rouge in neighboring Cambodia when the genocide and chaos threatened Vietnam's sense of regional stability. Tanzania finally put an end to dictator Idi Amin's brutality in Uganda only after Amin ordered his military to attack Tanzania in an effort to distract the Ugandan populace from domestic troubles. Vietnam and Tanzania justified their response wholly on national security grounds while India at first mentioned humanitarian need, then reverted to a national security argument. See Taylor B. Seybolt, *Humanitarian Military Intervention: The Conditions for Success and Failure* (New York: Oxford University Press, 2007), p. 10.

11. For the history of the Srebrenica massacre, see the Netherlands Institute for War Documentation report, April 10, 2002, on their website <http://193.173.80.81/srebrenica/>.

12. Peter D. Feaver and Christopher Gelpi, *Choosing Your Battles: American Civil-Military Relations and the Use of Force* (Princeton: Princeton University Press, 2003), pp. 95–149.

13. Taylor Seybolt, who has conducted the only systematic study of what works in humanitarian intervention, goes so far as to claim that countries should *only* intervene if they have political as well as altruistic reasons. "Governments that commit troops to help civilians should have political as well as humanitarian interests at stake (as long as the political interests do not overwhelm the humanitarian ones). The reason for this is that the local belligerents have their most cherished political interests on the line and often will fight to protect them. An intervener motivated solely by humanitarian interests will be likely to withdraw if the level of violence rises and its soldiers are killed. It is better not to intervene at all than to get involved and pull out when involvement leads to trouble." Seybolt, *Humanitarian Military Intervention*, pp. 20, 27.

14. Coady, "The Ethics of Armed Humanitarian Intervention," p. 10.

15. President George W. Bush tried to claim that the war in Iraq was a humanitarian war after his strategic rationales failed to gain traction. A glance at force deployment, the overwhelming destruction of civilian assets during the "shock and awe" campaign, and the lack of planning for postwar Iraq confirms that the war was not fought to protect the civilian population but that civilians were an afterthought in a war to depose a regime and to find presumed weapons of mass destruction.

16. In calculating America's willingness to sustain casualties, it is important to note that this tolerance tends to be higher than most Washington pundits suppose but drops in cases where the "national interest" does not appear to be at stake. Feaver and Gelpi's work suggests that Americans calculate their willingness to sustain casualties based on whether they think the effort is important and whether they think success is achievable. If those two factors are present, casualty tolerance is robust; if they are not, support plummets. With regard to humanitarian interventions, young troops in the Marines and Air Force (arguably the two groups most likely to be deployed for such missions) are more willing to tolerate casualties than those in the Army and Navy. See Feaver and Gelpi, *Choosing Your Battles*, pp. 95–149.

17. The Weinberger Doctrine is a series of conditions devised in the 1980s under the Reagan administration by Secretary of Defense Caspar Weinberger that must be met before the United States engages its military forces abroad. A response to the bombing of the Marine barracks in Beirut in 1983 during a U.S. "humanitarian" intervention in Lebanon, the doctrine requires that military engagement be the last resort, deploy an appropriate force to meet the size of the objective with the intention to win, have a clear exit strategy, and have the support of the U.S. people and Congress.

The Powell Doctrine is a similar set of guidelines formulated by former Secretary of State Colin Powell while he was chairman of the Joint Chiefs of Staff during the 1990–1991 Gulf War. The Powell Doctrine added the conditions of international support and changed "national security interest" to national security "threats," further reducing the scope for humanitarian action.

18. An operational objection sometimes raised to humanitarian intervention is that it will harm military readiness to fight wars because the more political humanitarian missions will dull troops' ability to use overwhelming force against an enemy. This reasoning made more sense when humanitarian intervention was seen as building schools and traditional warfare was viewed as using overwhelming force. But counterinsurgency operations in Iraq and Afghanistan require judgment on how to use force against enemies in urban environments while maintaining the support of civilian populations; humanitarian intervention in hostile areas requires similar judgment calls on using force while protecting civilians. Thus the missions are not only increasingly similar but coercive protection missions might augment troops' capacity to fight today's urban and counterinsurgency wars. For example, the Army's new counterinsurgency manual states that "Ultimate success in COIN [counterinsurgency] is gained by protecting the populace. . . . Using substantial force . . . increases the opportunity for insurgent propaganda to portray lethal military activities as brutal. In contrast, using force precisely and discriminately strengthens the rule of law that needs to be established." See the *U.S. Army/Marine Corps Counterinsurgency Field Manual* (Chicago: University of Chicago Press, 2006), pp. 47–48.

19. The 2005 Pew Global Attitudes Project survey (June 23, 2005) found that 79 percent of Indonesians said they had a more positive view of the United States as a result of American tsunami relief efforts. In a nationwide poll of Indonesians, 53 percent had a more favorable opinion of the United States following the U.S.S. *Mercy*'s mission. Nearly 48 percent said that the fact that the *Mercy* was a U.S. Navy ship made them more favorable (versus just 8 percent who felt less favorably because it was a Navy ship.) Those who believed that suicide bombings were sometimes justified declined from 27 percent to 9 percent and opposition to the U.S. war on terror dropped from 72 percent to 36 percent. "Unprecedented Terror Free Tomorrow Polls: World's Largest Muslim Countries Welcome the US Navy: New Results from Indonesia and Bangladesh" (2006) <http://www.terrorfreetomorrow.org/upimagestft/Final%20Mercy%20Poll%20Report.pdf>.

20. John Gaddis, *We Now Know: Rethinking Cold War History* (Oxford: Oxford University Press, 1997), pp. 256–258.

21. For a discussion of this issue, see Robert O. Keohane, "Introduction," in Holzgrefe and Keohane, *Humanitarian Intervention*, p. 1. For one such critic, see the writings of David Rieff, discussed in the introduction to *Civil-Military Relations, Nation-Building, and National Identity: Comparative Perspectives,* ed. Constantine P. Danopoulos et al. (Westport, Conn.: Praeger Publishers, 2004), p. 9.

22. United Nations General Assembly, *Organization of the Fifty-Fifth Regular Session of the General Assembly, Adoption of the Agenda and Allocation of Items: Report of the Secretary-General.* 55th Session, Supplement No. 1 (A/55/1) (August 30, 2000), p. 10. The United Nations Security Council was unable to reach agreement on intervention in Kosovo, given strenuous Russian objections to actions that it perceived as anti-Serb. In Rwanda, U.S. objections slowed UN troops on the ground from acting, and the UN ultimately was unable to authorize force in time to stop the genocide.

23. International Commission on Intervention and State Sovereignty, *The Responsibility to Protect* (Ottawa, Canada: International Development Research Center, 2001). The study drew on a body of thinkers, such as Francis M. Deng and Roberta Cohen, who had begun to articulate the notion of sovereignty as responsibility throughout the 1990s.

24. U.N. General Assembly, "2005 World Summit Outcome," A/Res/60/1 (October 24, 2005), p. 30. The year before a bipartisan task force mandated by Congress also upheld the responsibility to protect. United States Institute of Peace, "Task Force on the United Nations, American Interests, and UN Reform" (2004), p. 29.

25. A Brookings Institution study on the use of force found that elites in these countries still held strong attitudes toward sovereignty, in contrast to their own people. "Darfur at a Crossroads," p. 5. China has also worked to create a strong sovereignty belt across Asia by uniting the repressive governments in that region (four Central Asian republics, China, and Russia) into the Shanghai Cooperation Council, which has a central mission of upholding "nonintervention in the internal affairs of sovereign states."

26. "Darfur at a Crossroads," p. 5.

27. Ibid.

28. Fernando R. Teson describes this concept within the context of intervention in *Humanitarian Intervention: An Inquiry into Law and Morality,* 2d ed. (Dobbs Ferry, N.Y.: Transnational Publishers, 1997); Fernando R. Teson, "The Liberal Case for Humanitarian Intervention," Florida State University College of Law, Public Law Research Paper No. 39 (November .2001) <http://ssrn.com/abstract=291661 96=97/>.

29. Michael Byers and Simon Chesterman, "Changing the Rules About Rules," in Holzgrefe and Keohane, *Humanitarian Intervention,* pp. 177–203. For a careful and thoughtful discussion of this moral dilemma, see Donahoe, "Humanitarian Military Intervention: An Obscene Oxymoron?"

30. Donahoe, "Humanitarian Military Intervention: An Obscene Oxymoron?" p. 73. This argument is drawn from Donahoe's comprehensive overview of this problem.

31. These four categories are described in Seybolt, *Humanitarian Military Intervention,* pp. 39–43.

32. Of course, religious motives were among many others during the many wars that collectively were known as the Thirty Years' War but, as discussed earlier, few modern humanitarian interventions are unsullied by mixed motives as well.

33. Seybolt, *Humanitarian Military Intervention,* p. 269.

34. The EU fielded its first mission in 2003, sending troops to Macedonia in Operation Concordia to prevent the spillover of war. It has now fielded other significant missions in Bosnia and the Democratic Republic of the Congo, although the latter was basically a French mission with France providing most of the military personnel and the operational headquarters.

35. David Gompert, Richard Kugler, and Martin Libicki, *Mind the Gap: Promoting a Transatlantic Revolution in Military Affairs* (South Bend: Notre Dame University Press, March 1999), chap. 3. Also see Michael O'Hanlon, *Expanding Global Military Capacity for Humanitarian Intervention* (Washington, D.C.: Brookings Institution Press, 2003), pp. 51–85.

36. Seybolt, *Humanitarian Military Intervention,* p. 271.

37. Recent humanitarian interventions by these countries include the U.S.

and British mission to help the Kurds in Northern Iraq in 1991; the Nigerian-led interventions in Liberia in 1990 and 2003; U.S. and French intervention in Zaire in 1994; the UK's intervention in Sierre Leone in 1998; the Australian-led intervention in East Timor in 1999; the French-led EU mission to Congo in 2003; Australia's assistance to the Solomon Islands in 2003; and the French-led mission to Ivory Coast in 2004.

38. Victoria K. Holt and Tobias Berkman, *The Impossible Mandate? Military Preparedness, the Responsibility to Protect, and Modern Peace Operations* (Washington, D.C.: Stimson Center, September 2006), p. 128.

39. By "leasing" its airlift and other equipment to the UN at market rates, the United States has ensured UN failure by discouraging the UN from calling on reliable and fast transport options. Congressional reimbursement requirements on Department of Defense contributions to UN peace operations have discouraged the Department of Defense from assisting the UN. Moreover, in the mid-1990s the Pentagon killed the idea of a standing UN army or an on-call brigade-sized unit capable of rapid reaction. Moreover, President Clinton's plan to deploy regular combat units, rather than just deploying unique capabilities such as logistics, transportation, and intelligence, was dead on arrival at Congress. In Colin Powell's memorable phrase, "As long as I am chairman of the Joint Chiefs of Staff, I will not agree to commit American men and women to an unknown war, in an unknown land, for an unknown cause, under an unknown commander for an unknown duration." See Ivo Daalder, "Knowing When to Say No: The Development of U.S. Policy for Peacekeeping," in *U.N. Peacekeeping, American Politics, and the Uncivil Wars of the 1990s*, ed. William J. Durch (New York: St. Martin's Press, 1996), p. 43; and Sarah B. Sewall, "U.S. Policy and Practice Regarding Multilateral Peace Operations," Carr Center for Human Rights Policy Working Paper, Harvard University, February 2001.

40. United Nations General Assembly, 'A More Secure World: Our Shared Responsibility: Report of the High-Level Panel on Threats, Challenges and Change," A/59/565 (November 29, 2004).

41. The inherent structure of the UN includes a Security Council composed of great power countries whose interests will always diverge even if the council composition is altered; a General Assembly giving an equal vote to all the world's nations, regardless of whether they abuse the rights of their own people; and multinational peacekeeping forces that would need to share intelligence, whether constituted as a standing army or in the current ad hoc composition.

42. The *Report of the Panel on United Nations Peace Operations* (New York: United Nations, August 21, 2000), the conclusions of a panel chaired by Lakhdar Brahimi, offers a comprehensive list of reforms to the UN Department of Peacekeeping Operations. It enumerates changes such as an emphasis on conflict prevention, funding enhancements for immediate peacekeeping, and the sustained ability to continue to launch peacekeeping strategies. See <http://www.un.org/peace/reports/peace_operations/>.

43. *Report of the Panel on United Nations Peace Operations*, p. 63.

44. Coady, "The Ethics of Armed Humanitarian Intervention," p. 35.

45. "Darfur at a Crossroads," p. 5.

46. See the speech by Mark Malloch Brown, "The United Nations at a Crossroads: Debating the Use of Force in an Evolving World," Brookings Institution, October 12, 2006 <http://www.brookings.edu/~/media/Files/events/2006/1012global%20governance/20061012.pdf>.

47. Seybolt, *Humanitarian Military Intervention*, p. 271.

48. Chicago Council of Global Affairs, *The United States and the Rise of China and India: Results of a 2006 Multination Survey of Public Opinion* (2006) <http://www.thechicagocouncil.org/UserFiles/File/GlobalViews06Final.pdf>.

49. In his 2004 State of the Union address, President Bush declared that "America will never seek a permission slip to defend the security of our country." The "permission slip" accusation was successfully used in Bush's campaign speeches against Democratic presidential candidate John Kerry's support of multilateral approvals for military action.

50. Ruy Teixeira, "What the Public Really Wants," Center for American Progress/Century Foundation (April 16, 2007), citing a Pew Research Council/Center on Foreign Relations poll (October 2005).

51. In Africa the program incorporates predecessor programs including the Clinton administration's African Crisis Response Initiative, which trained troops but did not include weapons training; the Enhanced International Peacekeeping Capabilities Program, which included classroom training; and the Bush administration's more robust African Contingency Operations Training and Assistance Program, which includes weapons training for peace enforcement.

52. Nina M. Serafino, "The Global Peace Operations Initiative: Background and Issues for Congress" (Washington, D.C.: Congressional Research Service, June 11, 2007).

53. Sewall, "U.S. Policy and Practice Regarding Multilateral Peace Operations," pp. 32–33.

54. For instance, John Bolton, appointed by President Bush as ambassador to the UN, stated in 1994 that it wouldn't make "a bit of difference" if the UN lost "the top 10 stories from its [39-story] headquarters." Statements made during his brief tenure as ambassador to the UN continued this tone. See "Bolton: UN Riddled with 'Bad Management, Sex, and Corruption," Associated Press, February 25, 2006.

55. "G8 Action Plan: Expanding Global Capability for Peace Support Operations," Sea Island Summit, June 19, 2004.

56. Seybolt, *Humanitarian Military Intervention,* pp. 273–274.

57. Ivo Daalder and Robert Kagan, "America and the Use of Force: Sources of Legitimacy" (Muscatine, Iowa: Stanley Foundation, June 2007).

58. Michael Walzer, *Just and Unjust Wars,* 4th ed. (New York: Basic Books, 1977), p. 107.

59. But it is not impossible. Despite its failure in some high-profile cases, the UN has successfully and rapidly authorized missions, from the U.S. humanitarian action in Haiti in 1994 to the European Union's operation in Congo in the summer of 2003, the French-led Operation Licorne in Ivory Coast in 2003, the ECOWAS mission in that same country in 2003–2004, and the AU mission to Darfur since 2004.

60. Sewall, "U.S. Policy and Practice Regarding Multilateral Peace Operations," pp. 33, 37.

61. No mission is likely to be short term if the government does not provide consent. At times, however, government factions may be at odds or unable to provide consent, as in Albania in 1997, and the intervention can reasonably be seen as short term, as Italy's intervention there was.

62. This is, of course, the route the Clinton administration took in its intervention in Kosovo.

63. The Community of Democracies is already in existence. Scholars such as Anne-Marie Slaughter and G. John Ikenberry have discussed as part of the

Princeton Project on National Security's major study, *Forging a World of Liberty Under Law* (Princeton University, 2006) means to make this community into a "Concert" that could serve these purposes.

64. It is critical to remember America's own poor record of judgment in humanitarian intervention, particularly when we are considering acting against the wishes of the UN, the EU, and NATO. In the past we have helped the wrong side, as when we supported the Khmer Rouge in the United Nations even as it decimated the Cambodian population and when we sent a nuclear armed aircraft carrier to the Bay of Bengal to assist Pakistan during East Pakistan's war of independence after Pakistani troops had slaughtered as many as 3 million Bengali civilians and raped up to 200,000 women. In Iraq, an invasion not undertaken as a humanitarian mission has seen our presence, which lacks any larger legitimacy, galvanize opposition, create significant violence, upset the regional balance of power—and may eventually lead to more deaths than occurred even under Saddam Hussein. We have also been guilty of inaction. In World War II, even after genocide was publicly known and unfolding slowly, the American public was set against intervention. More recently, in Rwanda, it was, as we saw, the United States that obstructed Security Council action.

65. Walzer, *Just and Unjust Wars*, p. 107.

66. Chris Seiple, "The US Military/NGO Relationship in Humanitarian Intervention" (Carlisle, Penn.: United States Army Peacekeeping Institute, 1996). The Office of Post-Conflict Reconstruction should build systems and press for legislation allowing for the interchange of military service members and civilian aid practitioners from different countries. We should also increase the cadre of civil affairs officers who can bridge the military-aid divide. The military should make a concerted effort to reach out to the leadership of civilian aid organizations in order to improve working relationships throughout their structures. Officer training should include visits to humanitarian aid operations while leadership in humanitarian aid groups should be encouraged to attend appropriate events with military personnel.

67. Walzer, *Just and Unjust Wars*, p. 107.

Chapter 4

1. This data is derived from Gary C. Hufbauer et al., *Economic Sanctions Reconsidered*, 3rd ed. (Washington, D.C.: Institute for International Economics, 2004).

2. For the most comprehensive study of this issue, with an excellent review of studies that preceded it, see Joel A. Capellan and Simonpeter Gomez, "Foreign Aid and Human Rights: The Latin American Experience," *Revista de Ciencia Politica* 27:1 (2007), pp. 67–87.

3. The most comprehensive analysis of this diversity of goals is provided in David Cortright and George A. Lopez, *The Sanctions Decade* (Boulder, Colo.: Lynne Rienner Publishers, 2000); and David Cortright and George A. Lopez, *Sanctions and the Search for Security* (Boulder, Colo.: Lynne Rienner Publishers, 2002).

4. Both the aforementioned Institute for International Economics data and the Cortright-Lopez analysis of United Nations sanctions detail about a 33 percent success rate. But one celebrated study, employing more strict criteria of success, reported a rate of 5 percent. See Robert Pape, "Why Economic Sanctions Do Not Work," *International Security* 22:2 (Fall 1997), pp. 90–136.

5. This phrase was popularized by Richard N. Haas, "Sanctioning Madness,"

Foreign Affairs 76:6 (November/December 1997); and Richard N. Haas, ed., *Economic Sanctions and American Diplomacy* (New York: Council on Foreign Relations, 1998).

6. For the success of targeted sanctions see David Cortright and George A. Lopez, eds., *Smart Sanctions: Targeting Economic Statecraft* (Boulder, Colo.: Rowman and Littlefield, 2002); Peter Wallensteen and Carina Staibano, eds., *International Sanctions: Between Words and War in the International System* (New York: Routledge, 2005); and especially for the Libyan case, Thomas E. McNamara, "Unilateral and Multilateral Strategies Against State Sponsors of Terror" in *Uniting Against Terror*, eds. David Cortright and George A. Lopez (Cambridge: MIT Press, 2007), pp. 83–122.

7. Cortright and Lopez, *The Sanctions Decade*, pp. 3 -26.

8. Part of this argument is derived from Capellan and Gomez, "Foreign Aid and Human Rights"; and William Kaempfer, Anton Lowenberg, and William Mertens, "International Sanctions Against a Dictator," *Economics and Politics* 16:1 (2004), pp. 29–51.

9. The most articulate and consistent of these analysts is Joy Gordon, "Sanctions as Siege Warfare," *The Nation*, March 22, 1999; and "Cool War: Economic Sanctions as a Weapon of Mass Destruction," *Harper's* (August 2002).

10. See Wallenteen and Staibano, *International Sanctions*, pp. 165–241.

11. The most embarrassing example of this came in the March 2001 Senate Foreign Relations Committee hearings in which new Secretary of State Colin Powell simply had no useful response to committee chair Senator Jesse Helms (R-N.C.) when, in light of Powell's initial statement that the new Bush administration was trying to reconfigure coercive measures on Iraq and adopt smart sanctions, the senator quipped that he had not been aware that until the secretary's proposal the United States had imposed "dumb sanctions" on Iraq.

12. This is certainly not a new idea for a U.S. administration to embrace, since its use in a post-9/11 world was sketched for the difficult cases of Iran, Iraq, and Libya in Meghan L. O'Sullivan, *Shrewd Sanctions: Statecraft and State Sponsors of Terrorism* (Washington, D.C.: Brookings Institution Press, 2003).

13. See Cortright and Lopez, *Smart Sanctions*, pp. 3–41; Wallensteen and Staibano, *International Sanctions*, pp. 229–241.

14. David Cortright at al., "Sanctions," in *The Oxford Handbook on the United Nations*, eds. Thomas G. Weiss and Sam Daws (New York: Oxford University Press, 2007), pp. 358–361.

15. Michael Brzoska, "From Dumb to Smart? Recent Reforms of UN Sanctions," *Global Governance* 9 (2003), pp. 519–535.

16. As discussed in Cortright and Lopez, *Sanctions and the Search for Security*, pp. 61–74.

17. See ibid., chapters 5, 9, and 10.

18. For a comprehensive list of the correlates of both sanctions success and sanctions failure, see George A. Lopez, "UN Sanctions After Oil-for-Food: Still a Viable Diplomatic Tool?" Testimony provided to the Subcommittee on National Security, Emerging Threats, and International Relations, House of Representatives Committee on Government Reform, May 2, 2006.

19. George A. Lopez and David Cortright, "Bombs, Carrots and Sticks: The Use of Incentives and Sanctions," *Arms Control Today* (March 2005).

20. See George A. Lopez and David Cortright, "The Limits of Coercion," *Bulletin of Atomic Scientists* (November/December 2000), pp. 18–20.

21. Cortright and Lopez, *Sanctions and the Search for Security*, pp. 82–89.

22. One of the more astute observers of this reality has been Senator Richard Lugar (R-Ind.) who, as chair of the Senate Foreign Relations Committee, advocated that all economic sanctions have a two-year expiration date, at which point either Congress or the UN Security Council would need to endorse a new sanctions measure.

23. Cortright and Lopez, *The Sanctions Decade*, pp 87–105.

24. See for example Chado Makunike, "Sanctions: Mugabe's Red Herring," NewZimbabwe.com, October 2, 2007 <http://www.newzimbabwe.com/pages/chido27.16993.html>.

25. See David M. Malone, "The United States and the UN," in *The UN Security Council in the Post-Cold War Era*, ed. Thomas Weiss and Sam Daws (New York: Oxford University Press, 2006).

26. Created by UN Security Council Resolution 986 (1995), the oil-for-food program was the largest humanitarian venture in UN history. Between 1997 and 2001, the program approved and oversaw $28.6 billion in oil sales by Iraq in exchange for food, medicines, humanitarian goods, and critical infrastructure replacement parts that the country needed because of UN economic sanctions. See Cortright and Lopez, *Sanctions and the Search for Security*, pp. 27–33; and Lopez, "U.N Sanctions after Oil-for-Food."

27. For a full account of these details see McNamara, "Unilateral and Multilateral Strategies."

28. Ibid., pp. 110–112.

29. See Kofi Annan, *Uniting Against Terrorism: Recommendations for a Global Terrorism Strategy* (New York: United Nations General Assembly, Report of the Secretary-General, A/60/825, April 27, 2006).

30. United Nations General Assembly, *A More Secure World: Our Shared Responsibility* (New York, November 29, 2004).

31. A strong argument for this is made by David M. Malone, ed., *The UN Security Council: From the Cold War to the 21st Century* (New York: Oxford University Press, 2003), pp. 642–645.

Chapter 5

1. Thomas O. Melia, "The Democracy Bureaucracy: The Infrastructure of American Democracy Promotion," Discussion paper, Princeton University, Princeton Project on National Security, Working Group on Global Institutions and Foreign Policy Infrastructure, September 2005, p. 4 <http://www.wws.princeton.edu/ppns/papers/democracy_bureaucracy.pdf>.

2. Those interested in further reading on the merits of democracy promotion should refer to Tom Carothers, *Democracy Promotion During and after Bush* (Washington, D.C.: Carnegie Endowment for International Peace, 2007); and Michael A. McFaul and Francis Fukuyama, *Should Democracy Be Promoted or Demoted?* (Muscatine, Iowa: Stanley Foundation, 2007).

3. The United States can "intervene" even when it provides supposedly nonpolitical humanitarian and economic assistance. For example, many would argue that the decades of the United States providing such assistance helped to prolong authoritarian rule and preserve the status quo in the Middle East.

4. This chapter also draws on previous articles, including Jennifer Windsor, "Is Democracy Promotion the Answer?" in *Too Poor for Peace*, ed. Lael Branaerd and Derek Chollet (Washington, D.C.: Brookings Institution Press, 2007); Jennifer Windsor, "The Freedom Agenda: Time for a Recalibration?" *Washington*

Quarterly 26 (Summer 2006); and Jennifer Windsor, "Promoting Democracy Can Combat Terrorism," *Washington Quarterly* (Summer 2003). Paula Schriefer, Tom Melia, Bobby Herman, and Arch Puddington, all Freedom House colleagues who are democracy experts in their own right, made invaluable contributions and suggestions, as did Jerry Hyman, Tom Carothers, Sophie Richardson, and Peter Ackerman.

5. The attack on democracy assistance has been waged most vigorously by Russian President Vladamir Putin, who said in a July 2006 interview with French television, "If we go back 100 years and look through the newspapers, we see what arguments the colonial powers of that time advanced to justify their expansion into Africa and Asia. They cited arguments such as playing a civilizing role, the particular role of the white man, the need to civilize 'primitive peoples.' If we replace the term 'civilizing role' with 'democratization,' then we can transpose practically word for word what the newspapers were writing 100 years ago to today's world and the arguments we hear from some of our colleagues on issues such as democratization and the need to ensure democratic freedoms." See Steven Lee Myers and Andrew E. Kramer, "Group of 8 Talks, Like So Much These Days, Are All About Energy: Russia's Gas and Oil," *New York Times*, July 13, 2006 <http://www.nytimes.com/2006/07/13/world/europe/13summit .html?r=1&pagewanted=print&oref=slogin>. Also cited in Peter Ackerman and Michael J. Glennon, "The Right Side of the Law," *The American Interest* (Autumn 2007), pp. 1–6.

6. Carl Gershman and Michael Allen, "The Assault on Democracy Assistance," *Journal of Democracy* 17:2 (April 2006), pp. 37–51.

7. Those detained were released after they were forced to "confess" to trying to foment political change within the country. For a reminder of the history of coerced confessions in Iran, see <http://www.abfiran.org/english/document -300-708.php>.

8. For an example of voting patterns and trends at the UN Human Rights Council see <http://www.demcoalition.org/2005 html/undem offic.html>; Steven Edwards, "Canada under Pressure to Stand Firm in UN Rights Debate," *Ottawa Citizen*, November 6, 2007.

9. Thomas Carothers, "The Backlash Against Democracy Promotion," *Foreign Affairs* (March/April 2006) <http://www.foreignaffairs.org/20060301faes say85205/thomas-carothers/the-backlash-against-democracy-promotion.html>. The International Center for Not-for-Profit Law (www.icnl.org) has carried out path-breaking work detailing the increasing constraints placed on civil society in numerous countries around the world.

10. See <http://daccessdds.un.org/doc/UNDOC/GEN/N99/770/89/PDF/ N9977089.pdf?OpenElement>.

11. For more information on the Community of Democracies, see the Democracy Coalition Project's excellent website <http://www.demcoalition .org/2005 html/home.html>.

12. Ivo Daalder and James Lindsey, "Democracies of the World: Unite," *The American Interest* (Winter 2006).

13. Many fault the United States for engaging too late—and too ham-handedly—in the debates related to establishment of the new UN Human Rights Council, thereby alienating others who would have backed U.S. positions on the size and composition of the council. This still does not excuse the behavior of other democracies at the UN that folded during the negotiations and agreed to let repressive regimes onto the council. On June 19, 2007, in one of its last acts

in the first year of operation, the council abolished the special rapporteurs for Cuba and Belarus—in order, Western European diplomats asserted, to keep the special rapporteurs for Burma and North Korea. While its diplomats tried to influence this process, the United States had limited sway because it had chosen not to present itself as a candidate for election to the council. See Thomas O. Melia, "The United States in Opposition—Again: Revitalizing the International Democratic Faction," Testimony to the U.S. Senate Committee on Foreign Relations, International Operations and Organizations, Democracy and Human Rights Subcommittee, July 26, 2007. <http://freedomhouse.org/template.cfm?page=70&release=533>.

14. For an overview of the tensions and parallels between the two communities, see Tom Carothers, "Democracy and Human Rights: Policy Allies or Rivals?" *Critical Mission: Essays on Democracy Promotion* (Washington, D.C.: Carnegie Endowment for International Peace, 2004), pp. 9–23; and Mort Halperin, "Democracy and Human Rights: An Argument for Convergence" in *Realizing Human Rights: Moving from Inspiration to Impact,* ed. Samantha Power and Graham Allison (New York: St. Martin's Press, 2000), pp. 249–261.

15. There has been considerable debate about the State Department program to support democracy in Iran. The administration's decision to publicly announce the program (it was announced by Secretary Rice in February 2006 during congressional testimony while criticizing the Iranian government for its nuclear and other activities) led many to criticize the program as simply an attempt to change a regime which the administration found problematic. A State Department press release on the program released in June 2007 (see <http://www.state.gov/r/pa/prs/ps/2007/jun/85971.htm> for the actual text) further added to the controversy by asserting that funds had gone to groups inside of Iran. Critics maintained that the announcement of the program has led to crackdowns against the very elements in Iranian society that the program was designed to help. See Robin Wright, "U.S. Aid Compromising Iranian Human Rights Activists," *Washington Post,* April 27, 2007.

16. Arch Puddington, "Freedom in the World, 2007: Freedom Stagnation Amid Pushback Against Democracy" <http://www.freedomhouse.org/> (hereafter cited as Freedom House Survey).

17. *Countries at a Crossroads* provides detailed information on the state of corruption and rule of law in 60 countries. See <http://www.freedomhouse.org/template.cfm?page=140&edition=8&ccrpage=42>.

18. Given the importance of freedom of information as a subcomponent of freedom, Freedom House has produced a separate annual assessment of the state of press freedom around the world. See <http://www.freedomhouse.org/template.cfm?page=16>.

19. Carothers, "US Democracy Promotion."

20. Freedom House includes in its *Survey of Freedom* a broad range of criteria drawn directly from the Universal Declaration of Human Rights, separated into two broad categories: political rights and civil liberties. The category of political rights includes such questions as: Are there fair electoral laws, equal campaigning opportunities, fair polling, and honest tabulation of ballots? Are the voters able to endow their freely elected representatives with real power? Is there a significant opposition vote, de facto opposition power, and a realistic possibility for the opposition to increase its support or gain power through elections? Are the people free from domination by the military, foreign powers, totalitarian parties, religious hierarchies, economic oligarchies, or any other powerful group? The

civil liberties score is composed of three categories: freedom of expression and belief, association and organizational rights, and the rule of law and human rights. Some of the questions include: Is there an independent judiciary? Does the rule of law prevail in civil and criminal matters? Is the population treated equally under the law? Are the police under direct civilian control? Is there protection from political terror, unjustified imprisonment, exile, or torture, whether by groups that support or oppose the system? Is there freedom from war and insurgencies? See <http://www.freedomhouse.org> for further information and findings.

21. Larry Diamond has articulated the dimensions of democracy in many of his writings, including his chapter "Defining and Developing Democracy" in *Developing Democracy: Toward Consolidation* (Baltimore: Johns Hopkins University Press, 1999), pp. 1–23.

22. Freedom House regularly evaluates the United States along with all other countries in the world in its annual survey of freedom. In addition, in early 2008 Freedom House will publish a detailed analysis of the state of freedom as experienced by individuals within the United States in "Today's American: How Free?"

23. See Windsor, "Is Democracy the Answer?" for a fuller discussion of this point.

24. There are, however, numerous cases in history in which military action, undertaken for other reasons, has had the salutary benefit of paving the way for a more democratic future for a country. Beyond the most famous examples of post-World War II Germany and Japan, more recent cases include Panama after Manuel Noriega in 1989 and Argentina after the 1982 Falklands/Malvinas War. But as an instrument of democracy promotion, military action remains a theoretical proposition.

25. For an interesting analysis of the importance of nonviolent tactics to successful democratic transitions, see "How Freedom Is Won: From Civic Struggle to Durable Democracy," Freedom House, May 24, 2005 <http://freedom house.org/uploads/special report/29.pdf>. See also Michael A. McFaul and Anders Ashlund, *Revolution in Orange: The Origins of Ukraine's Democratic Breakthrough* (Washington, D.C.: Brookings Institution, 2006).

26. For an excellent discussion of the damage that has been done by linking democracy promotion to counter-terrorism, Carothers, "U.S. Democracy Promotion During and After Bush," pp. 24–27.

27. See Robert Packenham, *Liberal America and the Third World* (Princeton: Princeton University Press, 1977) for past missteps by the U.S. government in assuming automatic linkages between democracy, development, and other U.S. interests.

28. Tom Carothers, in "The Rule of Law Revival," *Critical Mission*, pp. 121–130, uses the term "elixir" to describe the fascination with rule of law by policy elites.

29. See Mort Halperin and Joseph Siegle, *The Democracy Advantage* (New York: Routledge, 2005); also discussed in more detail in Windsor, "Is Democracy the Answer?" See also a recent World Bank study, "Where Is the Wealth of Nations? Measuring Capital for the 21st Century," which concludes that, along with human capital, "the value of institutions (as measured by the rule of law) constitute the largest share of wealth in virtually all countries." Quoted in Ronald Bailey, "The Secrets of Intangible Wealth," *Wall Street Journal Online*, September 29, 2007.

30. Examples of standard setting include the passage of "right to democracy" resolutions at the UN during the Clinton administration and the specified criteria for inclusion in the Community of Democracies process. One of the most vexing challenges for successful standard setting are those cases in which governments have been elected through reasonably representative elections but are slowly backtracking on other crucial elements of democracy—as seen in the case of Hugo Chávez in Venezuela or Vladimir Putin in Russia.

31. Successful examples of Bush administration diplomacy include the suspension of $30 million of military assistance financing in response to the imprisonment of democracy advocate Saad Eddin Ibrahim in Egypt and the postponement of a visit by Secretary of State Condoleezza Rice to Cairo to encourage the release of opposition leader Ayman Nour. Many see that the U.S. willingness—at least publicly—to pressure the Egyptian government to make change—has diminished in the last year; see Peter Baker, "Bush: I Am a Dissident," *Washington Post*, July 20, 2007; and Michele Dunne et al., "Egypt—Don't Give Up on Democracy Promotion," Policy Brief 52 (Washington, D.C.: Carnegie Endowment for International Peace, June 2007).

The OAS democracy charter adopted in 2001 was one of the most ambitious pieces of standard setting although the implementation of the charter has been incomplete at best. Even OSCE, which, along with the OAS, provided one of the strongest examples of standards and their application, has been weakened because of the efforts of the Russian government to undercut it and the bid by Kazakhstan—a decidedly nondemocratic country—to head the organization beginning in 2009.

32. The EU is perhaps the most notable example of the use of leverage. The establishment of the Millennium Challenge Account, through which the Bush administration has linked significant amounts of foreign assistance to government performance on democratic governance, is a noteworthy addition to the tools with which the U.S. government can leverage positive change.

33. For an analysis of the Bush administration's fiscal year 2008 budget request of $1.45 billion for "governing justly and democratically," see the Freedom House report "Supporting Freedom's Advocates" at <http://www.free domhouse.org/uploads/press_release/FH_FY08_Budget_Analysis.pdf>.

34. AID is currently engaged in an extensive effort to evaluate the overall impact of its democracy assistance programs. As part of that effort, the University of Pittsburgh carried out a statistical analysis of the correlation between political change in societies and overall levels and types of USAID democracy assistance. See <http://www.pitt.edu/~politics/democracy/democracy.html>.

35. See, for instance, "Today's American: How Free?" a forthcoming special report by Freedom House.

36. See David Adesnick and Michael McFaul, "Engaging Autocratic Allies to Promote Democracy," *Washington Quarterly* 29:2 (Spring 2006), pp. 7–25.

37. See testimony by Jennifer Windsor, Tom Malinowski, and Mort Halperin before the Subcommittee on Democracy, Human Rights, and International Operations, House Foreign Affairs Committee, July 2007, on the issue of avoiding double standards without trying to achieve complete consistency in the application of human rights by U.S. policymakers.

38. See Tom Carothers, "The Sequencing Fallacy," *Journal of Democracy* 18:1 (January 2007); and Windsor, "Promoting Democracy." For a discussion of Islamist movements and democracy, see Nathan Brown, Amr Hamzawy, and Marina S. Ottaway, *Islamist Movements and the Democratic Process in the Arab World*

Experience: The Gray Zone (Washington, D.C.: Carnegie Endowment for International Peace, 2006).

39. See Tom Carothers, *Confronting the Weakest Link* (Washington, D.C.: Carnegie Endowment for International Peace, 2006) for an excellent analysis of political party assistance programs.

40. For a more thorough discussion, see Windsor, "Is Democracy the Answer?"

41. The principal sources of U.S. government funding for democracy promotion come from four major agencies or departments: the Agency for International Development, the Department of State, the Department of Justice, and the Department of Labor. Within the State Department at least four separate offices or bureaus provide funding: the Bureau for Democracy, Human Rights, and Labor; the Office of the Special Coordinator for Assistance to Europe and Eurasia; the Bureau for Cultural and Educational Affairs; and the Middle East Partnership Initiative. In addition, the National Endowment for Democracy is funded by a special congressional appropriation through the State Department although it maintains an independent board and decision-making capacity. For an analysis of the players involved in democracy promotion, see Melia, "The Democracy Bureaucracy"; see the website of the Princeton Project on National Security, <http://www.wws.princeton.edu/ppns/papers/democracy bureaucracy.pdf>, p. 4.

42. A case made persuasively in Melia, "The Democracy Bureaucracy."

43. The objective of the new foreign assistance planning and budgeting process (the so-called F process) is to try to craft a cohesive overall U.S. government strategy and budget for all foreign assistance, including democracy promotion, strategies that are then implemented by embassies, missions, or Washington-based units like MEPI or State's Democracy, Human Rights, and Labor bureau. It remains to be seen whether the new processes will lead to more effective democracy promotion efforts.

44. A grant is a method by which the U.S. government can provide funding for a program proposed by an NGO, but cannot direct how that program is carried out. A contract allows the government to dictate exactly how, where, and who should receive assistance.

45. Tom Carothers, Michael McFaul, and Francis Fukuyama have recently jumped into these debates about how to restructure U.S. democracy promotion. See Carothers, "U.S. Democracy Promotion," pp. 30–31; and McFaul and Fukuyama, "Should Democracy Be Promoted or Demoted?"

46. As Tom Melia has put it, "If, as the President has so powerfully said, the survival of liberty in our land can only be secured by strengthening democracy in other lands, then this ought to become a truly national mission, and not just another government program"—and not just the work of an administration that will soon reach the end of its term. See Melia, "The Democracy Bureaucracy."

Chapter 6

1. Beyond the obvious reference to the Charles Dickens novel, *A Tale of Two Cities* (New York: Knopf, 1993), I am borrowing and adapting the reference from Steven G. Calabresi, "Symposium: The Role of the Judge in the Twenty-First-Century: 'A Shining City on a Hill': American Exceptionalism and the Supreme Court's Practice of Relying on Foreign Law," *Boston University Law Review* 86 (2006), p. 1336, which describes "a tale of two cultures—an elite lawyerly culture

that favors things foreign and a popular culture that dislikes them." While Calabresi concludes that in contrast to the lawyerly elite, "most Americans think instead that the United States is an exceptional country that differs sharply from the rest of the world and that must therefore have its own laws" without engaging with the rest of the world, I believe the United States can be an exceptional nation and play an exceptional role in the world today by asserting its historic leadership in human rights through international cooperation and multilateralism.

2. I use the phrase "war on terror" because it is the rubric under which Bush administration policies in the aftermath of the September 11 terrorist attacks are commonly known. However, since the term could have indefinite elasticity in its usage leading to imprecision in, for example, its geographic and temporal scope, I use the term advisedly. For a cogent analysis of what the "war on terror" is (or should be) see Philip Bobbitt, *Terror and Consent* (London: Allan Lane, forthcoming, 2008).

3. See John Gerard Ruggie, "American Exceptionalism, Exemptionalism, and Global Governance" in Michael Ignatieff, ed., *American Exceptionalism and Human Rights* (Princeton: Princeton University Press, 2005), which claims, "More than any other country, the United States was responsible for creating the post-World War II system of global governance. See also Sarah Cleveland, "Our International Constitution," *Yale Journal of International Law* 31:1 (2006), which summarizes the literature documenting how the United States was the "primary instigator of the UN system and the creation of modern international treaties ranging from human rights and humanitarian law to international intellectual property and international trade."

4. See also, for example, Jose E. Alvarez, "Multilateralism and Its Discontents," *European Journal of International Law* 11 (2000), p. 399: "For some 35 years, within the United States, Republicans and Democrats alike adhered to a bipartisan consensus with respect to UN financing." And also see Stephen C. Schlesinger, *Act of Creation: The Founding of the United Nations* (Boulder, Colo.: Westview Press, 2003) pp. 62–63, which describes the bipartisan consensus at the founding of the United Nations.

5. Calabresi, "Symposium: The Role of the Judge," p. 1337.

6. Harold Hongju Koh, "America's Jekyll-and-Hyde Exceptionalism," in Ignatieff, *American Exceptionalism and Human Rights*, p. 112. See also Byron E. Shafer, ed., *Is America Different? A New Look at American Exceptionalism* (New York: Oxford University Press, 1991); John W. Kingdon, *America the Unusual* (New York: Worth Publishers, 1999); and Alexis de Tocqueville, *Democracy in America* (New York: Knopf, 1948), pp. 36–37.

7. Paul Kahn, "American Exceptionalism, Popular Sovereignty, and the Rule of Law" in Ignatieff, *American Exceptionalism and Human Rights*, p. 198. See also Catherine Powell, "Tinkering with Torture in the Aftermath of Hamdan: Testing the Relationship Between Internationalism and Constitutionalism," *New York University Journal of International Law and Politics* (forthcoming 2008), which dicusses "our constitutional ideals of democratic accountability, self-governance, and popular sovereignty."

8. Jed Rubenfeld, "Unilateralism and Constitutionalism," *New York University Law Review* 79 (2004), pp. 1976–91 discusses George Washington's desire to avoid "'foreign entanglements' [that] could drag the United States into 'bloody contests' in which the nation had no true interest" (citing Washington's Farewell Address).

9. For a discussion of this, see chapter 1 of Carol Anderson, *Eyes Off the Prize: The United Nations and the African American Struggle for Human Rights, 1944–1955* (New York: Cambridge University Press, 2003). Anderson discusses the prominent role of U.S. nongovernmental organizations, including, in particular, African American and Jewish organizations, in securing references to human rights in the UN Charter. See also Ruth B. Russell, *History of the United Nations Charter* (Washington, D.C.: Brookings Institution Press, 1958), chap. 39; and Ruggie, "American Exceptionalism," p. 305, n.2, which points out that "the Soviets and many others were happy to have this provision included."

10. Ruggie, "American Exceptionalism," p. 305. See also Anderson, *Eyes off the Prize*, chap. 1.

11. See Anderson, *Eyes off the Prize*, pp. 220–21, which describes how the Bricker amendment was an effort by southern Democrats, such as Senator John Bricker (R.-Ohio), to prevent the Genocide Convention from becoming a backdoor for an anti-lynching bill. See also Louis Henkin, "Editorial Comments: U.S. Ratification of Human Rights Conventions: The Ghost of Senator Bricker,", *American Journal of International Law* 89 (1995).

12. Rubenfeld, "Unilateralism and Constitutionalism," p. 1985, which recalls that "Hitler was elected, and Mussolini rose to power through parliamentary processes." See also Hannah Arendt, *The Origins of Totalitarianism* (New York: Harcourt Brace Jovanovich, 1973), which describes the broad popular support enjoyed by Hitler.

13. American leadership in post-World War II internationalism was motivated as much by a desire to expand American wealth and power globally as it was to secure American-style freedom and peace. See Rubenfeld, "Unilateralism and Constitutionalism," pp. 1987–88. Similarly, for Europeans, beyond exemplifying protection against a repeat of the horrors of World War II, "integration and international law are means of increasing economic efficiency and bringing the [U.S.] hyperpower to heel." Rubenfeld, "Unilateralism and Constitutionalism," p. 1984.

14. See Rubenfeld, "Unilateralism and Constitutionalism," p. 1974: "Because the point of the new international law was to Americanize, the United States, from its own perspective, did not really need international law (being already American)." He later notes that "international law would be American law, made applicable to other nations" (p. 1988). Rubenfeld characterizes this view by pointing to the work of Louis Henkin, who has contended that "the Universal Declaration of Human Rights, and later the International Covenant on Civil and Political Rights, are in their essence American constitutional rights projected around the world." Louis Henkin, "Rights: American and Human," *Columbia Law Review* 79 (1979) p. 415. While Henkin views the idea of human rights as rooted in Western (including American) philosophical thought, he is also firmly committed to the idea that the United States should apply human rights at home. See e.g., Henkin, "The Ghost of Senator Bricker," p. 341 and Catherine Powell, "Louis Henkin and Human Rights: A New Deal at Home and Abroad," an oral history of Louis Henkin's life contained in a chapter of a forthcoming book entitled *Bringing Human Rights Home,* ed. Catherine Albisa, Martha Davis, Cynthia Soohoo (Greenwood, Conn: Praeger Publishers, 2007). By contrast, the U.S. government has often viewed international law as a means through which to extend its conception of human rights, rule of law, and democracy to the rest of the world rather than as a vehicle for imposing international standards on the United States. Note, for example, that while the State Depart-

ment's annual country reports on human rights document human rights abuses that occur in countries around the world, they do not include human rights abuses that occur in the United States. See Catherine Powell, "Lifting Our Veil of Ignorance: Culture, Constitutionalism, and Women's Human Rights in Post-September 11 America," *Hastings Law Journal* 57 (2005), which shows how members of the Senate Foreign Relations Committee considered the possibility of U.S. ratification of the Convention on the Elimination of All Forms of Discrimination Against Women as a way to secure women's rights overseas—and primarily in the Arab world—rather than in the United States.

15. See, e.g., Cleveland, "Our International Constitution," p. 1; and Harold Hongju Koh, "Is International Law Really State Law?" *Harvard Law Review* 111 (1998).

16. Oona A. Hathaway, "Reflections on International Law and the Internal Point of View," unpublished ms., p. 1.

17. But see William H. Taft IV and Todd F. Buchwald, "Agora: Future Implications of the Iraq Conflict: Preemption, Iraq, and International Law," *American Journal of International Law* 97 (2003).

18. See respectively, (1) "Convention Against Torture or Other Cruel, Inhuman, or Degrading Treatment or Punishment," Dec. 10, 1984, *UN Treaty Series* (*U.N.T.S.*) 14, p. 85, International Legal Materials (*I.L.M.*) 23, p. 1027 (entered into force June 26, 1987) and (2) "Geneva Convention (I) for the Amelioration of the Condition of the Wounded and Sick in Armed Forces in the Field, "Aug. 12, 1949, *United States Treaties* (*U.S.T.*) 6, *U.N.T.S.* 75 (First Geneva Convention); "Geneva Convention (II) for the Amelioration of the Condition of Wounded, Sick and Shipwrecked Members of Armed Forces at Sea," Aug. 12, 1949, *U.S.T.* 6, *U.N.T.S.* 75 (Second Geneva Convention); "Geneva Convention (III) Relative to the Treatment of Prisoners of War," Geneva, Aug. 12, 1949, *U.S.T.* 6, *U.N.T.S.* 75 (Third Geneva Convention); and "Geneva Convention (IV) Relative to the Protection of Civilian Persons in Time of War," Aug. 12, 1949, *U.S.T.* 6, *U.N.T.S.* 75 (Fourth Geneva Convention). For convenience, cites to the Geneva Convention refer to the Third Geneva Convention, unless otherwise specified.

19. See, e.g., Memorandum of August 1, 2002 from Jay S. Bybee, Assistant Attorney General, Office of Legal Counsel, to Alberto R. Gonzales, Counsel to the President, "Regarding Standards of Conduct for Interrogation under 18 U.S.C. §§ 2340–2340A" (Aug. 1, 2004) <http://news.findlaw.com/nytimes/docs/doj/bybee80102mem.pdf>; Memorandum of January 9, 2002 from John Yoo, Deputy Assistant Attorney General, U.S. Department of Justice, Office of Legal Counsel and Robert J. Delehanty, Special Counsel, U.S. Department of Justice, to William J. Haynes II, General Counsel, Department of Defense, "Application of Treaties and Laws to Al Qaeda and Taliban Detainees," (reprinted in Karen J. Greenberg and Joshua L. Dratel, eds., *The Torture Papers: The Road to Abu Ghraib* [New York: Cambridge University Press, 2005], p. 38). See also Memorandum of January 25, 2002 from Alberto R. Gonzales, Counsel to the President, to President Bush, "Decision Re Application of the Geneva Conventions on Prisoners of War to Conflict with Al Qaeda and the Taliban" (reprinted in ibid., p. 118) in which Gonzales wrote, "In my judgment, this new paradigm renders obsolete Geneva's strict limitations on questioning of enemy prisoners and renders quaint some of its provisions requiring the captured enemy be afforded such things as commissary privileges, scrip (i.e. advances a monthly pay), athletic uniforms, and scientific instruments." But see David Stout, "Gonzales Disavows Torture as Confirmation Hearings Begin," *New York*

Times, Jan. 6, 2005, in which Gonzales is quoted as saying at his confirmation hearing to be attorney general: "Contrary to reports, I consider the Geneva Conventions neither obsolete nor quaint."

20. For a discussion of this, see Catherine Powell, "United States Human Rights Policy in the 21st Century in an Age of Multilateralism," *Saint Louis University Law Journal* 46 (2002).

21. President Clinton signed the treaty on December 31, 2000 without submitting it to the Senate for ratification. In May 2002 the Bush administration purportedly "unsigned" the treaty and informed the United Nations that it did not intend to become a party to the Rome Statute. See the letter from John R. Bolton, Under Secretary of State for Arms Control and International Security, to Kofi Annan, U.N. Secretary General, May 6, 2000 <http://www.state.gov/r/pa/prs/ps/2002/9968.htm>. See also Edward T. Swaine, "Unsigning," *Stanford Law Review* 55 (2003).

22. The United States signed the Optional Protocol on July 5, 2000 and ratified it on Dec. 23, 2002 with a declaration inter alia that: "The minimum age at which the United States permits voluntary recruitment into the armed forces of the United States is 17 years." See Multilateral Treaties Deposited with the Secretary-General <http://www.ohchr.org/english/law/index.htm>.

23. For an account of how the United States moved from supporting the "duty to pay" to one of unilateral withholding of UN dues, see Alvarez, "Multilateralism and Its Discontents," p. 400. After the September 11 terrorist attacks, the United States repaid most of the dues owed.

24. It should be noted, however, that President Jimmy Carter signed the ICESCR and sought its ratification. And President Clinton sought ratification of CEDAW. As Oona Hathaway has demonstrated empirically, more important than the question of nonratification is the question of noncompliance with the underlying norms. Oona A. Hathaway, "Do Human Rights Treaties Make a Difference?" *Yale Law Journal* 111 (2002), pp. 1935, 1977, 1980.

25. Harold Koh refers to this as "Swiss cheese ratification," meaning "ratification of multilateral treaties with so many reservations, understandings, and declarations that these conditions substantially limit the U.S. acceptance of these treaties." Harold Hongju Koh, "On American Exceptionalism," *Stanford Law Review* 55 (2003), n.17 and accompanying text.

26. I am borrowing the term "new sovereigntists" from Peter Spiro's "The New Sovereigntists: American Exceptionalism and Its False Prophets," *Foreign Affairs* (Nov/Dec. 2000).

27. Three prominent new sovereigntist scholars who have done tours of duty in the Bush administration include Curtis Bradley, Jack Goldsmith, and John Yoo. Their influential scholarship sets out the nationalist position. See, e.g., Curtis A. Bradley and Jack L. Goldsmith III, "Customary International Law as Federal Common Law: A Critique of the Modern Position," *Harvard Law Review* 110 (1997) and "The Current Illegitimacy of International Human Rights Litigation," *Fordham Law Review* 66 (1997), which argue against the status of customary international law as federal law. See also John C. Yoo, "Globalism and the Constitution: Treaties, Non-Self-Execution, and the Original Understanding," *Columbia Law Review* 99 (1999), p. 1961, which argues that the view that treaties are automatically enforceable in courts is not consistent with the framers' notions of democratic self-government and popular sovereignty; and John C. Yoo, "Treaties and Public Law Making: A Textual and Structural Defense of Nonexecution," *Columbia Law Review* 99 (1999), which asserts that constitutional

text and structure require implementation of treaty obligations by federal statute. But see Ryan Goodman and Derek P. Jinks, "Filartiga's Firm Footing: International Human Rights and Federal Common Law," *Fordham Law Review* 66 (1997); Harold Hongju Koh, "Is International Law Really State Law?" *Harvard Law Review* 111 (1998), p. 1825; Gerald L. Neuman, "Sense and Nonsense About Customary International Law: A Response to Professors Bradley and Goldsmith," *Fordham Law Review* 66 (1997); and Beth Stephens, "The Law of Our Land: Customary International Law as Federal Law After Erie," *Fordham Law Review* 66 (1997), all of which are responses to Bradley and Goldsmith. In response to John Yoo's scholarship, see, e.g., Martin Flaherty, "History Right?: Historical Scholarship, Original Understanding, and Treaties as 'Supreme Law of the Land,'" *Columbia Law Review* 99 (1999) and Carlos Manuel Vazquez, "Laughing at Treaties," *Columbia Law Review* 99 (1999), both of which persuasively refute Yoo's argument on the status of treaties.

28. Koh, "On American Exceptionalism," p. 1514, which notes that "the nationalist/ transnationalist debate now consumes much of the recent scholarship on international law in U.S. courts." See also Powell, "Tinkering with Torture," which explores the tension between the new sovereigntist embrace of democratic process as the litmus test for the legitimacy of law in the constitutional interpretation context, while running from the democratic process as an impermissible encroachment on the president's power to wage war as commander in chief in the "war on terror" context.

29. For an excellent discussion of the negative and positive faces of American exceptionalism, see Koh, "On American Exceptionalism," p. 1480.

30. President Ronald Reagan "Farewell Address to the Nation," *Public Papers* 2 (Jan. 11, 1989), p. 1722.

31. Remarks of Senator Barack Obama to the Chicago Council on Global Affairs, April 23, 2007. <http://www.thechicagocouncil.org/dynamic page .php?id=64>.

32. Margaret MacMillan, *Peacemakers: The Paris Conference of 1919 and Its Attempt to End War* (New York: Random House, 2001), which describes Woodrow Wilson's efforts to create a League of Nations (quoted in Koh, "On American Exceptionalism," p. 1480).

33. Joseph Nye, who coined the phrase "soft power" in the 1980s, examines the concept and its key role in American foreign policy in his book, *Soft Power: The Means to Success in World Politics* (New York: Public Affairs, 2004). See also Nye's *The Paradox of American Power: Why the World's Only Superpower Can't Go It Alone* (New York: Oxford University Press, 2002), p. 9.

34. Koh, "On American Exceptionalism," p. 1489.

35. Ibid., p. 1494.

36. The Annual Message to Congress (Jan. 6, 1941), in *The Public Papers and Addresses of Franklin D. Roosevelt*, ed. Samuel I. Rosenman, p. 663.

37. Ruggie, "American Exceptionalism," p. 304.

38. Ibid., which notes that Roosevelt's "vision drew on Woodson Wilson but was tempered by a pragmatic understanding of both domestic and international politics." For further discussion of Roosevelt's strategy of engagement and its legacy, see John Gerard Ruggie, *Winning the Peace: America and World Order in the New Era* (New York: Columbia University Press, 1996).

39. See generally Mary Ann Glendon, *A World Made New: Eleanor Roosevelt and the Universal Declaration of Human Rights* (New York: Random House, 2001), which describes the history of the Universal Declaration of Human Rights with a particular focus on Eleanor Roosevelt's role as chair of the drafting commission.

40. For further discussion, see Koh, "On American Exceptionalism," pp. 1497–98. Since September 11, however, "freedom from fear" has become the preeminent freedom for the Bush administration, which it has pursued by creating "extralegal zones" (Guantánamo Bay, Cuba) and "extralegal persons" ("enemy combatants") who are effectively stripped of all legal recourse. Koh, "On American Exceptionalism," p. 1498.

41. Schlesinger, *Act of Creation: The Founding of the United Nations,* pp. 62–63, which describes how President Franklin D. Roosevelt, "remembering the League of Nations fiasco of a quarter of a century ago," included a number of Republicans on the delegation to the San Francisco conference where the United Nations Charter was drafted.

42. Ruggie, "American Exceptionalism," pp. 305–06. See also Mary L. Dudziak, *Cold War Civil Rights: Race and the Image of American Democracy* (Princeton: Princeton University Press, 2000).

43. Ruggie, "American Exceptionalism," p. 306.

44. Koh, "On American Exceptionalism," p. 1483.

45. Ibid., which notes, for example, that the "judicial doctrine of 'margin of appreciation,' familiar in European Union law, permits sufficient national variance as to promote tolerance of some measure of this kind of rights distinctiveness. For a comparison of United States and international standards on hate speech, see Elizabeth Defeis, "Freedom of Speech and International Norms: A Response to Hate Speech," *Stanford Journal of International Law* 29 (1992).

46. Koh, "On American Exceptionalism," p. 1483.

47. Ibid., p. 1484

48. Ibid., p. 1485.

49. Ibid., p. 1484.

50. For a discussion of the concern that U.S. failure to ratify CEDAW would undermine women's rights abroad, see Powell, "Lifting Our Veil of Ignorance," pp. 361–62 which documents how members of the Senate Foreign Relations Committee considered the possibility of U.S. ratification of CEDAW as a way to secure women's rights overseas—and primarily in the Arab world—rather than in the United States.

51. Ibid., pp. 1485–86.

52. Ibid., p. 1486.

53. Ibid., pp. 1486–87.

54. Ibid., p. 1487. See also Tom Malinowski, "Overlooking Chechen Terror," *Washington Post,* March 1, 2003, p. A19, which notes that the United States has added three Chechen organizations to the State Department list of terrorist groups, apparently to avoid Moscow's veto of the Iraq resolution before the UN Security Council.

55. See "Declassified Key Judgments of the National Intelligence Estimate Trends in Global Terrorism: Implications for the United States" (dated April 2006) <http://www.dni.gov/press releases/Declassified NIE Key Judgments .pdf>: "The Iraq conflict has become the 'cause célèbre' for jihadists, breeding a deep resentment of U.S. involvement in the Muslim world and cultivating supporters for the global jihadist movement."

56. Koh, "On American Exceptionalism," pp. 1487 and pp. 1505–06, which discusses how U.S. opposition to the ICC has eroded support for American efforts to prosecute high-ranking Iraqi war criminals captured during the second Gulf War.

57. I would like to thank Susan Sturm whose thoughtful counsel helped me

develop this claim. See also G. John Ikenberry, *After Victory: Institutions, Strategic Restraint, and the Rebuilding of Order After Major Wars* (Princeton: Princeton University Press, 2001); Alexander Wendt, "Constructing International Politics," *International Security* 20 (1995), pp. 71–72, which notes that "the fundamental structures of international politics are social rather than strictly material . . . and that these structures shape actors' identities and interests, rather than just their behavior"; and John Gerard Ruggie, "What Makes the World Hang Together? Neo-utilitarianism and the Social Constructivist Challenge," *International Organization* 52 (1998).

58. Nye, *Paradox of American Power.*

59. Ibid.

60. See Oona Hathaway, "Between Power and Principal: An Integrated Theory of International Law," *University of Chicago Law Review* 702 (2005), p. 477, which classifies the existing compliance literature into two broad accounts: an "interest-based model" and a "norm-based model" and Ryan Goodman and Derek Jinks, "How to Influence States: Socialization and International Human Rights Law," *Duke Law Review* 54 (2004), p. 626, which discusses "coercion," "persuasion," and "acculturation" as three mechanisms through which international law influences state behavior. See also Harold Hongju Koh, "Why Do Nations Obey International Law?" *Yale Law Journal* 106 (1997), pp. 2649–52, which distinguishes "instrumentalist interest theories" from "constructivist international society approach." In international relations theory see Thomas Risse and Kathryn Sikkink, "The Socialization of International Human Rights Norms into Domestic Practice: Introduction," *The Power of Human Rights: International Norms and Domestic Change*, ed. Thomas Risse, Stephen C. Ropp, and Kathryn Sikkink (New York: Cambridge University Press, 1999), p. 11, which distinguishes "processes of instrumental adaptation and strategic bargaining" from "processes of moral consciousness raising, argumentation, dialogue, and persuasion," but warns against simplistic dichotomies such as "power versus norm" or "norms versus interests" (p. 9).

61. This section draws on and adapts my previous work in Powell, "United States Human Rights Policy," pp. 424–27.

62. See Hathaway, "Between Power and Principal," pp. 477–78, which notes that early accounts of this approach contend that international law is made and enforced only when it facilitates the interests of the most powerful states. For examples of recent legal scholarship that follows the interest-based or coercion model, see, e.g., Jack Goldsmith, "Sovereignty, International Relations Theory, and International Law," *Stanford Law Review* 52 (2000), p. 970; Jack L. Goldsmith and Eric A. Posner, "Moral and Legal Rhetoric in International Relations: A Rational Choice Perspective," *Journal of Legal Studies* 31 (2002), p. S124; Jack L. Goldsmith and Eric A. Posner, "A Theory of Customary International Law," *University of Chicago Law Review* 66 (1999), p. 1115; Andrew T. Guzman, "A Compliance-Based Theory of International Law," *California Law Review* 90 (2002), pp. 1865–68; and Oona A. Hathaway, "Do Human Rights Treaties Make a Difference?" *Yale Law Journal* 111 (2002), p. 1939. In political science and international relations scholarship, see, e.g., the work of Stephen Krasner.

63. Hathaway, "Between Power and Principal," p. 477. See also Goodman and Jinks, "How to Influence States," p. 626, which discusses the role of coercion in this account of compliance theory.

64. Harold Hongju Koh, "Transnational Legal Process," *Nebraska Law Review* 75 (1996), p. 192, describes realist international relations theorists in the con-

text of outlining the evolution of international scholarship and notes ironic similarity on this point between political realists and left-wing critical legal studies scholars.

65. Hathaway, "Between Power and Principal," p. 478, n.19, cites as examples of this view international relations theorists Hans J. Morgenthau, *Politics Among Nations*, 3rd ed. (New York, Knopf, 1966); Edward Hawllett Carr, *The Twenty Years' Crisis, 1919–1939* (London: Macmillan, 1946); and Hans J. Morgenthau, "Positivism, Functionalism, and International Law," *American Journal of International Law* 34 (1940).

66. John J. Mearsheimer, "The False Promise of International Institutions," *International Security* 19 (1994), p. 7.

67. For discussion, see Hathaway, "Between Power and Principal," pp. 478–79. For an example of this view in international relations theory, see Robert O. Keohane, "The Demand for International Regimes," p. 2 in *International Regimes*, ed. Stephen D. Krasner (Ithaca: Cornell University Press, 1995): "In general, we expect states to join those regimes in which they expect the benefits of membership outweigh the costs."

68. Robert O. Keohane, "Institutional Theory and the Realist Challenge after the Cold War," *Neorealism and Neoliberalism: The Contemporary Debate*, ed. David A. Baldwin (New York: Columbia University Press, 1993), p. 271.

69. Mearsheimer, "The False Promise," p. 17.

70. See William J. Aceves, "Institutionalist Theory and International Legal Scholarship," *American University International Law Review* 12 (1997), pp. 242–56, which summarizes a substantial amount of literature by scholars of international relations and game theory and discusses the prisoner's dilemma game theoretic within this scholarship.

71. "Even when competition or defection provides a short-term advantage, patterns of cooperation may nevertheless emerge from anarchy because 'the logic of collective action' convinces self-interested states that cooperation better serves their longer-term interests." Koh, "Transnational Legal Process," p. 200, which cites as examples of this view Robert Axelrod, *The Evolution of Cooperation* (New York: Basic Books, 1984); Robert O. Keohane, *After Hegemony: Cooperation and Discord in the World Political Economy* (Princeton: Princeton University Press, 1984); Mancur Olson, *The Logic of Collective Action* (Cambridge: Harvard University Press, 1971); Robert O. Keohane, "International Institutions: Two Approaches," *International Studies Quarterly* 32 (1988); and Krasner, *International Regimes*.

72. Goodman and Jinks, "How to Influence States," p. 634, describes this account of compliance theory.

73. For a thoughtful discussion of this point, see Hathaway, "Between Power and Principle," p. 479, which notes that this scholarship typically refers to such treaties as "cheap talk" inasmuch as powerful governments use these treaties to justify conduct that is actually motivated out of self-interest. For examples of this view, see Kenneth N. Waltz, *Theory of International Politics* (New York: McGraw-Hill, 1979), p. 118; Carr, *The Twenty Years' Crisis*; Morgenthau, "Positivism"; and John O. McGinnis and Ilya Somin, "Should International Law Be Part of Our Law?" *Stanford Law Review* 59 (2007), p. 1204.

74. The Third Geneva Convention requires that prisoners of war receive humane treatment; are not punished for not providing additional information beyond their name, rank, birth date, and serial number; and are entitled to be tried before the same courts with the same procedures that the detaining pow-

er's military personnel would face, offering "the essential guarantees of independence and impartiality."

75. Michael D. Gottesman, "Revising the Golden Rule: Toward a New Understanding of Reciprocity and Geneva Protections," *Yale Journal of International Law* (forthcoming).

76. This right can be found in the Vienna Convention on Consular Relations, bilateral agreements, and is considered to be a customary international law norm. See Vienna Convention on Consular Relations, April 24, 1963, Art. 42, *U.N.T.S.* 596, p. 261.

77. Angel Francisco Breard ICJ decision: Vienna Convention on Consular relations (*Paraguay v. United States of America*) Provisional Measures ICJ Reports 1998, p. 248; LaGrand ICJ decision: LaGrand (*Germany v. United States of America*) ICJ Reports 2001, p. 466; Avena ICJ decision: Avena and Other Mexican Nationals (*Mexico v. United States of America*) ICJ Reports 2004, p. 12.

78. *Sanchez-Llamas v. Oregon*, 126 S.Ct. 2669 (2006).

79. Catherine W. Brown, Assistant Legal Adviser for Counselor Affairs, State Department, Office of the Legal Adviser, Remarks at the American Society of International Law, 2001 Annual Meeting, International Law and the Work of Federal and State Governments, (April 4–7, 2001): "What I have been trying to do is to get federal, state and local law enforcement, judicial and other officials to comply with these notification requirements."

80. Jose E. Alvarez, "The WTO as Linkage Machine," *American Journal of International Law* 96 (2002), p. 146, which notes, "International regimes . . . enable parties to escape perennial prisoners' dilemmas by replacing short-term calculations of interest with long-term strategic analysis and mutual reliance on long-term regulation."

81. Ibid.

82. See Goodman and Jinks, "How to Influence States," pp. 635–38. Normative scholarship builds on the insights of "constructivist" theory in political science; see Hathaway, "Between Power and Principle," p. 481. For legal scholarship that emphasizes persuasion or the norm-based approach, see Thomas M. Franck, *Fairness in International Law and Institutions* (Oxford: Clarendon Press, 1995), pp. 7- 9; Abram Chayes and Antonia Handler Chayes, *The New Sovereignty: Compliance with International Regulatory Agreements* (Cambridge: Harvard University Press, 1995), 3–9; Harold Hongju Koh, "The 1998 Frankel Lecture: Bringing International Law Home," *Houston Law Review* 35 (1998), pp. 644–55; and Koh, "How Is International Human Rights Law Enforced?" pp. 1413–14. In political science international relations scholarship, see, e.g., Margaret E. Keck and Kathryn Sikkink, *Activists Beyond Borders: Advocacy Networks in International Politics* (Ithaca: Cornell University Press, 1998), pp. 16–25; Martha Finnemore and Kathryn Sikkink, "International Norm Dynamics and Political Change," *International Organization* 52 (1998), pp. 894–909; and Thomas Risse, " 'Let's Argue!': Communicative Action in World Politics," *International Organization* 54 (2000), p. 1.

83. Hathaway, "Between Power and Principal" p. 477. In international relations theory, see Risse and Sikkink, "The Socialization of International Human Rights Norms," p. 9, which distinguishes "processes of instrumental adaptation" from "processes of persuasion" but warns against simplistic dichotomies such as "power versus norm" or "norms versus interests."

84. For a discussion of this approach, see Hathaway, "Between Power and Principal,"p. 481. For examples of this view in international relations literature,

see Risse and Sikkink, "The Socialization of International Human Rights Norms," pp. 6–7; and Martha Finnemore, *National Interests in International Society* (Ithaca: Cornell University Press, 1996), p. 141, which argues that even "normative claims become powerful and prevail by being persuasive."

85. Risse and Sikkink, "The Socialization of International Human Rights Norms," pp. 6–7: "While materialistic theories emphasize economic or military conditions or interests in determining the impact of ideas in international and domestic politics, social constructivists emphasize that ideas and communicative processes define in the first place which material factors are perceived as relevant and how they influence understandings of interests, preferences, and political decisions." Compare with Goodman and Jinks, "How to Influence States," p. 634, which notes that since scholars who emphasize coercion assume that state interest can be deduced from the objective, material conditions the state confronts, under the logic of this view, international law and institutions "change the behavior of other states not by reorienting their preferences but by changing the cost-benefit calculation of the target state."

86. Hathaway, "Between Power and Principal," p. 483, notes that "norm-based scholarship offers an important corrective" by, for example, drawing attention to "the role and influence of nonstate actors [which are] often ignored in traditional interest-based accounts. See also p. 479, which describes traditional interest-based exclusive focus "on state-level interactions, with scholars largely ignoring substate dynamics."

87. Koh, "Bringing International Law Home," pp. 644–55. See also Koh, "How Is International Human Rights Law Enforced?" pp. 1413–14.

88. Koh, "Bringing International Law Home," pp. 626–27.

89. Koh, "Why Do Nations Obey International Law?" pp. 2599, 2657.

90. For a more exhaustive treatment of the question of torture, see Powell, "Tinkering with Torture."

91. See, e.g., the International Committee of the Red Cross report denouncing practices used by the United States at Guantánamo as "tantamount to torture."

92. Koh, "Bringing International Law Home," pp 626–27.

93. Harold Hongju Koh, "Can the President Be Torturer in Chief?" *Indiana Law Journal* 81 (2006), p. 1153.

94. Ibid., p. 1154. See also Eric Schmitt, "Bush Will Support McCain on Torture: Bipartisan Support Leads to Reversal," *San Francisco Chronicle*, Dec. 16, 2005, which reported that it was a "stinging defeat" for Bush when both chambers defied his veto threat to support McCain's measure overwhelmingly, especially since his party controlled both houses of Congress at the time.

95. Koh, "Can the President Be Torture in Chief?" p. 1154. Of course the combined effect of the president's signing statement, the Graham-Levin Amendment (which deprives detainees of habeas corpus rights) and, later, the Military Commissions Act, blunt the impact of the McCain Amendment.

96. Risse and Sikkink, "The Socialization of International Human Rights Norms," p. 14.

97. Ibid.

98. Ibid.

99. Putting to one side the legality of using these interrogation techniques, their efficacy in gathering reliable intelligence has been challenged. For discussion of the ineffectiveness of torture, see, e.g., Mary Ellen O'Connell, "Affirming the Ban on Harsh Interrogation," *Ohio State Law Journal* 66 (2005), pp. 1259–64 (quoting experienced interrogators).

100. Risse and Sikkink, "The Socialization of International Human Rights Norms," p. 14.

101. Ibid.

102. Goodman and Jinks, "How to Influence States," p. 639.

103. Ibid., p. 630.

104. Risse and Sikkink, "The Socialization of International Human Rights Norms," p. 11.

105. See, e.g., Goodman and Jinks, "How to Influence States," p. 621. Responding to skepticism over whether states, like individuals, can be socialized, Goodman and Jinks argue that "(1) states are purposive actors susceptible to empirical analysis as such, and (2) specific state practices are ultimately the product of socialization of relevant actors who in turn alter, or effect an alteration of, state policy." Ryan Goodman and Derek Jinks, *Socializing States: Promoting Human Rights Through International Law* (New York: Oxford University Press, forthcoming) acknowledges that "'states socialization' is a process grounded in the beliefs, conduct, and social relations of relevant individuals." For a skeptical perspective, see, e.g., José E. Alvarez, "Do States Socialize?" *Duke Law Journal* 54 (2005), a response to Goodman and Jinks.

106. Goodman and Jinks, "How to Influence States." See also Risse and Sikkink, "The Socialization of International Human Rights Norms," p. 11: "Because a state's political identity emerges not in isolation but in relation to and in interaction with other groups of states and international non-state actors, the concept of socialization may be useful in understanding how the international society transmits norms to its members."

107. See, e.g., Colum Lynch, "U.N. Official Faults U.S. Detentions," *Washington Post*, December 8, 2005, p. A27; UN Press Release: United Nations Human Rights Experts Express Continued Concern About Situation of Guantanamo Detainees," February 4, 2005.

108. Edith Lederer, "Close Terror Camp: Annan," *Advertiser* (Australia), February 18, 2006, p. 73.

109. "U.S. Admits Up to 50 'Extraordinary Renditions' E.U Lawmaker Says," Deutsche Presse Agentur International Services in English, May 17, 2006.

110. Goodman and Jinks, "How to Influence States," p. 641.

111. Mathew Lee, "White House Near Decision to Close Gitmo," Associated Press Newswire, June 21, 2007.

112. "A Sudden Sense of Urgency," *New York Times,* September 7, 2006, p. A28, which notes that "Mr. Bush admitted . . . that the Central Intelligence Agency has been secretly holding prisoners[, that] he was transferring 14 to Guantanamo Bay, [and that] he was informing the Red Cross about the prisoners, placing them under the Geneva Conventions." However, since then there have been reports that new detainees are being held secretly abroad. See, e.g., Sheryl Gay Stolberg, "Bush Defends Interrogations, Saying Methods Aren't Torture," *New York Times*, Oct. 6, 2007, p. A1.

113. See Goodman and Jinks, "How to Influence States," pp. 983, 992 (responding to José Alvarez and Harold Koh). Goodman and Jinks point to this decoupling of public conformity and private acceptance as a factor that distinguishes acculturation from norm-based accounts, which assume that the international norm is more genuinely internalized into domestic law (p. 993). Oona Hathaway refers to this type of decoupling as commitment without compliance to international law. See, e.g., Hathaway, "Between Power and Principal," p. 500, which references "the feedback effect between commitment and anticipated compliance."

114. Goodman and Jinks, "How to Influence States," pp. 995–96.

115. Note that the Bush administration recently brought its first prosecution under the Federal Torture Statute but against a foreign national.

116. For further discussion of the torture memos as well as the one that was rescinded, see Powell "Tinkering with Torture."

117. Goodman and Jinks, "How to Influence States," pp. 995–96.

118. The Supreme Court struck down the juvenile death penalty, citing the international trend away from this practice in *Roper v. Simmons*, 125 S.Ct. 1183 (2005).

Chapter 7

1. T. H. Marshall, "Citizenship and Social Class," reprinted in *Citizenship and Social Class*, ed. T. H. Marshall and T. Bottomore (London: Pluto Press, 1992), p. 10.

2. The language comes from the declaration adopted by the Second World Conference on Human Rights, held in Vienna in 1993. See United Nations, "The Vienna Declaration and Programme of Action," in *Report of the World Conference on Human Rights: Report of the Secretary-General*, UN doc. A/CONF.157/24, part I (New York: October 13, 1993), para. 5.

3. Cultural rights are largely absent from the analysis that follows. They have not been accorded significant attention by the relevant UN bodies that deal with ESCR as a whole nor have they been an important element in U.S. policy in this domain. Cultural rights are generally pursued through the lens of CPR rather than ESCR and are raised most often in the context of major violations of the CPR of those who would assert their cultural rights.

4. Cass R. Sunstein, *The Second Bill of Rights: FDR's Unfinished Revolution and Why We Need It More Than Ever* (New York: Basic Books, 2004).

5. "Eleventh Annual Message to Congress (January 11, 1944)" in *The State of the Union Messages of the Presidents, 1790–1966*, vol. 3, ed. Fred L. Israel (New York: Chelsea House, 1967), p. 2881. See generally Sunstein, *The Second Bill of Rights*.

6. The Bricker Amendment—after Republican Ohio Senator John Bricker—would have constitutionally restricted the ability of the president to negotiate and the Senate to ratify treaties with foreign powers. The amendment, which was designed to ensure that international law did not regulate or supersede domestic law, was defeated by a single vote in the Senate.

7. Conference on Security and Co-Operation in Europe, "Final Act" (Helsinki, August 1, 1975), para 1(a) VII <http://www.osce.org/documents/mcs/1975/08/4044_en.pdf>.

8. Conference on Security and Co-Operation in Europe, "Held on the Basis of the Provisions of the Final Act Relating to the Follow-up to the Conference," from *Concluding Document of the Vienna Meeting of Representatives of the Participating States of the Conference on Security and Co-operation in Europe*, International Legal Materials 28 (1989), p. 534, para. 14 (1989).

9. Ibid., p. 533, para. 13(a) and (b).

10. For a detailed and systematic review of the policies of the Reagan administration in relation to ESCR, see Philip Alston, "U.S. Ratification of the Covenant on Economic, Social and Cultural Rights: The Need for an Entirely New Strategy," *American Journal of International Law* 84 (1990), p. 365.

11. U.S. Department of State, "Introduction," *State Department Country Reports on Human Rights Practices for 1981* (1982).

12. Secretary Abrams was apparently unmindful of John Maynard Keyne's admonition that in the long term we are all dead.

13. Hearing Before the House Subcommittee on Human Rights and International Organizations, "Review of State Department Country Reports on Human Rights Practices for 1981," April 28, 1982, 97th Cong., 2d Sess., pp. 13–17.

14. See Marshall, "Citizenship and Social Class."

15. See generally Philip Alston, "The U.S. and the Right to Housing: A Funny Thing Happened on the Way to the Forum," *European Human Rights Law Review* 1 (1996), p. 120.

16. In a 1998 press conference, Ambassador George Moose, U.S. permanent representative to the UN in Geneva, affirmed that "the United States supports the whole principle of economic, social, and cultural rights. It's an integral part of the Universal Declaration of Human Rights. We supported the provisions on economic and social and cultural rights of the Vienna Declaration, as well as the provisions in that declaration regarding the right to development. We believe strongly that economic and social and cultural development is a fundamental part of creating international peace and stability." United Nations, "Press Conference on the Results of the 54th Session of the Commission on Human Rights," Transcript (April 24, 1998).

17. See for example this statement in regard to the Universal Declaration of Human Rights, which makes no distinction between the civil and political rights and the economic and social rights components of the declaration:

These reports describe the performance of governments in putting into practice their international commitments on human rights. These fundamental rights, reflected in the United Nations Universal Declaration of Human Rights, constitute what President Bush calls the "non-negotiable demands of human dignity." As Secretary Rice has said, the full promise of the UN Universal Declaration cannot be realized overnight, but it is urgent work that cannot be delayed.

Bureau of Democracy, Human Rights, and Labor, "Country Reports on Human Rights Practices: 2006" (March 6, 2007) <http://www.state.gov/g/drl/rls/hrrpt/2006/78717.htm>.

18. Remarks of Ambassador Richard Williamson, "Address to CHR, Item 17 Statement: Promotion and Protection of Human Rights," at the 60th Session of the United Nations Commission on Human Rights, April 16, 2004 <http://www.humanrights-usa.net/statements/0416Item17.htm>.

19. Remarks by Public Delegate Marc Leland, "Item 10: Economic, Social and Cultural Rights," at the 60th Session of the United Nations Commission on Human Rights, March 29, 2004 <http://www.humanrights-usa.net/statements/0329Leland.htm>.

20. Statement by Jeffrey de Laurentis, "Explanation of Vote on the Resolution on the Right to Food" at the 60th Session of the United Nations Commission on Human Rights, April 16, 2004 <http://www.humanrights-usa.net/statements/0421Food.htm>.

21. Statement of the United States of America delivered by Richard Wall, "Item 10: Economic, Social and Cultural Rights" at the 59th Session of the United Nations Commission on Human Rights, April 7, 2003 <http://www.us-mission.ch/humanrights/statements/0407Item10.htm>.

22. Leland, "Item 10: Economic, Social and Cultural Rights."

23. Ibid.

24. Intergovernmental Working Group for the Elaboration of a Set of Voluntary Guidelines to Support the Progressive Realization of the Right to Adequate Food in the Context of National Food Security, FAO Doc. CL 127/10-Sup.1, Annex 2 (Rome, September 23, 2004).

25. Ibid.

26. De Laurentis, "Explanation of Vote on the Resolution on the Right to Food."

27. Phyllis Schlafly, "Power Grab Through Executive Orders," *The Phyllis Schlafly Report,* May 1999 <http://www.eagleforum.org/psr/1999/may99/psrmay99.html>.

28. Committee on Economic, Social and Cultural Rights, "General Comment No. 9: Domestic Application of the Covenant," UN Doc. E/1999/22 (1998), Annex IV, para. 10.

29. Statement delivered by Wall, "Item 10: Economic, Social and Cultural Rights."

30. Leland, "Item 10: Economic, Social and Cultural Rights."

31. Writ Petition (Civil) 196 of 2001, *PUCL v. Union of India and others*; for further details, see <www.righttofood.com>.

32. Jean Drèze, "Democracy and the Right to Food," in *Human Rights and Development: Towards Mutual Reinforcement,* ed. Philip Alston and Mary Robinson (New York: Oxford University Press, 2005).

33. UN Committee on Economic, Social, and Cultural Rights Nineteenth Session, "General Comment No. 9: The Domestic Application of the Covenant," (Geneva, November 16–December 4, 1998).

34. The official statement argued that:

As a substantive matter, the idea of elaborating an optional protocol modeled on other conventions is ill-advised as economic, social and cultural rights are not justiciable in the same way as other rights. The Committee cannot be expected to have the capacity or experience to review the most fundamental resource allocation decisions of governments. These decisions, which are based on exceptionally complex facts and projections, involve everything from macroeconomic employment and monetary policy at the national level to the social welfare decisions of local governments. The Committee will be ill-equipped to review these decisions, leaving it with almost limitless discretion to opine on the essential resource and regulatory decisions of nation-states.

Statement delivered by Velia De Pirro, Political Officer, U.S. Mission, "U.S. Statement on the Optional Protocol to the ICESCR" to the Human Rights Council, June 27, 2006. <http://geneva.usmission.gov/Press2006/0627U.S.Statement ToICESCR.html>.

35. Ibid. In fairness it should be noted that U.S. opposition to the proposed optional protocol was also based on procedural grounds, including the fact that the working group responsible for drafting the protocol had not been able to reach consensus (in good measure due to U.S. opposition), and that the group had requested its chairperson to prepare a draft of the protocol rather than putting an initial draft together on the basis of diplomatic inputs.

36. See generally Michael A. Rebell, "Poverty, 'Meaningful' Educational Opportunity, and the Necessary Role of the Courts," *North Carolina Law Review* 85 (2007), p. 1467; and Goodwin Liu, "Education, Equality, and National Citizenship," *Yale Law Journal* 116 (2006), p. 330.

37. Statement by Ambassador Kevin E. Moley, Permanent Representative to

the United Nations in Geneva, "Item 4: The Report of the High Commissioner for Human Rights," at the 59th Session of the United Nations Commission on Human Rights, March 21, 2003 <http://www.us-mission.ch/humanrights/state ments/0321Moley%20Item%204.html>.

38. Ibid. There are currently 28 different thematic mandates, the first of which was set up in 1980. Not until 1998 was the first economic and social rights-based mandate established in the form of an independent expert on human rights and absolute poverty and a special rapporteur on the right to education. Subsequently, special rapporteurs were appointed to deal with human rights and foreign debt (2000), the right to food (2000), the right to housing (2000), and the right to health (2002). The U.S. government voted against the creation of most of these mandates.

39. "President Bush Addresses the United Nations General Assembly," White House Press Release, Sept. 25, 2007 <http://www.whitehouse.gov/news/releases/2007/09/print/20070925–4.html>.

40. See generally "'Why Veto a Popular Health-Care Bill?" *The Economist*, October 4, 2007. <http://www.economist.com/daily/news/displaystory.cfm?story id=9906843>.

41. Statement delivered by Wall, "Item 10: Economic, Social and Cultural Rights."

42. Statement by Paula Dobriansky, Undersecretary of State for Democracy and Global Affairs, "On-The-Record Briefing on the Release of the Annual Report, 'Supporting Human Rights and Democracy: The U.S. Record – 2006,'" April 5, 2007 <http://www.state.gov/g/drl/rls/rm/2007/82655.htm>.

43. For one of the early studies arguing in favor of a critical link of this type, see Sidney Ruth Schuler and Syed M. Hashemi, "Credit Programs, Women's Empowerment, and Contraceptive Use in Rural Bangladesh," *Studies in Family Planning* 25 (1994), p. 65.

44. Ricardo Hausmann, Laura D. Tyson, and Saadia Zahidi, *The Global Gender Gap Report 2006* (Geneva: World Economic Forum, 2006) <http://www.weforum .org/pdf/gendergap/report2006.pdf>.

45. See, e.g., Ylli Bajraktari, "Economic Empowerment of Women in Iraq: The Way Forward" (Washington, D.C.: United States Institute of Peace, May 2006) <http://www.usip.org/pbs/usipeace briefings/2006/0510 women iraq .html>: "Participants noted that most projects conducted so far have been focused mainly on empowering educated women, and not on supporting the larger number of women who are illiterate, handicapped, or marginalized by their location in remote areas."

46. Explanation of position by Miriam K. Hughes, Deputy U.S. Representative to the Economic and Social Council, on Human Rights and Extreme Poverty (A/C.3/61/L.21), November 21, 2006 <http://www.usunnewyork.usmission .gov/press_releases/20061121_354.html>.

47. Statement delivered by Velia De Pirro, U.S. Mission Political Counselor, "Report of the Special Rapporteur on the Situation of Human Rights in the Democratic People's Republic of Korea," at the 4th Session of the UN Human Rights Council, March 23, 2007 <http://geneva.usmission.gov/Press2007/0323DPRK.html>.

48. Statement by U.S. Ambassador Warren W. Tichenor on Zimbabwe, March 29, 2007 <http://geneva.usmission.gov/Press2007/0329StatementonZimbab we.htm>.

49. Testimony of Deputy Assistant Secretary Mark Lagon, Bureau of Interna-

tional Organization Affairs, Department of State, at a hearing on "UN Human Rights Council: Reform or Regression," House International Relations Committee Sub-Committee on Africa, Global Human Rights and International Operations, September 6, 2006 <http://usmission.ch/Press2006/0906LagonTesti monyHRC.html>.

50. "Bush to UN—U.S. is Pro-Family: A Report from the Front," Report from the United Nations, February 1, 2001 <http://www.hslda.org/docs/nche/ 000010/200104240.asp>, quoting the official statement by Michael Southwick, assistant secretary of state for international organization affairs. This statement and most others of this vintage have been removed from the official website of the U.S. mission to the UN, where one would have expected to find them.

51. Explanation from Ambassador Richard T. Miller, U.S. Representative to the UN Economic and Social Council, on UN Doc. 63 A/C.3/61/L.16: Rights of the Child, "Explanation of Vote Before the Vote," November 22, 2006 <http:// www.usunnewyork.usmission.gov/press_releases/20061122_407.html>.

52. There have been various attempts to analyze the arguments invoked to justify U.S. nonratification of the Convention on the Rights of the Child. See, for example, Howard Davidson and Cynthia Price Cohen, eds., *Children's Rights in America: UN Convention on the Rights of the Child Compared with United States Law* (Chicago: American Bar Association Center on Children and the Law, 1990); B. Hafen and J. Hafen, "Abandoning Children to Their Autonomy: The UN Convention on the Rights of the Child," *Harvard International Law Journal* 37 (1996); A. D. Renteln, "United States Ratification of Human Rights Treaties: Who's Afraid of the CRC?," *ILSA Journal of International and Comparative Law* 3 (1997); Susan Kilbourne, "The Convention on the Rights of the Child: Federalism Issues for the United States," *Georgia Journal of Fighting Poverty* 5 (1998), p. 327; Susan Kilbourne, "Placing the Convention on the Rights of the Child in an American Context," *Human Rights* (Spring 1999), p. 27; Andre R. Imbrogno, "Corporal Punishment in America's Public Schools and the U.N. Convention on the Rights of the Child: A Case for Nonratification," *Journal of Law and Education* 29 (2000), p. 125; and American Bar Association Project on the U.N. Convention on the Rights of the Child, "Briefing Paper: State Education Law Compared to the UN Convention on the Rights of the Child."

53. Inspiration in this respect can be drawn from Franklin Roosevelt's statement about the relationship among different rights:

> We have come to a clear realization of the fact that true individual freedom cannot exist without economic security and independence. "Necessitous men are not free men." People who are out of a job are the stuff of which dictatorships are made.
>
> In our day these economic truths have become accepted as self-evident. We have accepted, so to speak, a second bill of rights, under which a new basis of security and prosperity can be established for all—regardless of station, race, or creed.

"Eleventh Annual Message to Congress" in Israel, ed., *The State of the Union Messages of the Presidents.*

Chapter 8

1. Parts of this section draw on the author's earlier publication, "Foreign Investment and Human Rights," *Challenge* (January–February 1999), pp. 57–59.

2. See: V. I. Lenin, *Imperialism: The Highest Stage of Capitalism* (New York: International Publishers, 1939).

3. Stephen Hymer, "The Multinational Corporation and the Law of Uneven Development," in *Economics and World Order*, ed. J. W. Bhagwati (New York: Macmillan, 1971), pp. 113–40.

4. Ibid., p. 132.

5. Work along these lines includes Peter B. Evans, *Dependent Development: The Alliance of Multinational, State, and Local Capital in Brazil* (Princeton: Princeton University Press, 1979); Volker Bornschier and Christopher Chase-Dunn, *Transnational Corporations and Underdevelopment* (New York: Praeger, 1985); and George W. Shepherd, Jr., and Ved P. Nanda, eds., *Human Rights and Third World Development* (Westport, Conn.: Greenwood Press, 1985).

6. International Monetary Fund, Balance of Payments Statistics.

7. U.S. Department of Commerce, Bureau of Economic Analysis, "U.S. Direct Investment Abroad: Country and Industry Detail for Capital Outflows" (2007) <http://www.bea.gov/international/usdiacap.htm>.

8. Morton Winston, "NGO Strategies for Promoting Corporate Social Responsibility," *Ethics and International Affairs* 16 (March 2002), pp. 71–87; Carla C. J. M. Millar, Chong Ju Choi, and Stephen Chen, "Global Strategic Partnerships Between MNEs and NGOs: Drivers of Change and Ethical Issues," *Business and Society Review* 109 (Winter 2004), pp. 395–414; and A. Rani Parker, "Prospects for NGO Collaboration with Multinational Enterprises," in *Globalization and NGOs: Transforming Business, Government, and Society*, eds. Jonathan P. Doh and Hildy Teegen (Westport, Conn.: Praeger, 2003), pp. 81–105.

9. There are, of course, significant differences between individual countries; these conclusions are based on averages. See David Dollar and Aart Kraay, "Growth Is Good for the Poor," World Bank Policy Research Working Paper no. 2587 (Washington, D.C.: World Bank, April 2001); Martin Ravallion, "Growth, Inequality, and Poverty: Looking Beyond Averages," World Bank Policy Research Working Paper no. 2558 (Washington, D.C.: World Bank, February 2001); and Michael Klein, Carl Aaron, and Bita Hadjimichael, "Foreign Direct Investment and Poverty Reduction," World Bank Policy Research Working Paper no. 2613 (Washington, D.C.: World Bank, June 2001).

10. On the particular human rights challenges posed by extractive industries, see the discussion in Spar, "Foreign Investment and Human Rights," pp. 60–62.

11. I am borrowing the term "bebop" from my colleagues Michael Chu and V. Kasturi Rangan, who coined the word (an acronym for "business at the bottom of the pyramid") and teach an innovative course at Harvard Business School with this name. For more on their work on this subject, see: V. Kasturi Rangan, Dalip Sehgal, and Rohithari Rajan, "The Complete Business of Serving the Poor: Insights from Unilever's Project Shakti in India," in *Business Solutions for the Global Poor: Creating Social And Economic Value*, eds. V. Kasturi Rangan et al. (San Francisco: John Wiley, 2007), pp. 144–154; V. Kasturi Rangan and Arthur McCaffrey, "A 'Customer-Centric' View of Global Economic Development," in *Multinational Corporations and Global Poverty Reduction*, eds. Subhash C. Jain and Sushil Vachani (Northampton, Mass.: Edward Elgar Publishing, 2006), pp. 177–203; and Michael Chu, "Commercial Returns at the Base of the Pyramid," *Innovations* (Winter/Spring 2007), pp. 115–146.

12. See C. K. Prahalad, *The Fortune at the Bottom of the Pyramid: Eradicating Poverty Through Profits* (Upper Saddle River, N.J.: Wharton School Publishing, 2005) and Rangan, *Business Solutions for the Global Poor*, esp. pp. 128–189.

13. "Underserved Communities: Case Study—Project Shakti," *Brand Strategy* (December 18, 2006) and V. Kasturi Rangan and Rohithari Rajan, "Unilever in

India: Hindustan Lever's Project Shakti—Marketing FMCG to the Rural Consumer," HBS Case no. 9-505-056 (Boston: Harvard Business School, 2005).

14. Ian Limbach, "Keeping It Local in Africa And Asia—Wireless in the Developing World," *Financial Times,* July 13, 2005, p. 6.

15. Kathryn Kranhold, "GE Pins Hopes on Emerging Markets," *Wall Street Journal,* March 2, 2005, p. A3.

16. "Underserved Communities"; Rangan and Rajan, "Unilever in India."

17. Steve Coll, "In the Gulf, Dissidence Goes Digital," *Washington Post,* March 29, 2005, p. A1; Craig Skehan, "Message Waiting: Join the Revolution," *Sydney Morning Herald,* January 22, 2001, p. 8.

18. Michael Kremer, "Pharmaceuticals and the Developing World," *Journal of Economic Perspectives* 16 (Fall 2002), pp. 67–90; Chris Papageorgiou, Andreas Savvides, and Marios Zachariadis, "International Medical Technology Diffusion," *Journal of International Economics* 72 (July 2007), pp. 409–427; Thomas Reardon et al., "The Rise of Supermarkets in Africa, Asia, and Latin America," *American Journal of Agricultural Economics* 85:5 (December 2003), pp. 1140–1146; and William A. Jácome, Luis E. Loría, and Luis Reyes Portocarrero, "Multiahorro: Barrio Store," in *Business Solutions for the Global Poor,* pp. 128–134.

19. See, for instance, B. Marulanda and M. Otero, *The Profile of Microfinance in Latin America in 10 Years: Vision and Characteristics* (Boston: ACCION International, 2005); "The Hidden Wealth of the Poor," *Economist,* November 5, 2005; and Marguerite Robinson, *The Microfinance Revolution: Sustainable Finance for the Poor* (Washington, D.C.: World Bank, 2001).

20. See Chu, "Commercial Returns," p. 118.

21. Masud Karim, "Nobel Prize Winner Changes Lives in Bangladesh," Reuters News, October 16, 2006; and Harry Hurt III, "A Path to Helping the Poor, and His Investors," *New York Times,* August 10, 2003.

22. Susy Cheston and Lisa Kuhn, "Empowering Women through Microfinance," in *Pathways Out of Poverty: Innovations in Microfinance for the Poorest Families,* ed. Sam Daley-Harris (Bloomfield, Conn.: Kummarian Press, 2002), pp. 167–228; Naila Kabeer, "Money Can't Buy Me Love: Reevaluating Gender, Credit, and Empowerment in Rural Bangladesh," IDS Discussion Paper No. 363 (Brighton, UK: Institute of Development Studies, University of Sussex, 1998).

23. See Debora L. Spar, "Hitting the Wall: Nike and International Labor Practices," HBS Case no. 9-700-047 (Boston: Harvard Business School, 2002), p. 2.

24. Farhan Haq, "U.S.-Labor: Nike Campaign Strikes at Firm's Record in Asia," Inter Press Service, October 30, 1996.

25. Farhan Haq, "U.S.-Labor: Nike Not Worried at Criticism," Inter Press Service, October 21, 1997.

26. "Nike, Inc. Code of Conduct" <http://www.nike.com/nikeresponsibility/tools/Nike_Code_of_Conduct.pdf >; "The Reebok Human Rights Production Standards" <http://www.reebok.com/Static/global/initiatives/rights/business/standards.html>.

27. "Nike FY05–06 Corporate Responsibility Report," Nike, Inc. <http://www.nike.com/nikebiz/nikeresponsibility/#workers-factories/audittools>.

28. According to a major study completed in 2006 for the United Nations under the direction of John G. Ruggie, only 36 percent of a sample of more than 300 firms recognize the right to a minimum wage. See Michael Wright and Amy Lehr, "Business Recognition of Human Rights: Global Patterns, Regional and Sectoral Variations" (Geneva: United Nations, December 12, 2006), p. 7.

29. Ibid.

30. For more on this effect and its implications, see Debora L. Spar, "The Spotlight and the Bottom Line," *Foreign Affairs* (March/April 1998), pp. 7–12.

31. Mark Suzman, "Body Shop Launches Audit with Social Conscience," *Financial Post*, February 2, 1996.

32. For a discussion of this campaign and its implications, see Debora L. Spar, "Continuity and Change in the International Diamond Market," *Journal of Economic Perspectives* 20:3 (Summer 2006), pp. 195–208.

33. Melody Petersen, "Novartis Agrees to Lower Price of a Medicine Used in Africa," *New York Times*, May 3, 2001, p.1; and Joe Nocera, "Can a Vision Save All of Africa?" *New York Times*, June 16, 2007.

34. For a more in-depth discussion of this phenomenon, see Debora Spar and David Yoffie, "Multinational Enterprises and the Prospects for Justice," *Journal of International Affairs* 52:2 (Spring 1999), pp. 557—581.

35. Mike Dolan, "World Bank's IFC Recasts Social, Environmental Rules," Reuters News, February 21, 2006.

36. Stephen L. Kaas and Jean M. McCarroll, "The Revised Equator Principles," *New York Law Journal* 236 (September 2006), p. 3.

37. Kristi Ellis, "Cambodian Trade Deal Renewed with Labor Caveat," *Women's Wear Daily*, January 3, 2002; and Joseph Kahn, "Labor Praises New Trade Pact with Jordan," *New York Times*, October 25, 2000, p. 1.

Chapter 9

1. ILO Declaration on Fundamental Principles and Rights at Work, International Labor Conference, 86th Session, Geneva, June 18, 1998.

2. There is a substantial body of evidence demonstrating the economic benefits of guaranteeing freedom of association and the right to organize in both developing and developed nations. See, e.g., Dani Rodrik, "Democracies Pay Higher Wages," *Quarterly Journal of Economics* 114 (1999); Joseph Stiglitz, "Democratic Development as the Fruits of Labor," Keynote Address to the Industrial Relations Research Association, Jan. 2000; Josh Bivens and Christian Weller, "Rights Make Might: Ensuring Workers' Rights as a Strategy for Economic Growth," *Economic Policy Institute Issue Brief*, No. 192 (2003); Toke Aidt and Zafiris Tzannatos, *Unions and Collective Bargaining: Economic Effects in a Global Environment* (Washington, D.C.: World Bank, 2002).

3. 29 C.F.R. § 570.2(b).

4. See ILO Convention (No.100) Concerning Equal Remuneration for Men and Women Workers for Work of Equal Value, June 29, 1951, *United Nations Treaty Series* (*UNTS*) 165, Art. 2.

5. See "Equal Remuneration: Report of the Committee of Experts on the Application of Conventions and Recommendations," International Labor Conference, 72nd Session, Geneva, 1986, Report III (Part 4B), para. 20.

6. See generally, Congressional Research Service, "Pay Equity Legislation in the 109th Congress," May 11, 2005. See also *Spaulding v. University of Washington*, 740 F.2d 686 (9th Cir. 1984) (denying a comparable worth claim by members of the female nursing faculty at a university); *AFSCME v. State of Washington*, 770 F.2d 1401 (9th Cir. 1985) (finding that Title VII does not obligate a state to eliminate economic inequality it did not create by assuring equal pay for dissimilar jobs of comparable worth).

7. See ibid.

8. See, e.g., Human Rights Watch, *Unfair Advantage: Workers' Freedom of Association in the United States under International Human Rights Standards* (New York: Human Rights Watch, 2000).

9. U.S. Department of Labor, Bureau of Labor Statistics, "Union Members Summary," Jan. 25, 2007.

10. Richard Freeman, "Do Workers Still Want Unions? More Than Ever," *Economic Policy Institute Briefing Paper*, No. 182 (2007).

11. *Oakwood Healthcare Inc.*, 348 *National Labor Relations Board* (*NLRB*) No. 37 (Sept. 29, 2006); *Golden Crest Health Care Center*, 348 NLRB No. 39 (Sept. 29, 2006); *Croft Metal, Inc.*, 348 NLRB No. 38 (Sept. 29, 2006).

12. See, e.g., UDHR, General Assembly (G.A.) Res. 217A(III), U.N. Doc. A/810, p. 71, Dec. 10, 1948, art. 23; ICCPR, G.A. Res. 2200A (XXI), 21 U.N. General Assembly Official Record (GAOR) Supp. (No. 16), p. 52, U.N. Doc. A/6316, 999 UNTS 171, Dec. 16, 1966, Art. 22.

13. ILO Committee on Freedom of Association, "Complaint against the Government of the United States presented by the UFCW, the AFL-CIO and the International Federation of Commercial, Clerical, Professional and Technical Employees (FIET)," Report No. 284, Case No. 1523, Vol. LXXV, 1992, Series B, No. 3, para. 199(a).

14. ILO Committee of Freedom of Association, "Complaint against the Government of the United States presented by the AFL-CIO," Report No. 278, Case No. 1543, Vol. LXXIV, 1991, Series B, No. 2, para. 92.

15. *Hoffman Plastic Compounds, Inc., v. National Labor Relations Board*, 535 U.S. 137 (2002).

16. ICCPR, arts. 2(2), 3(a); International Labor Office, *Digest of Decisions and Principles of the Freedom of Association Committee of the Governing Body of the ILO* (Geneva: ILO, 2006), paras. 763–64.

17. See, e.g., *NLRB*, "Seventieth Annual Report of the National Labor Relations Board for the Fiscal Year Ended September 30, 2005," May 1, 2006, table 23.

18. ILO Committee on Freedom of Association, "Complaints against the Government of the United States presented by the AFL-CIO and the Confederation of Mexican Workers (CTM)," Report No. 332, Case No. 2227, Vol. LXXXVI, 2003, Series B, No. 3, paras. 610, 611.

19. "1994, Freedom of Association and Collective Bargaining: Promotion of Collective Bargaining, Report of the Committee of Experts on the Application of Conventions and Recommendations," International Labor Conference, 81st Session, Geneva, 1994, Report III (Part 4B), para. 262.

20. ILO Committee on Freedom of Association, "Complaint against the Government of the United States presented by the United Electrical, Radio and Machine Workers of America (UE), supported by Public Services International (PSI)," Report No. 344, Case No. 2460, Vol. XC, 2007, Series B, No. 31 paras. 997, 998.

21. H.R. 800, 110th Cong., 1st Sess. (March 1, 2007).

22. U.S. Department of State, Havana Charter for an International Trade Organization, 32 (1948), Pub. No. 3206.

23. WTO, Singapore Ministerial Declaration, Dec. 13, 1996, 36 *International Legal Materials* (*ILM*) 220, p. 221.

24. Constitution of the International Labor Organization, June 28, 1919, 49 Stat. 2712, 225 Consolidated Treaties and International Agreements (CTIA) 373, art. 33.

25. The ILO recommended, inter alia, that members "review . . . the relations that they may have with the member State concerned and take appropriate measures to ensure that the said Member cannot take advantage of such relations to perpetuate or extend the system of forced or compulsory labour." "Resolution concerning the measures recommended by the Governing Body under article 33 of the ILO Constitution on the subject of Myanmar," International Labor Conference, 88th Session, Geneva, June 14, 2000.

26. It is beyond the scope of this chapter to review all of the proposals that have been made for integrating workers' rights protections into international trade rules. However, some useful references include Michael J. Trebilcock and Robert Howse, *The Regulation of International Trade*, 2nd ed. (New York: Routledge, 2002), pp. 441–463; Steve Charnovitz, "Trade, Employment and Labour Standards: The OECD Study and Recent Developments in the Trade and Labour Standards Debate," *Temple International and Comparative Law Journal* 11 (1997); Daniel S. Ehrenberg, "From Intention to Action: An ILO-GATT/WTO Enforcement Regime in International Labor Rights," in *Human Rights, Labor Rights, and International Trade*, ed. Lance A. Compa and Stephen F. Diamond (Philadelphia: University of Pennsylvania Press, 1996).

27. A challenge could argue, for example, that such measures violate the WTO principle of nondiscrimination among members (most favored nation treatment).

28. For example, while section 301 of U.S. trade law authorizes the United States to take trade measures against countries that deny fundamental workers' rights (see 19 U.S.C. § 2411(d)(3)(B)(iii)), if such unilateral action were to result in withdrawing market access guaranteed under WTO rules, the measures could lead to a WTO challenge against the United States.

29. See, e.g., Agreement Between the United States of America and the Hashemite Kingdom of Jordan on the Establishment of a Free Trade Area (U.S.-Jordan FTA), Art. 6(4)(b); Dominican Republic-Central America-United States Free Trade Agreement (DR-CAFTA), Art. 16.2(b).

30. See, e.g., Trade Promotion Agreement between the United of America and the Republic of Peru (U.S.-Peru FTA), Arts. 17.2, FN 1; 17.3(a). The new provision expands on its predecessors to include conduct affecting investment as well as trade.

31. The U.S.-Jordan FTA contained similar but much weaker and less absolute language.

32. See, e.g., U.S.-Peru FTA, Arts. 17.2, 17.3.

33. See, e.g., Sandra Polaski, "Serious Flaw in U.S.-Singapore Trade Agreement Must Be Addressed," *Carnegie Endowment for International Peace Issue Brief* (2003).

34. U.S. Department of State, Bureau of Democracy, Human Rights, and Labor, "2006 Country Reports on Human Rights Practices: Indonesia," March 6, 2007 <http://www.state.gov/g/drl/rls/hrrpt/2006/>.

35. Free Trade Agreement Between the United States of America and the Republic of Korea (U.S.-South Korea FTA), Annex 22-B, para. 3.

36. See, e.g., Human Rights Watch, "The US-Korea Free Trade Agreement Annex 22-B: A Missed Opportunity on Workers' Rights in North Korea," Aug. 2007.

37. FTA investment provisions are subject to distinct enforcement procedures that create a private right of action to challenge government actions affecting investors' rights. No such procedures exist for the other commercial obligations or for labor obligations.

38. See, e.g., Human Rights Watch, "Labor Rights and Trade: Guidance for the United States in Trade Accord Negotiations," Oct. 2002.

39. See, e.g., North American Agreement on Labor Cooperation Between the Government of the United States of America, the Government of Canada, and the Government of the United Mexican States (NAALC), Art. 30; DR-CAFTA, Art. 20.7; U.S.-Peru FTA, Arts. 21.7, 21.8.

40. Under GSP, the president may not designate a country a beneficiary if that country has not taken or is not taking steps to afford internationally recognized worker rights and the president shall take into account whether such steps have been taken when reviewing eligibility. See 19 U.S.C. §§ 2462(b)(2)(G) and (c)(7). Under the Caribbean Basin Trade Partnership Act and the Andean Trade Promotion and Drug Eradication Act, the president must take into account the extent to which countries provide internationally recognized worker rights when determining country eligibility. See 19 U.S.C. §§ 2703(b) (5)(B)(iii) and 3203(b)(6)(B)(iii). Under the African Growth and Opportunity Act, the president can only designate a country a beneficiary if the president determines that the country has established, or is making continual progress toward establishing, protection of internationally recognized worker rights. See 19 U.S.C. § 3703(a)(1)(F).

41. For an analysis of the workers' rights conditionality of the GSP program, see Lance Compa and Jeffrey S. Vogt, "Labor Regulation and Trade: Labor Rights in the Generalized System of Preferences: A 20-Year Review," *Comparative Labor Law and Policy Journal* 22 (2001).

42. Because unilateral preference programs are by definition not negotiated with beneficiary countries, the United States has exclusive discretion to establish strong workers' rights criteria.

43. The preference program that would be created under the proposed New Partnership for Development Act of 2007 would largely fulfill these recommendations. See H.R. 3905, 110th Cong., 1st Sess. (Oct. 18, 2007).

44. Ibid.

45. The evaluation could include, as appropriate, in-country monitoring visits and public hearings.

46. The World Bank and most of the regional development banks have policies that call for an analysis of core labor standards in country strategy documents and the provision of technical assistance to improve workers' rights. However, these policies do not impose binding safeguards to ensure that all lending complies with core workers' rights. Many of these mandates have resulted from replenishment negotiations. In the thirteenth replenishment of the World Bank's International Development Association (IDA), for example, the IDA deputies called on the bank to include an assessment of compliance with fundamental workers' rights in the core diagnostics included in Country Assistance Strategies. "Additions to IDA Resources: Thirteenth Replenishment," Report from the Executive Directors of IDA to the Board of Governors, Sept. 17, 2002, p. 22 <http://siteresources.worldbank.org/IDA/Resources/FinaltextIDA13Report.pdf>.

47. See, e.g., AFL-CIO, "The World Bank and Workers' Rights," in *Responsible Reform of the World Bank: The Role of the United States in Improving the Development Effectiveness of World Bank Operations* (2002), pp. 13–15 <http://www.essential action.org/imf/worldbank_report/IDA_FINAL_REPORT. pdf >.

48. Unfortunately, the embrace of workers' rights in project financing continues to stand in contrast to policy recommendations from the World Bank that

prioritize the deregulation of labor markets over core labor standards compliance, creating a disconnect that sends mixed signals to countries seeking IFI advice and assistance. See, e.g., World Bank, *Doing Business 2007: How to Reform* (Washington, D.C.: World Bank, 2006) (ranking countries according to the degree to which they have deregulated their labor markets and other areas of their economies).

49. See International Finance Corporation, "Performance Standard 2: Labor and Working Conditions," April 30, 2006 <http://www.ifc.org/ifcext/enviro.nsf/Content/PerformanceStandards>.

50. See International Trade Union Confederation, "World Bank Takes Major Step on Labour Standards," Dec. 13, 2006 <http://www.ituc-csi.org/spip.php?article491&var_recherche=world%20bank>.

51. 22 U.S.C. § 2191a. The OPIC criteria require that a country merely be "taking steps to adopt and implement laws that extend internationally recognized worker rights."

52. OPIC's accountability and advisory mechanism only investigates whether OPIC itself complies with its own statutory mandates and policies—the mechanism does not accept complaints regarding violations of contract conditions by the private companies financed by OPIC. See, e.g., Harvey A. Himberg, "The New Accountability and Advisory Mechanism of the Overseas Private Investment Corporation: The Application of International Best Practices of the International Financial Institutions," in *Conference Proceedings of the Seventh International Conference on Environmental Compliance and Enforcement* 1 (Washington, D.C.: International Network for Environmental Compliance and Enforcement, 2005), p. 311.

53. U.S. law already requires the USEDs (who represent the United States on the boards of IFIs) to use their voices and votes to maintain and improve workers' rights through IFI programs, but the vigor and effectiveness of their efforts is difficult to ascertain given the lack of transparency of IFI board discussions. See 22 U.S.C. §§ 262o-2(a)(9) and 262p-4p.

54. See Millennium Challenge Corporation, "Indicators Home," no date <http://www.mcc.gov/selection/indicators/index.php>. For a proposal on monitoring and measuring core workers' rights compliance, see Committee on Monitoring International Labor Standards, *Monitoring International Labor Standards: Techniques and Sources of Information* (Washington, D.C.: National Research Council, 2004).

55. See U.S. Office of Management and Budget, *Budget of the United States, Fiscal Year 2006*, Department of Labor Annex, p. 742; U.S. Office of Management and Budget, *Budget of the United States, Fiscal Year 2008*, Department of Labor Annex, p. 703. ILAB appropriations for 2007 were kept steady at 2006 levels.

56. See U.S. Agency for International Development, "Trade Capacity Building Database," no date <http://qesdb.cdie.org/tcb/index.html>.

Chapter 10

1. Various Bush administration spokespeople have asserted that the United States has made the promotion of women's human rights a foreign policy priority. To mark International Women's Day in 2005, for example, First Lady Laura Bush stated that President George W. Bush had made the advancement of women's human rights a "global policy priority." Remarks of Laura Bush on the

Occasion of International Women's Day, March 8, 2005 <http://usinfo.state
.gov/dhr/Archive/2005/Mar/08–835440.html>.

2. In numerous speeches President Bush, Laura Bush, and Secretary of State
Condoleezza Rice have claimed that women's rights are better protected in postinvasion Iraq and Afghanistan. In comments in 2005 for International Women's
Day, all three pointed to the "gains" in freedom and opportunity enjoyed by
women following the U.S. invasions of both Afghanistan and Iraq. For an alternative view, see Yifat Susskind, *Promising Democracy, Imposing Theocracy: Gender-
Based Violence and the US War on Iraq* (New York: Madre, 2007). Susskind concludes that women's lives and rights have suffered greatly in postinvasion Iraq
given increased physical insecurity and the rise of Islamist factions seeking to
restrict women's rights.

3. World Public Opinion, a project of the University of Maryland, has synthe-
sized and reported on numerous polls indicating that support for gender equality among Americans has grown steadily over the past 30 years. Similarly, strong
majorities of Americans believe that promoting the rights of women in other
countries should be a priority for the United States and its foreign policy. See
<http://www.americans-world.org/digest/global_issues/women>.

4. Isobel Coleman, "The Payoff from Women's Rights," *Foreign Affairs* (May/
June 2004).

5. Remarks of Secretary of State Colin L. Powell, March 8, 2002. Powell
asserted that the "worldwide advancement of women's issues . . . is strongly in
our national interest. . . . Women's issues . . . are ingredients of good government and sound economic practice. They go to the heart of what makes for successful, stable societies and global growth. . . . It is not just popular opinion, but
plain fact: countries that treat women with dignity, that afford women a choice
in how they live their lives, that give them equal access to essential services, give
them an equal opportunity to contribute to public life—these are the countries
that are the most stable, viable and capable of meeting the challenges of the new
century."

6. World Bank, *Engendering Development* (New York: Oxford University Press
2001).

7. Augusto Lopez-Claros and Saadia Zahidi, *Women's Empowerment: Measuring
the Global Gender Gap* (Geneva: World Economic Forum, 2005). The 58 countries
evaluated represent all regions of the world and all stages of economic and political development and include Sweden, Canada, the United States, New Zealand,
Poland, Colombia, China, Israel, Jordan, Turkey, Brazil, South Africa, Russia,
and Zimbabwe.

8. Press statement from Yakin Erturk, special rapporteur of the United
Nations Human Rights Council on Violence against Women, July 27, 2007.
Official estimates place the number of sexual violence cases in South Kivu, a
region of Congo, at 4,500 in the first six months of 2007—likely a low number
given that many women live in isolated areas, are afraid to report, or did not
survive.

9. *Arab Human Development Report 2005: Towards the Rise of Women in the Arab
World* (New York: United Nations Development Programme, 2006), p. 5.

10. See <http://www.state.gov/g/wi/rls/18767.html>.

11. Quoted by Ambassador Ellen Sauerbrey, U.S. Representative to the Commission on the Status of Women, "U.S. Statement to the Forty-ninth Session of
the United Nations Commission on the Status of Women," March 2, 2005.

12. All four teams concluded that UNFPA actually was playing a critical role in efforts to *end* coercive population control practices in China.

13. Obstetric fistula is a devastating physical consequence of prolonged labor that is particularly common among girls and young women with bodies not ready for childbearing and no access to medical care during childbirth. After many hours and sometimes days of labor, bodies rupture, leaving women and girls with this condition unable to control the passage of fluids and waste from their bodies.

14. Remarks of Secretary of State Colin L. Powell to mark International Women's Day, March 8, 2002 <http://usinfo.state.gov/scv/Archive/2005/May/18–298320.html>.

15. United Nations Convention against Transnational Organized Crime, Protocol to Prevent, Suppress and Punish Trafficking in Persons, Especially Women and Children, 2000.

16. News reports indicating that the numbers of trafficked persons claimed by the U.S. government and others have not been substantiated by the evidence underscore the need to understand trafficking as one part of a broader problem and craft remedies that respond not just to the most egregious cases—which may be relatively small in number—but to the range of practices that discriminate and abuse women in the migrant and trafficking streams. See "Human Trafficking Evokes Outrage, Little Evidence," *Washington Post*, September 23, 2007.

17. World Bank, "The International Migration Agenda and the World Bank: Managing Risks, Enhancing Benefits" (September 2006) <www.worldbank.org/migration>.

18. Women now comprise roughly half of the world's 200 million migrants. As many as 50 to 75 percent of the legal migrants leaving Indonesia, the Philippines, and Sri Lanka are women.

19. Nisha Varia, "Globalization Comes Home: Protecting Migrant Domestic Workers' Rights," in *Human Rights Watch World Report 2007* (New York: Human Rights Watch, 2007). In many countries the legal status of migrants who are domestic workers is tied to their employer. This makes it difficult for them to leave or negotiate an abusive situation.

20. One of President Bush's first acts in 2001 was to reinstate the Mexico City Policy, also called the global gag rule, which prohibits U.S. aid to foreign nongovernmental organizations that provide any abortion-related information or services, even if those activities are funded with other money.

21. The anti-prostitution pledge or "loyalty oath regarding prostitution" requires nongovernmental organizations receiving U.S. Agency for International Development funding to adopt a policy explicitly opposing prostitution and sex trafficking throughout their programs, regardless of funding source. Public health, human rights, and faith-based advocates have all expressed concern that the oath restricts programs from using best practices to prevent HIV/AIDS among sex workers and trafficked persons.

22. In 2006 two federal district courts ruled that the anti-prostitution oath requirement violates the first amendment rights of U.S.-based organizations.

23. Critics of the anti-prostitution pledge have gathered evidence to show that these "ideological litmus tests" interfere with sound public health practices and run afoul of human rights standards. See Center for Health and Gender

Equity, "Implications of U.S. Policy Restrictions for Programs Aimed at Commercial Sex Workers and Victims of Trafficking Worldwide" (November 2005).

Chapter 11

1. Madeleine Albright, *The Mighty and the Almighty* (New York: Harper Collins, 2006), p. 9.

2. Any limitations must be "prescribed by law" and "necessary to protect public safety, order, health or morals, or the fundamental rights and freedoms of others." Article 18 (3), International Covenant on Civil and Political Rights. For text, see Tad Stahnke and J. Paul Martin, eds., *Religion and Human Rights: Basic Documents* (New York: Columbia University Center for Human Rights), p. 74.

3. UN General Assembly, Summary Record, No. 36, December 1981, paras 9–12.

4. Felice Gaer, "Human Rights: What Role for US Policy?" *Great Decisions* (New York: Foreign Policy Association, 1998), p. 35.

5. Allen D. Hertzke, *Freeing God's Children* (New York: Rowman and Littlefield, 2004), p. 12.

6. Ibid.

7. Hertzke, *Freeing God's Children*, p. 1; J. Heilbrunn, "Christian Rights," *The New Republic* (July 7, 1997), pp. 19–24.

8. IRFA, Sec. 2(1).

9. Felice Gaer, "Protecting Religious Liberty," Issues of Democracy 3:3 (October 1998) <http://usinfo.state.gov/journals/itdhr/1098/ijde/gaer.htm>.

10. See General Comment 22 on Article 18, ICCPR, in Stahnke and Martin, *Religion and Human Rights,* p. 93

11. Gaer, "Protecting Religious Liberty."

12. See "Religious Persecution as a US Policy Issue," Trinity College, 1999 <http://www.trincoll.edu/depts/csrpl/Religious%20Persecution/relperse.pdf>; Peter G. Danchin, "US Unilateralism and the International Protection of Religious Freedom: The Multilateral Alternative," *Columbia Journal of Transatlantic Law* 41 (2002), pp. 33–136; John Shattuck at the Pew Forum on Religion and Public Life, May 8, 2007 <http://pewforum.org/events/?EventID=139>; and Heilbrunn, "Christian Rights."

13. Four countries have been recommended by USCIRF for CPC status but have not been designated: Turkmenistan; Pakistan, Laos and, after the pogroms in Gujarat, India—a country USCIRF later removed from its list.

14. See Sections 401, 405 of IRFA

15. USCIRF 2007 report, pp. 93ff. Secretary Rice announced the Eritrean sanction in September 2005; Ambassador John Hanford announced the confirmation of policies by Saudi Arabia in July 2006 and stated that the secretary had left in place a waiver "to further the purposes of the act."

16. Press conference, "On the Record Briefing on the Release of the Dept. of State's Annual Report on Religious Freedom," September 15, 2006 <www.state.gov/g/drl/rls/rm/2006/72303.htm>.

17. 2004 IRF report.

18. 2007 IRF report, p. 137.

19. <http://www.youtube.com/watch?v=k2CfXeoMlsE>.

20. <www.queme.net>, August 23, 2007 (report from IBIB).

21. USCIRF memo, "Vietnam: Religious Freedom Briefing Note," October 22-November 1, 2007 delegation.

22. <www.state.gov/g/drl/rls/irf/2006/71284.htm>.

23. <www.state.gov/g/drl/rls/irf/2007/90159.htm>.

24. 2007 CIRF report, p. 137.

25. See <http://commdocs.house.gov/committees/intlrel/hfa91795.000/hfa91795_0f.htm>.

26. Interview September 15, 2004. Available at <usinfo.state.gov/xarchives/display,html? = washfile-english&y = 2004&m = September&x = 2004091618322>.

27. Press Briefing by Ambassador at Large John Hanford, "International Religious Freedom Report and Countries of Particular Concern," Washington, D.C., September 15, 2004 <http://fpc.state.gov/fpc/36238.htm>.

28. Department of State, Nov. 9, 2005 daily press briefing by Adam Ereli, deputy spokesman <http://www.state.gov/r/pa/prs/dpb/2005/56716.htm>.

29. "Ambassador at Large for International Religious Freedom Briefs Congress on US-Saudi Discussions on Religious Practice and Tolerance" <www.state.gov/r/pa/prs/ps/2006/69197.htm>.

30. "U.S.-Saudi Discussions on Religious Practice and Tolerance," July 19, 2006 (circulated in typescript by fax).

31. USCIRF press release, November 13, 2006 available at <www.uscirf.gov>.

32. "Commission Members Probed for Forced Entry and Murder," *Arab News,* May 27, 2007; "Fair Probe Promised," *Arab News,* May 28, 2007; "Cooperation from Government Bodies Lacking," *Arab News,* May 30, 2007; "Five Commission Members Held in Tabuk," *Arab News,* June 4, 2007; "Court Clears Two Commission Members of Wrongdoing," *Arab News,* November 29, 2007.

33. "Religious Freedom Casualty of War in Iraq, Lantos Notes," Sept. 14, 2007. Available at <www.lantos.house.gov>.

34. For a contrasting view, see Tom Farr's speech at the Pew Forum on Religion and Public Life, May 8, 2007 <http://pewforum.org/events/?EventID = 139> in which Farr argues it is time to train U.S. State Department personnel in a "religion" *sub*specialty.

35. See testimony by Harold Hongju Koh before the U.S. House of Representatives Foreign Affairs Committee, March 2007.

36. Executive Summary, IRF 2007 report <http://www.state.gov/g/drl/rls/irf/2007/90080.htm>.

37. See Section 101(c)(2) of IRFA.

38. See A/HRC/1/107 (June 2006) and A/HRC/4/9 (March 2007) in the council; E/CN.4/RES/2005/3 in the Commission on Human Rights.

Chapter 12

1. "Asylum Cases Filed with USCIS: Applications Received and Backlog, FY 1980–2004," *Refugee Reports* 25:9 (December 31, 2004), citing DHS, U.S. Citizenship and Immigration Services, Asylum Division, p. 5.

2. "Asylum Levels and Trends in Industrialized Countries, 2006," UNHCR, Division of Operational Services, March 23, 2007, table 1, p. 10 <www.unhcr.org/statistics/STATISTICS/460150272.pdf>.

3. "Updated Prior Years Disposition of Cases," *DHS Report to Congress on Detained Asylum Seekers, FY 2003*, DHS (on file with author).

4. Ibid.

5. "Asylum Cases Filed with US Citizenship and Immigration Services District Directors and Asylum Officers: Fiscal Years 1973–2004," *Yearbook of Immigration Statistics 2004* (Washington, D.C.: DHS, Office of Immigration Statistics), table 16.

6. Ibid.

7. Calculated from fiscal year reports from 2000 through 2005, Department of Justice, Executive Office of Immigration Review, Office of Planning, Analysis, and Technology, Immigration Courts Asylum Statistics (on file with author).

8. The Immigration Act of 1990, Pub. L. No. 101–649 (1990).

9. One such case involved an 81-year-old Haitian pastor, Rev. Joseph Dantica, who arrived with valid travel documents at Miami International Airport on October 29, 2004. He was subjected to mandatory detention because he said that he was seeking asylum. He died five days later while in U.S. immigration custody. See "Pastor's Death in Custody is Probed," *Miami Herald*, December 10, 2004.

10. The UNHCR *Handbook on Procedures and Criteria for Determining Refugee Status Under the 1951 Convention and the 1967 Protocol Relating to the Status of Refugees* presumes that legitimate refugees generally do not carry valid passports and provides guidance for recognizing the exceptional cases of people with valid passports who are, indeed, refugees. See paragraphs 47–50.

11. 8 C.F.R. § 1003.19 (h)(2)(i)(B).

12. *From Persecution to Prison: The Health Consequences of Detention for Asylum Seekers* (Cambridge: Physicians for Human Rights and the Bellevue/NYU Program for Survivors of Torture, 2003).

13. See "Illegal Aliens: Opportunities Exist to Improve the Expedited Removal Process," GAO/GGD-00–176; "Report on the First Three Years of Expedited Removal," Center for Human Rights and International Justice, University of California, Hastings College of Law, May 2000.

14. "Report on Asylum Seekers in Expedited Removal: Volume I: Findings and Recommendations" and "Report on Asylum Seekers in Expedited Removal: Volume II: Expert Reports," United States Commission on International Religious Freedom (February 2005).

15. USCIRF report, Vol. I, p. 41.

16. USCIRF report, Vol. I, p. 6.

17. USCIRF report, Vol. I, p. 31.

18. "DHS Announces Expanded Border Control Plans," DHS, August 10, 2004 <http://www.dhs.gov/vnews/releases/press_release_0479.htm>.

19. See note 13.

20. <http://www.cbp-gov/xp/cgov/toolbox/about/mission/guardians.xml>.

21. "DHS Budget in Brief, FY 2008," DHS, p. 26 <http://www.dhs.gov/xlibrary/assets/budget_bib-fy2008.pdf>.

22. "Remarks by Secretary of Homeland Security Michael Chertoff . . . on the Secure Border Initiative," DHS, Office of the Press Secretary, August 23, 2006 <http://www.dhs.gov/xnews/releases;pr_1158351672542.shtm>.

23. "Annual Immigration to the United States: The Real Numbers," Migration Policy Institute, May 2007 <http://www.migrationpolicy.org/pubs/FS16_USImmigration_051807.pdf>.

24. Average of years 2002 to 2006, based on "Admissions Comparison Graph," Department of State, Bureau of Population, Refugees and Migration, Office of Admissions <http://www.wrapsnet.org/LinkClick.aspx?fileticket= v2cNaoRr820%3d&tabid= 211&mid=630>.

25. Average of years 2002 to 2006, based on "Asylum Levels and Trends in Industrialized Countries, 2006," UNHCR, Division of Operational Services, March 23, 2007, table 1, p. 10 <www.unhcr.org/statistics/STATISTICS/4601 50272.pdf>.

26. "Statement of the Honorable Michael Chertoff, Secretary US Department of Homeland Security Before the United States Judiciary Committee," DHS, February 28, 2007 <http://www.dhs.gov/xnews/testimony/testimony _1172853501273.shtm>.

27. Pub. L. 107-56, 115 Stat. 272 (October 26, 2001).

28. INA § 212(a)(3)(B)(iii)(V)(b).

29. INA §212(a)(3)(B)(vi)(III).

30. INA § 212(a)(3)(B)(iv)(VI).

31. *Matter of S-K-*, transcript of oral arguments before the Board of Immigration Appeals, January 26, 2006, p. 20 (on file with the author).

32. *In re S-K-*, 23 I&N Dec. 948 (BIA 2006).

33. *Colombia: Displaced and Discarded: The Plight of Internally Displaced Persons in Bogotá and Cartagena*, Human Rights Watch, October 2005, p. 14.

34. INA § 241(b)(3)(A).

35. INA § 241(b)(3)(ii).

36. UNHCR Executive Committee Conclusion No. 7 (1977).

37. *UNHCR Handbook*, paragraph 154. The U.S. Supreme Court has determined that although the *Handbook* is not legally binding on U.S. officials, it nevertheless provides "significant guidance" in construing the 1967 protocol. (*INS v. Cardoza-Fonseca*, 480 US 421, 439, n. 22; 107 S.Ct. 1207, 1217 (1987)).

38. Article 1F(b), which excludes from refugee status persons who "committed a serious non-political crime outside the country of refuge."

39. *UNHCR Handbook*, paragraph 155.

40. Unpublished letter from Thomas Albrecht, deputy regional representative, UNHCR, Washington, D.C., January 6, 2006, on file with author.

41. See "Forced Apart: Families Separated and Immigrants Harmed by United States Deportation Policy," Human Rights Watch, July 2007, p. 53.

42. *McAllister v. Ashcroft*, 2004, U.S. Dist. LEXIS 29598 (D.N.J. July 21, 2004), p. 81.

43. Ibid., p. 54.

44. *In re Sejid Smriko*, 23 I&N Dec. 836 (BIA 2005).

45. *Matter of B-Y-*, unpublished decision, U.S. Immigration Court, York, Pennsylvania, November 19, 2004, on file with author.

46. Ibid.

47. INA § 241(b)(3)(B)(iv).

48. *Matter of A-H-*, 23 I&N Dec. 774,788 (A.G. 2005).

49. Ibid.

50. 8 C.F.R. § 1208.18

51. *In re B-Y-*, unpublished BIA decision, dated August 26, 2005, on file with the author.

52. Letter to B-Y- from the Office of Detention and Removal Operations, Immigration and Customs Enforcement, DHS, dated July 19, 2006, on file with author.

53. *Matter of B-Y-*, p. 8.

54. 8 USC. § 1362 (2001).

55. Andrew I. Schoenholtz and Jonathan Jacobs, "The State of Asylum: Representation: Ideas for Change," *Georgetown Immigration Law Journal* 16 (Summer 2002), p. 1.

56. *Gideon v. Wainwright,* 372 US 335,344 (1963).

57. *In re Gault,* 387 US I, 41 (1967) and *Vitek v. Jones,* 445 US 480, 100 (1980).

58. *Ardestani v. INS,* 502 US 129 (1991), p. 138.

59. Ibid.

60. Schoenholtz and Jacobs, "The State of Asylum," p. 5.

61. INA § 235(b)(1)(B).

62. USCIRF report, Volume II, p. 189.

63. Ibid.

64. Ibid., p. 190.

65. Ibid.

66. *In re: David Joseph,* In Bond Proceedings, BIA, March 13, 2003 (on file with author).

67. *In re D-J-* 23 I&N Dec. 572 (A.G. 2003).

68. "Budget-in-Brief, FY 2008," DHS, pp. 2–3 <www.dhs.gov/xabout/budget/>.

69. "Annual Flow Report, Refugees and Asylees: 2006," table 6, p. 4.

70. Ruth Ellen Wasem, "US Immigration Policy on Haitian Migrants," Congressional Research Service, January 22, 2007, p. 3.

71. "US Policy Unjust to Haitians Fleeing Violence," *Miami Herald,* January 9, 2006, cited by Wasem, "US Immigration Policy," p. 4.

72. Canada has taken some of the Haitians at Guantánamo. In April 2007 the United States and Australia announced a deal to swap mostly interdicted Haitian refugees at Guantánamo for mostly Sri Lankan and Burmese refugees that Australia interdicts and holds on Nauru Island in the South Pacific. See "US/Australia: Refugee Deal Trades in Human Lives: Agreement to Swap Refugees Flouts International Law," Human Rights Watch, April 18, 2007 <http://hrw.org/english/docs/2007/04/18/usint15736.htm>.

73. U.S. Committee for Refugees and Immigrants, *World Refugee Survey 2007* (Washington, D.C., 2007), pp. 2, 3, and Internal Displacement Monitoring Center <http://www.internal-displacement.org/8025708F004CE90B/(httpPages)/22FB1D4E2 B196DAA802570BB005E787C?OpenDocument&count=1000>.

74. *World Refugee Survey 2007,* p. 4.

75. "Implementation of General Assembly Resolution 60/251: Report of Special Rapporteur on the Right to Food, Jean Ziegler, UN doc. A/HRC/4/30, January 19, 2007, pp. 20–21.

76. Ibid.

77. Gil Loescher and John A. Scanlan, *Calculated Kindness: Refugees and America's Half-Open Door: 1945–Present* (New York: Basic Books, 1986).

78. "Syria Tightens Rules to Stem Refugees," *Financial Times,* September 5, 2007 <http://www.ft.com/cms/s/0/b94fd040–5b48–11dc-8c32–0000779fd2ac.html>.

79. Averages based on "Refugee Arrivals Fiscal Years 1980 to 2006," Department of State, Bureau of Population Refugees and Migration, Office of Admissions, Refugee Processing Center, table 13 <http://www.dhs.gov/xlibrary/assets/statistics/yearbook/2006/Table13.xls>.

80. Refugee figures are from "Cumulative Summary of Refugee Admissions," Department of State, Bureau of Population Refugees and Migration, Office of Admissions, Refugee Processing Center <http://www.wrapsnet.org/LinkClick.aspx?fileticket=VlvfLwFZ%2fRQ%3d&tabid=211&mid=630>.

81. "Summary of Refugee Admissions FY 2003-FY 2007, as of June 30, 2007," Department of State, Bureau of Population Refugees and Migration, Office of

Admissions, Refugee Processing Center <http://www.wrapsnet.org/LinkClick
.aspx?fileticket=gAw0p3CjfKI%3d&tabid=211&mid=630>.

Chapter 13

*In preparing this chapter, I benefited from the perspectives of a variety of
former officials and other experts. I am particularly grateful for the thoughtful
editorial comments and suggestions provided by Stephen Rickard on the incentive structures at the State Department. On general bureaucratic issues, there
has long been debate on the relative importance of individuals *versus* institutional arrangements. Studies such as *Bureaucratic Politics and Foreign Policy*, by
Morton Halperin and Priscilla Clapp, with Arnold Kanter (Washington, D.C.:
Brookings Institution Press, 2006, 2nd ed.), have convincingly demonstrated
that institutional arrangements can dramatically impact incentives and hence
policy outcomes. This chapter will consider not only institutional structure, but
also distribution of authorities and practices relating to personnel.

1. The National Security Act of 1947, Sec. 101.

2. See National Security Presidential Directive 1, February 13, 2001, para. 3
<http://www.fas.org/irp/offdocs/nspd/nspd-1.htm>.

3. In the current administration, the vice president has attended NSC principals' meetings as well. Under National Security Presidential Directive 1, issued
by President Bush in February 2001, the vice president may also be asked by the
president to chair meetings of the NSC.

4. Senior directors head up regional or functional offices at the NSC, while
assistant secretaries run regional or functional bureaus at the State Department.

5. Interview with administration official, August and September 2007. See
also Peter Baker, "As Democracy Push Falters, Bush Feels Like a 'Dissident,'"
Washington Post, August 20, 2007. According to an administration official who
was involved in the process, this democracy review was also meant to incorporate
human rights. One observer has written that the review was led by the undersecretary of state for democracy and global affairs. See Thomas O. Melia, "The
Democracy Bureaucracy: The Infrastructure of American Democracy Promotion," Discussion paper for the Princeton Project on National Security, Working
Group on Global Institutions and Foreign Policy Infrastructure, 2005, p. 11.

6. See Freedom House, "Supporting Freedom's Advocates? An Analysis of
the Bush Administration FY 2008 Budget Request for Democracy and Human
Rights," April 2007 <www.freedomhouse.org>.

7. Executive Order 13107, December 10, 1998.

8. See DOD Directive 3000.5, "Military Support for Stability, Security, Transition and Reconstuction (SSTR) Operations," November 28, 2005. Also of note is
a Defense Department public briefing of the new Africa Command (Africacom),
where it is stated that Africom tasks will include "work with African states,
regional organizations and other partners to . . . enhance humanitarian assistance . . . and . . . foster respect for human rights" <www.defenselink.mil/
home/pdf/AFRICOM_PublicBrief02022007.pdf>.

9. For information on the NSC structure in the second term, see Memorandum on National Security Council Staff Reorganization, March 28, 2005 <www
.fas.org/irp/news/2005/03/nsc-reorg.pdf>. The global democracy position
seems to have been tailored to the background and expertise of Elliott Abrams,
and it is hard to argue that, as a general matter, the Near East and North Africa
should be the *only* NSC regional office that comes under the authority of a deputy

national security adviser for global democracy programs. The reestablishment of an NSC staff with many deputies is an issue that goes beyond the scope of this paper. But if a multideputy structure is maintained, a major focus of one deputy should be human rights and democracy.

10. Interview with Washington-based official of international human rights NGO, August 2007.

11. Interview with former NSC official, August 2007. NSC influence on the Egypt cases would certainly have also resulted from the formal responsibility for Middle East issues retained by Elliott Abrams, the deputy national security adviser for global democracy programs. As discussed earlier, however, this institutional arrangement does not necessarily provide a model for future administrations.

12. The logic of this approach would also require that responsibility for the State Department Bureau of International Narcotics and Law Enforcement Affairs, which was recently transferred from the undersecretary for democracy and global affairs to the undersecretary of state for political affairs, be returned to Democracy and Global Affairs.

13. Most of these offices would come under the area of responsibility of the Bureau of Democracy, Human Rights, and Labor.

14. Information provided by the Department of State, Office of the Undersecretary for Democracy and Global Affairs, September 2007.

15. I reach this conclusion based on my personal involvement in the deliberations on Haiti in 1994, while a staff member at the NSC.

16. Michael Bowman, Gary Freeman, and Kay Miller, *Passing By: The United States and Genocide in Burundi, 1972* (New York: Carnegie Endowment for International Peace, 1973), cited in Samantha Power, *A Problem from Hell: America and the Age of Genocide* (New York: Basic Books, 2002), p. 89.

17. For a brief discussion of this issue, see Melia, "The Democracy Bureaucracy," pp. 18–19.

18. PL 107–228, Section 663, September 30, 2002.

19. See Steven E. Finkel, Aníbal Pérez-Liñán, and Mitchell A. Seligson, with the assistance of Dinorah Azpuru, "Effects of US Foreign Assistance on Democracy Building: Results of a Cross-National Quantitative Study," January 12, 2006, version No. 34, Vanderbilt University and the University of Pittsburgh <www.usaid.gov/our_work/democracy_and_governance/publications/pdfs /impact _of_democracy_assistance.pdf>.

20. A description of funding through the Human Rights and Democracy Fund may be found at the State Department website at <http://www.state.gov/g/drl/p/> .

21. For a history and description of the NED, its four affiliated institutions and other related programs, see the NED website at <http://www.ned.org/about/nedhistory.html>.

22. See Summary and Highlights, International Affairs, Function 150, at <www.usaid.gov/policy/budget/cbj2008/fy2008cbj_highlights.pdf>. At the time this chapter was drafted, the NED budget was still under consideration by Congress.

23. As described elsewhere in this paper, the NSC has a deputy national security adviser for global democracy; the State Department has an undersecretary for democracy and global affairs; and AID has a Bureau for Democracy, Conflict, and Humanitarian Assistance.

Contributors

Philip Alston is John Norton Pomeroy Professor of Law at New York University School of Law. He was the first rapporteur of the UN Committee on Economic, Social, and Cultural Rights from its inception in 1987 through 1990 and was chair of the committee from 1991 to 1998.

Alexandra Arriaga is Associate Deputy Executive Director for Advocacy and Director of Government Relations at Amnesty International USA.

Elizabeth Drake is a trade attorney at the law offices of Stewart and Stewart. She served for six years as an international policy analyst at the American Federation of Labor and Congress of Industrial Organizations, where she worked on a range of trade and other international economic policy matters for the U.S. labor movement.

Bill Frelick is the Refugee Policy Director for Human Rights Watch. He served previously as the Refugee Program Director for Amnesty International USA and the Director of the U.S. Committee for Refugees.

Felice D. Gaer is the Director of the Jacob Blaustein Institute for the Advancement of Human Rights of the American Jewish Committee. She has served since 2001 on the U.S. Commission on International Religious Freedom and has also been chair of the commission.

Rachel Kleinfeld is the Executive Director of the Truman National Security Project. She served previously as a consultant to the Center for Strategic and International Studies where she addressed issues in bioterrorism, homeland security, intelligence reform, and postconflict preparation.

George A. Lopez holds the Reverend Theodore M. Hesburgh Chair in Peace Studies at the Joan B. Kroc Institute for International Peace Studies at the University of Notre Dame. With David Cortright he has been coeditor and coauthor of six books and dozens of articles on economic sanctions.

Elisa Massimino, Washington Director of Human Rights First, has taught international human rights law at the University of Virginia Law School and now teaches human rights advocacy at Georgetown University.

Carol Pier is the senior labor rights and trade researcher for Human Rights Watch, where she conducts fact-finding missions to document labor rights violations and engages in advocacy on workers' rights and trade issues in the United States and abroad.

Catherine Powell is an Associate Professor of Law at Fordham Law School, specializing in international law, human rights, and comparative constitutional law. She served previously on the faculty of Columbia Law School, where she was the founding executive director of the Human Rights Institute.

Regan E. Ralph is the founding Executive Director of the Fund for Global Human Rights. Previously she helped build and ultimately ran the women's rights program at Human Rights Watch.

William F. Schulz, a Senior Fellow at the Center for American Progress, is former Executive Director of Amnesty International USA and former President of the Unitarian Universalist Association of Congregations.

Eric P. Schwartz is the Executive Director of the Connect US Fund. He has served as the UN Secretary General's Deputy Special Envoy for Tsunami Recovery; Chief of Office for the UN High Commissioner for Human Rights; and Senior Director and Special Assistant to the President for Multilateral and Humanitarian Affairs at the U.S. National Security Council.

John Shattuck, CEO of the John F. Kennedy Library Foundation, was Assistant Secretary of State for Democracy, Human Rights, and Labor and Ambassador to the Czech Republic under President Bill Clinton.

Debora L. Spar is the Spangler Family Professor at Harvard Business School, where she works on issues of business-government relations and the political environment of international commerce.

Jennifer L. Windsor is the Executive Director of Freedom House. Previously she worked at the U.S. Agency for International Development on democracy and governance programs.

Acknowledgments

This book would not exist were it not for the support provided its editor by the Center for American Progress and in particular its executive vice president for policy, Melody Barnes, and its former vice president for national security, Peter Rundlet. In addition, staff member Michael Fuchs read each of the chapters for content and Sarah Dreier and Tamara Chao did the painstaking task of checking each note for accuracy and consistency. Thanks go as well to the Carr Center for Human Rights Policy at Harvard's Kennedy School of Government, where I served as a Fellow in 2006–2007 and in whose stimulating environment many of the ideas in my introduction to the book were incubated.

Penn Press, with whom I have happily published before, is always a delight to work with. Peter Agree, the press's editor in chief, believed in the book even before its contents had been agreed upon and development editor Bill Finan honed those contents to the point that we trust they prove worthy of Peter's faith. Without our authors, however, Bill would have had nothing to hone and to them we reserve our deepest thanks.

Finally a word of appreciation to two human rights activists to whom this book is dedicated, Bob and Pat Flynn, with whom I worked at Amnesty International USA and who embody the conviction that democratic governments change when their citizens care enough to make them change. We hope that in some small way this volume may help realize that vision.

William F. Schulz